Business Finance

a value-based approach

We work with leading authors to develop the strongest educational materials in business finance, bringing cutting-edge thinking and best learning practice to a global market.

Under a range of well-known imprints, including Financial Times-Prentice Hall, we craft high quality print and electronic publications which help to understand and apply their content, whether studying or at work.

To find out more about the complete range of our publishing, please visit us on the World Wide Web at: www.pearsoned.co.uk

BUSINESS FINANCE
a value-based approach

Bill Neale and Trefor McElroy

Reader in Financial
Management, School of
Finance & Law,
Bournemouth University

Head of Accounting,
School of Finance & Law,
Bournemouth University

FINANCIAL TIMES

An imprint of **Pearson Education**
Harlow, England · London · New York · Boston · San Francisco · Toronto · Sydney · Singapore · Hong Kong
Tokyo · Seoul · Taipei · New Delhi · Cape Town · Madrid · Mexico City · Amsterdam · Munich · Paris · Milan

Pearson Education Limited
Edinburgh Gate
Harlow
Essex CM20 2JE
England

and Associated Companies throughout the world

Visit us on the World Wide Web at:
www.pearsoned.co.uk

First published 2004

ISBN 0201-61904-0

British Library Cataloguing-in-Publication Data
A catalogue record for this book is available from the British Library.

10 9 8 7 6 5 4 3 2 1
08 07 06 05 04

Typeset in 9/12pt Stone Serif by 25.
Printed and bound in Great Britain by Henry Ling Ltd, The Dorset Press, Dorchester, Dorset.

The publisher's policy is to use paper manufactured from sustainable forests.

CONTENTS

CHAPTER 3 STRATEGIC MANAGEMENT FOR VALUE CREATION

CHAPTER 4 PROJECT APPRAISAL I: THE BASICS

CHAPTER 5 PROJECT APPRAISAL II: THE TRICKY BITS

CHAPTER 6   THE RATE OF RETURN REQUIRED BY OWNERS

CHAPTER 7   WORKING CAPITAL MANAGEMENT

CHAPTER 11 RETURNING VALUE TO OWNERS

CHAPTER 12 MANAGING RISK

CHAPTER 13 MEASURING PERFORMANCE

LIST OF FIGURES

PREFACE

The market for UK-oriented textbooks in financial management, while not crowded, is certainly more densely populated than when one half of the present writing team entered the field with *Corporate Finance & Investment* in the early 1990s. Over the past decade or so, not only have more UK-related texts become available, but their average length has expanded, even the ones that initially set out to offer a concise treatment of the subject.

Paradoxically, the expansion in book length (and price) has coincided with the truncation of many courses in order to fit into an ever-expanding curriculum. The rise of semesterisation, incorporating course durations of typically 10–15 weeks, has meant that attempting to do justice to the ground covered in the typical text is a daunting task for staff and students.

In addition, the focus of many finance courses has shifted towards corporate and business strategy, not only within educational institutions but also on professional courses, e.g. the Financial Strategy course at CIMA final level. The convergence of finance and strategy has probably been most marked on MBA courses where many of us teach courses called something like Strategic Financial Management. One wag (a Strategy lecturer) noted that no self-respecting MBA course is credible without words like 'Strategy' and 'Strategic' in the title. More seriously, we recall another colleague saying, 'Of course, we all teach Strategy now'. And, of course, we, in the finance area, always have done, not least because of our awareness that no strategy is deliverable unless due attention is given to the fundamentals of financial analysis, financial planning and evaluation of financial performance, all curiously neglected in many strategy textbooks.

This book, therefore, addresses what the authors perceive to be a need for a textbook shorter than most, and suitable for use on a semester-length course within a programme that has a strong orientation towards strategy. This role definition most obviously fits MBA and similar courses, e.g. the rapidly growing Masters in Business courses, but it also fits many undergraduate courses. It does require prior exposure to an elementary accounting course, although not a prior course in strategy. The reader will find a strong emphasis on value and value creation, reflecting our view of the appropriate contribution of financial managers to setting out and achieving corporate and business strategy. In this respect, we acknowledge our debt to writers such as Alfred Rappaport who have attempted to marry finance and strategy in the past.

Readers will also find that the emphasis adopted by the authors is on application of the principles of finance in a strategic setting. To this end, we have used copious mini-cases, both within the text and also for end-of-chapter work. The vast majority of these relate to situations that have arisen over the past three or four years, a time of great turbulence (and hence great interest) in business and financial markets. To us, this provides the essence of finance – it is a living subject and important developments occur almost daily.

Of course, it is not exciting all of the time – there is a certain amount of groundwork that needs to be laid before some of the more interesting applications can be examined. No course, and no book, can totally neglect the underpinnings of the subject, and some will say that we have cut too many corners and omitted too much core material (for example, only after a great amount of soul-searching did we decide not to include Modigliani-Miller's capital structure models). For the purists, this is undoubtedly true. However, we hope we have struck the right balance between academic rigour and real-world applicability. We leave you, the readership, to judge. Any feedback – preferably constructive – would be welcome via our respective e-mail addresses:

bneale@bournemouth.ac.uk
tmcelroy@bournemouth.ac.uk

OUTLINE OF THE BOOK AND HOW TO USE IT

The outline

A synopsis of each of the chapters will give a broad indication of the scope of this book.

Chapter 1, Setting the scene, introduces the subject matter of finance.

Chapter 2, The meaning of shareholder value, explains how the term value is used in finance. This involves development of the concept of present value, an important building block for many later chapters. A simple valuation model is presented pinpointing the two main drivers of value, namely expected cash flows and their degree of risk. The valuation of a firm in the capital market is also explained in the context of the *Efficient Markets Hypothesis*. Attention is given to constraints on value creation in the form of the *agency problem*, the difficulty faced by owners of ensuring that managers will act in their best interests.

Chapter 3, Strategic management for value creation, explains the strategic context in which financial managers operate. The distinction between corporate strategy and business strategy is made. The importance of *core competences* of a business and how they are harnessed to enable value creation is explained. The chapter also looks at a well-known model for evaluating the attractiveness of a particular industry – Michael Porter's Five Forces Model. Particular emphasis is given to how firms can protect value by building entry barriers.

Chapter 4, Project appraisal I: the basics, looks at how and why firms evaluate capital projects. It looks at the structure of the typical investment decision, the information inputs, and the variety of evaluation techniques that are commonly used in practice. Attention is given to the drawbacks of each method, together with an overview of the role of appraisal in the investment decision-making process.

Chapter 5, Project appraisal II: the tricky bits, looks at aspects of an investment appraisal that often complicate the analysis and that are often 'swept under the carpet'. These are addressed separately to enable a sound understanding of the basic methods to be obtained in Chapter 4. The 'tricky bits' are the treatment of inflation, the incorporation of taxation and investment allowances and ways of tackling risk and uncertainty. The chapter relies extensively on numerical analysis for illustration, although only the more common and less complex methods of risk analysis – use of probabilities, and sensitivity analysis – are examined.

Chapter 6, The rate of return required by owners, looks at how the shareholders of the firm will stipulate the rate of return they require on their investment and hence the discount rate that should be used when evaluating the cash flows of an all-equity-financed project, an issue that was side-stepped in Chapters 4 and 5. The two key methods examined are the Dividend Valuation Model and the Capital Asset Pricing Model. The treatment, although numerical, does not rely on intensive use of complex mathematics. The emphasis is on how to use the Beta coefficient generated by the CAPM. Recent empirical evidence on the equity premium is discussed.

Chapter 7, Working capital management, swings the focus away from investment towards financing. Although it does look at why firms invest in short-term assets – cash, stock and debtors – the primary attention is on how these items can be managed and thus improve the liquidity position of the firm. In this respect, the focus is on financing issues, since more liquidity means less need for external finance. Different working capital policies, and their strategic implications, are discussed. Finally, the important issue of overtrading is explained and illustrated.

Chapter 8, Raising long-term finance, is a largely descriptive survey of the main methods of raising finance that the firm expects to be using for several time periods. The major categories discussed are equity, borrowing and various hybrids. Attention is given to the advantages and disadvantages of borrowing, especially to the gearing phenomenon. An extensive worked example brings in many of the aspects covered in this and the preceding chapter.

Chapter 9, The required return on investment, examines the determination of the required return when the firm uses a mixture of methods of finance, specifically debt and equity. To develop the so-called Weighted Average Cost of Capital, it is necessary to examine the cost of debt, and then show how it is combined with the owner's required return. The impact of using debt on the required return and on the value of the firm is explored, especially the issues of whether there is an optimal gearing ratio and the limits to debt finance.

Chapter 10, How to value companies, examines alternative approaches to valuing both quoted and unquoted firms. Although quoted firms have a market value, unless the stock market is efficient, this valuation may be unreliable. Hence, both quoted and unquoted firms can be valued by approaches such as the Net Asset Value Method, Price Earnings Approach, and Discounted Cash Flow. A major part of this chapter is devoted to the *Shareholder Value Analysis* approach devised by Rappaport. This is used to value both ungeared and geared firms.

Chapter 11, Returning value to owners, focuses on the dividend decision, whether to pay a dividend and, if so, how much. The pure theory of dividend policy, the Irrelevance Theory, is examined as a benchmark before giving attention to the real-world factors, such as personal taxation, that firms must consider in practice. A feature of the chapter is the inclusion of material on share repurchases.

Chapter 12, Managing risk, reflects the increasing attention being given, following the Turnbull Report in 1999, to the issue of how firms identify and manage the risks they face. It gives an overview of the major risks facing firms at both the operational and financial levels. Two types of financial risk, foreign exchange risk and interest rate risk, are selected as vehicles to explain how risk can be managed by the firm wishing to insulate itself against adverse contingencies.

Chapter 13, Measuring performance, the culminating chapter, looks at how to assess how well firms have managed their financial decisions by analysing various ways of assessing company performance. It begins by questioning the validity of profit-based measures before explaining modern measures of performance including Total Shareholder Return and Economic Value Added. It also examines the case for a more 'rounded' view of performance measurement by discussing Kaplan and Norton's balanced scorecard.

How to use this text

Apart from reading the basic text, you will find a number of other learning aids incorporated in the book. In each chapter, you will find a selection of the following:

- *A set of self-assessment activities (SAAs)*. These are placed *in situ* to test your understanding and ability to apply what you have just read. Answers for most of these are contained at the end of each chapter. (The exception is a series of 'go and find out' questions.)

- *Worked examples* (depending on the nature of the topic analysed). These aim to incorporate as many as possible of the key ideas and techniques covered in the body of the chapter.

- *End-of-chapter questions and mini-cases*. These aim to emphasise the everyday relevance of finance by utilising materials from the web and from newspapers and other publications. Wherever possible, these relate to actual firms, although in some instances, more traditional exercises or quiz questions are provided, depending on the nature of the subject covered in the particular chapter. Most of this material has been 'road tested' with students on a variety of courses.

- *Between-chapter case studies*. These are longer cases, strategically placed in between chapters. Most are designed to draw together several strands of the book studied up to the point in question. The final case, focusing on the Dutch airline KLM, is a full strategic and financial evaluation that brings out many of the issues encountered in the preceding chapters.

- *References and further reading*. As explained in the preface, this book is designed for a relatively brief exposure to finance. Therefore, our treatment of several topics is necessarily brief. Readers who wish to explore topics more deeply are guided to a range of widely used textbooks. Their full titles are given in chapter 1, but in subsequent chapters we refer only to the authors. Because this book is not designed for an intensive study of finance, we do not give an extensive reading list, but copious suggestions for further reading can be found in the texts cited.

A website to accompany this book with resources for lecturers is available at www.booksites.net/nealemcelroy.

You will find that many of the *SAAs* are focused on a real company, what is described as 'a company of your choice' or 'your company'. To obtain maximum benefit from studying financial management, it is always useful to have a set of accounts to hand so that you can see how 'your company does it', e.g. how it raises finance, what it invests in, how efficient it is at working capital management, and so on. You can obtain company reports free of charge by logging on to the *Financial Times* website (www.ft.com) and accessing its company reports service.

Alternatively, you can visit the website of your chosen company. Most large companies post their annual report and accounts on their websites. These are easy to locate, generally under the label of www.companyname.com or www.companyname.co.uk for a British firm. Using the figures of a real company and visualising the firm in question in its strategic context will significantly enhance the value of your learning experience.

You do not have to be a fully qualified accountant to obtain this value. Anyone with a basic understanding of simple company financial statements (which is what this book assumes as a prerequisite) can benefit in this way. If you are in doubt about accounting terminology, we recommend *Pocket Accounting* by C Nobes (Economist Publications).

AUTHOR'S ACKNOWLEDGEMENTS

The authors wish to acknowledge the kind assistance of the following who have consented to use of material:

Tim Bond – Barclays Capital
Stephen Devany – Tomkins plc
Sarah Pelling – Cadbury Schweppes plc
Patricia Rowham – London Business School.

In addition, our deepest thanks to the following who have contributed case material:

Maurice Brown – aviation industry consultant
Martin Kelly – The Management Institute.

Bill Neale
Trefor McElroy

PUBLISHER'S ACKNOWLEDGEMENTS

We are grateful to the following for permission to reproduce copyright material:

Figure 3.1 adapted with the permission of The Free Press, a Division of Simon & Schuster Adult Publishing Group, from Figure 1.1 on p. 4, *COMPETITIVE STRATEGY: Techniques for Analyzing Industries and Competitors*, by Michael E. Porter (1998). Copyright © 1980, 1998 by The Free Press. All rights reserved; Figure 3.2 extensively adapted from figure *The MOST Acronym* from, *Contemporary Strategic Analysis: concepts, techniques, applications, 4th Edition*, Blackwell Publishing, (Grant, R.M., 2001); Table 6.1 from *Constituents of FT 30 Share Index, July-September 2002*, reproduced by kind permission of the London Business School, (2002); Table 6.2, from table from Barclays Capital web site (*www.barcap.com*), Barclays Capital, (2002); Table Ch 10 Appendix 1 from *easyJet plc Annual Report and Accounts for the year ended 31 December 2001*, easyJet plc, (2001); Figure 13.1 adapted from Figure 15.18, p. 674 from *Corporate Financial Management, 2nd Edition*, Prentice Hall (Pearson Education), (Arnold, G., 2002); Figure 13.2 adapted with the permission of The Free Press, a division of Simon & Schuster Adult Publishing Group, from Figure 2.1, p. 56 from *CREATING SHARE-HOLDER VALUE: a Guide for Managers and Investors*, by Alfred Rappaport. Copyright © 1986, 1998 by Alfred Rappaport. All rights reserved; Figure 13.2 also adapted from a figure from *Corporate Finance and Investment, 4th Edition*, Financial Times Prentice Hall, (Pearson Education), (Pike, R.H. and Neale, C.W., 2003); Figure 13.3 adapted from Exhibit 17.1, p. 637 from *Corporate Strategy, 3rd Edition*, Financial Times Prentice Hall (Pearson Education), (Lynch, R.L., 2003); Figure 13.3 also based on information from *The Balanced Scorecard: translating strategy into action*, by Kaplan, R.S., and Norton, D.P., Harvard Business School Press, Boston, MA (1996), Reprinted by permission of Harvard Business School Press. Copyright © 1996 by the Harvard Business School Publishing Corporation; all rights reserved; Tables Ch 13 pp. 397 and 398 *DTI Value Added Scorecard 2003* from *DTI Value Added Scorecard 2003*, (www.innovation.go.uk/finance), © Crown Copyright 2002. Crown Copyright material is reproduced with the permission of the Controller of Her Majesty's Stationery Office and the Queen's Printer for Scotland; Tables Ch 13 pp. 415–416 adapted from table from *Change in Market capitalization of Companies 1997–2001, and comparison of Coca-Cola and PepsiCo* from www.sternstewart.co.uk, Copyright © 1997–2001 Stern Stewart & Co.; Tables 1, 2, 3 and 4 Case study Ch 13 from *Report and Accounts of KLM Royal Dutch Airlines*, KLM Royal Dutch Airlines, reproduced by kind permission; Table 3 Case Study Ch 13 and Table Appendix 1 Ch 13 Case Study from *Report and Accounts of British Airways 2001* and *1997 to 2001*, British Airways, reproduced by kind permission; Table 3 Case Study Ch 13 and Table Appendix 1 Ch 13 Case Study from *Report and Accounts of Delta Air Lines 2001* and *1997 to 2001*, Delta Air Lines, Inc., reproduced by kind permission; Table 3 Case Study Ch 13 and Table Appendix 1 Ch 13 Case Study from *Report and Accounts of Continental Airlines 2001* and *1997 to 2001*, Continental Airlines, Inc., reproduced by kind permission; Table 3 Case Study Ch 13 and Table Appendix 1 Ch 13 Case Study from *Report and Accounts of Deutsche Lufthansa AG 2001* and *1997 to 2001*, Deutsche Lufthansa AG, reproduced by kind permission; Table 3 Case Study Ch 13 and Table Appendix 1 Ch 13 Case Study from *Report and Accounts of SAS Group 2001* and *1997 to 2001*, SAS Group, reproduced by kind permission; Table 3 Case Study Ch 13 and Table Appendix 1 Ch 13 Case Study from *Report and Accounts of Northwest Airlines 2001* and *1997 to 2001*, Northwest Airlines, Inc., reproduced by kind permission.

ACCA for a selection of questions from various examination papers; American Media Inc. for an extract from "'Time-traveller' busted for insider trading" by Chad Kultgen published in *Weekly World News* 19th March 2003; Cadbury Schweppes for extracts from their *Annual Report 2001*; Elsevier Limited for a selection of questions from various examination papers from CIMA (IFIN) & CIMA Finance (IFIN) by CIMA. Reprinted by permission of Elsevier Limited; SAB Miller plc for extracts from their *Report and Accounts 2001*; and Tomkins plc for extracts from their *Report and Accounts 2003*.

Mini-case study p. 22 from 'Go staff share £53m windfall in easyJet tie up', © *Financial Times*, 17 May 2002; Mini-case study p. 234, from UK is Europe's worst in corporate liquidity, © *Financial Times*, 6 November 2002; Mini-case study p. 236 from Cash flow, Lex Column, © *Financial Times*, 3 December 2002; Appendix 2 easyJet plc share price movements six months to April 2001, from FT.com, © *Financial Times*.

In some instances we have been unable to trace the owners of copyright material, and we would appreciate any information that would enable us to do so.

SETTING THE SCENE

Value creation in action

Mannesmann AG, a German conglomerate with extensive interests in both engineering and telecommunications, was a relatively late convert to the notion of creating and releasing shareholder value. Its entry into telecoms in the late 1980s had begun to bear fruit a decade later, but the fit with the traditional automotive and engineering (A&E*) business was not obvious. Telecoms also guzzled huge sums for development in a fast-moving sector, thus starving the A&E side of investment capital.

Mannesmann had borrowed large amounts to finance the acquisition of two Italian telecoms firms, Omnitel and Infostrada, operators of mobile phone and fixed-line services respectively. Facing mounting pressure to sell off the A&E side, it surprised the markets by announcing, in September 1999, its intention to divide the company into two separate entities, focused on A&E and telecoms respectively. Behind this decision was the suspicion that the stock market viewed the group essentially as a traditional slow-growing engineering combine. This tended to undervalue the telecoms side at a time when market valuations of telecoms operators in Germany and elsewhere were reflecting highly optimistic growth expectations.

The result of this 'financial engineering' was a share price increase of 8 per cent. The split would be effective at the end of 2000, with each company to have separate market listings from 2001.

This was just the start of the fun. In October 1999, Mannesmann bid £20 billion for Orange, the third largest British mobile phone operator. Including £2 billion of Orange debt, the total value of the offer was £22 billion. Orange shares, floated in the UK at £2.05 in 1996, now stood at

£14.60. Mannesmann offered £16.30 in a combination of cash and shares, reflecting a premium of some 21 per cent on the pre-announcement market price. New finance for the deal would come from a €12 billion bridging loan and an issue of ordinary shares worth €4 billion.

Market reaction was harsh. Mannesmann's shares reversed the September appreciation, falling 8 per cent to €147 on concerns that it was over-paying. Investors feared the German company was over-reacting to the challenge thrown down by its arch-rival, Deutsche Telekom, acquirer of Orange's smaller British rival One2One in August 1999 in a bidding contest from which Mannesmann itself had walked away, saying the bidding had gone too high. Observers were concerned that Mannesmann was now paying 2.6 times the price paid for One2One and that the acquisition terms would reduce earnings per share during 2000–1. Mannesmann justified its bid by arguing that Orange had much faster earnings growth potential than One2One. Chief executive Klaus Esser said a 'full price' had to be paid to win Orange's shareholders' support for perhaps one of the last entry tickets into the then booming British market. Mannesmann's bid was supported from Hong Kong conglomerate Hutchinson Whampoa, 45 per cent share-holder in Orange, destined to hold over 10 per cent of the enlarged company. The managing director of Hutchinson Whampoa said the Orange bid was 'excellent value' for his shareholders.

Critics of Mannesmann alleged the Orange bid was a defensive strategic move, based on the fear of a hostile takeover. Other observers wondered whether Mannesmann had over-extended itself, leaving itself even more vulnerable to a bid from Vodafone-AirTouch, already its partner in joint ventures in Germany, Italy and France. Meanwhile, Mannesmann's position was undermined by publication of 'mixed results' in November 1999 for the previous nine months that highlighted both its strengths and weaknesses. Telecoms sales from continuing business had risen 31 per cent (73 per cent, including the contribution of the Italian acquisitions). However, automotive sales had risen by only 5 per cent, while engineering sales were flat. Telecoms accounted for 95 per cent of Mannesmann's €15 billion invest-ment spending. The shares rose 3 per cent in value to €179, reflecting renewed expectations of a hostile takeover bid. The bid from Vodafone for Mannesmann duly arrived a month later, in what became the first-ever suc-cessful hostile bid for a German company by a foreign company, the world's then largest takeover at €175 billion, to create the world's largest telecoms group.

(* Note: in Britain, A&E is also a medical abbreviation for Accident & Emergency.)

Objectives:

The objectives of this chapter are to:

- explain the meaning of value as used in finance

- discuss the role and expectations of different stakeholders in business enterprises

- focus on the possible conflicts between owners of firms and business managers

- explain the notion of shareholder wealth maximisation, and contrast it with the stakeholder approach

- define the historical context of modern financial management

- outline the scope of this book, and how the reader should use it.

1.1 Introduction

The introductory cameo endeavours to convey the capacity of financial issues to excite strong emotions. It shows how high-profile firms, often household names, make financial decisions likely to affect us all. Mixed in with the Mannesmann episode are issues of financial performance, corporate strategy and national culture that transcend the monetary measurements underpinning the decision making by the key players.

This may seem far removed from people's typical conceptions of accountancy and finance. In common parlance, the terms accountancy and finance are often used synonymously and interchangeably, and often greeted with incomprehension. Observe that financial affairs are invariably covered at the tail-end of news bulletins. Why is this? How fair is it? Has the world of finance received a bad press?

First, two definitions: 'Accountancy' is a profession and a body of expertise, while 'accounting' refers to the *practice* of accountancy. In accounting, where the emphasis is largely on reporting (or 'accounting for') past performance, there are usually definable solutions, although accountants have some latitude over which accounting policy to follow. Balance sheets balance (or can be made to!), reflecting the principle of double-entry book-keeping that provides a continuous check on accuracy and completeness of records. The fact that the answer is in there somewhere often gives people a degree of comfort – while difficult to find in some cases, there is solace in the notion that the maze does have an exit.

In finance, this comfort is absent. In accounting (and financial accounting, in particular), the emphasis tends to be historical, i.e. reporting on past events in the form of the firm's trading and financial experiences. While past behaviour and performance are measurable, the opposite is true in finance. Finance looks

at financial decisions in terms of their capacity to generate desirable *future* outcomes that create wealth.

But, of course, none of us can foretell the future! Yet what we *can* do is to make reasoned assessments about future likelihoods, based on sensible assumptions and coherent arguments. And although we are almost certain to be wrong, this should not daunt us. The test of a financial decision is not in how correct it was in predicting the future but in how intelligent an assessment was made in the first instance. Some find this approach frustrating, others find it exciting – however it is for you, you will not deny the roles of insight, initiative and flair in financial analysis.

1.2 Value and wealth

This book is about value, what it means, how it can be created by firms on behalf of their owners and how it can be delivered to these owners. But what gives a company value, and how can it increase this value?

Value, as used in finance, is rather different from 'wealth'. Someone's overall stock of wealth includes non-monetary blessings like health and happiness, certainly things to 'value'. It also includes financial investments, e.g. a share of a company's value. Although Financial Management can have little impact on the first wealth component, it suggests how firms, by enhancing their own values, can enhance the people's financial wealth component.

Value/wealth comes in many forms, ranging from cash to physical assets. But assets other than cash are valuable financially only if they can be turned into cash (like a valuable painting) or if they contribute to the production of goods and services that can be sold for cash (like a machine) in the future. This brings us to an important observation: namely that business value and individual wealth have two components – assets and cash held today, and the expectation of future cash inflows. A man with no cash in his pocket today but who is expecting to inherit £1 million in a year's time would be considered wealthy by most of us.

Similarly, the value of any company is based upon assets owned today and expectations of future cash inflows. Many factors add value to a company by improving its prospects for future cash inflow. The list includes:

- quality and range of products produced
- assets used
- brand name
- quality of workforce and management
- prevailing economic and market conditions.

The feature common to all these factors is their capacity to improve the future financial prospects of a business. Any business decision that enhances these future prospects increases value today, e.g. investing in a new product range or spending on staff training. Improving the future financial prospects, and thus adding value to a business, is the primary role of financial managers.

It is commonly thought that most company value resides in the assets it holds right now. But often, most of a company's value derives from expectations about future incomes. In 2002, the accounts of Microsoft, the giant US computer software company, disclosed a book value of net assets of $41 billion. However, its total market value based upon its share price was $285 billion! This gives some indication of the importance of future prospects when valuing any business. In this case, the market values the prospect of future sales driven by the power of the brand, the prospect of new products and the ideas and marketing skills of Bill Gates. Microsoft exemplifies the 'new economy' firm, most of whose value is based on the future and especially on people's ability to exploit future (often as yet unrevealed) opportunities rather than the tangible assets held at any one time.

People also rank among the most important assets of a business. Reflect on why Real Madrid paid £25 million for the English footballer David Beckham in 2003. The value is clear – Beckham, widely regarded as one of the best footballers in the world, will help his team earn huge TV revenues and fill the Bernabeu stadium by winning cups and championships. Moreover, his name will increase the sale of football shirts bearing his squad number, and other merchandise. The fee paid for him reflects confidence that Beckham will be a financial as well as a footballing asset for many years. But we must always be careful to talk of expected future returns – there are few guarantees in life. Consumer demand will change, new products or processes will inevitably appear, so that what was once valuable may cease to be so. What would happen to the value of Beckham if he lost form? Or broke his leg? Value and risk go hand in hand.

Every financial decision should seek to achieve or move a firm nearer to its defined objective. Finance centres on the creation of value. The concept of value is thus critical to an understanding of finance. But what is meant by this term? The poet and dramatist Oscar Wilde defined an economist as 'someone who knows the price of everything and the value of nothing'. This suggests that whereas prices are readily identifiable, value is rather more esoteric and intangible. This distinction is an interesting one. As applied to firms, we can find their current prices by looking in the financial press, but often we suspect – and indeed company chairmen often tell us – that their true values are different (invariably higher!) than these published prices. How can this be?

This raises questions such as 'How is value measured in finance? How can it be created? What factors limit the ability of managers to create value?'. These are the key issues both in this introductory chapter and in the whole book. But first, we look at the question of 'value for whom'. This requires discussion of the respective roles and interests of the **stakeholders** who comprise the community of interests that make up the modern business enterprise.

1.3 Owners, managers and other stakeholders

A firm is owned by its shareholders and is operated by managers (sometimes the same people), but who calls the shots? In whose interests should the business be operated?

UK legislation says that directors have a 'fiduciary' duty to act in the best interests of the owners of the enterprise, but the precise nature of this duty is undefined. Any firm is a highly political entity consisting of lots of different groups of people, all with vested interests. These 'stakeholder' groups will make various claims and demands on the firm, presenting the directors with a range of competing demands to be reconciled. The main stakeholder groups and their demands can be identified as follows:

● *Shareholders* are the legal owners of a company. They become shareholders by investing money through the purchase of ordinary shares. Investment is the sacrifice of present consumption in the expectation (but not the guarantee) of a future return. Shareholders get this return in the form of cash dividends paid out and in the form of a capital gain (through a rising share price).

● *Managers* ostensibly manage the company on behalf of the owners, the shareholders, but are likely to have their own agenda as well. This may relate to financial rewards, career opportunities or a concern for power and status within the organisation. They are often shareholders as well.

● *Employees* clearly have a vested interest in the company through their jobs, careers and remuneration. Employees want to improve all three aspects and may be organised into trade unions to represent them when these issues are discussed.

● *Lenders* banks and bondholders lend money to a company to earn interest. They will demand liquidity as a sign of its ability to meet the interest payments and security for their lending in case of company failure. Banks also wish to extend the relationship by offering other services to companies, such as financial advice.

● *Suppliers* in the short term want assurance that they will get paid for any recent deliveries. In the longer term, they will be hoping for regular orders.

● *Customers* mostly seek value for money, i.e. top quality at the keenest prices. When purchasing a good that will last some time, consumers also want to see the manufacturer maintain continuity of supply in case any parts need replacing or servicing.

● *The government* takes an active interest in the business and financial affairs at both the general and the individual level. The perceived financial health of companies influences economic policy. At another important level, the government will be concerned that companies pay their taxes.

- *The local community* will always feel the impact of business activities. Some of these impacts are, of course, benign, such as provision of employment and local taxation revenue, but others may be more troublesome, such as smoke and noise pollution. Local communities seek protection against these harmful effects, along with care for the local environment in general. Many firms regard it as good public relations to promote community projects.

Conflicting stakeholder interests

Typically, stakeholders will disagree as to what, or whose, is the paramount interest. For example:

- Shareholders want dividends and capital gains. They also want high returns and low risk.
- Employees want high wages and salaries, and maximum security of employment and their pensions.
- Customers want high quality and low prices.

There is thus considerable scope for conflict between these various stakeholder groups.

Stakeholders in conflict	Reasons for conflict
Managers *vs.* shareholders	Are managers worth their high remuneration and benefits?
	Do managers make decisions in the best interests of shareholders?
Customers *vs.* shareholders	Customers want low prices, shareholders want high profits
Employees *vs.* shareholders	Employees want good working conditions and high salaries, that shareholders may prefer not to pay
Lenders *vs.* shareholders	Interest has to be paid even if no profit is earned, and it is paid before dividends are paid to shareholders. (It's a 'prior charge')
Government *vs.* employees	The government may impose taxes on a firm which may affect future growth of employment

Shareholders versus managers: the principal/agent problem

In many ways, the deepest and most interesting conflict is that between owners and managers. The potential conflict between shareholders (as owners or *principals*) and managers (as *agents*) in particular is well recognised in both the theory and the practice of financial management. Many factors can cause conflict:

(i)   Managers exercise the day-to-day control of running the business. Because shareholders own but do not have the time, expertise or inclination to manage the business themselves, they appoint managers as their agents.

(ii) Managers will tend to maximise their own benefits (remuneration, working conditions, benefits, status), some of which may not obviously be in the interests of shareholders in that they have not earned them. In addition, managers may be unwilling to take risks that might jeopardise their positions or employment, whereas shareholders can spread their risk by investing in many different enterprises. This means that managers may turn down value-creating investment opportunities because of the perceived risks involved.

(iii) Managers have detailed information about the firm that is generally unavailable to shareholders. This is called **information asymmetry**.

(iv) Managers may be highly focused on the short-term whereas many investors buy shares as a long-term investment. This presents a problem if firms seek short-term gain at the expense of long-term value.

Self-seeking managers can behave in illegal ways. The most notorious example of this was the scandal perpetrated by Robert Maxwell, who raided his company's pension fund to fund an illegal share price support programme. The government took this as a signal that it must intervene to protect the general public. Subsequently, a series of committees of investigation were set up to establish better and more open corporate governance procedures, as embodied in the successive reports of the Cadbury (1992), Greenbury (1997), Hampel (1999) and Higgs (2003) committees.

Shareholders also need to protect themselves against management fraud and self-interest. They can monitor the actions of managers through internal and external auditing, and they can ask questions and vote at the annual general meetings. Such monitoring will of course cost time and money. One common strategy is to turn managers into shareholders by paying bonuses in shares or share options. Share options allow managers the option to buy shares at a stated price – known as the **exercise price** – so the higher they can 'manage up' the market price, the more valuable the options become (if the market price is less than the exercise price, the options are worth nothing).

Ultimately, of course, if shareholders are unhappy with the management of their company, they can sell their shares.

1.4 **Business goals**

Firms need to decide and prioritise an overall set of goals from all of the varying demands from stakeholders. Many companies present their aims in two ways: mission statements and statements of objectives.

Mission statements

These tend to be overarching statements usually couched in very general terms. A clear mission statement should accurately explain a firm's *raison d'être*, and what it hopes to achieve in the future. It articulates the firm's essential nature, its values, and its activities. Here are three examples, all of leading supermarkets.

- *J Sainsbury plc*: 'Our mission is to be the consumer's first choice for food, delivering products of outstanding quality and great service at a competitive cost through working "faster, simpler and together".'

- *Safeway plc*: 'Our goal is to be the first choice for those customers who have the opportunity to shop locally in a Safeway store. To deliver this goal, we will focus on:
  - product and price, and be
  - best at freshness
  - best at availability, and
  - best at customer service.'

- *Tesco plc*: 'Our core purpose is to create value for customers to earn their lifetime loyalty.'

Notice that in none of these examples is reference made to owners. Are these firms really in business to make consumers' lives as pleasant as possible?

Statements of objectives

These tend to detail the targets that the company will try to meet or better to achieve the mission. Thus both Sainsbury and Tesco place emphasis on providing customers with value for money and good service, alongside the necessary conditions of well-trained staff, product choice and pleasant, hygienic shopping conditions.

Typical objectives found in company annual reports include:

- financial – to increase profits/reduce borrowings/increase dividends/increase share price

- market – to increase market share/enter new markets/maintain market leadership
- product – to increase product range/diversify into new product areas
- technology – to increase expenditure on research and development
- employment – to ensure security of employment/reduce staff turnover
- environmental – to reduce pollution/use more recycled materials.

In extremis, under hostile trading conditions, even survival may be a valid objective, although companies would not explicitly state this so blatantly to avoid alarming customers, suppliers and investors. It is stated in other ways such as announcing a series of profit warnings, as in the cases of Marconi, the telecoms equipment company (2001) and HP Bulmer, the cider manufacturer (2002). Investors are left to read between the lines.

Self-assessment activity 1.1

Look up mission statements and objectives in the annual reports of firms from different sectors, and compare these with the supermarket objectives above. You can find most annual reports on company websites (often found under 'Information for investors'). Annual reports can be ordered free of charge from ft.com.

1.5 Shareholder wealth maximisation

But what is (or should be) the *paramount* aim of the firm? A moment's thought will confirm that the owners are the group responsible for setting up the firm, and they did not usually do so out of altruism. This is reflected in the basic assumptions of finance theory, viz:

(a) Shareholders are the most important stakeholder group, because:

   (i)   they are the owners – in the same way that you would view yourself as the most important stakeholder if you set up your own business
   (ii) they bear the ultimate risk of loss, sometimes total loss.

(b) From this stems the main objective, that of *maximising* the returns to shareholders. Thus the key focus of financial management is the theory and practice of making investment and financing decisions that maximise shareholder wealth (**shareholder wealth maximisation**).

Decisions that add value to the firm increase the wealth of the shareholders who own that firm. A share in a company is rather like a slice of a cake. The bigger the cake, the bigger the slice will become. The more valuable the firm, the more valuable each share will be.

The role of financial managers thus becomes making decisions that increase the value of the firm. Shareholders will benefit from increased value through higher dividends and/or increasing share prices. Cadbury Schweppes plc, the subject of the short case study on pages 24–6, typifies companies that adopt this focus.

There are major advantages in identifying shareholders as the primary stakeholder group, as identified by a former chief executive officer (CEO) of Chase Manhattan Bank:

'The principal objective of a business enterprise is to generate economic returns to the owners. The notion that the board must somehow balance the interest of shareholders against the interest of other stakeholders fundamentally misconstrues the role of directors. It is, moreover, an unworkable notion because it would leave the board with no criterion for resolving conflicts between interests of shareholders and of other stakeholders, or among different groups of stakeholders.'

(Walter Shipley, CEO Chase Manhattan Bank 1997, quoted by Al Ehrbar, 1998)

Shipley is saying that CEOs can make decisions when focusing on one group (in this case, whether the decision will add value for shareholders) but do not know how to balance out the varying demands if all groups are taken into account.

Furthermore, it is often argued that although the primary objective of shareholder wealth maximisation benefits shareholders, everybody benefits from added value. This view, dating from Adam Smith, is echoed by others:

'The business man ... by pursuing his own interests, frequently promotes that of society more effectually than when he really intends to promote it.'

(Adam Smith, 1776)

'The business of business is business.'

(Commonly attributed to Milton Friedman, US economist)

'We have a precise focus on why we exist: to create real value for our shareholders over the long term.'
'Coca-Cola provides value to everyone that touches it.'

(Coca-Cola annual report 1995)

These views argue that all stakeholders can benefit from a focus on shareholder wealth maximisation. If the cake is bigger, everyone can have a bigger slice. To take one stakeholder group as an example, it is easy to see that it may make sound business sense to pay employees good salaries and provide good working conditions to make them more efficient and more likely to add value in their work.

1.6 The stakeholder approach

An alternative focus is known as the **stakeholder approach**, where businesses make decisions after considering all stakeholder groups, having tried to reach a consensus of views. This approach is illustrated as follows:

> 'Maximising shareholder wealth has always been way down the list of our priorities. Yes, profit is the cornerstone of what we do, but it has never been the point in and of itself. The point in fact is to win, and winning is judged in the eye of the customer and by doing something that you can be proud of. There is a symmetry of logic in this. If we provide real satisfaction to real customers – we will be profitable.'

(John Young, former CEO, Hewlett-Packard)

Here shareholders appear to be secondary (at least in public) to customers and other stakeholders. Maybe it was no coincidence that HP steadily lost market share in the 1990s and was forced into a defensive merger with Compaq in 2002.

A more powerful version of this is displayed in the mission statement of Body Shop plc:

> 'To dedicate our business to the pursuit of social and environmental change.
>
> 1 To creatively balance the financial and human needs of our stakeholders – employees, franchisees, customers, suppliers and shareholders.
>
> 2 To courageously ensure that our business is ecologically sustainable, meeting the needs of the present without compromising the future.
>
> 3 To meaningfully contribute to local, national and international communities in which we trade, by adopting a code of conduct which ensures care, honesty, fairness and respect.
>
> 4 To passionately campaign for the protection of the environment, human and civil rights and against animal testing within the cosmetics and toiletries industry
>
> 5 To tirelessly work to narrow the gap between principle and practice whilst making fun, passion and care part of our daily lives.'

(www.thebodyshop.com)

There is considerable disagreement about the advantages of the approach articulated here, and there are interesting socio-economic differences between countries in this debate.

1.7   A little historical background

Firms in 'Anglo-Saxon' economies (broadly, the USA and the UK plus many of the 'old' Commonwealth countries) have traditionally operated with a strong shareholder-oriented focus. This is largely due to the fact that the bulk of corporate finance in these countries is provided by equity – that is, investment by shareholders. Dividend payouts tend to be high, and firms wanting additional **capital** for strategic investment have had to compete on the financial markets for more capital. To attract more capital requires the firm to show, in addition to strong future prospects, a track record in creating and delivering value. Instead of attracting capital, firms with poor track records frequently become takeover targets for other companies and alternative managerial teams that offer to utilise the corporate assets more effectively, or even break up the firm.

In many other countries, such as France and Germany, a more consensus-seeking stakeholder model was established as part of the post-1945 socio-economic restructuring of those countries. Here, companies tend to be regarded as social institutions, not just as the property of their shareholders. Employees, trade unions and various other stakeholders have a strong say in corporate governance and in labour relations through legal requirements for power-sharing and through the traditional principle of consensus-seeking. In these countries, finance for industry has been provided to a far greater degree by the banking system and, in France, from family sources. Dividend payouts have been lower and more funds typically invested in research and development with uncertain and long-term payoffs. Far fewer companies use the stock markets for finance; indeed, far fewer companies are quoted on local stock markets. A major benefit of this orientation has been a friendly investment climate, with fewer pressures to deliver short-term performance. Indeed, this stability was presented as one underpinning of the impressive record of economic progress once boasted by Japan and Germany. Against this, it discouraged flexibility and responsiveness to change with slower and more cumbersome management decision making, with little threat of inefficient management being taken over.

In the 1980s, several things happened to make the Anglo-Saxon focus seem more appealing:

- The US stock market embarked on the longest bull run in history.

- The breathtaking rate of technical progress emanating from Silicon Valley both fuelled the recovery of the US economy and provided the locomotive force behind the stock market rise, which saw small start-ups such as Microsoft, Intel, Cisco Systems and Oracle grow from acorns to giant oaks.

- Tax changes, notably in the USA and UK, introduced by more rightward-leaning administrations, and eagerly adopted elsewhere, removed, or moderated, the typical fiscal discrimination against dividend payments.

- The removal of official regulations in key sectors, notably telecommunications and airline operation, lowered barriers to new competition and expansion of markets.

- The widespread privatisations of state-owned assets, involving massive stock market flotations, greatly increased the number of shareholders, and enabled many investors to make significant sums of money. (As well as generating substantial revenues for governments.)

- The deregulation of many stock markets (such as the 1986 'Big Bang' on the London Stock Exchange) and the removal of restrictive practices and barriers to overseas participation strengthened the hand of investment bankers in pressurising corporations for higher levels of performance.

- The increasing power of institutional investors, anxious to swell the size of funds under their management, also exerted greater pressure on managers to perform.

It is impossible to weigh the separate contributions of all these factors, but together they created a vastly different business and investment climate. Managers, themselves increasingly rewarded in the form of stock options, became far more keenly aware of their responsibilities and duties towards their employers, i.e. the shareholders. As already observed, such a focus can generate substantial economic benefits for all.

1.8 The Vodafone/Mannesmann case – a seminal event?

The Vodafone/Mannesmann episode reflects changing views and priorities in a country where, until quite recently, it would be fair to say that shareholder interests had not been given the utmost prominence. The notion of running a company primarily in the interests of any single group has been slow to take root in Germany. German post-war reconstruction was based on an unwritten consensus that companies were coalitions of mutually reinforcing interests and all stakeholders were to be considered, if not equal, at least fairly. As a result, industrial relations were relatively harmonious and firms developed close working relationships with banks, which provided a major part of corporate equity as well as loan capital. Dividends were typically parsimonious and expenditures on R&D were high, at least by Anglo-Saxon standards.

Companies were governed by two-tier boards, the supervisory board, 50 per cent of whose members were elected by the workforce, acting as a check on the actions and policies of the executive board, or the board of management. German executives had always been somewhat dismissive of the inclination of US and UK firms to grow by acquisition rather than by internal means, and pointed to the so-called German economic miracle as justification. However, this miracle was beginning to fade – German economic growth was distinctly sluggish in the1980s and 1990s, prompting widespread calls for restructuring of finance and industry along more dynamic lines. According to critics, German industry had become complacent and enveloped in excessively cosy relationships with both the banking system and its labour force, to the relative neglect of shareholder interests.

People began to realise that the almost decade-long era of growth in the USA might have something to do with the concern showed in that country for the owners of companies, and the practice of rewarding managers via generous stock options designed to align their interests more closely with those of shareholders, among whose number they now featured prominently. It seemed 'the times they were a-changing' in the hitherto staid confines of German industrial circles. But, as we explain next, the pendulum may already be swinging in reverse.

1.9 2000-3: stock market slump and corporate scandals

Europe's shift towards the Anglo-Saxon focus on shareholders looked to have become a strong trend by the end of the 1990s. The impending introduction of the euro, the continuing development of the single market, and an increasingly global business perspective all reinforced the momentum. But just as the old European stakeholder model was being written off, events have led to a significant reappraisal. The major world stock markets slumped by 40–50 per cent following the bursting of the 'dotcom bubble' and worsening economic conditions amidst continuing instability in the Middle East.

Many managers have been left with share options which now look worthless. In addition, the financial world was rocked by scandals surrounding the huge failures of companies such as Enron, Global Crossing and WorldCom in the USA, Holzman and Kirch in Germany, and Marconi and Railtrack in the UK. Inevitably, this tarnished the attraction of equity investment for investors, including the army of small, and now disillusioned, ones.

Even the right-wing governments of Italy and France signalled a return to their traditional consensual, social welfare models. The Italian finance minister stated that his government's position was 'private if possible, public if necessary'.

Struggling companies, such as Fiat and France Telecom, are now being bailed out by government packages rather than being left to their own devices (see www.bbc.co.uk, Fiat 15 October 2002, France Telecom 4 December 2002). Another indication of this reappraisal is that the EU has found it difficult to reach agreement on a **takeover** code to operate in the European single market. The Mannesmann takeover, far from starting a trend of mainland European companies being taken over, has served instead to bolster defences. Germany's first mandatory takeover code, which became law in 2002, includes protections from hostile takeovers. Among these is the use of 'poison-pill' defences which make taking over a company unattractive, such as allowing shareholders to sell their shares back to the company at a premium if such a takeover takes place.

For many people, recent events may signal a need to return to basic principles or, to use a cricketing metaphor, 'line and length'. Arguably, directors have been diverted from the real business of business, i.e. to create permanent, rather than transitory, increases in wealth. This requires a focus on the fundamental principles of finance rather than attempting to manipulate value by 'wheeling and dealing'. As ever, cash is at the fountainhead of wealth. Many failed businesses of recent years were in poor cash positions, but were often able to disguise the nature of their difficulties by clever exploitation of prevailing accounting regulations, e.g. Enron and Worldcom (see *Financial Times* 10 October 2003).

1.10 The focus of finance – the big three issues

Whatever the focus of financial management, its exponents face the task of meeting goals using the (usually) limited resources available to them. All businesses are engaged in deploying real resources to optimal effect and also in augmenting those resources. In financial management, the key resource is cash. Hence, financial managers want to utilise cash to maximum effect. This hinges on three key decision areas:

- *The investment decision* – in what assets should the firm invest money in order to add value? This involves identifying the activities that generate cash inflows.

- *The financing decision* – having decided what to invest in, how best can the firm pay for it? This, of course, involves cash outflows, the smaller the better.

- *The payout or dividend decision* – having successfully managed the financial resources at their disposal, how best can managers return value to owners? Should they pay a dividend, and if so how much, and thus how much should they retain in the firm? This deals with the distribution of the net inflows of cash, sometimes called **free cash flows**, because they are free of all other obligations.

Any decision should be aimed at a coherent objective, and judged according to how well it meets that aim. Financial decisions should be judged according to whether they create value, and how much.

Investment decisions are essentially a search for projects that are worth more than they cost to exploit thus creating value. Value usually stems from the exploitation of opportunities to produce new products before other firms spot the gap in the market or to serve new market segments currently ignored by others. These opportunities arise only because of imperfections – gaps in the range of products offered, or in the markets served – and will eventually be eliminated by the arrival of new competition. Until that happens, the first arrival can enjoy '**first mover's advantage**'. A spectacular example of this is the development and marketing of the Viagra drug by the US pharmaceutical giant Pfizer. Pfizer will want to prolong this advantage as long as possible by deterring competition. One way of doing this is to erect barriers to entry, such as tying up the rights to produce the product in patents. These issues are examined in more detail in Chapter 3.

In the case of financing decisions, the same aim applies: seeking ways of financing operations that are worth more than they cost. This implies a search for 'cheap' financing, although there is a strong body of thought that denies that this is possible. Unlike product markets, where effective R&D, for example, can lead to the introduction of a novel product of genuine value to customers, financial markets are far more perfect and, given increasing globalisation, linkage of markets and the revolution in communications, are likely to become increasingly so.

In other words, any disparity between borrowing costs in different locations is likely to be quickly eliminated as people (known as **arbitrageurs**) move money in the direction of greatest return. This pushes down interest rates in the receiving location and pushes them up in the sending location as capital becomes scarcer, until the cost of finance (allowing for inflation) becomes the same in every location.

Moreover, providers of finance are increasingly able to price in the true risks of lending to different categories of client and for different time spans. In modern financial systems, a structure of interest rates is established across the world financial markets that faithfully reflect the risks involved in different types and durations of loan. This is a reflection of **market efficiency**, discussed in Chapter 2. We will see that an efficient market fully incorporates the risk and return characteristics of different securities into their relative market prices. Financing decisions are discussed in Chapter 7.

Finally, the payout or distribution decision is a more tricky issue. People invest money in companies in order to receive higher levels of value, but this value can be delivered in different ways, essentially either in the form of cash dividend or in the form of capital appreciation, should the company invest wisely. The awkward issues involved in this decision are presented in Chapter 10.

It is helpful to visualise the financial manager as operating at the interface of the firm's operations, actual and projected, that drive the firm's *demand for finance* and the financial markets that provide the *supply of finance*. The financial manager's tasks are to provide the right amounts of finance at the optimum cost and at the right times, as well as to advise on the viability of different courses of action.

Figure 1.1 Managing cash flows

In Figure 1.1, arrow 1 represents the flow of finance into the firm, arrow 2 represents the allocation of funds to projects, arrow 3 represents the return flow of cash from successful projects, and arrow 4 represents the return of cash to investors in the form of interest payments and dividends. In most firms, the amount returned to investors is less than the cash generated from operations, as firms wish to retain funds for reinvestment in attractive opportunities.

The figure encapsulates the essence of financial decision making:

● what to invest in – the investment decision

● how to pay for it – the financing decision

● what to do with the proceeds – the dividend decision.

In the next chapter, we will examine the notion of value, as used in finance, in more depth, and how successful decisions in the first of these three areas can enhance it.

References and further reading

Textbooks

Arnold, G (2002) *Corporate Financial Management* (Prentice Hall), chapter 1.
Brealey, R A and Myers S C (2000) *Principles of Corporate Finance* (McGraw-Hill), chapter 1.
Pike, R H and Neale, C W (2003) *Corporate Finance and Investment* (Prentice Hall) chapter 1.
Samuels, J M, Wilkes, F M and Brayshaw, R E (1999) *Management of Company Finance* (Chapman & Hall), chapter 1.
Watson, D and Head, A (2002) *Corporate Finance – Principles and Practice* (Prentice Hall), chapter 1.

Other

Ehrbar, A (1998) *EVA The Real Key to Creating Wealth* (Wiley).

Friedman, M (1962) *Capitalism and Freedom*.

Henderson, D (2001) 'Misguided Virtue: False Notions of Corporate Social Responsibility', Institute of Economic Affairs.

Jensen, M C (2001) 'Value maximisation, stakeholder theory and the corporate objective function', *Journal of Applied Corporate Finance*, Vol. 14, No. 5.

Nobes, C (2001) *Pocket Accounting* (Economist Publications).

Parkinson, J E (1999) *Corporate Power and Responsibility* (Oxford University Press).

Sternberg, E (1999) 'The stakeholder concept: a mistaken doctrine', www.ssrn.com

Vinten, G (2001) 'Shareholder versus stakeholder – is there a governance dilemma?' *Corporate Governance*, Vol. 9, pp. 36–47.

Questions and mini-case studies

1 Should management try to maximise the book, or accounting, value of capital as shown on the balance sheet, or the market value of a company? Why might the two be different?

2 Why might it not be in the best interests of the shareholders for the company to maximise accounting profit?

3 Many company executives now earn in excess of £1 million in basic salary. How might shareholders feel about that?

4 In *Capitalism and Freedom* (1962), Milton Friedman argued that in a free economy, there is one, and only one, social responsibility of business: to use its resources and engage in activities designed to increase its profits so long as it stays within the rules of the game, which is to say, engages in open and free competition without deception or fraud. He further stated that social responsibility is 'fundamentally subversive'. Is finance theory right to emphasise shareholders over other stakeholders? Does managing for shareholders mean exploiting other groups?

5 How useful in practice are mission statements?

Mini-case study - Rentokil

On 18 August 1999, Rentokil, the business services group involved in cleaning and pest control, announced that it was to abandon its long-standing target of increasing profit by 20 per cent per annum. It was being replaced by the less ambitious target of substantially outperforming the sector as measured by total shareholder return, although the required level of outperformance was not revealed. 'One of the benefits of this objective is that it is not quantifiable until after the event,' said the chief executive, Clive Thompson, who made the announcement. In addition the company announced that it was to sell non-core assets, which accounted for about 15 per cent of the group's profits, and return the proceeds to shareholders. Thompson blamed the reduced profit performance on the fact that a lot of Rentokil's business was low-margin; attempts to raise prices had resulted in a loss of some contracts.

Thompson was known in the City as 'Mr 20 per cent'. His formula for this 20 per cent growth was to achieve 7 per cent from sales growth, 8 per cent from cost savings and 5 per cent from acquisitions. He still expected earnings growth this year to be in excess of 10 per cent, although this was more cautious than the 10–15 per cent expected growth that he had announced three months before.

This more cautious stance about future earnings, and the official abandonment of the 20 per cent growth target, was taken badly by the market. The market was unhappy that the company's statement to the Stock Exchange contained just two paragraphs and gave insufficient detail about what was going wrong. Shares in the company fell by nearly 20 per cent on the day of the announcement. One analyst stated that the company's organic growth had been weak for some time and the target had been increasingly achieved by making acquisitions to 'buy' profit.

Thompson said that he expected that the company's remuneration committee (comprising only non-executive directors) might wish to amend the senior executive bonus scheme in the light of his announcement. At that time the bonus was paid if the company's annual profit rose by more than 10 per cent.

Required

(a) Give reasons why you think Rentokil's share price fell so much after these announcements.

(b) Compare the new target relative to the old one – was it an 'improvement'?

(c) How might the remuneration committee view these changes at its next meeting?

Source: For further information see *The Times* 19 August 1998

Mini-case study – Bradford City FC

The financial plight of many football clubs provides a stark demonstration of the potential for conflict among stakeholders, especially when the going gets tough. In 2002, many of the clubs in the Nationwide League struggled financially, particularly with the collapse of the ITV Digital contract, which was worth £178 million to the Nationwide clubs. This resulted in clubs such as Bradford City and Leicester City going into administration.

Administrators run the club for the protection of the creditors while a buyer is found. They will often insist on cost-cutting measures while a sale is negotiated. Cutting the major cost of players' wages is difficult since all clubs are obliged under an agreement with the players' union to meet player contracts, often negotiated in the good times and worth up to £20,000 per week in Bradford's case. When these clubs were relegated into the Nationwide from the Premiership, they lost a considerable income, measured in millions of pounds. The collapse of ITV Digital completed the misery as the clubs contemplated sky-high player contracts, falling income and smaller crowds. Some of the bigger clubs in the Nationwide were nego-tiating for a bigger split of the money available from television, but this upset the smaller clubs, which would inevitably be hit by any such deal.

A further problem has been the collapse of the transfer market as all clubs, big and small, fear that the golden financial era of football may be over, and that future TV deals will be smaller than before. Thus, clubs find that they are unable to sell high-contract players and often end up giving them free transfers just to save the wages. Leeds United, which in 2001 reached the semi-finals of the European Champions League, revealed the full financial cost of that effort with debts in excess of £70 million at one point. By failing to reach Europe in 2002, the club was forced to sell and even give away players to compensate for the resulting loss in revenue.

The chairmen of these clubs often carry the can for the failures. By betting heavily on success through spending extravagantly on transfer fees and giving lucrative contracts, but then failing to deliver success on the pitch, they often come under heavy criticism, and usually leave. They also stand to lose a lot of money themselves – Bradford's chairman Geoffrey Richmond calculated that he would lose up to £15 million.

Going into administration has its critics. Gordon Taylor of the Professional Footballers Association was quoted as saying: 'To go into administration and write off your debts totally destroys your credibility. There should be no place in the league for a club run according to the chairman's whims.'

Required
Identify as many stakeholders as you can who are affected in this case. For each stakeholder group, outline their demands and where conflicts are likely to occur.

Mini-case study – easyJet plc

Read the following *Financial Times* article and comment on how each of the stakeholder groups is affected by easyJet's takeover of Go in May 2002.

easyJet is taking over Go in a deal that creates Europe's largest low-cost airline and makes millionaires of six Go executives, including Barbara Cassani, its chief executive.

Ms Cassani, who has strongly opposed the sale to easyJet, will receive £9.5 million for her 4 per cent stake. She told staff in a recorded telephone message that she would leave the group by early July.

The takeover, valuing Go at £374 million, will see easyJet leap-frog Ryanair to become leader of the European no-frills airline sector.

It is to be financed in part through a deeply discounted rights issue to raise £276.7 million, and in part through £113.3 million cash.

The terms of the deal were welcomed by investors, who sent easyJet's share price up 11 per cent, or 50p, to close at 510p.

The deal will trigger a fierce battle between Boeing and Airbus for one of the biggest aircraft orders this year.

Both easyJet and Go were already negotiating multi-billion-dollar aircraft orders before the takeover, and the combined group is expected to order more than 100 aircraft within two months.

The transaction is a coup for 3i, the UK venture capital group, which backed a £110 million management buy-out of Go from British Airways only 11 months ago.

It will help to compensate for the losses that 3i has suffered on technology investments.

3i said it would receive £149 million from the deal, a 156 per cent gain on the £58 million it paid for a 40 per cent stake last June.

Together with associated funds, 3i controls a 67.5 per cent stake in Go, with Barclays Private Equity holding 10 per cent and Go management and staff 22.5 per cent.

However, the Go management team, which Ms Cassani said last week was '100 per cent' behind her, has split over the deal.

Ms Cassani said four leading Go executives were quitting, including Andrew Cowen, chief financial officer, while three were staying to take positions at easyJet. These include Ed Winter, chief operating officer, who will become acting Go chief executive and will lead the transition team at easyJet.

In total, Go's 800 staff would receive a £53 million windfall for their 22.5 per cent stake, Ms Cassani said. Staff would pay 10p for options on shares that were now worth more than £14 each.

She said it had been 'very difficult' for the Go management team but she believed Go was 'a better company' than easyJet and urged her staff to take the 'Go spirit' to carry out 'a reverse culture takeover'.

easyJet said it was making a 4 for 11 rights issue at 265p a share, a 42.4 per cent discount to Tuesday's closing price of 460p.

Stelios Haji-Ioannou, easyJet founder and chairman, and his brother and sister, who control 58.5 per cent of easyJet's equity, will only take up shares to the value of their rights. After the deal, they will control 48.3 per cent, with Mr Haji-Ioannou's stake falling from 26.7 per cent to 22.8 per cent.

Go has £116.4 million of net cash on its balance sheet, giving it an enterprise value of £257.6 million, or £668 million, adjusted for capitalised leases on 26 aircraft.

Source: Kevin Done, 'Go staff share £53m windfall in easyJet tie up',
Financial Times, 17 May 2002

Required

(a) Analyse the main stakeholder groups that have been affected by this takeover
(b) Discuss
   ● the basis of the current market valuation of Go
   ● the basis of easyjet's bid price for Go.
(c) As an analyst what are the strenghts and possible problems surrounding this takeover. Include an analysis of the share price reaction in your answer.

Self-assessment answers

1.1
Over to you.

Case study: Cadbury Schweppes plc

Company reports and accounts are an excellent source of examples to illustrate the strategies, and progress towards achieving them, of the firms in question. The following extract is from the report and accounts of the leading UK snacks and beverages firm Cadbury Schweppes. It clearly states the overriding objective of the firm – its true mission – and the strategies that it follows in trying to achieve it.

You will find indications of substantial 'wheeling and dealing' as the firm divests peripheral activities and concentrates resources on selected market arenas. Inevitably, there are terms used here that are not dealt with until a later stage in the book, so you will find it helpful to use the glossary, and also perhaps to read ahead a little. You will certainly find it useful to familiarise yourself with key terms and concepts used in the financial world.

Cadbury Schweppes annual report 2001

Cadbury Schweppes' governing objective is growth in shareowner value. The actions of the entire organisation, from top to bottom, around the world, are directed to this objective. The strategy by which we will achieve this objective is:

- Focusing on our core growth markets of beverages and confectionery.

- Developing robust, sustainable market positions which are built on a platform of strong brands with supported franchises.

- Expanding our market share through innovation in products, packaging and route to market where economically profitable.

- Enhancing our market positions by acquisitions or disposals where they focus on strategy, value-creation and available market opportunities.

Managing for value is the process which supports the achievement of our strategy. In 1997, we made our public commitment to this process and set clear financial objectives for 1997 through to 2000.

- To grow **earnings per share** (EPS) by at least 10 per cent per annum.

- To generate at least £150 million of free cash flow.

- Whilst accepting that it was not totally within our control, striving to double **total shareowner return** (TSR) every four years.

At the end of this first four-year tranche, on average, in the four years from 1997 to 2000, underlying earnings per share grew by 11 per cent, free cash flow averaged £252 million and total shareowner return grew by 84 per cent. To double shareowner value in four years is a stretching objective and we are pleased to have come so close to our goal.

Managing for value - Phase 1 results: 1997-2000

	1997	1998	1999	2000	Average	Total
Underlying EPS growth*	10%	11%	8%	13%	11%	**49%**
Free cash flow	£157m	£157m	£292m	£401m	£252m	**£1,007m**
TSR growth	+14%	+57%	+2%	+2%	+16%	**+84%**

* at constant currencies and excluding restructuring, goodwill amortisation and exceptional items

Growing for value

As we enter the next four-year phase of this process, we have committed to challenging objectives once again. While our earnings per share and total shareowner return objectives remain the same, we have increased the free cash flow target to £300 million per year. Greater emphasis is being put on growth, and management is being incentivised to focus on promoting 'good' (that is, *economically profitable*) growth through innovation - in products and packaging - and extending the availability of our products into new channels of distribution. This formula applies equally to developed and emerging markets.

Recent strategic developments

Over the past 18 months, we have acquired a number of leading brands and companies from around the world. In 2001, acquisitions to date include the confectionery brand Mantecol in Argentina, Slush Puppie, the frozen non-carbonated beverage, in the United States, and Spring Valley, a leading fruit juice and flavoured milk producer in Australia. In July, we announced the acquisition of La Casera, Spain's third largest soft drinks manufacturer, and in August, the acquisition of the ReaLemon and ReaLime brands in the United States. We also purchased Carteret, a contract packer of Snapple in the United States.

In September 2001, we acquired Pernod Ricard's soft drinks brands such as Orangina and Yoo-Hoo and businesses in Continental Europe, North America and Australia.

In 2000, we acquired Mauna La'i tropical juice and Snapple, the zany and innovative natural flavours drink in the United States, which has added a leading brand in the non-carbonated beverages market in the United States to our portfolio, providing a greater platform for growth in that market. We also acquired the Pepsi Lion Nathan joint venture bottling business in Australia. In confectionery, we made our largest ever acquisition with Hollywood in France and acquired Trebor Wuxi in China that included local trademarks such as SPORTLIFE and POLI sugar-free and low-sugar chewing gum, and we also bought out our minority interest in our confectionery operations in South Africa.

In 1999, the $1 billion sale of our beverages brands in 160 markets where our presence was modest enabled us to focus our resources on three markets – North America, Europe and Australia.

Required

Answer the following questions:

1 Whom does Cadbury Schweppes see as its primary stakeholder group?

2 What strategies is it following to meet the demands of this group?

3 How might these strategies affect other stakeholder groups for this company?

4 How well has the company performed against these objectives?

5 Are the strategies:
   ● qualitative or quantitative?
   ● primary and secondary?
   ● short-term and long-term?
   ● financial and non-financial?
   ● specific and general?

For further information on Cadbury Schweppes' corporate social responsibility policy:

http://www.cadburyschweppes.com/social_responsibility/index.html

Source: Website: www.cadburyschweppes.com;
Cadbury Scheppes, Annual Report 2001

2

THE MEANING OF SHAREHOLDER VALUE

Veba to devote energy to shareholders

In the mid-1990s, Veba AG (now part of Eon) was a widely diversified German conglomerate, rooted in the energy and chemical industries. Until the 1990s, its markets were largely protected by government-mandated barriers to entry but they are now characterised by deregulation and mounting competition. Veba was a comparatively early convert to the shareholder value principle, as suggested by the following statement:

'By investing in shares, investors are fully aware that they are limiting their role to that of providers of capital. In return, they expect their investment to be managed professionally, require comprehensive information on corporate strategies and adequate disclosure of company results, and not least, expect an appropriate return on the capital they have made available.

To formulate a policy according to shareholder value principles is not only in the interests of shareholders but also is a solid base for any enterprise. After all, the adoption of value-oriented objectives ensures that all corporate divisions generate an adequate return according to their respective business risks. In general, financial resources will be made available only to operating units that achieve the required returns. Business activities that destroy value by failing to meet these essential targets have to be restructured. Our primary objective is a long-lasting enhancement of corporate value. Our shareholder-oriented policy does not therefore aim simply to make a "quick buck".'

Source: annual report 1994

Objectives:
This chapter aims to:

- explain how value is measured in finance

- introduce the concepts of present value and net present value

- identify the twin determinants of value

- explain the function of stock markets

- explain how efficient stock markets record the value of firms

- discuss the agency issues that may hinder value creation.

As with several of the subsequent chapters, we make reference to the accounts of the 'company of your choice' – it will be useful to have its report and accounts to hand.

2.1 Introduction

The first chapter explained the range of decision problems financial managers face and sketched out the concept of value, as it is used in financial management. Remember that the value attributed to any item today, or its 'present value', is likely to include the prospect of future cash inflows. How to assess the 'present value' of future expected cash flows is the first task of this chapter. This will allow us to identify which financial decisions will add value and which will not.

Any rational investor will require a return to compensate them for giving up money now. Most people really prefer to spend money now and enjoy the benefits of what is bought rather than save it for the future. The return required in order to make this sacrifice of saving will depend on three factors:

- *The size of the present sacrifice.* A rich man may be content to earn 5 per cent p.a. on an investment of £100; an impoverished student will want a much higher return because saving £100 involves a much greater sacrifice in the present.

- *The rate of inflation.* Inflation erodes the value of money – if an investment earns merely the rate of inflation, the investor is no better off in real terms. The return that he/she earns is merely keeping the investor 'standing still'.

- *The returns available on other investments.* These returns will include the general level of interest rates in the economy, plus an appropriate 'risk premium'. The higher the perceived risk, the higher the risk premium that an investor requires. The best available alternative return for a comparable risk is called the **opportunity cost** – this is the value given up, i.e. opportunity forgone, by investing in one firm rather than in the best alternative.

Some of these concepts are brought out in the example in the next section – for the moment, we assume that there is no inflation.

2.2 The touchstone of success - the pursuit of shareholder value

Put in simple terms, a successful financial decision is one that creates value – that is, it is worth more than it costs to implement. Naturally, investors are attracted by the prospect that their company will create wealth for them, but how do we measure the wealth-creating potential of the activity? Consider a simple example.

A newly formed company invites subscriptions of £1,000 per share from investors who require an annual return of 15 per cent. The money raised is to be invested in a short-term project with a single cash return after one year.

What minimum cash flow is necessary to make investors no worse off? This is easy – in order to meet the minimum required return of 15 per cent, the end-year cash flow per share must be no lower than:

£1,000 (1 + 15%) = £1,150

Our investor is indifferent between £1,000 now and £1,150 in a year's time. Only when the investment earns more than 15 per cent (i.e. returns more than £1,150 in a year's time) will the investment add value or wealth to the investor and thus make him better off. Now imagine that based on the available information, a future cash flow of £1,300 is envisaged in a year's time. This clears the bare minimum by a margin of £150, so will be attractive to this investor. But how much better off will he now be?

To answer this question, the investor must appreciate that £1 received in the future is worth less than £1 received now simply because if received now, it can be invested elsewhere. In other words, £150 extra in a year's time is not worth £150 in 'today's money'. To calculate the **present value** of £150 receivable in a year's time, we ask: 'What amount of money invested today for one year will be worth £150 in a year's time?' This can be found using the following formula and inserting the return that can be achieved on any investment today:

$$\text{Present value (PV)} = \frac{\text{future value (FV)}}{(1 + \text{rate of interest})}$$

Assuming that any money invested today can earn 15 per cent, this formula

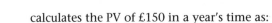

calculates the PV of £150 in a year's time as:

$$PV = \frac{£150}{(1+0.15)} = £130 \text{ (to the nearest whole number)}$$

In other words, if one invested £130 today at 15 per cent, then in one year the investment would be worth £150 as a result of compounding at 15 per cent. £130 is the present value of £150 in a year's time if the rate of interest is 15 per cent. In this example, this is the increase in value or wealth to the investor of this investment as it is the excess over the required return of £1,150 in present day equivalent pounds.

It is more usual to calculate this added value by looking at the total cash flows, and to deduct the initial outlay from the present value of the future inflow.

The present value of the total cash inflow is simply:

$$PV = £1,300 \times \frac{1}{1.15} = \frac{£1,300}{1.15} = £1,130$$

This result is known as the *gross present value (GPV)*. It signifies the value of the whole activity, although it does not measure the value actually *created* by it. To generate a GPV of £1,130 requires an initial outlay of £1,000. The added value can then be found by netting off from the GPV the outlay required to undertake the activity. The resulting figure, known as the *net present value (NPV)*, measures the amount of wealth created:

$$NPV = (£1,130 - £1,000) = £130$$

This result reflects the fact that before the project is announced, the investor's wealth is £1,000. Once the investor invests in this investment, he expects £1,300 in a year's time, which has a present value of £1,130. As a result of this investment, the investor is wealthier by £130. An investment will have a NPV if the return on the investment is greater than the investor's required return.

Self-assessment activity 2.1

When can the investor realise his increase in wealth?
(answer at end of chapter)

Company managers acting in the best interests of owners should operate in exactly the same way – their aim is to maximise the additional wealth for owners. This means undertaking all available investment projects that have a positive NPV, or if forced to choose between projects, undertaking the ones with the highest NPVs.

Notice that to find the present value we have applied a *discount factor*, or conversion factor, equal to 1/(1.15). Finding a present value is called *discounting*, which involves, in effect, applying the 'exchange rate' between money received now and money receivable in a future year. This is akin to finding, say, the sterling value of a given amount in US dollars by applying the sterling/dollar exchange rate. If this rate of exchange is, say, \$1.50 per £1, then in sterling terms, \$300 is worth \$300/1.50 = £200. We thus find the sterling equivalent of the \$300 by discounting the dollars at the exchange rate, namely the ratio [1 : 1.5].

Discounting, and the reason for doing it, reflects one of the most fundamental concepts in finance – the *time value of money*. Quite simply, money received or held now has a greater value than money receivable in the future. Notice that this proposition is independent of any inflation of the price level that would undermine future purchasing power. The need to compensate people for the cost of waiting for their money (sometimes called the *price of time*) applies even in the absence of inflation, unless lenders are exceptionally altruistic! Inflation merely adds to the case for offering compensation for waiting.

2.3 The meaning of the NPV

Finding an NPV figure is simple, but what does the NPV signify? Projects with positive NPVs offer three things to investors. Using our simple project as an example, its cash flow of £1,300 is high enough to:

- recover the initial outlay of £1,000, *and*

- meet the finance charge, i.e. the minimum required return of (15% × £1,000) = £150, *and*

- offer a surplus of £150

The meaning of this surplus return after capital recovery and the finance charge is crucial. When discounted at the required return, we find:

$$\text{PV of £150 in one year} = \frac{£150}{(1.15)} = £130$$

Notice that this is the NPV of the project – the NPV is thus the discounted or present value of the activity after meeting all finance charges, including return of initial capital. It measures how much better off the shareholders become due to the company investing in the project. In theory, this should be reflected in the market value of the shares, i.e. the equity, or ownership stake of the company. If they do not want to wait for completion of the project, the owners could sell out at this higher value to other investors (assuming they wanted a similar return).

To repeat, the value of a project is the discounted value of its *total* returns, while the value created is the discounted value of its *net* returns. The link with project value and the value of a whole enterprise should now be easy to grasp. A company is a collection of projects, so the value of the whole firm is the value of all its future discounted cash flows, and the value created by the managers is the value over and above the required return of the funds invested by owners. When the stock market sets a value on a company, it is implicitly discounting the future cash flows at a rate of discount that reflects investors' opportunity costs and attitude to risk.

Self-assessment activity 2.2

A firm has a one-year contract to sell goods that cost £100,000 to buy now, at a price of £180,000 in one year. Profits tax of £20,000 is payable on the deal. Shareholders require a return of 12 per cent. How much value is created by this venture?
(answer at end of chapter)

Capitalisation

The discounting process is also called *capitalising* – setting a single capital value on a stream of future income payments. This is why the market value of the total issued shares of a company is called its **capitalisation**, or **market capitalisation**, which is simply the market price per share times the number of shares in issue. Of course, discounting in order to capitalise cash flow streams over more than one year is a more complex operation. We defer this until Chapter 4, which examines investment appraisal in detail.

To illustrate capitalisation, on 31 December 2002 the closing price per ordinary share of Six Continents plc, the UK-based global hotels and pubs group, was 502p. This price, multiplied by the number of issued shares (867 million), gave a capitalisation of:

867 million × £5.02 = £4.352 million

Self-assessment activity 2.3

Consult a quality newspaper with a comprehensive financial coverage.
What is the share price, and the capitalisation, of your chosen company?
By implication, how many shares have been issued?
Cross-check your answer by reference to the report and accounts. This will detail the number of shares in issue.
What happened to the share price yesterday?
Why do you think the price changed?

Section 2.4 examines the behaviour of markets and looks at some of the factors that cause share prices to vary.

2.4 **The twin determinants of value**

The key determinants of company value are expressed in diagrammatic form in Figure 2.1. Put at its simplest, these two key value determinants are, first, the investment policy of the firm, which, if successful, determines the future cash flows, out of which dividends may be paid, and second, the rate at which these cash flows are discounted (the required rate of return).

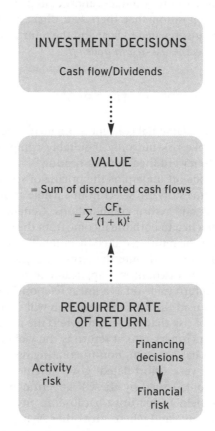

Figure 2.1 The twin determinants of value

The discount rate depends on the time value of money and the inherent risk of the company's chosen activity. Some lines of business are inherently less risky than others. For example, the supply of bulky commodities such as cement and aggregates which are expensive to import and have relatively stable demands is less exposed to risk than, say, consumer electronics, which is import-intensive and subject to rapid changes in technology. The fluctuation in returns due to purely business-related factors is called *business or activity risk*.

In addition, the required return may also depend on the financial policy of the firm. As we will see in Chapter 8, some methods of financing pose more risks than others.

Using borrowed money is more risky than equity because lenders have a prior claim on profits and can insist on receiving interest even in a bad year. This may plunge the poorly-performing firm into insolvency. Moreover, short-term debt is more risky than long-term debt as it can be withdrawn more rapidly. To compensate for these financial risks, investors generally require additional returns i.e. there will also be a financial risk premium built into the discount rate facing firms that borrow.

This discussion introduces another important building block in finance – the simple proposition that there is a direct relationship between the risks that investors are prepared to bear and the return they require as compensation. This is known as the *risk–return trade-off*.

The risk-return trade-off

This is a fundamental concept in finance – the notion that people are prepared to undertake risk but only if suitably compensated by a risk premium high enough to reward them for risk-bearing.

This trade-off underpins the pricing of securities in capital markets. In these markets, investors can select from a whole array of securities, each reflecting different risk and return combinations. Generally, the higher the risk or uncertainty attached to both the income from the security and its future capital value, the higher the return required by rational investors. The importance of this relationship is that it defines the terms on which firms have access to capital, and therefore the discount rate applicable to future cash flows. Figure 2.2 portrays the risk–return trade-off as a linear relationship.

As you read through this text, you will encounter different concepts of risk. The type of risk that is relevant here is the risk of fluctuations in the returns.

The benchmark rate of return is the yield on an (effectively) risk-free asset because it has a certain, non-fluctuating return. This is usually taken to be the yield on very short-dated government securities, such as three-month Treasury bills issued by the UK government. These securities are risk-free if they are held to maturity because an investor knows exactly the payment he will receive and when. Any other securities have to offer an extra yield to compensate for risk.

Corporate bonds are more risky than government bonds because firms are more likely to default than governments, while even riskier are ordinary shares, or equities. Holders of ordinary shares receive a return only after all other claimants have been paid – indeed, there is no *obligation*, legal or moral, even in a year of good profits, to pay a dividend at all.

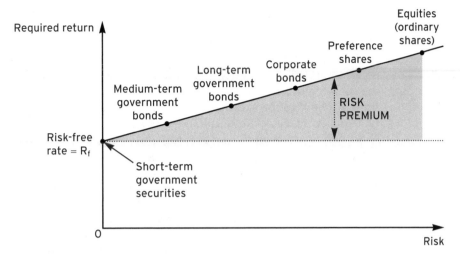

Figure 2.2 The risk–return trade-off

Moreover, in the event of insolvency, the ordinary shareholder, being last in line for payment from the proceeds of liquidating the firm's assets, could well receive nothing. Conversely, the risk to the company is low since failure to pay a dividend will not provoke legal action as with non-payment of interest on bonds.

It is useful to remember the two-sided nature of the risk attaching to securities. Bonds are risky for the firm but far less so for the investor, while equities are risky for the investor but not for the firm. Of course, if the firm persistently paid no return to investors, the board of directors should not be surprised to receive demands for their resignation from shareholders or takeover offers from other firms.

The shape and position of the trade-off is not set in stone. For example, if the monetary authorities decide to increase interest rates, the benchmark rate will rise and the schedule will bodily shift upwards, while if increasing economic uncertainty made people less prepared to accept risks, i.e. become more risk-averse, the schedule might become steeper, i.e. it would pivot.

Self-assessment activity 2.4

What impact did the events of 9/11 have on the risk–return trade-off in world financial markets?
(answer at end of chapter)

In summary, identifying the risk–return trade-off is important for the financial manager as it defines the rates of return which investors require on different types of security which drives the cost of capital, the denominator in the valuation expression. Also, it provides a reminder that investors are (mostly) risk-averse, that is, they will undertake risk, but only if suitably compensated. This should not be confused with risk-avoidance, which involves seeking to *minimise* risk.

The required return that investors expect from their holdings in a firm thus depends on market conditions, and these, of course, can vary. This means that the valuation of a firm, and thus the value of the owners' wealth tied up in that firm, is subject to the vagaries of stock market fluctuation. Quite simply, when share prices change, market capitalisations also change.

So, why do share prices change? Share prices (and hence the total value of the company – its market capitalisation) change because people's expectations about the amount of future cash flows (and hence future dividend-paying capacity) alter and/or people look for higher or lower returns than hitherto (perhaps due to a change in the perception of the risk of those future cash flow expectations).

There is an obvious relationship between company financial decisions and the stock market value of the equity – decisions that are perceived to be sound create favourable expectations about company prospects. It is, therefore, important to keep the stock market informed about the company's operations, without, of course, releasing commercially sensitive information. A stock market which responds accurately and rapidly to new information made available about the company (good or bad!) is said to be 'efficient'. The next section examines in more detail another concept fundamental to understanding value, the so-called *Efficient Markets Hypothesis*.

2.5 The Efficient Markets Hypothesis (EMH)

What is a financial market? What are its functions? The following story illustrates superbly how financial markets behave – essentially they set prices of stocks and shares by processing information.

> Within an hour of the Challenger Space Shuttle crash in 1986 the market had pinpointed Morton Thiokol Inc., manufacturer of the infamous O-ring, as the culprit. The firm's one-day decline of 12 per cent was quick and permanent and corresponded to the subsequent losses in terms of legal liability, repair costs and lost future business. By contrast, the other firms involved in the Shuttle programme suffered only temporary stock price setbacks that recovered for the most part by the end of trading on the day of the crash.
>
> It remains unclear exactly how the market received information about Morton Thiokol's O-ring problems before the enquiry had even been launched and concluded. Although there had been previous concerns by NASA regarding the seals on the Space Shuttle, this information was not publicly available.
>
> *Source*: Based on Maloney and Mulherin, 2003

The importance of financial markets

The EMH is most usually discussed in relation to the efficiency of capital markets. Capital markets are the markets in long-term finance linking providers of long-term funds with those who require long-term finance. The highest-profile capital market is the Stock Exchange where investors provide long-term finance by purchasing company shares, debentures and government securities. As well as the main markets, such as the New York and London Stock Exchanges, there are markets that provide for the financing of smaller firms, such as the Alternative Investment Market (AIM) in the UK.

It is useful to appreciate that capital markets perform two main functions:

- *The primary function* – to allow firms to raise new capital for investment purposes by selling new securities, e.g. equity and debt. This is the new issue market, on which **initial public offerings** (IPOs) are made.

- *The secondary function* – to enable people to realise their assets by selling existing securities to others wanting to expand, or rearrange, their portfolios.

Self-assessment activity 2.5

Look out for news of an impending IPO in your local or some other stock market.
How much of the firm's equity is being floated? At what price?
At what level is the firm being valued? Would you want to invest in this one? If not, why not?
Plan to look back at some stage and see whether the flotation was a success.

In fulfilling these functions, the role of price is crucial – unless people are confident that share prices accurately reflect the value inherent in companies, they will be reluctant to use the markets. In other words, they need reassurance that the valuation of financial assets genuinely reflects company earnings prospects. Financial managers also will want to look to the markets both for reliable signals to guide investment and financing decisions and for the market's assessment of how well they are performing in existing activities.

A market is deemed efficient when prices instantaneously and fully reflect all relevant available information in an unbiased way. A disreputable second-hand car dealer might put a 'For Sale £4,000' sticker on the windscreen of one of the cars on the forecourt. This price would be unlikely to be efficient in that it would not reflect all information relevant to the value of the particular car. In particular, it would be difficult to spot defects in the vehicle without a detailed inspection of the bodywork and the engine. Also casual inspection would give little information about the service history of the car.

Share prices on the Stock Exchange must not be like this car price sticker, otherwise investors will not trade shares through the market and companies will experience difficulty raising the necessary finance they need.

Among the requirements for a market to be efficient are:

- a large numbers of buyers and sellers (no individual dominates the market)

- transaction costs do not discourage trading

- cheap and ready access to up-to-date information.

A good example of an efficient market with which you will be familiar is the housing market. On housing estates, with standard models, it is possible to get a reasonable 'feel' for what a particular house might be worth, based on recent transactions. Even the market in second-hand cars may display evidence of efficiency in many cases (disreputable car dealers excepted). By looking around, it is possible to estimate how much a particular model of a particular year might cost – anything much above indicates it is overpriced, and anything much below is likely to arouse suspicion. The efficiency of many other second-hand markets, e.g. for computers or golf clubs, may suffer from lack of sufficient numbers of buyers and sellers. In such cases, prices for second-hand goods can be very low.

It is therefore important that investors are assured that the price they pay for any security such as share is a fair reflection of the value that the share represents. Otherwise, investors will be deterred from buying. This could be a particular problem if the buyer thinks that the seller knows something that he, the buyer, does not. In other words, stock markets will function adequately only if both sides feel that there is no hidden information. Different levels of 'information efficiency' have been investigated.

The three forms of market efficiency

Fama (1970) identified three forms of information efficiency for stock markets:

1 Weak-form

In a weak-form efficient market, today's prices fully reflect all information about past share price movements. Hence, a study of past share price movements will *not* earn investors abnormal returns because all of this information is already included in the price. This means that past share price movements are no guide to future share price movements. The statistical proof of this proposition was given by Kendall (1953) who showed that share prices follow a *random walk*.

Random walks
In the 1950s, it was commonly believed that share price graphs showed patterns and trends that would be repeated in the future. This meant that if the trends

could be spotted early on, investment decisions could be made accordingly to profit from it. However, Kendall found that security prices, e.g. shares, actually followed a random walk, i.e. there was no relation between changes in the price today and changes yesterday. Thus, yesterday's price change gives no prediction about today's foreseeable change – there are no trends or patterns.

A good example of a 'random walk' is tossing a coin. I may have tossed ten consecutive heads, but of course the next toss could be a head or a tail. The fact that I have just tossed ten consecutive heads (a trend of heads) was pure chance and gives no prediction about the next toss. Nasser Hussain, former England cricket captain, once lost eleven tosses in a row.

Self-assessment activity 2.6

A friend gleefully informs you that the EMH must be nonsense as her investment adviser has managed to outperform the market in each of the last four years. As a believer in the EMH, how do you respond? (answer at end of chapter)

Old ideas die hard. **Technical analysts**, or **chartists**, still like the old ideas and look at the past to predict the future. At its simplest, a coin-tossing chartist would predict the next toss by examining the pattern of past tosses. Share chartists are more sophisticated than this, but the principle is the same – intensive scrutiny of graphs of share prices to try to predict future movements or patterns. For example:

- they use various 'filter rule' (e.g. buy if the share goes up by more than 1 per cent for two consecutive days in the belief that this heralds the start of a trend)
- they look for patterns in the share price over time, such as a 'head and shoulders' pattern
- they look for price 'breakouts' from a specified price range.

But random walks cannot be predicted, however sophisticated the statistical analysis of share price graphs employed by Chartists. Their sole source of information is the graphs of past share prices. One famous chartist of old is said to have put up boards on his office windows so that he was not distracted by other information, such as what the weather was like that day.

The basic fact is that even if it is successful, the winner has no understanding of why he wins, simply because his success is down to luck, and like all streaks of luck, they run out. If a persistently successful dealing rule existed, other investors would realise the opportunity and the loophole would soon be closed.

For example, if share prices always went up on 1 May, what do you think would happen? Of course, people would anticipate this annual event and buy in April, thus creating an 'April effect' and most likely taking their profits on or before 1 May when history suggests that share prices will be high. Instead, however, prices will now fall on 1 May!

Forecasting share prices – a mug's game?

The year 2002 was the worst ever recorded for UK equities. The FTSE 100 index ended the year at 3,940, above its worst, but still reflecting a loss of 25 per cent of its start-year value (4,925) and a third successive annual decline. During the whole of the 20th century, a decline in the overall market for three straight years had been recorded only once before. Following declines in 2000 and 2001, many experts were convinced that 2002 would see a reversal in stock market fortunes, especially as memories of 9/11 faded. Well, it was not to be. So, what will happen in 2003? Surely, there cannot be a fourth successive fall!

By the time this book goes to print, you will have a pretty good idea. Meanwhile, in the table below we give the forecasting record for three brave souls (names, but not employers, withheld to protect the innocent!) who gave their forecasts at the end of 2002 for the upcoming year. For the record, their predictions for 2002 are also recorded. (Notice that Expert A did actually predict a fall for 2002.)

	Forecast for end-2002	Forecast for end-2003
Expert A (Credit Suisse)	4,600	4,200
Expert B (HSBC)	5,700	4,200
Expert C (Deutsche Bank)	6,200	5,000
Expert D (Legal & General)	6,000	4,600
Expert E (Bear Stearns)	5,800	5,000

Information flows – for better or for worse

The reason why share prices follow a random walk is because of the unpredictability of the arrival of new information on to the market. At any point in time, share prices include all available information. They will move only if there is new relevant (i.e. price-sensitive) information. This information could be:

- positive – improving future prospects, increasing today's price
- negative – worsening future prospects, reducing today's price
- neutral – no change in future prospects, no reason for the price to move.

Figure 2.3 shows the possibilities. Today's share price is X, but what will happen tomorrow? Who knows? The share price may increase above X or drop below X

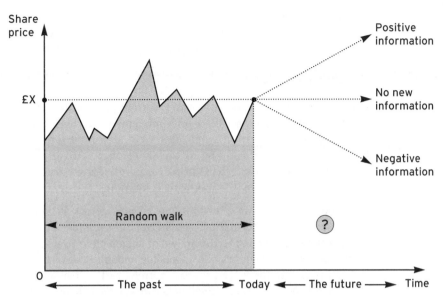

Figure 2.3 How share prices respond to new information

according to the type of new information. Possible examples of price-sensitive information include:

● company financial results

● appointment of a new chairman

● introduction of a new product

● rumours of a takeover bid

● general economic indicators, such as inflation or the exchange rate

● political events such as a general election

● actions of a competitor.

Notice that some types of information are specific to the firm in question and others affect the prospects of all firms in the market, although probably to different degrees.

Given that there are so many potential kinds of information which can affect a firm's share price at any particular time, it is clearly not possible to predict the future pattern of any share price. This also helps to explain why many share prices are so volatile and change by the minute.

However, it should be noted that the share price will react in an entirely rational way to any new piece of information – positively to good news and negatively to bad news. Given the mass of evidence demonstrating that share prices follow a random walk, it would appear that there is little to gain in employing the services of a technical analyst. However, the fact that they exist suggests that some people believe they have a value. Indeed, some would argue that there is evidence that the market does not price properly.

2 Semi-strong form

In a semi-strong form efficient market, current prices reflect all publicly available information as well as past share price movements. If this is true, trading on publicly available information would not yield abnormal returns since all of this information would already be in the share price. This is reinforced by much empirical evidence that share prices respond to new information extremely quickly, as suggested by the following quotation.

> 'Market efficiency is a description of how prices in competitive markets respond to new information. The arrival of new information to a competitive market can be likened to the arrival of a lamb chop to a school of flesh-eating piranha, where investors are – plausibly enough – the piranha. The instant the lamb chop hits the water, there is turmoil as the fish devour the meat. Very soon, the meat is gone, leaving only the worthless bone behind, and the water returns to normal. Similarly, when new information reaches a competitive market there is much turmoil as investors buy and sell securities in response to the news, causing prices to change. Once prices adjust, all that is left of the information is the worthless bone. No amount of gnawing on the bone will yield any more meat, and no further study of old information will yield any more valuable intelligence.'
>
> (Higgins, 1992)

Fundamental analysts spend their time poring over various sources of information trying to find undervalued and overvalued shares to buy and sell. In most cases, analysts will be too late trading on the information they find, i.e. it is likely that the information is already in the price and all that remains is 'the bone'. However, what drives fundamental analysts on is the hope of finding something before the rest of the market and thereby earning an abnormal return by trading on it. This is unlikely to happen, but the market hopes they keep looking. The paradox of an efficient market is that most fundamental analysis will not earn abnormal returns, but the fact that so many analysts keep trying ensures that information gets into the price quickly.

Semi-strong form efficiency relies on all publicly available information being incorporated into the price so quickly that most investors cannot profitably exploit any new information. Gordon Brown, Chancellor of the Exchequer at the time of writing, once made a speech at the Stock Exchange in front of a bank of screens displaying share prices. As he announced some disappointing economic data, the screens behind him turned red before he had barely finished the sentence. Dealers with three phones on each ear are quick to react to any snippet of information by buying or selling shares. Indeed, it has been estimated that there are around 1,000 analysts per share on the New York Stock

Exchange – they act like a giant vacuum cleaner sucking up any piece of relevant information and trading on it. It is difficult to keep relevant information from the market given the number of analysts and the speed of information dissemination.

However, this was not always the case, as the following story illustrates.

Oh, for the wings of a dove!

When the Battle of Waterloo took place in 1815, nobody in England knew for 72 hours who had won. However, Nathan Rothschild, who had already established his bank, had a contact at the battlefield who informed him of the result by using carrier pigeons. On getting the message before anybody else that the English had beaten the French, Rothschild instructed the agents of his bank to sell off British government bonds. Other dealers saw this as a bad signal, assumed the French had won and sold as well so that the price of these bonds plummeted. Rothschild quickly instructed his agents to buy as many as they could get their hands on at the low price. Once news of the English victory hit the market, Rothschild had established his fortune.

Rothschild's strategy relied on a principle that still exists today. If you know something that the market does not, it is possible to trade and earn abnormal returns. The difference between then and now is the speed of information to the market. If the Battle of Waterloo had taken place today, instead of the market having to wait 72 hours for information, it is likely analysts would be watching live pictures on their TV screens, probably with a CNN reporter interviewing the protagonists.

The EMH has implications for fund managers who invest our pensions and savings. Many funds are actively managed in the sense that the fund tries to pick undervalued and overvalued shares to trade in. In an efficient market, the share price is a fair price in that it offers a normal return based on the risk, i.e. there is no such thing as an undervalued or overvalued share. If this is true, it is impossible to consistently beat the market. It is not possible to keep correctly guessing future share prices. In addition, if investors have to pay for this type of fund management, they will end up losing in the long run (although some might win by being lucky with their guesses). Active funds are therefore relatively expensive as a consequence of all the buying and selling (the transaction costs) and of the requirement to pay the fund managers themselves for their 'expertise' in trying to pick winners. It is a salutary fact that each year 75 per cent of actively managed funds fail to perform as well as the market itself.

In December 2000, Hargreaves Lansdowne, a major UK broker, recommended to its clients 18 shares to sell and 34 shares to buy. Six months later the 18 'sell' shares had risen by an average of 9 per cent (an excellent performance given that the market had fallen by 10 per cent during this period) whereas the 34 'buy' shares had fallen by 10 per cent on average. In Hargreaves Lansdowne's defence, all share recommendations are for medium-term investment of at least five years.

Tracker funds, on the other hand, in effect buy the index (FTSE 100 or FTSE All Share Trackers are the most common) – instead of trying to beat the market, they simply ride it. Consequently, they beat over 75 per cent of actively managed funds and are much cheaper because there are fewer transactions.

The EMH also has implications for companies indulging in **'creative accounting'**, i.e. reporting higher profits than the facts warrant. The semi-strong EMH states that the market will see through any attempt by companies to 'pull the wool over its eyes'. Indeed, Kaplan and Roll (1972) demonstrated many years ago that companies' attempts to boost share prices by changing the method of depreciation in the accounts did not work (since depreciation will not affect cash flows in that it is allocating past costs). Nevertheless, hindsight suggests the market was fooled by the creative accounting of some of the dramatic failures such as Enron and WorldCom.

Do market prices always include all publicly available information?

There have been suggestions that trading on the following market inefficiencies will yield abnormal returns in certain cases. Some examples of so-called 'anomalies' are:

1 *Timing effects* – some studies have shown abnormal returns by trading on Fridays, in January or during the first hour of trading.

2 *Small firms' capitalisation.* The price : earnings ratios of small firms (about which there is generally limited information) at one time looked much lower than for large firms in the same industry, prompting people to buy up such shares. However, investing in small firms has been discouraged by the large price falls suffered during the market collapse of the early 2000s, a reflection of the often higher risk of small firms.

3 *Value investing*, which is based upon searching for companies with, for example, low price/earnings ratios, high book to market ratios, high dividend yields, strong asset backing.

4 *Bubbles* such as the 1999/2000 dotcom spree. Many of these companies no longer exist, or have share prices sitting at less than 10 per cent of their peak values – the notorious '95 per cent Club' of firms whose shares have fallen by 95 per cent or more. As all West Ham fans appreciate, all bubbles eventually burst and fade away.

At the very least, these examples provide some evidence that the market may not always value fairly, based upon publicly available information. Many winning investors in the market, such as Warren Buffett, the 'Sage of Omaha', would agree; his investment vehicle, the Berkshire Hathaway fund, increased in value from \$19.46 per share in 1964 to \$40,442 by the end of 2000. He is famously contemptuous of EMH:

'I'd be a bum in the street with a tin cup if the markets were efficient'.

Warren Buffett is celebrated for not having invested in dotcom firms, which he claimed not to understand. Perhaps he understood them perfectly?

Self-assessment activity 2.7

Look out for news of the performance of Berkshire Hathaway. Buffett's investment performance is so exceptional that announcement of its results usually receives great press attention.

3 Strong-form

In a strong-form efficient market, current prices reflect all information, whether publicly available or not. If this were true, it would never be possible to consistently earn abnormal returns, even on insider trading, since all public and private information would already be in the share price.

In reality, it is apparent that insider trading *does* earn abnormal returns. In other words, stock markets are not reckoned to be strong-form efficient. Of course, insider trading is illegal (but difficult to prove). Most major markets are regarded as semi-strong, but not strong-form efficient.

The following piece, found on www.weeklyworldnews.com, offers an interesting slant on insider trading.

'Time-traveler' busted for insider trading

Wednesday March 19, 2003
by Chad Kultgen

NEW YORK - Federal investigators have arrested an enigmatic Wall Street wiz on insider-trading charges - and incredibly, he claims to be a time-traveler from the year 2256! Sources at the Security and Exchange Commission confirm that 44-year-old Andrew Carlssin offered the bizarre explanation for his uncanny success in the stock market after being led off in handcuffs on January 28.

'We don't believe this guy's story - he's either a lunatic or a pathological liar,' says an SEC insider.

'But the fact is, with an initial investment of only $800, in two weeks' time he had a portfolio valued at over $350 million. Every trade he made capitalized on unexpected business developments, which simply can't be pure luck.

'The only way he could pull it off is with illegal inside information. He's going to sit in a jail cell on Rikers Island until he agrees to give up his sources.'

The past year of nose-diving stock prices has left most investors crying in their beer. So when Carlssin made a flurry of 126 high-risk trades and came out the winner every time, it raised the eyebrows of Wall Street watchdogs.

'If a company's stock rose due to a merger or technological break-through that was supposed to be secret, Mr Carlssin somehow knew about it in advance,' says the SEC source close to the hush-hush, ongoing investigation.

When investigators hauled Carlssin in for questioning, they got more than they bargained for: a mind-boggling four-hour confession.

Carlssin declared that he had traveled back in time from over 200 years in the future, when it is common knowledge that our era experienced one of the worst stock plunges in history. Yet anyone armed with knowledge of the handful of stocks destined to go through the roof could make a fortune.

'It was just too tempting to resist,' Carlssin allegedly said in his video-taped confession. 'I had planned to make it look natural, you know, lose a little here and there so it doesn't look too perfect. But I just got caught in the moment.'

In a bid for leniency, Carlssin has reportedly offered to divulge 'historical facts' such as the whereabouts of Osama Bin Laden and a cure for AIDS.

All he wants is to be allowed to return to the future in his 'time craft'.

However, he refuses to reveal the location of the machine or discuss how it works, supposedly out of fear the technology could 'fall into the wrong hands'.

Officials are quite confident the 'time-traveler's' claims are bogus. Yet the SEC source admits: 'No one can find any record of any Andrew Carlssin existing anywhere before December 2002.'

Source: Extract from Kultgen, C. (2003)
'Time-traveller busted for insider trading', in *Weekly World News*,
Wednesday 19 March, 2003. See www.weeklyworldnews.com

The conclusion from the discussion of the EMH is that, yes, capital markets do exhibit volatility, and sometimes wild swings, and sometimes stock market valuations may look irrational. But in the longer term, the markets are efficient processors of information and get valuations about right. Meanwhile, managers should focus on getting the fundamentals right, concentrating on developing the strategies that are most likely to deliver value to shareholders over the longer haul, and not worry too much about day-to-day or even year-to-year fluctuations.

If they feel that the market does undervalue their companies, the remedy is often in their own hands – the market relies on clear, unambiguous information signals and evidence of management competence. If the company is 'undervalued', directors have probably failed to define and deliver an acceptable strategy or to explain it coherently to the market.

The vagaries of the stock market may be seen in some quarters to impose an external constraint on the ability of managers to create, or at least sustain, value. Yet there is another, more insidious constraint emanating from within the firm, and stemming from the behaviour of managers themselves.

2.6 Internal constraints on value maximisation - agency issues

One reason why shareholder aims may not be given top priority stems from the so-called *agency problem*. In most large companies, ownership is widely dispersed among thousands of shareholders, who can meet only once a year at the AGM. In reality, attendance at AGMs, for understandable reasons of time and access, is woeful, although the proportion of ownership represented is usually quite high, due to the importance of institutional owners. Small shareholders send in their votes by post, if they bother at all.

Newcastle United plc was criticised in 2002 for holding its AGM in London, 300 miles from its ground at St James' Park, starting at 9am – a significant deterrent for small shareholders.

Thus both day-to-day control of the business and effective control over strategy are vested in a small cadre of paid managers. This group has the power and the opportunity to pursue their own interests at the expense of overt value maximisation. It is, of course, not in their personal interests to run the business into the ground (although some do), but so long as they achieve acceptable levels of performance, i.e. not seriously out of line with those of comparable firms, they can retain shareholder support. Having achieved a satisfactory performance (termed *satisficing*), they can seek personal aims such as self-aggrandisement, higher pay and benefits, job security, plush offices and superfluous staff reporting to them, all of which are enhanced by size of firm.

 The impact of managerial prestige as a motivator was illustrated by the breakdown of **merger** negotiations between Glaxo and SmithKline Beecham in 1998. The merger was supposed to generate cost savings worth £10 billion but foundered due to the inability of the two chief executives to agree on the allocation of post-merger jobs. Only after Jan Leschly, the former tennis champion and CEO of SmithKline, announced his forthcoming retirement was the merger consummated in 2000.

A major problem that most owners face is lack of information. They simply do not have sufficient information to judge the intensity of effort expended and the quality of the work performed by managers. Managers have more information about past performance, investment opportunities and business prospects, information which it is in their interests not to disclose. The managers (*agents*) have a built-in advantage over the owners who appoint them (the *principals*), stemming from **information asymmetry**. The problem facing the owners is how the agents can be coerced or encouraged to work effectively and energetically in their interests, i.e. to secure *goal congruence*.

One way of binding the agent to the principal is to express what is required from managers and how they are to be rewarded in the form of a contract. Inevitably, however, due to incomplete information, such contracts are incomplete – managers have the upper hand regarding available information – and due to imperfect foresight, it is impossible to cover all contingencies in a legally binding contractual relationship.

A second way of solving this '*principal–agent problem*' is to police managers' behaviour by rigorous auditing of their conduct. As we have seen, German companies operate a two-tier board system, with the executive board's conduct and performance scrutinised by a densely populated supervisory board. Moreover, the extensive cross-shareholding among German companies, and particularly holdings by banks, means that major shareholders can exert relatively rapid pressure on managers. However, this is cumbersome and expensive, and by no means guaranteed to place shareholder interests at the pinnacle.

Linking management performance to shareholder value

The preferred approach in Anglo-Saxon economies, and one which is increasingly being adopted in mainland Europe, is to reward managers according to measures linked with shareholder value. Indeed, there is evidence that managers whose remuneration packages are weighted more towards bonus elements rather than basic salary tend to achieve higher returns for shareholders.

In some companies, bonuses are related to measures such as increases in profits or growth in earnings per share, but as these are expressed in accounting terms, they can be manipulated through 'creative accounting'. Accountants often have some flexibility – particularly in the UK, which tends to downplay rigid accounting rules – over how some items, such as inventory value, can be accounted for. This creates temptations for directors to select the accounting policy which shows company performance in the most favourable light, with the danger that managers come to be rewarded not for genuine performance but for accounting sleight of hand.

In addition, if remuneration depends on annual performance, it is likely to encourage a short-term perspective. A simple example is when people are rewarded by achieved return on assets. Although this could be defined in various ways, consider the following definition:

$$\text{Return on assets} = \frac{\text{Operating profit}}{\text{Fixed assets} + \text{current assets}}$$

Asset values decline over time as firms depreciate equipment, so return on assets is likely to increase under stable market conditions. This provides a disincentive for managers to invest in new equipment because to do so would create a higher asset base, and hence a higher depreciation charge that would drag down operating profits.

To avoid both creative accounting and short-termism, it is more sensible to base remuneration, at least partially, on shareholder value creation, the most obvious indicator being share price movement. While some managers would argue that this exposes their remuneration to the short-term vagaries of the stock market, it has the virtue of objectivity and also overcomes the short-termism problem. This is because share values hinge on the long-term cash-generating ability of the company, which is hard to disguise by accounting obfuscation. Moreover, share values depend on how clearly the firm communicates its long-term strategy to the market and how credible this appears to market players.

Share options

Share options work in a simple fashion. They carry the right for managers to buy a specified number of ordinary shares at a specified time in the future at a price fixed now. Ideally, the purchase price or exercise price should represent a challenging but not infeasible target. The time period before which the options should be exercisable should be reasonably long, say three years, but not so long as to lose meaning as a target. If share prices fall, perhaps the option might be re-expressed in terms of share price movement relative to some peer group of companies or to the stock market as a whole. Indeed, critics of such schemes argue that this should apply to the topside as well to guard against managers being rewarded not for exceptional performance but because the whole market has risen.

Some option schemes have been criticised as being too undemanding. Many managers have been able to win millions of dollars or pounds by exercising options for quite ordinary performance, or even when the share price has fallen relative to other companies. A safeguard introduced by the Cadbury Committee, to whose recommendations listed firms are supposed to conform, is that executive pay should be determined by a remuneration committee, made up mainly or entirely of non-executives. This seems to have been ineffective as one firm's

executives tend to be another firm's non-executives, i.e. they have similar interests in driving up rewards.

Legislation which might force boards to submit pay schemes for approval by shareholder vote was promised by the incoming Labour administration in 1997 but became effective only in 2003. Meanwhile, very few AGMs are presented with sufficiently detailed pay schemes to appraise, although occasionally institutional investors are consulted and are able to express their opposition to excessively generous schemes, which are then sometimes withdrawn. However, the financial institutions still tend to stick by the incumbent managers, however woeful their performance.

In April 2003, 45 per cent of the shareholders of the troubled financial news service Reuters voted against a controversial executive pay scheme. When the proxy votes of the institutions were added in, 77 per cent of voters had supported the scheme, although 40 per cent of all shareholders failed to vote.

There is no question that abuse is rife or, regrettably, that the opposition mounted against 'corpulent felines' is often feeble, although in 2003, the Association of British Insurers expressed its determination to stamp out excessive payouts on termination of contract – so-called 'rewards for failure'.

Self-assessment activity 2.8

Look out in the press for examples of alleged over-payment of top executives. How are they paid, and why was their particular package criticised?

Executive option schemes, while based on the sound principle of aligning shareholders' and managers' interests by making managers into shareholders, appear to have got out of hand. The **agency costs** involved in, to put it crudely, paying managers to do their jobs properly are now taking up a rising and unacceptable proportion of shareholder value. In some areas, such as internet technology, such payments can be justified as the return on an increasingly scarce resource, i.e. managerial talent, but this argument is far-fetched in sectors relatively free from technical change or economic turbulence.

In 1997, *The Economist* said: 'Choose the right person and give him *[sic]* lots of shares: it is hard to think of a simpler rule, or a more effective one.' Just two years later, in August 1999, it was writing about 'the trouble with stock options' and the need in the UK to record, as in the USA, performance-related stock options as a cost against profits in order that shareholders can appreciate the full extent to which they are relinquishing their equity. Many US firms have begun to do this, Coca-Cola being an example, but there remains much controversy over the appropriate way to measure the costs involved.

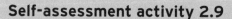

> ### Self-assessment activity 2.9
>
> Look again at the report and accounts of your chosen company.
> Does it have a remuneration committee? What is stated about executive remuneration? Have options been granted? What are the terms, the exercise date and the exercise price?

2.7 Words of warning

Emphasis on shareholder value has not found favour in all quarters, at least in the way it may be interpreted by some managers. It is alleged that too many UK managers confuse value with profitability and think that increasing profitability will increase shareholder returns. It is relatively easy to raise short-term profits by cutting R&D and training budgets, reducing overheads and leaning on suppliers. Some even say this is due to the preponderance of accountants on UK boards, which results in financial prudence overcoming marketing flair.

Value is not necessarily related to short-term profits. Value stems from exploiting long-term growth potential by spotting market opportunities and investing accordingly, with less concern for current profits and dividends. This is the key to building long-term competitive advantage. It may explain why firms in the 'industries of the future' which are exploiting internet technology can be valued much more highly by the stock market than firms in traditional sectors like engineering and packaging, even though the profitability of the former is frequently much lower (and often negative) than the latter.

The trick that older firms have to pull off is to push investment into the newer areas and demonstrate their awareness and use of new business opportunities, while maintaining a suitably high rate of return to satisfy the markets. This is the lesson of companies like Mannesmann with its excursion into mobile telephony and the UK retailer Dixons, which launched the most extensive internet portal service Freeserve and thus transformed both its strategic direction and its share price. As ever, presentation – presenting strategy to the market in a convincing fashion – is essential.

2.8 Summary

Based on the introduction to the concept of wealth in Chapter 1, this chapter explained in more detail how wealth is based on the concept of present value.

It examined the twin determinants of value and discussed the factors which underpin these. It then discussed the way in which the stock market is likely to respond to company investment and financial decisions according to the

Efficient Markets Hypothesis. Finally, it discussed the extent to which managers can be relied upon to pursue shareholder aims.

The next chapter looks more closely at the first of the key financial decision areas, investment appraisal and decision making. Again, you will find that the concept of present value is crucial.

References and further reading

Textbooks

Arnold – chs 9 and 14.
Brealey & Myers – chs 2, 3, 5 and 13.
Pike & Neale – chs 2 and 3.
Samuels, Wilkes & Brayshaw – chs 4 and 13.
Watson & Head – ch 2.

Other

Fama, E (1970) 'Efficient capital markets: a review of theory and empirical work', *Journal of Finance*, May.
Fama, E 'Efficient capital markets II', *Journal of Finance*, Vol. 46, December, pp. 1575–1617.
Higgins, R C (1992) *Analysis for Financial Management* (McGraw-Hill).
Kaplan, R and Rolls, R (1972) 'Investor evaluation of accounting information: some empirical evidence', *Journal of Business*, April, pp. 225–57.
Keane, S (1983) *Stock Market Efficiency – Theory, Evidence and Applications* (Phillip Allan).
Kendall, R (1953) The analysis of Economic Time Series, *Journal of the Royal Economic Society*, Vol. 69, pp. 11–25.
Maloney, M and Mulherin, H (2003) 'The stock price reaction to the challenger crash', *Journal of Applied Corporate Finance*.
Roberts, H V (1964) 'Stock market patterns and financial analysis: methodological suggestions', in P. Cootner (ed.) *The Random Character of Stock Market Prices* (MIT Press, Cambridge, MA).
Schwarz, D (1998) *The Schwarz Stock Market Handbook*, 3rd edn (Burleigh Publishing).
Smith (1992) *Accounting for Growth* (Century Books).

Questions and mini-case studies

1   In June 2002, the UK defence group BAe bid for TRW, a US aerospace group. BAe's shares fell by 16p on the day of the bid. The shares of TRW rose. Why do you think this happened?

2   In what circumstances may a 'fair' price not correctly value a company?

3   With markets falling and nervous in 2002, many planned new issues of shares were withdrawn. Is this logical?

4   When Ford beat General Motors to buy Jaguar cars in 1989, it paid nearly 700p a share. Prior to the takeover, Jaguar shares were trading at around 250p. After the takeover, a senior manager from Ford in Detroit visited the main Jaguar factory in Coventry and declared that it was the worst factory he had seen outside of Eastern Europe.

    Offer your views on the above, including suggestions as to why Ford bid for this company.

5   'If financial managers are to achieve their corporate goals, they require well-developed financial markets where transfers of wealth from savers to borrowers are efficient in both pricing and operational cost.' (Pike & Neale).

    Explain and discuss the view expressed in this statement.

Mini-case study – Vodafone and British Airways

Two good examples of 'shareholder abuse' were provided in mid-July 2000. First, Vodafone had decided to award CEO Chris Gent a bonus of £10 million after completing the takeover of Mannesmann. Half of this was a cash bonus and half was payable in shares if Vodafone achieved 'significant' earnings growth targets. Lex in the *Financial Times* described the former element of this 'gentrification' 'impossible to justify', a reward merely for pulling off a big and complex deal (a 'finder's fee') rather than a reward for creating shareholder value. (Vodafone's share price had actually fallen since the takeover.)

All this so upset the National Association of Pension Funds (NAPF) that it urged its 1,450 members to protest against the bonus by abstaining from the AGM vote to be taken on Vodafone's remuneration policy. The NAPF admitted this was a 'slap on the wrists', justifying the abstention rather than a vote against because it was otherwise happy with Vodafone's policy (presumably, the performance-related element). Not so the Pensions Investment Research Council (PIRC). The PIRC adopted a firmer approach by urging its clients to actually vote against the policy, on the grounds that the documentation supposed to detail Gent's performance targets contained only vague generalisations.

Meanwhile, on the very same day that the NAPF's wrath was reported, British Airways faced a barrage of opposition from shareholders over its decision to award former CEO Bob Ayling a £2 million compensation package for loss of office following his dismissal in May 2000 over the airline's poor performance. Many critics labelled this a clear case of 'rewarding failure'.

Mini-case study – Martha Stewart

In October 2002, Martha Stewart, a household name in the USA, whose Home Design company is seen as the model of good taste and quality, is under investigation for insider dealing. US securities regulators have told Martha Stewart they plan to bring a civil case against the home design guru stemming from their probe of insider trading at ImClone, the biotechnology company.

The Securities and Exchange Commission has informed Ms Stewart's lawyers of the likely charges and asked for their response. The onus is now on the home design guru and her lawyers to convince regulators why they should not bring charges. The SEC action would represent the first formal charges against Ms Stewart in a scandal that has already tarnished her image and knocked hundreds of millions of dollars from her company's market value. Ms Stewart is the public face of a global home design empire spanning merchandise, magazines and television shows.

The charges could bolster a parallel criminal investigation of Ms Stewart being carried out by the US attorney's office. They may also increase pressure on Ms Stewart to step down from the company she founded.

Authorities have been probing whether Ms Stewart relied on insider information in December when she sold her stake in ImClone for $227,000 the day before the Food and Drug Administration publicly rejected Erbitux, the company's promising anti-cancer drug, and sent the shares spiralling. She has denied any wrongdoing and stated that her decision to sell was based on a pre-arranged agreement with her broker.

Shares in her own company have fallen more than 60 per cent since the scandal erupted in June.

Sam Waksal, ImClone founder and Ms Stewart's close friend, pleaded guilty to several insider trading charges. Mr Waksal pleaded guilty to some – but not all – of the charges in an August grand jury indictment, including securities fraud, perjury, and obstruction of justice. He admitted in a federal court that he called his daughter, Aliza, and ordered her to sell ImClone shares shortly before the biotechnology company made its announcement about Erbitux. He also admitted forging the signature of the company's general counsel to cover up a $44 million bank loan he secured using ImClone stock options he had already pledged to another creditor.

'I deeply regret what happened. I was wrong,' Mr Waksal said outside the courthouse. Government prosecutors said they might bring additional charges against Mr Waksal, and indicated that they were widening their net. Michael Schachter, assistant US attorney, said the government had developing 'compelling evidence' that Mr Waksal tipped others. The government was exploring a $600,000 share sale on 28 December by 'a close friend' of Mr Waksal and another totalling $30 million that began the previous day.

In July 2003, Mr Waksal received a 7 year jail sentence for insider training – the maximum that could have been imposed.

What are the main issues of this case in the context of:

(a) the Efficient Market Hypothesis?

(b) the prosecution of cases involving alleged insider dealing?

Quiz on the Efficient Markets Hypothesis

1 The weak form of the EMH means that share prices are randomly (i.e. irrationally) priced. True or False?

2 If a capital market is efficient, can an investor make:

(a) abnormal returns?
(b) positive returns?

3 Does capital market efficiency mean that all investors:

(a) know all there is to know about any security?
(b) have the same expectations?

4 If share prices are low, is it logical for a company to wait for prices to pick up before it makes an issue of new shares?

5 Throughout 2002, the management of ICI complained that the market had consistently underpriced its shares. How logical is this statement in the light of capital market efficiency?

6 The *Sunday Times* tips ABC plc as an undervalued share. Should you rush out and buy it on Monday morning?

7

	Company A	Company B
Share price 1 May	250p	250p
Share price 31 May	125p	500p

Which share should I buy on 31 May?

8   True or false?

(a) Tests have shown that there is an almost perfect correlation between successive price changes.
(b) The semi-strong form of EMH says that prices reflect all publicly available information.
(c) In an efficient market, the expected return on each share is the same.
(d) The fact that some investors have made a fortune on the stock market shows that you can beat the market.

9   You have £50,000 to invest. You visit a stockbroker for advice. How can she help you?

10 Does the evidence that 75 per cent of unit trusts do not match the FTSE 100 index suggest that you should avoid using them?

11 The following will increase accounting profit. Will they also increase the share price?

(a) Reducing the provision for depreciation.
(b) Reducing expenditure on research and development.

12 'If the FTSE 100 index can stay above the critical 4750 level this month, I can see no reason why it cannot close the year around 5000.' Does this make sense?

13 The following prices held at the close of business on 22 May 2002:

High	Low		Price
824	565	Lloyds TSB	750
632	360	Barclays	602
922	575	HSBC	842
354	244	Bradford & Bingley	342

If you decide that you want to introduce a bank share into your portfolio and assuming that all of the above are of equal risk, which one should you choose?

14 The following statement contains several errors. Identify and explain them.

'According to the EMH, all share prices are correct at all times. This is achieved by prices moving randomly when new information is announced. New information from published accounts is the only deter-minant of the random movements in share prices. Fundamental and technical analysts of the stock market serve no function in making the market efficient and cannot predict future share prices. Corporate finan-cial managers are also unable to predict future share prices.'

Source: ACCA Financial Management Exam June 1989, question 3

15 What is the likely effect on a company's share price if the following happens:

    (a) The company announces an unexpected loss for the year.
    (b) Interest rates rise.
    (c) The £ falls against the US$.
    (d) The company announces that it will invest in a highly profitable new report.
    (e) The company revalues the assets on the balance sheet.

Self-assessment answers

2.1
It is tempting to answer 'at the end of one year'. However, if it is possible to sell the rights to receive future benefits from investment, and if market participants agree with this assessment of the value of the project, then it can be sold right now (although there are likely to be transactions costs).

2.2
$$\text{NPV} = -£100{,}000 + [£180{,}000 - £20{,}000]/(1.12) = -£100{,}000 + £142{,}857$$
$$= +£42{,}857 = \text{wealth created by the project.}$$

2.3
Your call.

2.4
The atrocities perpetrated on 9/11 shook the financial markets, making people generally more concerned about the future, i.e. they became more risk-averse, reflected in a sell-off of ordinary shares. Governments throughout the world tried to support financial markets by reducing interest rates. Thus there were two effects: the trade-off became steeper but the risk-free rate, the intercept, was reduced.

2.5
Over to you.

2.6
Assuming the friend is not lying – like inveterate gamblers, people often lie about investment winnings – first, ask about charges: what is the 'expert's' performance in net terms? Assuming it is still ahead of the market in each year, now work out the probability of beating the market average four years in a row.

    Because the chance of beating the market average in any one year is 50 per cent, the answer is: $(0.5) \times (0.5) \times (0.5) \times (0.5) = 0.0625$, i.e. 6.25 per cent.

This is a good performance, but about 6 per cent of market players will also have achieved this level of performance – probably tens of thousands of people across the world. What did the adviser achieve prior to this run? And what will he/she do next year? Note that the chance of outperforming next year is still 50 per cent!

2.7, 2.8 and 2.9
Your call.

STRATEGIC MANAGEMENT FOR VALUE CREATION

3

Didn't Dell do well!

By 2001, Dell Computers had grown its share of the global PC market to 13 per cent, and its share of the US market to 40 per cent, while other competing firms struggled – Gateway made losses, Compaq and Hewlett-Packard rationalised through a defensive merger, and IBM left the consumer market altogether. Dell's success, achieving 10 per cent p.a. growth in a market contracting by 9 per cent p.a., is based on manufacturing skills rather than technological excellence. Since 2000, its manufacturing space had halved but production had increased by 30 per cent. Dell manufactures most of its own products (whereas IBM and Compaq outsource most of their production to Taiwan), it builds to order (half its orders arrive via the internet) and holds little inventory (average one week compared with competitors' four weeks). Dell uses just-in-time stock management, having developed the necessary close relationship with suppliers. Its operating expenses are only 10 per cent of revenue (compared with 20 per cent at HP), and it relies on standardised technology and high-volume production.

Whereas Apple's recent strategy has been to create demand through innovation, Dell serves the existing market. But component prices are starting to rise, exerting a double squeeze on profits in a declining market. Two ways for Dell to increase growth are to merge (like Compaq), and to widen the range of services it provides to customers from basic support to professional services. But the company does not have a competitive advantage in its quality of services, and merging may lose focus. It may choose to stick to what it does best – manufacturing quality computers at a competitive price.

Dell's recent successes are only a continuation of an ongoing success story that has enriched those investors astute enough to buy the stock when it listed on NASDAQ in 1982. Allowing for a series of stock splits, the ordinary shares had risen in price 300 fold by December 2002 – $1,000 invested in the flotation would have grown to $298,000!

Objectives:
This chapter aims to:

- discuss the particular advantages a business enjoys over its competitors

- explain how these core competences can provide competitive advantage

- explain how these competitive advantages can be protected from competitors

- identify the type of market in which a company is most likely to earn abnormal returns.

As with Chapter 2, it will be helpful to have the report and accounts of 'your' company to hand to help you with the SAAs, all of which are qualitative rather than numerical.

3.1 Introduction

Dell's almost fantasy-like story of financial success is a textbook example of effective financial management based on solid strategy. So what does Dell get right? The explanation is simple but achieving it is less so!

Dell has never lost sight of the overarching financial objective of a company, namely to maximise shareholder wealth, the best way of doing this being to invest in activities or projects that add value. Value-creating projects provide the business with a future return in excess of the required return, thus offering an *abnormal return*, reflected in positive net present value. However, abnormal returns will attract competitors as they seek to seize some of the value available. To create sustainable value for owners, firms have to offer value to customers.

This chapter looks at the factors that enable businesses like Dell Computers to add value in their projects and investments, and conversely some of the reasons why businesses may lose value. Knowledge of these factors will enable companies to take strategic views about the future development of their business. Explaining this strategic view is the main objective of this chapter.

The chapter is also a reminder that financial management is not merely a theoretical exercise. The reality is that businesses of all shapes and sizes have to make decisions that will affect their future. But in competitive markets and uncertain economic conditions, future prosperity is not guaranteed. The many examples in this chapter are an indication of the practice built on the theory.

3.2　Levels of strategy

Once a firm has defined its objectives, the next stage is to make plans to achieve them. These plans will shape the nature of the business and the types of markets the business should be operating in. Such plans embody its business strategy and thus they define the relationship the business has with its competitors in its chosen market environment.

By definition, strategy involves competing – if you have no opposition, you do not need a strategy. However, strategy can be conducted at different levels. Writers in the strategy field distinguish between corporate and business strategy. As the labels suggest, the former relates to corporate-level issues, in particular the question of what fields the firm should operate in, or 'domain selection'. The latter turns on the issue of how a firm should operate in its chosen field, or 'domain navigation'. Hence strategy is essentially about *where* to compete and *how* to compete. In terms of value creation, this translates to asking in what fields should the business seek to create value, and in what ways should it seek to create value?

Strategy is therefore a continuous process of making decisions about the deployment of resources, i.e. how to apply the existing and readily accessible resources to the market environment. Effective execution of strategy will help the business achieve abnormal returns in the marketplace, thereby adding value to the business. Strategic decision makers therefore need to:

- identify, develop and exploit the strengths, often called the **core competences**, of the business which will give it a competitive edge over its competitors

- identify the markets where these resources can be best deployed

- remedy any shortages in required capabilities by investment in fixed and human capital, respectively

- apply the available resources to the markets where these competences can be most effectively exploited

- erect barriers to stop competitors encroaching into these areas of added value.

Given the assumed business imperative of adding value, financial management assists in the strategic approach by providing the financial backcloth for the decision making. Nevertheless, the financial manager must appreciate that although his input is likely to be significant, there are factors other than the purely financial to reckon with in most decisions.

The first requirement of strategy is to understand what assets the firm already possesses, its resources and capabilities; in effect what it is good at. Identification of these strengths is part of a strategic audit of the business.

> ### Self-assessment activity 3.1
>
> What are the major sectors in which 'your' company operates?
> Has it entered any new ones recently? Were reasons given for such ventures?

3.3 Core competences

At the simplest level, companies create value by investing in activities that require skills that they can perform more ably than other companies. These skills represent the distinctive capabilities the company possesses over its competitors. They underpin the firm's ability to outperform the competition. It is not enough to merely be as good as the competition, i.e. to have *threshold competences*; a business must have exceptional advantages, or *distinctive competences*, to give it 'an edge' over competitors. By exploiting these advantages, a business can earn above-average, or abnormal, returns.

A business may be seen as a set of competences rather than as a group of activities. Honda's core competence lies in making engines, which helps to explain why it has been successful in manufacturing motorcycles, cars and lawn-mowers. Canon's core competence in optics underpins its production of cameras and copiers. Core competences are often a significant factor allowing companies to stretch their particular expertise into different areas.

Core competences are often long established in businesses and come to define what the company is renowned for. Others emerge as the business, and the market it serves, evolve over time. Often, a successful company may have only one or two competences to give it a particular attraction to customers.

There are many examples of core competences that can be harnessed to add value:

- customer relationships
- supplier relationships
- quality of management
- product reliability

- human resources management

- innovative ability

- information technology capability.

These are now examined in turn.

Customer relationships

Chapter 1 explained that companies have to operate within a context of continual demands from a variety of stakeholder groups. These relationships need to be harmonious to encourage the value-adding process. If not encouraged and maintained, they can become dysfunctional and hinder the attainment of the primary objective of adding value. Once established, good practice needs to become embedded in the organisation. The way in which a business interacts with its stakeholders is an important potential source of core competence.

There has been a huge shift in the structure of the UK economy over the past 40 years or so. The service sector of the economy increased from 50 per cent of the economy to occupy around 80 per cent in 2002. The increased importance of the service sector over manufacturing has affected the 'service culture' of this and many other countries. Many businesses have recognised that good service attracts customers, many of whom are willing to pay extra for outstanding service.

Former state airlines such as British Airways now advertise the services they provide as they strive to win back customers from the 'no-frills' airlines like easyjet and Ryanair. These advertisements emphasise the extra services on offer to customers, such as teams of staff available at airports, free meals on board, more flexibility in ticketing, better airport facilities, more flights, and more convenient airports. Other airlines have tried to attract premium-paying business-class customers with the offer of chauffeured cars to and from the airport, superior departure lounges, quick routes through passport and baggage and, once on the aircraft, more leg-room.

Service as a core competence can mean different things to different firms in the same sector. In the retail sector, several service levels are discernible. Large supermarkets like Sainsburys can offer assistance with packing at the till, help in carrying the shopping to the car and an extensive product range, whereas corner shops can offer a more personal and less-pressured service to customers to compensate for their more limited product range and higher prices. Tesco actually does both, having set up the Tesco Metro chain of small stores.

Quality and speed of service revolutionised the fast-food industry in the UK in the 1970s, following the entry of McDonald's. Its near-instant service 'pressed the right buttons' for many consumers in an increasingly busy world. Over the years, this core competence has become a threshold competence (i.e. an assumed requirement) for businesses offering fast-food.

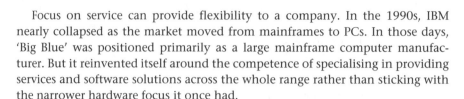

Focus on service can provide flexibility to a company. In the 1990s, IBM nearly collapsed as the market moved from mainframes to PCs. In those days, 'Big Blue' was positioned primarily as a large mainframe computer manufacturer. But it reinvented itself around the competence of specialising in providing services and software solutions across the whole range rather than sticking with the narrower hardware focus it once had.

Supplier relationships

A major lesson taught over the past 30 years by Japanese companies operating in Europe and North America, particularly in manufacturing, is the value of a strong working relationship with suppliers. Japanese companies, led by the example of Toyota, taught manufacturers in the West that instead of trying to squeeze the last penny from suppliers, it might be good business to financially support them and invest in them and give them long-term contracts. All of these things help to ensure the quality of their output and the continuity of supply to the manufacturer, as well as reducing stock management costs.

The UK service sector offers more positive examples of good supplier relations than does manufacturing. An often-cited example of a UK company having a good relationship with suppliers is the clothing retailer Marks and Spencer, which for many years obtained nearly all its stock from British clothing manufacturers. M&S was such a dominant force on the UK high street that it was often the only customer for many clothing suppliers. This gave M&S significant control over the type and quality of garment that it wanted to sell on the shop floor. Nevertheless, suppliers actively sought contracts with Marks to obtain regular business as well as profit.

However, recent years have seen a significant change in the company's strategy. This particular core competence became expensive to maintain – a cost that customers, and eventually the company, were no longer willing to bear. As the economies of Asia and the Far East developed, it became possible to obtain supplies from there at a fraction of the cost of the UK. Thus in the late 1990s, M&S effectively dismantled its long-established core competence by not renewing many of its contracts with UK suppliers and instead obtained stock from the cheaper manufacturers abroad. This significantly dented the M&S image. It then faced the major task of winning back dissenting customers by offering clothing at more competitive prices without sacrificing quality. After some difficult years following this new policy, the company had begun, at the time of writing, to recover at least some of its former pre-eminence in retailing.

Quality of management

Successful companies have usually developed an organisational structure that allows and encourages managers to make value-adding decisions. When dominant positions are lost, quality of management is an important ingredient required to recover the situation. Obviously, with senior management, individual personalities have to be considered, from the inclusive approach of Jeff Bezos of Amazon to the strong, centralised approach characteristic of Simon Marks, builder of Marks and Spencer. There have been many examples in corporate finance where the manager himself has been a core competence to the business. Leaders such as Richard Branson for Virgin, Lord Hanson for Hanson, Jack Welch for American conglomerate General Electric, and Larry Ellison of Cisco Systems all used their ability to spot investment opportunities and exploit them to add value to the companies that they ran.

However, the culture beneath the senior team is also important. Businesses must avoid the agency problems discussed in Chapter 2. Value-destroying dysfunctional decision-making may add money to the manager's wallet, increase the size of his department or raise his status in the organisation, but reduce shareholder wealth. A transparent system of management which makes managers accountable and which also encourages them to add value needs to be put firmly in place. Regular audits and transparent corporate governance can report on the quality of the decision making, among other things. The remuneration of managers and the way in which their performance is assessed are all-important areas to be looked at in any business that wants to add value.

Product reliability

Reliability became a core competence of Japanese car manufacturers. As well as being founded on close links with suppliers, this competence was reinforced by their commitment to what became known as total quality management – or getting it 'right first time'. As the example of Marks and Spencer demonstrated, core competences do not last for ever. European and US car manufacturers soon realised that they needed to manufacture to the same standard of reliability and quality if they were to compete with the Japanese car firms. Thus, as with customer service, a core competence which could add value has now become a threshold competence which is necessary simply to survive in tough markets.

Quality, nevertheless, is still a powerful attraction for customers. The cachets attached to the Rolls-Royce and Mercedes-Benz brands were built up over many years and still have considerable value.

Human resources management

Many managers glibly state that employees are their most valuable assets. It is common to find statements to this effect in many company reports. However, like everything in business, this resource needs to be nurtured and invested in

for staff to add value as a core competence rather than simply allow the company to stay in the market.

The US chemicals group DuPont recognised this requirement when it shifted the measurement of its employee training from the numbers attending training courses to a measurement based upon the business impact of such training. Training began to be run as a profit centre rather than being levied as a fixed charge to the business. As departments now had to pay for their own training, they became more interested in defining their own training needs rather than merely picking from a standard menu drawn up by the centre. Not surprisingly, training sessions started to focus on real business issues, such as customer service and retention, growing market share and sales, along with financial concerns such as improving cash flows and cutting costs.

Investing in staff or workforce development is likely to improve customer relations and generate more business. Effective workforce development and training can improve morale, make staff more productive and assist in retaining key staff within the organisation.

Innovative ability

Some companies specialise in constantly innovating and bringing new products to the market. TMT (high-technology, media and telecommunications) companies have offered good examples of this in recent years. Indeed, companies in these sectors live or die by their ability to provide new products.

Nokia, the mobile phone company, creates customer demand by constantly providing phones with new facilities and technologies. This does not happen by accident. Diversity and risk-taking are encouraged throughout the organisation, and occasional failure is accepted as a natural part of this process. It is also the responsibility of managers at Nokia to ensure that new ideas and knowledge are effectively transferred through the company – a process it calls 'competence investment'. This is intended to encourage staff to be innovative and creative and allows everyone in the business to share successes.

Another IT company, Casio, changes its products every six months, and even long-established companies such as Gillette are constantly innovating around basic products like razors – around 50 per cent of Gillette's annual sales are from products developed in the last five years.

Information technology capability

A culture of incorporating IT and an ability to use it effectively can often enhance the value-adding capability of businesses. In manufacturing, technology can help efficiency, flexibility, quality and cost reduction. In stock control, the use of the internet in particular can reduce stockholding levels and cut down the possibility of stock-outs.

In 'new economy' companies like Amazon.com, the whole business model relies on harnessing and utilising IT to attract customers and process orders. It has been said that the real core competence for Amazon is the experience it creates for customers – one-click purchasing, selling a range of products that consumers want, and offering them a good deal. It is this mix that provides an attractive virtual marketplace for customers to buy in. In addition, the budget airlines established a business model on customers booking flights over the internet rather than using travel agents.

Examples of core competences

The following are examples taken from annual reports.

Hampson plc (2002) – this British firm is a specialist engineering company, including aerospace. It identifies a core competence of manufacturing smaller-dimensioned precision components. The company states that it regards the constant change in its market as presenting unique opportunities for strong suppliers like itself to gain further competitive advantage by moving quickly to implement and consolidate new ways of working.

(www.Hampson.co.uk)

Ascom plc (2000) – this British communications company defines co-operation between its different business units as a core competence. The company states that this co-operation permits a critical mass to be achieved in research and development, marketing, sales and production areas.

(www.Ascom.co.uk)

British Airways plc (2002) – 'Anyone can fly air planes but few organisations can excel in serving people ... [this is] a competence that's hard to build, it's also hard for competitors to copy or match.'

(BA plc Annual Report and Accounts 2002)

Another, more generic example of changing core competences is occurring in the financial services sector. Banks are increasingly moving towards risk management as a core competence. This meets the demands of their customers for this service and reflects the increasing sophistication of risk management techniques being developed and the availability of capital markets in which to operate.

Self-assessment activity 3.2

Identify the core competences of 'your' company. Do any threshold competences apply in its major activities?

3.4 How core competences add value

Core competences give businesses an edge, or a **competitive advantage**, over their competitors. Net present values arise when a firm's core competences are applied to make products or provide services that the market wants. In other words, having a core competence allows the company to offer products or services at a price or a quality or in a style that other businesses cannot match. This competitive advantage may provide an opportunity for the company to charge a premium price and earn 'abnormal returns' – returns above the level required to keep the company in business.

In general, core competences allow a business to add value through adopting one of the strategic stances identified by Michael Porter (1985):

- *Cost leadership* – a core competence is likely to allow a company to produce something or provide a service at a lower cost than its competitors can. The core competence will allow the company to be more efficient and more able to drive down production and other costs as far as possible.

- *Differentiation* – companies can broadcast their superiority over competitors so that they are perceived as being unique in the eyes of customers. Very often, this differentiation will be recognised by criteria such as the quality of the service or the product. Such differentiation is often encapsulated in a brand name. By being perceived as unique, companies can exploit an effective monopoly position by charging premium rates.

- *Focus (or niche)* – whereas the two previous strategies involve appealing to all customers in a market, some firms may elect to target a narrower segment within an industry as the best strategy to exploit the advantage that the core competences give them. They are likely to adapt their strategy to serve that particular segment more effectively than their competitors. Focus strategies can involve cost leadership ('cost focus') or differentiation.

Core competences become particularly valuable when:

- they are applicable to a wide variety of products, e.g. Honda and Casio
- they help to produce output which the market wants
- they are difficult for competitors to imitate.

All of these factors allow companies to exploit core competences in the market to add value in a potentially significant way over a potentially significant time. In particular, if the competence is difficult to imitate, this gives the company time to exploit its advantage in the market.

Prahalad and Hamel (1990), who formulated the concept of core competence, argue that companies have to be increasingly creative as they adapt to ever-changing market conditions. It has already been noted that core competences do not provide abnormal returns for ever. In a business environment where speed and innovation are increasingly important, core competences need to be nurtured and adapted. In addition, new markets (the ageing population, increased globalisation) and new approaches to business (the internet, greater access to information) offer opportunities for competitive advantage through the development of new core competences to meet the demands of these new markets.

Companies and their competitive advantages

The links between competences, competitive advantage and value should be clear. Core competences are the skills that enable firms to compete strongly and thus build up competitive advantage. Successful exploitation of competitive advantage adds value for owners of the enterprise. It is instructive to observe firms that appreciate this nexus.

Haraeus, a 150-year-old German private company, has a multitude of businesses developed around its core competence of a wide expertise in high melting point materials. The company buys a variety of minerals (gold, platinum, quartz) for use in manufacturing a variety of products from light bulbs to pen nibs. Its expertise, built up over many years, also enables it to supply the IT industry with components. The company actively trades in metals for its production requirements and employs specialised teams of traders. The company sees the integrated nature of its business, with its traders linked directly to the product divisions, as a further competitive advantage.

Astute firms often provide public evidence that they understand the importance of maintaining their competitive advantage in their markets. The following are some examples of statements:

- The Chloride Group, once best known for its automotive batteries but which now specialises in 'the manufacture and sale of power protection solution', states: 'We continue to give priority to investment in technology to maintain the competitive advantage of our high-quality, innovative products and solutions.'

  (Chloride Group Interim report 2002)

- The financial services group Aviva plc: 'Our financial strength, broad product range and growing distribution continue to give us competitive advantage.'

  (Richard Harvey, Chief Executive Aviva, October 2002))

- The aluminium producer Nordic Aluminium plc: 'Close co-operation with customers in product development builds competitive advantage.'

  (Annual Report 2000)

- The micro-technology company Pace plc, that makes set-top decoders: 'Keeping the overall level of overheads low gives us a competitive advantage compared to others with high operating costs.'

  (Interim Report 1999)

Self-assessment activity 3.3

Does 'your firm' enjoy competitive advantage mainly by cost leadership or by product differentiation? Can you see how its core competences confer competitive advantage?

3.5 Core competences as a basis for strategy

Since core competences can provide value to businesses, it is important that businesses manage their development and exploitation effectively. BTG plc is a firm that has identified its core competence and articulated its strategy for exploiting this. A world leader in commercialising technology, it stated in its annual report:

'Our business model and strategy is firmly based around our core competence, the commercialisation of Intellectual Property Rights through selectively:

- acquiring rights to high-potential technologies

- investing in early-stage development activities where the potential for return is high, and

- licensing technology, creating ventures or selling patents.

We continue to build on our established market position to take advantage of the many opportunities created by the explosion in IPR awareness. To capitalise on these market developments, we are accelerating our strategy in a number of ways.

We are strengthening the business groups to handle a larger number of technologies and to take a lead where technical discoveries and market changes create new commercial opportunities.

We are putting in place both the people and structures to implement more early-stage ventures, expanding and investing in existing and new partnerships, and creating strategic alliances with companies whose businesses are complementary to BTG.

We are also upgrading our internal systems to improve our global operations.'

(BTG annual report and accounts 2000)

Concentration on a single core competence can add further strength. Intel has achieved dominance by focusing on its core competence, its technical and manufacturing resource, and has become the world's largest producer of microprocessors. This concentration allowed it to switch out of memory production into processors in the mid-1980s. Its immediate future was secured when IBM adopted the Intel processor in its architecture so that it became an industry standard. The company continues to play a high-risk strategy of 'putting all your eggs in one basket and trying to win big' (Burgelman, 2002).

However, a single core competence can leave a company vulnerable should anything go wrong. Huntingdon Life Sciences, a drug-testing company, established its core competence around its scientific test data bank. When there were accusations that this was being falsified, not only were relationships with pharmaceutical suppliers affected but the company also lost clients. This led to a considerable loss in business. It is not unknown for a firm to misunderstand its own core competences, as in the case of Fiat – see the mini-case study on page 87.

Companies must also be aware of the limitations of any core competences they possess. Hanson became a huge transatlantic company through taking over and restructuring poorly performing businesses. But its success occurred in traditional mature businesses such as bricks, pipes and concrete. When it tried the same trick with Ever Ready, the battery manufacturer, it found it had acquired a company needing much new investment in highly competitive markets. When Hanson eventually sold the company, it had presided over a loss in its market share from 80 per cent to 30 per cent.

3.6 Divestment - a return to core competence?

Although there are potential benefits in diversifying, this often results in companies moving from areas where they have core competence into areas where they have none. In 2003, Invensys, once a FTSE top ten firm with sales of nearly £9 billion in 1998, announced its latest round of sell-offs. Its market value had fallen from £8 billion in 1998 to barely £500 million. In order to refocus around its production management and rail business, it was shedding once key businesses in appliance and climate controls and metering systems that would reduce group revenue to just £1.7 billion. Among the businesses on the block was the Dutch-based software business Baan, a heavy loss-maker which, in 2000, in an attempt to diversify, Invensys had acquired for £470 million, even though it was on the brink of insolvency.

Financial history is littered with similar examples of companies straying into areas where they had no core competence, losing money and returning to the safe haven of their core business, poorer and sometimes wiser. Daimler-Benz's brief foray into aerospace and micro-electronics in its attempt to become an 'integrated technology group' is a further example. It quickly realised that its core competence remained in manufacturing luxury cars. Ironically, British Aerospace made the opposite but similarly misplaced journey from its core area of aerospace into car-making when it took a stake in Rover cars. The culture of the troubled car firm was completely at odds with the quasi-military hierarchy in British Aerospace. British Aerospace eventually sold Rover to BMW in 1994 for £1, another purchase with a troubled history.

Some firms make a comeback. In the 1990s, Logica designed and fitted bespoke IT systems, which it regarded as its core competence. However, the company then set up a mobile phone venture that destroyed value. The company's strategic shift back to its core competence resulted in it winning a huge £200 million contract to manage the technology requirements of the UK Crown Prosecution Service.

These actions reflect the view that when **diversification** is suspected of destroying value, it may make strategic sense for diversified companies to return to what they do best and refocus on their original competence. Indeed, this is the conclusion of a study by Deloitte (2002) which suggests that demerging often adds value – it is often the way to undo a mistake that should never have been made in the first place.

Although demerging may reduce economies of scale, and add to duplication as demerged businesses set up their own structures, there are potentially significant advantages. It allows businesses to focus on their core competence, i.e. adding value by concentrating on what they are good at. Greater independence creates greater motivation; decision making becomes clearer, more flexible and more focused.

Often the best way to increase shareholder value is to keep managers focused on their core competence. The drinks group Diageo sold Burger King in December 2002 for $1.5 billion to the US venture capital firm Texas Pacific. It now sees its core expertise in the production and marketing of drinks, not food.

An extreme case is Anadolu, Turkey's leading brewing company (www.anadolugroup.com). The company also manufactures cars, light trucks, pencils, and runs a bank! However, the company has now sold off many of these other interests. As one analyst said, the company suddenly realised that it was 'very good at beverages, but not so good at other things, such as banking'. This strategic **divestment** stemmed from two key environmental factors – a 10 per cent decline in Turkey's gross domestic product (GDP) in 2001 and the prospect of stiffer competition with Turkey possibly joining the EU. It is often the case that tougher economic conditions highlight areas where companies are not adding value and encourage a return to their strengths.

However, diversifications based upon core competences can be very successful. Examples include General Electric (whose output ranges from engines to broadcasting, based upon a core competence of innovation) and 3M (which produces Post-it notes to magnetic tape, based upon its core competence with sticky tape). At a time when conglomerates are out of favour, these are exceptional companies that the market values highly as diversified conglomerates.

But if the market is unsighted, the company may choose the wrong options. Tyco is a highly diversified American company involved in many areas from financial services to fire extinguishers, a diversification that was highly successful. It identified those resources and competences which could be applied across a range of businesses. These were:

- quality management based upon a system of devolved decision making
- substantial and uncapped financial incentives for staff
- a robust system of financial control.

However, lack of transparency in Tyco's accounts meant investors could not identify clearly the results of its value-adding activities. Where the market feels unsighted, it tends to downgrade the stock because of the potential risk, especially since the Enron collapse. Coupled with the alleged financial wrongdoing of the former CEO, this lack of transparency is starting to destroy Tyco's value as fast as the company is creating it (see *Financial Times* 27 June 2002). Tyco suggested that it might break up the company into four stand-alone companies to stop the decline in its share price. However, this announcement hit the share price even more. The market did not see a break-up as a solution since the diversification of the company is not the problem. Instead, Tyco has to try to shine more light into the financial positions of its various activities.

Self-assessment activity 3.4

Has 'your' company divested any activities recently? What reasons were given?

3.7 Selecting the markets in which to exploit core competences

Firms find that different markets offer different opportunities for them to exploit the core competences that add value. In some markets, it will be easier to earn abnormal returns than in others. Porter (1985) provided a framework (often called his **Five Forces Model**, or 5FM) which identified the factors that determined the degree of attractiveness, in terms of expected profitability, of an industry, including the 'rivalry' or level of competition within any market. The more intense the rivalry, the more difficult it will be to exploit the core competences that add value. Thus intense rivalry will tend to produce a market where profit margins are low.

The five forces, illustrated in Figure 3.1, are as follows:

1 *Intensity of rivalry among existing firms.* This depends largely on the number and closeness of substitutes for the product. The implication of this is that customers are willing to buy similar products to what any one company is offering to the market. Thus, prices will tend to be competitive as companies attempt to attract customers to their product rather than a substitute. Newspapers and supermarkets often get involved in price wars as customers demonstrate their fickleness between the options available. The less differentiated the product is, the more intense the competition is likely to be. Two examples are the ever-falling price of video tapes and aspirin.

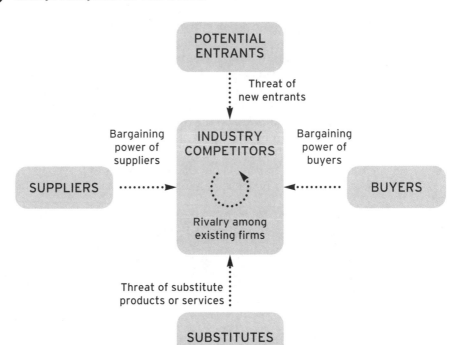

Figure 3.1 Porter's Five Forces Model

Source: Adapted with the permission of the Free Press, a Division of Simon & Schuster Adult Publishing Group, from Figure 1.1 on p. 4, *Competitive Strategy: Techniques for Analyzing Industries and Competitors*, by Michael E Porter (1998). Copyright © 1980, 1998 by The Free Press. All rights reserved.

However, it is not unknown for firms to 'buy off' competition by arranging some form of collusive arrangement such as a cartel. Cartels are usually illegal as they lay down secret agreements to maintain prices or otherwise restrict competition. OPEC is the most well-known example of a cartel, although its activities are hardly secret.

2 *Customers' bargaining power*. Where customers are strong, the market is likely to be competitive. Suppliers will expend time and money competing among themselves to obtain orders from the customers, since there is likely to be little to be gained by putting pressure on the customers themselves. Thus governments handing out large contracts and supermarkets looking for products are both strong customers who will unleash very competitive market conditions for the businesses seeking to supply them. If the customer is weak, on the other hand, the supplier can charge a premium price. Most modern PCs fit Intel processors – Intel knows the quality stamp that it gives to a PC and the customers (the computer manufacturers) realise what a critical part of their product this represents. Intel can drive home the advantage that it possesses when it negotiates prices with manufacturers.

Customers have become stronger when purchasing utilities such as telephone, electricity and gas. Where it used to be difficult and time-consuming to switch suppliers, the companies concerned now make it much easier by doing much of the switching administration themselves. This has encouraged competition among the various utility companies. Banks are similarly trying to entice customers from competitor banks by offering the same ease of switching. Yet most consumers continue to exhibit inertia in this area because of the effort involved – people are more likely to get divorced than to change bank accounts!

3 *Suppliers' bargaining power.* Similarly, a market where suppliers are strong is likely to be competitive. This is the flip-side of customer strength. Suppliers will tend to be strong and charge higher prices if there are high switching costs such as changing a bank account as just mentioned. Suppliers are strong if they are few in number or have a distinctively good product to offer. For example, if the supplier has a valuable branded product which the market demands, a brand confers monopoly power, as in the case of Intel's Pentium chips or Microsoft's Windows operating system. Both factors contribute towards the PC market being highly competitive.

4 *The likelihood of a substitute product emerging.* The threat of substitutes will increase competition within any market and limit the price that can be charged because substitutes offer alternatives to the consumer. In a sense, the threat of substitution is almost limitless in that there are many demands on our money. At any time, someone could be considering spending money on a new car, or a foreign holiday or a new kitchen.

The key to the risk of substitution in the Five Forces Model is when competitors move into a market from outside to provide a service in a different manner. The straight choice between a Ford car or a Nissan is covered under the power of buyers, and the threat of a new car manufacturer from China will come under the same heading because the Chinese company will aim to satisfy demand in the same manner as its competitors. But existing car manufacturers do face a substitution threat from the development of electric cars. Similarly, Eurotunnel was a substitution threat to the shipping and airline companies because it was satisfying need in a different way. Substitutes provide the same or similar service in a different manner. Thus glass, plastic, aluminium and carton manufacturers are all substitutes to provide containers for beverages. Even the OPEC cartel faces the long-term threat of the development of hydrogen fuel cells as an alternative to oil.

5 *Barriers to entry.* High barriers to entering a market, such as cost or level of technology, protects those businesses already in the market from outsiders entering. One of the major problems facing dotcom companies as they try to build high-value businesses has been the comparative ease with which competitors can enter the market and offer a similar service. This will start to occur as soon as abnormal profits are identified in a market, attracting competitors like bees round the honey-pot. This is the main reason why leading dotcom businesses spend so much money trying to erect the one

significant barrier that they can establish: their brand name. Amazon, Yahoo, Google and Lastminute.com all spend considerable sums on marketing in order to establish their names in the market so as to attract customer loyalty, which may deter competitors.

Lowered barriers = value destroyed

An example of the role of barriers to entry is provided by the case of the financial news agency Reuters plc. Founded in 1851 by Julius Reuter, Reuters enjoyed a virtual monopoly position for over a century until the early 1990s, when Michael Bloomberg, later to become mayor of New York, founded a fledgling news agency. By 2003, Bloomberg had become market leader with 42 per cent market share compared with Reuters' 39 per cent. In 2002, Bloomberg had increased its own sales by 1 per cent at a time of rising unemployment among investment bankers. In 2003, Reuters reported its first ever loss, while the share price had plummeted from over £11 in early 2001 to barely £1 by April 2003.

Reuters was reported to have admitted privately that it had seriously underestimated the challenge from Bloomberg, relying far too heavily on what it perceived as the superiority of its own financial news service. The complacency of Reuters' management was summed up by an analyst who said: 'It was easier to reproduce that news service than they thought.'

Nevertheless, despite the welter of bad news, chief executive Tom Glocer was paid a £612,000 bonus. In defence of this apparent 'reward for failure', the Reuters chairman was quoted as saying: 'There is a market price for expertise.'

The five forces determine the degree of competition and hence the scope to make profits found in any market. They will become particularly powerful if the market has no growth. In a stagnant market, the only way a firm can add value is at the expense of another – a situation likely to intensify competition. Rivalry is also likely to be intense if companies are reluctant to leave the market due to the financial expenditures they have already made and the low prices they would get for their assets. For both of these reasons, steel-makers often stay in markets where they are barely covering operating costs in the hope that prices will rise in the future, or that competitors will 'blink first' and close down.

Nevertheless, if market conditions are too hostile, it may be necessary to 'bite the bullet' however much money has been spent. In 1998, the German company Siemens closed a brand new computer chip manufacturing facility in the northeast of England after less than one year in operation. Even though it had spent £1.2 billion on the facility, world prices of computer chips had collapsed to such a low level that Siemens could not see the investment ever making a satisfactory return.

> ## Self-assessment activity 3.5
>
> Conduct a 'five forces' analysis of the main market in which your company operates.

The ideal market?

The ideal market, in which profits are easiest to make, is one with:

- weak inter-firm competition
- low customer power
- low supplier power
- little prospect of a substitute product emerging
- high barriers to entry.

The problem firms face in reality is that these circumstances rarely coincide – some forces may be favourable and others adverse. Part of the art of strategy is to weigh up the overall situation by balancing one factor against the others. It may be that all bar one factor look highly promising, but the exception is so unappealing that the industry appears thoroughly unattractive. For example, at the time of writing, many forces seem to favour the tobacco industry, but few firms would want to diversify into cigarette production given the prospect of litigation of increasing severity.

> ## Self-assessment activity 3.6
>
> Suggest some strategic decisions that may weaken the five forces.
> (answer at end of chapter)

3.8 Protecting competitive advantage

Core competences give a company a competitive advantage over its competitors – exploiting them enables it to earn abnormal returns. However, abnormal returns will attract competitors and if allowed to enter the market, competitors will erode value until a level of profitability is established that will no longer attract further entrants. This is why it is helpful if the competences are difficult for competitors to imitate.

Having established a competitive advantage, wherever possible the company should try to defend it against new entrants by building barriers to entry. Doing this will protect the value niche and will prolong a company's ability to add value. As Steve Ballmer, the chief executive of Microsoft, put it: the ability to make profits critically depends on 'how good is the moat you can build around the company to protect its position'. Indeed, Bill Gates himself has stated that 'profit is not a natural state for companies'. His genius has been to establish the Windows operating system as a formidable moat (not without criticism!).

Once investment opportunities arise, managing for value requires that the business then creates, preserves and even enhances its competitive advantage by protecting its value 'honey-pot'. Warren Buffett, the legendary investment guru, has said that the main thing he looks for in any company in which he is thinking of investing is sustainable competitive advantage.

There are many possible barriers to entry which may protect such advantage.

Cost advantages

At its simplest, being able to provide goods and services at a cheaper price than competitors always offers important market protection. In these cases, competitors see no prospect of earning abnormal returns and so are not attracted into the market in the first place.

There are various ways in which cost advantages can be achieved. Economies of scale, synergistic production, and distribution and marketing rationalisations may all provide low costs of production which competitors may struggle to match. In addition, some businesses require high capital investment (heavy engineering) or a high level of expenditure in research and development (pharmaceuticals or aerospace). These factors may present considerable hurdles for any new company contemplating entering the market.

Low-fare airlines operate a low-cost structure to provide competitive advantage. Ryanair operates mainly from out-of-city airports, achieves quick turnarounds, operates an internet booking system (removing the requirement for the airline to pay travel agents or to set up a more expensive alternative booking facility) and offers little by way of frills. Despite, or because of, this, Ryanair is valued at double the market value of British Airways and is the most highly capitalised airline in Europe. It even eclipses the American equivalent, Southwest Airlines, by carrying twice the passengers per employee. Ryanair's share price has doubled since 11 September 2001, while many other airlines, particularly the highly geared 'hub-and-spoke' network operators, have tumbled. Some, like Sabena and Swissair, have even gone bust.

Product differentiation

At most supermarkets, it is possible to find an own-brand can of cola selling for less than half the price of a can of Coca-Cola, yet people still buy the Coca-Cola. This is the power of the brand and the experience it promises – 'It's the real thing'. Brands are constantly reinforced by substantial advertising. But they create in the minds of the consumer a monopoly where the brand itself is the only product, i.e. Coca-Cola is a unique product, not just another cola. This allows the manufacturer to charge the premium price, which customers are willing to pay.

At another level, Unilever and Procter and Gamble use product differentiation as a barrier to entry. If they produced just one brand of detergent each, a new entrant could expect to fight for up to a third of the total market. This is one reason why the two companies each produce around a dozen brands of washing powder. This minimises the likely market that any new entrant can pitch for.

Legal protection through patents and trademarks

This is a powerful incentive offered to businesses that create new products or processes. To encourage innovation and invention, the government allows legal protection against competition for a period of years to allow the inventing company time to recover its costs and earn a profit from its endeavours.

Patents are thus extremely valuable and are fiercely protected. Aventis, the Franco-German pharmaceutical company, values its patents at around 35 per cent of total company assets. Significantly, it also gives details of the expiry date of each patent in its annual report – the day when competitors are allowed into the market and can take some of the value away from Aventis for themselves.

By keeping out competitors, a patent can add value in many different ways – by providing the company with a monopoly product for which it can charge a premium price or by providing the opportunity to sell the right of use for royalties (this has the advantage of establishing a product in the market). The vacuum manufacturer Dyson chose to produce its own 'bag-less' vacuums based upon the inventions patented by the company's founder, James Dyson. Dyson took Hoover to court for infringing that patent when Hoover marketed its own 'bag-less' model, winning £4 million in damages for the breach. Hoover itself was once a powerful brand in electrical appliances.

Stopping others from using a product by taking out a patent is not always the best approach. Apple computers did not allow others to use its operating system and protected it legally. Microsoft, on the other hand, allowed the Windows operating system to be used by others and has been rewarded by seeing it become the industry standard, which allows Microsoft to sell its other software to users. Microsoft reinforces this advantage by keeping the source code for Microsoft Windows a secret (in the same way as Coca-Cola's recipe is kept in a safe in Atlanta).

It is not just companies that seek legal protection. In order to establish a competitive advantage over other countries in e-business and information and communication technologies, in October 2002 the Republic of Ireland government proposed the establishment of e-courts to provide a secure and just legal process for patents, copyright and other intellectual property issues. By doing this, the government was encouraging new IT companies to set up in Ireland where they can be sure of legal protection for any patents on IT products.

Access to distribution channels

Manufacturers and other businesses need to be able to get their product to the market. The existence of a distribution infrastructure can be a valuable asset as well as acting as an important barrier against competitors entering the market.

There are many examples of companies making strategic decisions which impacted on this area. Many years ago, the French car company Peugeot was trying to establish itself in the UK market. One of its major problems was that the company had no distribution network in which it could sell its cars, and existing dealers were tied to other motor manufacturers. The company was at a considerable competitive disadvantage to the other manufacturers. The company needed a strategy to rectify the situation. Obviously, it could have started from the beginning and gradually built up a network of dealers. Instead, Peugeot took over the US manufacturer Chrysler which had an established UK dealership network, so as to give it an 'instant' dealer network through which it could sell its cars.

The long-running battle between Virgin Airlines and British Airways has revolved around the competitive advantage that BA enjoys because of the number of flight slots allocated to the airline, particularly at Heathrow. This reduces the number of take-off slots available to its competitors and therefore the number of flights they can schedule. In addition, BA has a predominance of the take-off slots at London's second airport, Gatwick. One of the reasons for this is that BA took over the failing charter airline Dan-Air. BA paid £1 for the company (it also took responsibility for its considerable debt), not because it wanted its ageing aircraft, but because Dan-Air owned a large number of allocated take-off slots at the airport. The value in the deal as far as BA was concerned was embedded in these take-off slots.

Prudential, the financial services group, sought competitive advantage by agreeing a deal which allowed it to sell its with-profit bonds through the Abbey National Bank. The Prudential said the deal reflected 'our strategy of building multi-channel distribution'. This meant it would be much easier for customers to buy this product now that it was available at branches of the Abbey National.

We have already referred to the value-adding abilities of Microsoft. In effect, by allowing use of its Windows operating system, the company created its own distribution network for all of its software products, such as the Office suite of programs.

Companies need to be alert to any threats to their distribution network. Many advertisers are concerned that the proposed merger of the two big television companies Carlton and Granada will present them with a monopoly situation when they negotiate rates for TV advertising. (The date of the merger is still unknown as the case is under investigation by the Competition Commission.) Unilever, anticipating the merger, agreed a four-year deal to advertise Birds Eye, Dove, Wall's and Persil 'to secure a competitive advantage through a period of continuing change', i.e. to reach agreement with the TV companies in anticipation of the advertising rates being pushed up after the merger.

Government regulation

Government regulation often restricts new entrants and protects existing businesses. For example, farming quotas may be allocated to existing farmers or fishermen and do not allow new entrants into the market.

In recent years, governments have greatly restricted the building of out-of-town shopping centres partly because of the impact they are having on traditional town-centre shops. However, those already built benefit from the fact that other sites are now unlikely to be developed.

The relationship between business and governments does of course vary around the world. The link with the government enjoyed by Singapore's state-owned companies, such as Singapore Airlines, the two main telecoms operators and the biggest bank on the island, gives them considerable competitive advantages. They can recruit the best graduates, they can obtain cheaper (government-backed financing), and they have the security of being able to plan for the long term. However, these advantages have not brought guaranteed success; in fact, despite the growth in the economy, these companies have performed relatively poorly. Perhaps the government link is too protective and the advantages it bestows must be balanced against stifling the entrepreneurial culture in the companies concerned.

Location

Location – being in the right place – can be an important competitive advantage. Companies such as Marks and Spencer are very careful to locate their stores at just the right place on the high street, and on the right side of the road.

Location can also be important for islands and areas like the Isle of Man. Financial services on the Isle of Man have one notable competitive advantage over the Channel Islands of Guernsey and Jersey as a tax-free centre – the island can attract labour due to the relative ease of obtaining work permits and accommodation compared with the restrictions on labour mobility imposed by the Channel Islands. All three areas are successful financial centres, but there are problems in their dependence on this industry. In particular, the relationship of the UK with the EU, including the possible introduction of the euro, will have huge implications for the islands. On another level, Jersey has been reluctant to comply with international pressure to increase the financial transparency of tax havens such as itself in case it concedes competitive advantage to Switzerland, which is maintaining a high level of banking secrecy.

Self-assessment activity 3.7

To what extent do these barriers operate in the main market of your chosen company?

The following mini-case involves creation of entry barriers.

From dot.gone to dot.come – a Lastminute success story

The share flotation of Lastminute.com at the start of 2000 represented the peak of the UK dotcom boom. Investor interest in the issue was so high that, very unusually, the financial advisers of the company actually raised the offer price just a couple of weeks before the deadline for applications. Investors who had applied at the original 340p had to confirm that they were still interested in applying at the higher 380p eventually imposed. By the start of 2002, the shares stood at 26p, having fallen to below 20p at one stage. Incredibly, it became the best performing share on the London market in 2002, finishing the year at 105p and finding itself back in the FTSE 250 index of leading British companies. By September 2003, the company share price had risen to 270p.

Behind this turnaround is the core competence of technology that the company has developed. The company has reached a critical mass so that the £15 million per year that it is spending on technology now represents a barrier to entry. This is in addition to the brand name that is often the only barrier that dotcoms try to establish to keep out competition.

But competition remains strong. Expedia, a US company, has a market capitalisation ten times that of Lastminute, and it has its eyes on Europe. In addition, the budget airlines have developed sophisticated online booking systems that have significantly reduced the flight bookings now going through Lastminute's website. Lastminute has responded by spending £60 million on three overseas online businesses which have given the company a wider presence and a critical mass in more high-margin business areas such as hotels and package holidays. The company has reduced its staff base to 800 and it now outsources parts of the business. Lastminute.com reported its first pre-tax profit in the quarter ending September 2002, and its first positive net cash flow in the quarter ending March 2003. Lastminute is starting to look like a regular business!

Self-assessment activity 3.8

Lastminute.com is a survivor, unlike 90 per cent of the dotcoms floated at the turn of the century. Other survivors are Amazon, Yahoo and e-Bay. Select one of these and try to account for its survival, i.e. what market opportunity did it exploit, what competences were required to do so, are there any entry barriers, etc?

3.9 Overview of the key ideas in strategic management

It is easy to get bogged down in jargon in the strategy field. However, the key ideas are very simple. Firms are in business to create value for their owners. They do this by selecting the most appropriate field in which to operate, and by utilising their existing assets in the most effective way, buying in more assets if they perceive gaps in skills or resources.

This can be shown by the MOST schema used by Grant (2000). MOST is an acronym standing for Mission-Objectives-Strategy-Tactics, viz:

- The *Mission* is the overriding purpose of the firm. Whatever is stated in public, this means maximising value for owners, although it may be qualified by mention of other stakeholders.

- The *Objectives* of the firm are the targets it lays down. These are selected for their impact in achieving value creation, and thus provide measuring rods for progress.

- The *Strategy*, as explained, involves selecting the markets in which to operate and how to compete, e.g. by pursuing cost advantage or product differentiation.

- The *Tactics* adopted are the operating policies implemented to secure the chosen competitive advantage, e.g. Dell's production management policies designed to meet supply schedules.

The elements of the acronym are brought together, with examples, in Figure 3.2.

The same ideas can be shown from the bottom up. Certain skills, or competences, are required to enable effective implementation of the chosen tactics, which, if effectively implemented, will help managers achieve the key objectives. This sequence of relationships is shown in Figure 3.3.

As you progress through the book, it may be helpful to refer back to these figures to see how the particular financial skill examined fits into the strategic management of the firm. For example, in the next chapter we examine investment appraisal – this is the set of techniques used to evaluate whether new resources, fixed and other assets, should be acquired to supplement the firm's resource base and help it to deliver its strategies and achieve its mission of adding value.

MISSION	(e.g.) Maximise shareholder wealth	
OBJECTIVES	Financial	(e.g.) 'Raise EPS by 8% p.a.' 'Achieve an ROE of 25% p.a.'
	Marketing	'Increase turnover by 5% p.a.' 'Achieve no. 1 or 2 position for every product'
STRATEGY	Corporate strategy	What markets to serve?/ What products to produce?
	Business strategy	How to compete in chosen markets? (e.g.) Product differentiation *vs.* cost advantage?
TACTICS	(e.g.) ● Rapid delivery, right first time quality control ● Discounts for bulk purchase and early payment ● Just-in-time stock management ● Flexible production scheduling	

Figure 3.2 The dimensions of competition: the MOST acronym

Source: Based on Grant (2000)

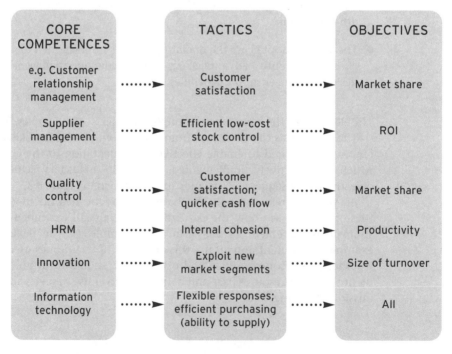

Figure 3.3 Business objectives and the exploitation of core competences

3.10 Summary

There is no magic wand to guarantee value creation. Companies can add value by identifying where their strengths are relative to those of their competitors and exploiting that advantage in the right markets. This is a continual process in an ever-changing world and value must be protected and nurtured. The recent huge declines in the value of companies such as Reuters, Marconi and Cable & Wireless clearly demonstrate the requirement for all businesses to maintain and renew their value. Value can collapse almost overnight. The single best way to add value is by making good investments, the subject of the next chapter.

References and further reading

Textbooks

Arnold – ch 15.
Brealey & Myers – ch 11.

Other

Burgelman (2002) *Strategy is Destiny: How Strategy-making Shapes a Company's Future* (Free Press).
Deloitte (2002) *Demerger Study: Analysing the Value of Demergers through Share Performance* (Deloitte & Touche).
Grant, R M (2001) *Contemporary Strategic Analysis: concepts, techniques, applications*, 4th edn, (Blackwell Publishing).
Porter, M E (1980) *Competitive Strategy* (Free Press).
Porter, M E (1985) *Competitive Advantage* (Free Press).
Porter, M E (1987) 'From competitive advantage to corporate strategy', *Harvard Business Review*, May–June.
Prahalad, C and Hamel, G (1990) 'The core competence of the corporation', *Harvard Business Review*, Vol. 68, No. 3, May–June, pp. 79–93.

Questions and mini-case studies

1 Corporate strategy has often been compared to military strategy. Do you think this is a good comparison?

2 Most of us are familiar with supermarkets. From your experience, identify what you consider to be a 'well-performing' or successful supermarket and a 'badly performing' one. Using the concepts in this chapter, identify the

reasons that distinguish the good supermarkets from the bad ones. In your opinion, what can the poorer ones do to improve?

Mini-case study – McDonald's

In 2003, McDonald's, the fast-food chain, reported its first ever loss – £222 million for the quarter (although much of this was down to restructuring costs). The company announced a series of measures to reverse the company's fortune:

- appointment of a new chairman, Jim Cantalupo, a 28-year McDonald's veteran

- plans to divest its stakes in 'partner brands' such as Prêt-a-Manger and Chipotle Burritos. Although these have contributed in excess of $1 billion sales, they now are regarded as a management distraction from the core business, as well as requiring considerable capital spending

- closure of 719 underperforming restaurants

- dampening shareholder expectations about the future, even though shares were trading at a ten-year low, at just $12 compared with its peak of $48 in 1999. It announced that a future growth rate of 10–15 per cent was no longer realistic

- adoption of a 'back to basics' policy to refocus on service and cleanliness, following negative feedback from customer surveys. As an example, it aimed to replace its new system of cooking to order with its old system of cooking in advance. Although the new system produced higher-quality, fresher food it was slower and was causing longer waiting times – customers did not appreciate the wait! However, the company intended to continue to provide more healthy options, such as salads and yoghurts, on its menu.

Required

(a) What do you think are the main core competences of McDonald's?

(b) Analyse the strategies for re-establishing its competitive advantage over its rivals.

Source: 'McDonalds: Back to Buns', *The Guardian*, 8 April, 2003

Mini-case study - Fiat

Fiat is the sixth largest maker of cars and trucks in the world, selling 2 million units annually worth €30 billion. But size does not necessarily provide value. In 2001, it lost €445 million. Unfortunately for Fiat, its main output is in markets where there is fierce competition, e.g. small hatch-backs and family saloons, and is concentrated in Italy, where it sells 57 per cent of its European output, although it now enjoys less than a 50 per cent share in a market it once dominated. It has no niche high value-added product.

So what are Fiat's core competences, and why are things going wrong? It could be argued that Fiat's core competence has nothing to do with car production as such. Instead its strength has been that this is a 'family' firm that has always been well connected both politically (an essential require-ment for a successful Italian company) and financially in the Italian socio-economic system. Major problems have now emerged which are threatening the survival of this famous name.

The conflict between family interests and strategic interests relating to its products in the market is now causing problems. Thus, alliances with other companies are difficult given the primacy of family interests and the loss of control that this might bring. Changes in the political land-scape in Italy have ruptured the privileged relationship that the company once had with the government. Two further problems have been the eco-nomic downturn in Europe at the start of the new millennium, and the issue of succession following the death of the dominant chairman Gianni Agnelli.

All of these factors have diluted the core competence that this company had. This has resulted in part of the company being sold to the US auto giant General Motors, a strategy that has succeeded in upsetting the family, the government and most of Italy. The Italian prime minister was so incensed by this sale that he intervened to try to stop the deal, an action which led to the chairman of Fiat calling the prime minister 'crazy'.

Required

(a) Analyse the rise and fall of Fiat as indicated in this case.

(b) What strategies should the company be considering for the future?

Source: Adapted from Peter Martin 'Decline of the Turin Empire', *Financial Times*, 14 May 2002, and the article by Fred Kapner *Financial Times*, 12 December 2002

Mini-case study – BT Group plc

In 2002, BT's new chairman pleased the City with a series of announcements:

- it would resume dividend payments following the cut in 2001
- it expressed its intention to pull out of loss-making ventures in Europe and elsewhere, despite substantial book losses
- it was to refocus its management by setting more rigorous revenue targets based on extending the business into 'adjacent areas where we have capability and understanding' (in particular, the growth of broadband) rather than focus on cost-cutting.

Underpinning these announcements is a realisation that BT's core competence is access provision (broadband and high-speed internet) rather than the provision of content. BT has recognised that consumers and businesses are increasingly willing to conduct business online. A spokesman for the company said: 'I think we are trusted with our core competence of network and communication solutions.'

In May 2002, BT sold off 6,700 properties such as telephone exchanges for £2.38 billion. John Pike, head of Property Partners (a business unit within BT), explained the reason for this sale: 'Debt reduction was a key aim, but there was also a desire to focus on our core competences, of which property management is not one.'

For companies like BT, saving maintenance costs, the reduction of staff required and saving the 'hidden' cost of underutilising buildings are among the advantages of selling superfluous properties. The staff involved often prefer to work for a specialised property company rather than BT because of the greater career opportunities available to them.

Required

(a) Comment on the three specific points announced by BT's new chairman.

(b) In the past, BT has attempted to:
  - merge with other telecommunications companies, such as MCI in the US
  - link with European banks, such as Banco Santander in Spain and Banca Nazionale del Lavaro in Italy.

  Offer strategic advice to BT as to whether it should continue to look out for similar opportunities.

(c) Some analysts argue that in fast-moving businesses like telecommunications, it is not worth having strategic plans for the future. Comment on this point of view.

Source: Adapted from Fiona Harvey 'Survey-Corporate Real Estate',
Financial Times, 17 May 2002

Mini-case study - eBay

eBay is one of the 10 per cent or fewer that got away - a dotcom firm that survived. It was set up as a trading platform for bargain hunters, collectors and sellers from anywhere in the world, taking a fee for every item listed and commission on every sale. By 2003, it claimed 62 million registered users, had stakes in businesses in 27 countries, and reckoned that 100,000 small businesses operated solely on its platform.

eBay was founded in 1997 by Frenchman Pierre Omidyar, not in a garage but in a bedroom, to provide an online auction house for people wanting to sell almost anything. In the early days, its main business was in collectibles, with Beanie Babies accounting for over 10 per cent of its turnover. By 2003, collectibles were matched in importance by computers, electronic goods, books and CDs. Its fastest growing sector was second-hand cars, accounting for about 1 per cent of all used car sales in the largest market in the world.

By 2003, eBay was forecasting revenue of $1.9 billion, well on the way to the $3 billion it forecast (rashly, in some eyes) at the peak of the dotcom bubble, when revenues were $425 million. It was also sitting on that rare dotcom commodity - cash of $1.5 billion. Its shares stood at $89, almost 500 per cent higher than the price at flotation in 1998, reckoned to be the fifth most successful IPO ever.

eBay's business model is as unusual as its success story:

- it is open 24/7 worldwide
- it holds no stock
- it has no delivery costs
- it needs negligible capital expenditure
- it operates from modest offices in out-of-town San Jose, California.

Taxation aside, its revenues feed directly into profits and thence into cash. Chief executive Meg Whitman (meg@ebay.com) said:

> 'It's really different from most businesses. The R&D lab here is our community of users and it's an undirected R&D lab - they figure out how to best use this platform. We didn't sit in a room five years ago and say, "Let's have our users get into the used car business" - they did it on their own. The diversification of the platform happened organically.'

(Quoted in *The Guardian*, April 12 2003)

Required

(a) How do you account for eBay's success?

(b) What are its core competences?

(c) What is the source of its competitive advantage?

Mini-case study – Boots

Boots, the UK's largest high street retail chemist, surprised the City in March 2003 when it announced that it was closing down its Wellbeing Clinics and its Pure Beauty upmarket cosmetic stores. The clinics provided a variety of services including Botox injections and laser hair removal. Wellbeing had lost £140 million over the previous three years. In addition, Boots would close its remaining shops in Europe, and in future would only operate concessions in the Far East. These changes were to result in 700 jobs lost and cost around £55 million.

This marked the end of a sorry tale of attempted diversification by the company. Failed ventures in the past included:

- Boots for Men, specialising in men's grooming
- Halfords, a car parts and servicing business
- Bootsphoto.com, an online photograph developing service
- Boots outlets sited in Sainsbury's, the UK's second largest supermarket chain
- Children's World, a chain of shops stocking children's clothes, toys and books.

But the biggest failure of all was the company's venture into the growing do-it-yourself business. Its failed operation of the Do-It-All chain cost Boots around £300 million.

Boots management is hoping that the move back to the high street and to its core business will lead to better times. After being an attractive 'buy' in the 1990s, the shares have plummeted in price recently. When asked if there was limited growth in its core business, the managing director said: 'I always thought that it was not the business that was mature, but the managers.'

Nevertheless, future success is not guaranteed. Boots' lucrative £1 billion p.a. pharmacy business was threatened after an investigation by the Office of Fair Trading (Report on Community Pharmacy, February 2003). Although 40 per cent of its sales are own-label, the 12 per cent profit margins have attracted competition from the supermarkets. Signalling that there is no easy solution, the market price fell by 6 per cent on the above announcement.

Required

(a) What do you think was the reasoning behind each of Boots' attempts at diversification outlined above?

(b) How would you suggest that Boots expands its core business? How can it compete with the supermarkets?

Self-assessment answers

(All but self-assessment activity 3.6 involve a focus on your chosen firm.)

3.6
- *Internal rivalry*: make collusive agreements.
- *Customer power*: engage in advertising, produce related products to lock in buyers to the product line.
- *Supplier power*: engage in JIT, acquire a major supplier.
- *Intensity of inter-firm rivalry*: differentiate the product, take over competitors, make collusive agreements.
- *Appearance of substitute products*: reduce dependence on original product, invest in competing activities.
- *Entry barriers*: build artificial barriers, e.g. tie up distribution channels by supplier incentives, engage in a high level of R&D to quicken technical progress, and raise entry costs.

Case study: the Quaker story

Brand games

This case describes the story of the Quaker Oats company over the 1990s. Quaker was an early convert to the shareholder value philosophy, although it found itself a takeover target in 2000, due partly to flagging overall performance, but primarily due to having developed a highly attractive product coveted by the two major players in the soft drinks market, Coca-Cola and PepsiCo. Quaker subsequently found itself caught up in the perennial power struggle for supremacy in the soft drinks industry between the two market leaders. A key element in this story is the value of brands and market share in pursuing business strategy.

Introduction: Quaker and its mission

The prominent US food and drinks manufacturer Quaker Oats was one of the first firms to wholeheartedly embrace the shareholder value principles propounded by writers like Rappaport. In its 1990 annual report, the chairman declared:

> 'Our objective is to maximise value for shareholders over the long term. As a worldwide marketer of grocery products, value is embodied in our strong portfolio of brands. Management is empowered to oversee the investment in, and maintenance of, our brands to maximise their growth and profit potential. In all lines of business, Quaker managers must weigh the impact of strategic issues on investment decisions. Ultimately, our goal is the goal of all professional investors – to maximise value by generating the highest cash flows possible.
>
> There are two challenges created by this goal. The first is to pursue business strategies that strike the proper balance between profitability and growth in each of our brands. The second challenge is to invest in projects that will allow us to consistently deliver cash flows to shareholders at rates in excess of our cost of capital and better than our competitors.'

It would be difficult to find a clearer or more convincing espousal of the shareholder value philosophy. In the same report, Quaker supplemented this declaration of philosophy by documenting its mission, strategies and objectives.

Business mission

To maximise value for our shareholders as a successful, independent marketer of leading consumer brands.

Business strategy

To maximise value by generating the highest cash flow possible through internal product development and acquisitions and making strategic decisions to invest where growth and returns are most attractive.

Financial goals

1   Achieve return on equity of 25 per cent or more.

2   Achieve 'real' earnings growth of 7 per cent p.a. over time.

3   Increase dividends, consistent with earnings growth, in 'real' terms.

4   Maintain a strong financial position as represented by Quaker's current bond and commercial paper ratings.

Operating strategies

1   Continue to be a leading marketer of strong consumer brands.

2   Achieve profitable, better-than-average 'real' volume growth in our worldwide grocery business.

3   Improve the profitability of low-return businesses or divest them.

By the end of the subsequent decade, a re-reading of several of these bold words and phrases like value, growth and independence might appear quite ironical.

Value destruction: the Snapple acquisition

In 1994, Quaker's commitment to shareholder value came under sharp scrutiny when it paid $1.7 billion for Snapple, a soft drinks company that made strawberry iced tea and other exotic cocktails. Snapple was generally perceived as being well past its market peak, with sales flagging. A common view was that Quaker had paid at least $1 billion too much for a fading star. As it turned out, both Quaker and the experts were wrong.

Quaker itself proceeded to invest more money in the Snapple brand. Yet despite marketing ploys like giving away free drinks, sales failed to revive, falling by 8 per cent to around $550 million during 1996 and inflicting operating losses of $100 million on its new parent, depressing the Quaker share price. The share price recovered in March 1997 when it announced that it had swallowed its pride in selling Snapple for just $300 million to Triarc, a New York-based food and drinks group.

Triarc clearly saw something in Snapple that Quaker was unable to exploit and that the pundits had overlooked. Sales grew strongly at over 10 per cent p.a. on average during the next three years to reach $770 million by 2000, generating earnings before interest, tax and depreciation of $111 million, raising the possibility of a stock market flotation. However, following the third year of strong growth, Triarc announced in September 2000 that it had sold Snapple to the UK food, confectionery and soft drinks group Cadbury-Schweppes for $1.45 billion, nearly five times its initial outlay. The deal would increase the US earnings of Cadbury, already the owner of cola and carbonated drinks producer Dr Pepper, 7-Up and juice producer Motts, to more than 60 per cent of the group's total profits.

Cadbury was to pay a total outlay which included $910 million in cash, the assumption of debt and other liabilities of $420 million and buying out employee share options worth $120 million. It estimated that synergies from the deal would amount to between $10 million and $15 million in the first year, rising to $50 million by year three. In defending the decision, Cadbury's chief executive, John Sunderland, said:

'You don't get good food brands cheaply. You can buy duff things for tuppence but this is a great brand.'

This seemed to reassure investors as, despite the magnitude of the outlay, the deal was well received by the London market. On the expectation that Snapple would immediately enhance Cadbury's earnings, the share price rose over 5 per cent to 404 pence.

Independence threatened

A mistake on such a major scale as Quaker's throws into question the credibility of its management and its strategy, raising the possibility of further sales or even takeover. However, following the Snapple fiasco, in which it lost and failed to recover shareholder value of over $1 billion, Quaker was nurturing a gem of its own under a new chairman and CEO, Robert Morrison. In response to questions about the company being bought or making its own acquisitions, Morrison said he would always be in favour of any deals that made economic sense and produced shareholder value:

'Deals need to make strategic sense and provide new growth opportunities.'

Meanwhile, the likelihood of just such a deal was increasing.

In October 2000, it emerged that PepsiCo, which had smaller market share than Coca-Cola in the world soft drinks market, was talking to Quaker about a takeover for nearly $14 billion. Although these talks were inconclusive, they raised the possibility of flushing out alternative acquirors. The news that Quaker was 'in play' served to increase Quaker's share price from around $82 to $90, driving its market capitalisation to a shade below $12 billion.

The attraction for Pepsi was Quaker's sports drink brand Gatorade, which accounted for 86 per cent of this segment of the US market, a colossus when set beside the brands of Pepsi (All-Sport) and Coca-Cola (Powerade). According to John Sicher, editor of *Beverage Digest*, the industry trade newspaper:

'Quaker has a valuable jewel in Gatorade. At this time in the beverage industry, non-carbonated beverages are growing more quickly and gaining importance both strategically and in terms of revenue and profits. If Gatorade is available, it would be hard to imagine why Coke and Pepsi wouldn't be taking a very, very hard look at it.'

The reason was clear – while carbonated drinks were still the mainstay of both the giants' drinks empires, they were growing at a snail's pace compared with non-carbonated drinks. Moreover, Gatorade had a highly efficient distribution system which could be used to place other brands on supermarket shelves.

The value of Gatorade to Quaker was such that by 1999 it accounted for 40 per cent of its sales and profits.

The not-too-surprising news that Coke was also a suitor broke in early November 2000, when the Atlanta-based company was reported to have offered $15.8 billion in a deal that valued Quaker at about $115 per share. Around the same time, it was reported that French food group Danone SA, which was cash-rich after recently selling its beer brand Kronenbourg to the UK brewing and hotels group Scottish & Newcastle, had also expressed interest in acquiring Quaker, although it subsequently backed out.

Coca-Cola's CEO was Douglas Daft, who had taken over in February 2000, bringing two grand strategic ideas: first, to make Coke more responsive to local markets, and second, to shift its focus from colas to the faster-growing 'functional' drinks markets – teas, waters and juices – which claim to offer health benefits. Acquisition of the Gatorade brand would have given Coke a major lead in a rapidly growing sector and helped cement a decisive advantage over the ever-present threat from PepsiCo, reflecting the dominant influence on Coke's strategy. Whereas sales of these functional drinks had risen by over 60 per cent by volume in the preceding five years, sales of fizzy drinks were flat, actually falling in some markets (e.g. Germany and North America) in 1999.

However, the Coke proposal failed to survive a five-hour meeting of its board, during which the legendary private investor Warren Buffett ('the Sage of Omaha'), leader of Coke's independent directors, was fierce in his opposition. Buffett's opposition was motivated by the high cost involved in issuing shares that would significantly dilute the holding of existing investors.

Independence conceded

The cycle completed a full revolution in December 2000 when Pepsi re-appeared as the successful bidder in a $13.4 billion, $97.5 per share deal that gave it a distinct edge over Coke in the non-carbonated beverages market.

With control of Gatorade, and other brands including the Tropicana juice business and Lipton iced-tea line acquired from Seagrams in 1998, its pur-chase of SoBe herb-enriched energy drinks and its internally-developed water brand Aquafina, PepsiCo would have over a quarter of the USA's non-carbonated soft-drinks market. This segment showed growth of 8–9 per cent p.a. compared with just 2–3 per cent for fizzy drinks.

PepsiCo announced that the Quaker deal would add 1–2 cents to growth in earnings per share in the first year after the deal, raising the growth rate from 12–13 per cent to 13–14 per cent, and that profits would rise by $170 million within five years. The Pepsi share price rose over 5 per cent to $45. The deal would raise the market value of the combined entity to $80 billion, placing it among the world's five largest consumer products companies. Roger Enrico, PepsiCo's chairman and CEO, said:

> 'Bringing together Quaker and PepsiCo creates a wealth of exciting growth opportunities as well as important cost and selling synergies. It is also very consistent with our sharp focus on convenience food and beverages.'

The completion of the deal heralded significant managerial changes. Rather than see through the acquisition integration process, Enrico stepped down from his combined posts earlier than planned, relinquishing his position early in 2001 rather than at year-end. On completion of the takeover, Enrico and Morrison became vice-chairmen of PepsiCo, PepsiCo president Steven Reinemund assumed the new company's chairman and CEO, while Indra Nooyi, PepsiCo's chief financial officer, who was highly regarded on Wall Street, became the additional post of president.

Enrico's early departure looked surprising. He had just propelled PepsiCo into an unusual position of market leadership over Coca-Cola, without engaging in a bidding war. In fact, the value of the deal was virtually the same as PepsiCo's original offer. Coca-Cola's abortive entry into the fray had left it in some disarray after Warren Buffett's intervention, leaving doubts as to who actually controlled its strategy.

However, as *The Economist* put it, as well as having learned the art of successful delegation to able subordinates like Reinemund, who doubled growth at Frito-Lay, the savoury foods business, Enrico had probably acquired the wisdom to leave at the high point, especially as the hard work of integrating Quaker and disposing of its presumably unwanted, unexciting food business was about to begin.

Required

1 To what extent is the value of a firm driven by the value of the brands it controls?

2 Does ownership of successful (or promising) brands guarantee financial success?

3 To what extent is it possible to estimate/assess the value of a brand? How would you attempt to assess this?

Sources: based on information from Quaker Inc Annual Report and Accounts, 1990;
Guardian 28 March 1997; Gulf News (UAE)/Evening Standard 19 September 2000;
Gulf News/Reuters 2 November 2000; Gulf News/Reuters 5 December 2000

4

PROJECT APPRAISAL I: THE BASICS

Boeing and Airbus – same markets, different visions, different aircraft

Seattle-based Boeing in the US and the European consortium comprising Airbus have sharply divergent views on the future of commercial airliners. In 1997, Boeing, builder of the 747, the 'Jumbo', decided to pull its latest version, codenamed the 747–400. This new plane would have seated 550 passengers. The reason given was the lack of firm orders from airlines, only British Airways and Singapore Airlines having expressed any interest. BA, ever in the vanguard of operating new planes – until 2003 it continued to operate Concorde, the fastest-ever commercial airliner – was interested in the super-Jumbo for its transatlantic routes. Boeing itself acknowledged concern about the logistics of flying such huge numbers on one plane. Turnaround times, airport capacities and safety were among the operational issues likely to arise with these passenger loads.

At the time of writing, however, Airbus was still proceeding with its project to build a 555-seater, codenamed A380. Airbus does not offer a comparable model to the Jumbo at the moment; its largest plane, the A330, has 330 seats. By 2002, Airbus had received 97 firm orders for its new A380, due to enter service with Singapore Airlines in 2006. Airbus's success in obtaining orders led Boeing to reconsider its earlier decision to pull out at one stage. However, it reconfirmed its decision in 2001 when it unveiled its new project, a 'sonic cruiser'.

Airbus estimated the development costs of the A380 at around $11 billion. Boeing originally costed its project at around $2 billion as it was based upon the proven technology of the existing 747. But Boeing saw costs rise to an estimated $7 billion as airlines demanded new features, such as 'fly-by-wire' electronic technology, unavailable on the existing 747. Even so, Boeing reckoned Airbus could not match its own technological advantages and estimated that Airbus would have to spend nearer $12 billion to build its new plane. It also accused Airbus of receiving massive aid from European governments to help it build the new plane. Airbus rebutted both of these claims. Indeed, Airbus was trying to establish industrial partnerships to help meet the development costs, particularly in Japan. Unfortunately for Airbus, Boeing was already well ensconced there, with leading Japanese aerospace groups participating in existing Boeing production and supplies. By offering Japanese firms up to 30 per cent of the development and production work, Airbus hoped to entice orders from Japan Airlines and All Nippon Airways, both loyal Boeing customers.

Boeing also suggested the old 'hub and spoke' system of flying was breaking down, with passengers using more airports, requiring more and smaller planes. This explained why Boeing thought the market for 'super' planes was so flat – it expected that fewer than 500 super-Jumbos would be demanded by airlines up to 2014, yet Airbus estimated the demand at 1,400.

After finally deciding against the super-Jumbo, Boeing concentrated on developing its sonic cruiser – a smaller plane with around 250 seats but one that would go faster at just under the speed of sound, aiming to reduce travel times by around 20 per cent. The company developed technology that would allow this plane to travel further (allowing London–Sydney non-stop for the first time), higher (less turbulence) and more quietly (easier on the environment). Some airlines expressed scepticism, implying this was Boeing's idea rather than emanating from the airlines. Airlines tend to emphasise cost efficiency rather than speed and range. However, Boeing was confident that firm orders would start to appear in 2002.

In November 2002, Boeing decided to put development of the sonic cruiser on hold after disappointing feedback from the major airlines in a specially constituted panel. Airlines were not convinced that business passengers would pay a 15 per cent premium on existing business fares for more speed. Instead, Boeing announced it would now develop a 'super-efficient' aircraft based on the conventional designs of the 767 and 777. However, because of new lightweight material and a more aerodynamic design, the aircraft would burn 20 per cent less fuel than the 767. The downside was that it would travel at only 80 per cent of the speed of the sonic cruiser. Walt Gillette, a vice-president said: 'If we do decide to do a super-efficient aircraft first, it does not rule out a sonic cruiser.' But he added: 'Boeing is not really thinking about launching two aircraft simultaneously.'

Both firms have to cope with a rapidly changing world. September 11th had a hugely depressing impact on the airline industry. But Airbus has gone from strength to strength. At the time of writing, it was taking more orders than Boeing, and in 2003, for the first time, Airbus expected to deliver more aircraft than its rival.

Objectives:
This chapter aims to:

- explain the importance of investment decisions

- identify the ingredients of an investment project evaluation

- examine non-discounting methods of project appraisal

- examine discounted cash flow (DCF) methods of appraisal

- discuss problems with DCF methods

- offer an overall assessment of the merits of different approaches to project appraisal.

4.1 Introduction

The introductory cameo drives to the heart of the problems facing a firm wanting to invest in a new product. It needs to analyse the likely demand for its product, ensuring that it produces what customers require rather than simply what it finds convenient to offer. It needs to consider the cost of developing the product and over what time-span. The longer it takes, the greater the danger of competing products emerging embodying better technology. And all the time funds are tied up, funds that are costly to finance. The task facing the Big Two in aircraft manufacturing has hardly been made easier by the terrorist acts of 9/11 that make people more reluctant to fly and airlines less willing to invest their money. And this is before we begin to consider *sources* of finance.

In previous chapters, we identified the investment decision as one of the key decision areas of financial management. To begin this chapter on investment decisions, it is helpful to define the term 'investment'. The word usually evokes images of spending on 'clunky' things like machinery, buildings, vehicles and so on, capital assets that can be found in a firm's capital budget and subsequently on its balance sheet. However, firms 'invest' in many other ways. In general, an investment is:

> '… any course of action that involves sacrifices now or in the near future in anticipation of higher future benefits'.
>
> (Pike and Neale, 2003)

This definition covers a wide variety of expenditures on items ranging from plant, machinery and buildings to advertising and promotion and training schemes, i.e. it ranges far beyond expenditures on physical or tangible assets, and thus transcends a simple distinction based on the difference between capital and revenue expenditure.

Investment decisions are important because:

- they (usually) involve substantial long-term commitments of capital

- they are often irreversible, except at great cost. Once these decisions are implemented, they may often erect barriers to exit, either real or psychological

- they define the future operating capability of the firm

- they shape its long-term strategic options

- the future benefits may be substantial but they are usually highly uncertain.

The investment decision is perhaps the *most* important of all decisions a firm makes. As the Boeing/Airbus cameo shows, because there are strategic, technical and political issues as well as financial aspects to grapple with, it involves more than simply number-crunching the relative financial costs and benefits. Often, many costs and benefits are difficult if not impossible to quantify. Moreover, the numbers are often secondary – what determines whether a project is accepted or not depends on the strategic direction the company wants to pursue. Further, the approval of projects may hinge on the nature of the decision process within the firm, i.e. project approval in reality is often a question of 'internal politics', 'selling' a new project to often sceptical superiors.

4.2 The role of strategy

Investment appraisal is often referred to as 'capital budgeting'. This is because, once approved, projects enter the overall budget for the upcoming planning period and often far beyond. The annual budget is the short-term path to how a firm plans to achieve its long-term strategy – today's capital expenditure is the vehicle for attaining the long-term strategy.

The investment expenditure budget sub-heading of a company's budget typically reflects two categories of expenditures:

- *Regular expenditures of a routine nature such as the investment required to replace worn-out assets or those which have become obsolete.* These are expenditures required to maintain intact a firm's operating capability. However, if an improved version of the asset is acquired as replacement, it may well enhance capability, e.g. a new computer system with greater processing and storage (often at lower cost). Notwithstanding this reservation, these expenditures are often lumped together as 'replacement investment'. In effect, these are the expenditures required to maintain the firm's existing capacity to create value.

- *Expenditure required for implementing the strategic decisions made in previous years.* Strategic investment, almost by definition, enhances operating capability and hence the ability to create additional value. In effect, these are the expenditures required to increase the firm's capacity to create value.

Firms commonly give outline approval for major projects some time in advance of commencement in order to collect more information and enable clarification of market trends. Whether the provisionally accepted project eventually goes ahead or not is at the discretion of some higher decision-making body – hence the term 'discretionary investment'. Some companies have a body called the operating board, which scrutinises key strategic proposals and then submits accepted ones to the main board for final approval, often largely a rubber-stamping exercise.

Self-assessment activity 4.1

(a) Try to discover the procedure whereby investment projects are approved in your own firm (or in one you have knowledge of), before being incorporated into the overall budget.

(b) Few private-sector firms actually disclose their capital budgets. One exception is the German energy and chemicals group Eon (formerly Veba), which explains, in outline form in its annual report, its capital expenditure plans over the forthcoming few years and, moreover, how these fit into its longer-term strategy. This is well worth reading.
The Eon website is located at www.eon.com

Hierarchical organisations in both the public and the private sectors usually impose restrictions on how much investment can be approved at the lower levels. Beyond specified ceilings, authorisation for investment projects has to be obtained by transmitting projects upwards for consideration. Investment approval levels might resemble the following:

- Regional manager – approval for expenditures up to £50,000.

- Divisional manager – approval for expenditures up to £250,000.

- Operating board – approval for expenditures above £250,000.

To obtain approval, managers must demonstrate that a project possesses 'strategic fit' or that it is necessary to maintain capacity by replacing old or obsolete capital assets. Many companies classify projects into various categories in which different amounts of information are required as inputs into the evaluation process. A simple project classification, arranged according to relative risk, might be:

- replacement – low risk

- expansion – medium risk

- new product development – high risk.

New product development may also be sub-divided into 'new to the world' products, i.e. generically new products, in which the firm will take market leadership and hope to exploit 'first mover's advantages' on the one hand, and 'copy-cat' products, replicas of those already produced by other firms, on the other. The pharmaceutical industry provides many examples. Viagra, pioneered by US pharmaceutical giant Pfizer, was totally new to the world but it will be copied by many other firms when (and probably well before) its patent protection expires in 2017. The time and resources required to develop totally new products makes these relatively far more risky than the replicas. It is easier to produce 'generic' drugs that are out of patent than to pioneer new ones that have only around a 10 per cent chance of successful commercialisation.

Self-assessment activity 4.2

Consult the report and accounts of the company whose accounts you selected earlier.

(i)   What statement(s) did it make regarding its investment strategy?

(ii) How much capital expenditure did it undertake in its past financial year?

(iii) How was the investment broken down, e.g. equipment, buildings, vehicles, etc?

4.3 The ingredients of an investment appraisal

There are three key components of an **investment appraisal**:

(a) the objective(s) which the firm is seeking to pursue via the project

(b) information on the project's costs and benefits

(c) the techniques of evaluation.

We discuss all of these in this section but give greater attention to the appraisal methods in the next two sections.

(a) Objectives

Investment decisions, like any others, should be evaluated according to whether they contribute to achieving the firm's objective(s). Advocates of new projects need to acknowledge two kinds of objective. First, the overall aim of the firm, which the project is supposed to enhance, and second, the aim of the particular project – how is it supposed to contribute to achieving the overarching aim?

As ever, the most appropriate overall aim is assumed to be value creation for the owners of the enterprise. Strategic decisions are designed to contribute to value creation. New projects can create value in various ways, e.g. by:

● Identifying an unsatisfied demand for an existing product or service

● Erecting a barrier to make it harder for other firms to compete

● Producing a product or service at a lower cost than competitors

● Enabling the firm to be the first to develop and exploit a new product and thus to exploit first mover's advantage.

(b) Project costs and benefits

Information is also required regarding the costs incurred by the project and the benefits it is expected to deliver. There are a number of guidelines to determine what data are relevant in evaluating new investment and what is not.

Generally, *relevant* costs and benefits are those that result from undertaking the project, i.e. those which would not be incurred or received if it is decided not to proceed with the project (hence the term *decision costs*). Usually, only cash flow costs are relevant, such as the capital expenditure required to erect a new factory, and the costs of the materials required to manufacture the additional output. (Later in this chapter we will find one important exception to this rule, namely the treatment of interest payments.)

However, all costs are **opportunity costs** – if you spend money in one area, you may be prevented from spending money elsewhere. If you pursue one course of action, it may preclude another one. If I spend £30 going to watch a rock concert, the opportunity cost is what else I could have spent the money on.

There is a qualification to the above point about cash flows – it is possible that no cash changes hands but there is still an opportunity cost. The point is that cash could have changed hands had an alternative action been followed – opportunity costs are not always cash flows but they *might* have been.

Self-assessment activity 4.3

A firm can sell a machine for £1 million now, but chooses to repair it at a cost of £500,000, planning to operate it for a further five years, after which it expects it to have a resale value of £200,000.
Identify the opportunity cost(s) involved in the firm's decision to prolong the operation of this machine.
If the relevant discount rate is 12 per cent, what is the present value of this decision? (Ignore any operating cash inflows.)
(answer at end of chapter)

Irrelevant costs include *sunk costs*, e.g. those already incurred or those to which the firm is contractually committed, and are therefore inescapable, while *apportioned fixed costs* are those that would have been incurred anyway. Sunk costs include items such as the cost of already completed market research or a feasibility study undertaken in advance of more formal appraisal of a project.

A classic example of sunk costs was the penalty for early closure that worked against earlier termination of the London Millenium Dome project. The Dome operation was already committed to certain contractual costs so that any income received above everyday operating costs represented a contribution towards recovery of the sunk costs. Although in accounting terms, the Dome was a hopeless loss-maker, it was cheaper to continue it up to the first penalty-free closure date. Similarly with Concorde, another huge accounting loss-maker. As long as Concorde could generate revenues which exceeded the cost of flying to and from the US, it was worth continuing, and contributing towards the sunk R&D costs. In 2003, BA took the decision to stop flying Concorde as even these flying costs were no longer being covered by passenger revenues.

An example of *apportioned costs* is central administration costs which are unaffected by a new project but which, for accounting purposes, are shared out among all the firm's activities. Some decision makers might (wrongly) want to attribute some of these costs to a new project when evaluating it. Clearly, these are irrelevant because they would be incurred anyway – they do not give rise to incremental cash flows.

This is not to say that fixed administrative costs are necessarily irrelevant in project appraisal. The level of these each year may be affected by the project, i.e. there may be *incremental* overhead costs to consider, such as the appointment of an additional controller to monitor the implementation of a new project.

Similar principles apply to defining relevant project benefits. Table 4.1 summarises these points.

Table 4.1 Relevant and irrelevant costs

Costs relevant to the decision are:	Costs that are irrelevant are:
Incremental	Costs paid in the past
Additional	Costs committed to in the past
Escapable	Non-cash costs (except opportunity costs)
Avoidable	Apportioned overheads
Opportunity costs (cash or otherwise)	
Cash flows	

Self-assessment activity 4.4

Indicate which of the following are true or false:

(i)   All relevant costs are cash costs.

(ii) All relevant costs are incurred in the future.

(iii) Overhead costs are irrelevant.
      (answer at end of chapter)

(c) Investment appraisal techniques

The third input relates to the choice of evaluation criterion. This partly depends on the type of decision problem in hand. There are three broad categories of investment decision problems for which suitable appraisal techniques are required:

● *Screening* – rough and ready evaluation to determine whether a project is obviously unacceptable or worthy of further examination.

● *Choosing whether or not to do a project* – i.e. the accept or reject decision.

● *Choosing between alternatives* – decisions about the best among competing projects. Projects can range from those leading to higher revenues to those that promise cost savings. In all cases, the best project is the one that promises greatest wealth creation.

But what should a 'good' appraisal technique do? The key attributes of a sound appraisal technique are:

● it ranks projects in meaningful order of value-creating potential

- it provides a clear decision, including a 'cut-off point' beyond which no further investment is worthwhile

- it is consistent with, and helps to achieve, the company's objectives, particularly value creation.

The various methods of appraisal are normally divided into two groups:

- Those not involving discounting cash flows – principally, payback and the return on investment method (often called the accounting or average rate of return method). These *do not* incorporate the time value of money concept.

- Discounted cash flow methods – the most common are net present value and internal rate of return. These *do* incorporate the time value of money concept.

It will be useful for you to compare the main methods of appraisal to examine the extent to which they are capable of performing the three key functions. You will see that only the discounting methods satisfy all these criteria. But first, the non-discounting varieties are examined.

4.4 **Non-discounting methods**

(i) Payback

Payback is simplicity itself, which is perhaps why, in practice, it is the most popular method of all. It involves calculating how quickly the cash flows generated by the project recover the initial outlay. If this time period is within or equal to a stipulated time period, the project is accepted. For example, if a project requiring an outlay of £10 million generates annual cash flows of £2.5 million, it will pay back the investment after four years (assuming end-year cash flows). This will be acceptable to a firm demanding payback within, say, five years.

There are several reasons why payback is used:

- It is simple and understandable by managers at all levels. It thus provides a means of communicating minimum acceptable project standards. The notion of the time required to break even – how quickly you get your money back – is a powerful one.

- It is biased in favour of quick-returning projects and thus provides a safeguard against two forms of risk:

  (a) Risk of total market collapse – for example, it might be used when evaluating entry into a risky overseas market.
  (b) Risk of financial failure through illiquidity, i.e. inability to meet short-term financial obligations. The more rapid the payback of cash,

the greater the ability of the firm to withstand exceptional demands on its financial resources.

For this reason, it may be helpful where the company has difficulty in raising external finance (**capital rationing**).

● It is useful for 'screening' projects, i.e. providing a rough assessment of their validity before exposing them to more detailed scrutiny.

Problems with payback

However, there are significant problems with payback. Some of these are highlighted with the following example:

Project outlay £m	Cash flow Year 1 £m	Cash flow Year 2 £m	Cash flow Year 3 £m	Cash flow Year 4 £m
A (15)	5	5	5	5
B (15)	5	5	5	
C (15)	8	2	5	5

● Which is the better project, A or B? Both pay back in three years so look equally acceptable, but A offers a cash flow in Year 4 as well. The problem is that payback ignores the cash flows beyond the point of payback. Against this, it does relax the pressure for forecasting accuracy, i.e. the decision maker needs to forecast only over the payback period.

● Which is the better project, A or C? Both offer the same total cash flows and each pays back in three years, but C offers a faster recovery of capital outlay. The problem is that payback ignores the timing of cash flows over the payback period, i.e. cash flows are not discounted. Having a faster cash inflow allows earlier reinvestment of cash.

● Firms often apply very short, arbitrarily chosen payback periods, unrelated to a required rate of return.

● Neglecting the true cost of finance can lead to rejecting worthwhile projects. For example, a company able to raise finance at 15 per cent but imposing a two-year required payback period would reject all the above projects, even though their implied annual returns are 33 per cent (because they pay back over three years, i.e. 100/3 = 33% p.a.).

● Perversely, it could lead to accepting more risky projects. Quick-returning projects are favoured by payback and these could carry the greatest risk, given that risk and returns are typically directly related. Some types of long-term project involve secure contractual cash flows, but most projects offer expected, but not guaranteed, cash flows in the future.

- Payback does not measure profitability (or indeed liquidity), merely the time taken to recover capital.

A halfway house: discounted payback

One way to 'rescue' the payback method is to discount the cash flows at the cost of finance and then investigate how quickly the firm can recover the initial outlay via the stream of discounted cash flows. This allows for the time value of money while retaining the appeal of the payback philosophy, i.e. speed of recovery.

Self-assessment activity 4.5

A firm requires a discounted payback in three years. A new project requires an outlay of £1 million and offers cash flows of £350,000 p.a. over the next six years. Using a cost of finance of 10 per cent, determine whether the project is acceptable.
(answer at end of chapter)

(ii) Accounting or average rate of return (ARR) method

This method uses data on expected accounting profits rather than cash flows. Because it relates profits generated by the project to its capital requirements, it is the forward-looking counterpart of the return on investment concept. Broadly, the accounting profit is the cash flow figure less the depreciation charge, viz:

Accounting profit = cash flow – depreciation

Depreciation is an accounting allocation of cost, and is not itself a cash flow. Hence, the ARR =

[Average accounting profit/investment] × 100

Investment may be initial capital invested or an average measure.

Remember that, because of the accruals convention in accounting, there are many other reasons why cash flows and accounting profits differ, e.g. working capital movements, but the implication here is that these will average out over time and can be ignored, leaving the depreciation charge as the main point of difference.

The most common way to express the ARR is to calculate the average profit over the project's lifetime, then express this as a proportion of the initial outlay. The project is acceptable if the ARR calculated exceeds some specified target rate of return.

Example

The initial project outlay is £12,000 and the firm uses straight-line depreciation. The project lifetime is three years. Zero resale value is assumed.

Figures in £	Year 1	Year 2	Year 3	Total
Cash flow	8,000	8,000	8,000	24,000
Depreciation	(4,000)	(4,000)	(4,000)	(12,000)
Profit	4,000	4,000	4,000	12,000

In this example, the ARR, defined as average profit divided by initial capital, is:

$$ARR = [£4,000/£12,000] \times 100 = 33.3\%$$

However, if we use the average investment as the denominator (i.e. average of starting and ending capital employed = $[£12,000 + 0]/2 = £6,000$) the ARR would be:

$$ARR = [£4,000/£6,000] \times 100 = 66.7\%$$

The average investment in the project is the average of the starting figure of £12,000 and the ending figure of zero, after fully depreciating over three years.
There are several reasons why the ARR is used:

● It is based on the return on investment (ROI) concept, well known to most business people, incorporating 'familiar' terms like 'profit' and 'capital'.

● Business people like to work in percentage terms (so they say!).

● It is consistent with the way in which many managers are rewarded, i.e. according to ROI achieved.

● The impact of the project on the profit and loss (P&L) and the balance sheet can be projected. The ARR computations can thus be incorporated into the budgeting process.

Problems with the ARR

As with payback, there are many problems with the ARR:

● Like payback, it ignores the timing of returns.

● It is imprecise – 'profit' can be defined in many ways (and therefore manipulated by creative accounting).

- The target return is often arbitrarily selected, bearing little relationship to the cost of capital. Typically, it is based on past performance, not on what it is reasonable to expect in the future.

- It uses accounting profits (generally lower than operating cash flows, after deduction of depreciation) rather than cash flows and hence is likely to understate project profitability (see later).

Self-assessment activity 4.6

To appreciate how the ARR might be manipulated, imagine that you are an ambitious young manager. Consider the two definitions of the ARR above, based on initial capital and average capital employed. Which definition would you use (i.e. which ARR) when presenting the project proposal to your superiors for approval?
(answer at end of chapter)

Theoretically, the most acceptable method approach to project evaluation is to evaluate cash flows.

4.5 Discounting methods/discounted cash flow

As well as focusing on cash flows, DCF methods all have the common advantage of incorporating the rate of return required by the investor based on their time preference, i.e. their relative preference for money now as compared with money in the future, the *time value of money*. This embodies the notion that sums of money received at different points in time cannot be added together. Most people prefer to receive money sooner rather than later for various reasons:

- it allows us to reinvest in other projects earlier

- we generally prefer consumption now rather than later

- money received earlier is perceived to be less risky

- inflation erodes the value of money.

A project is worthwhile only if it generates a rate of return above the minimum rate of return required by investors. Many companies ignore this simple truth, and as a result they destroy value for their owners. (Specifying the required return is a separate issue which we defer to Chapter 6 for more detailed consideration.)

There are several variants of the DCF approach. First, the net present value method is examined.

Net present value (NPV)

The NPV method is founded on the concept of the time value of money. This concept, and hence the rationale for discounting future flows of cash, was introduced in Chapter 2. It was explained that £1 received today is worth more than £1 receivable in, say, one year's time because the earlier one receives a payment, the quicker it can be reinvested to earn a return, i.e. converted into a higher sum. The method operates as follows.

All future cash flows are discounted at a rate reflecting the return required by the investor, and added together to yield the gross present value (GPV) of the project. This is compared to the investment expenditure required to undertake the project (including working capital requirements). If the GPV exceeds the outlay required, the NPV is positive, signifying that the project is acceptable, i.e. the project provides a return greater than the required return. In a choice situation, the project with the highest NPV should normally be undertaken since NPV is expressed in terms of the 'present' value of money.

In general, the NPV is given by:

$$\text{NPV} = \sum_{t=1}^{n} \frac{CF_t}{(1+r)^t} - I_0$$

where

CF_t denotes each cash flow in each year t
r is the required rate of return
I_0 is the initial investment expenditure.

Calculation short cuts

Discount tables show the *discount factors* for any (plausible) combination of discount rate and number of years. An example is given in Appendix 1. The present value tables (or present value interest factor tables, PVIF for short) show the present value of a payment of £1 received in n years at $r\%$. For example, the discount factor for one year at 10 per cent is 0.909, so the present value of a payment of £1,000 after one year is (£1,000 × 0.909) = £909, after two years (£1,000 × 0.826) = £826, and so on. Note that the tables assume end-of-year receipts. Present values are the flipside of the coin to compound interest tables. With an interest rate of 10 per cent p.a., a sum of £909 invested for one year will compound to £909 (1 + 10%) = £1,000. Similarly, £826 invested over two years will also compound to £1,000 (= £826 (1 + 10%)(1 + 10%)).

Golden rules in project appraisal

Two golden rules in calculating the NPV both need to be set in stone. These are:

- *RULE ONE. Do not deduct interest payments from the operating cash flows.*
  The operating cash flows reflect the investment decision, while the discount rate reflects the financing decision. By discounting, you are testing whether the project can tolerate a specified cost of finance. If the NPV is positive, the return on the project exceeds the cost of finance. This may seem confusing because interest payments are a cash outflow in reality, but to reduce the cash flows for interest in the calculation, and then to discount the resulting (smaller) figures, would involve double-counting for the cost of finance.

- *RULE TWO. Depreciation is not a cash flow.*
  Depreciation is simply an accounting adjustment undertaken to spread the initial (cash outflow) cost of acquiring the asset over its expected lifetime, thus reflecting the **matching** principle adopted in accruals accounting. The relevant cash flow for evaluating the decision is the cash paid when purchasing the equipment and the cash received (if any) when selling it. Making an annual depreciation charge results in double-counting for the initial outlay and poses the risk of rejecting a worthwhile investment.

  Remember that, over the long term, the net cash flow will equal the profit – only the timing of the two will differ. In investment appraisal, we are concerned with discounting cash flows not profits.

Self-assessment activity 4.7

A firm spends £12,000 on a new machine and pays cash. Assuming a four-year lifetime and no scrap value, show that the impact on cash flow and the impact on profits are identical over the four-year period.
(answer at end of chapter)

Variations on the NPV theme

The NPV calculation is highly versatile. Some applications you may encounter include the following three cases.

The annuity

An annuity is an investment with a constant annual cash flow. To calculate the present value of an **annuity**, the annuity tables (or present value interest factors for annuities, PVIFA for short) can be used as another short-cut. These add up the individual discount factors. The discount factor for a series of two annual payments of £1 at 10% = (0.909 + 0.826) = £1.735. Hence, the present value of a series of payments of £1,000 p.a. for two years = (£1,000 × 1.735) = £1,735, and so on. Annuity tables are shown in Appendix 2.

The straight perpetuity

A perpetuity is an investment with a constant cash flow that goes on for ever – a 'perpetual annuity'. Its present value is:

$$\text{Annual cash flow} \times \left(\frac{1}{\text{discount rate}}\right)$$

For example, the present value of a perpetual flow of £1,000 at 10% = £1,000/0.10 = £10,000. Pure perpetuities are rare, but many series are effectively perpetuities if they involve high(-ish) discount rates and long(-ish) periods. For example, the PV of a payment of £1,000 in 20 years at 20% is only (£1,000 × 0.026) = £26, so any subsequent payments would add little to the total. Remember that most of the future cash figures are merely estimates in practice, so the errors introduced by this sort of simplification are unlikely to impose serious distortions.

The growing perpetuity
This is where the perpetuity grows at a constant annual rate. Denoting the annual growth rate as g, the formula for its present value is:

$$\text{Net cash flow} \times \left(\frac{1}{r-g}\right)$$

For example, if this year's cash flow is £500, g is 5 per cent p.a. and investors require a return of 15 per cent, the present value of all future cash flows is:

$$\frac{£500(1+g)}{15\% - 5\%} = \frac{£525}{10\%} = £5,250$$

An interesting application of this is the case of valuing a share in a firm that is expected to generate a stream of increasing dividends over time. An efficient capital market would set a price (P) on the shares of a company with a *constant* dividend (*D*), viz:

$$P_0 = D/k_e$$

where k_e = the shareholder's required return

When the dividend is growing, the formula becomes

$$P_0 = \frac{D_0(1+g)}{(k_e - g)}$$

$$= \frac{D_1(1+g)}{(k_e - g)}$$

where

P_0 = today's market price per ordinary share
D_0 = this year's dividend per share
g = expected annual rate of growth of dividends
D_1 = the dividend expected next year.

Self-assessment activity 4.8

What is the market price of an ordinary share on which a cash dividend of 40p is paid? Dividend growth in recent years has averaged 5 per cent. Shareholders require a return of 12 per cent p.a.
(answer at end of chapter)

The **profitability index** (PI)

This is a variation on the NPV that is used when the company faces limited access to finance, i.e. capital rationing. It is defined as

either $\dfrac{\text{NPV}}{\text{initial outlay}}$ i.e. the NPV per £ invested

or $\dfrac{\text{GPV}}{\text{initial outlay}}$ i.e. the GPV per £ invested

In the first form, the rule is accept the project if the PI > 0 and in the second, accept if the PI > 1.0. Each version will give the same answer to the accept/reject decision. The PI gives an indication of the project's 'efficiency' in terms of the productivity of capital invested in the project. It is biased in favour of relatively productive projects which is a desirable property when capital resources are limited.

Self-assessment activity 4.9

For practice, work out the PI in both forms for a project with initial expenditure of £10 million and annual cash flows of £2.0 million over seven years. Discount at 12 per cent.
(answer at end of chapter)

The annuity method

This variation on the NPV converts the cash flows into an *equivalent annuity*, i.e. the constant annual cash flow which yields the same present value. The project is acceptable if the equivalent annuity exceeds the annuity required to at least break even. It is useful when projects have different lifetimes and one wants to appraise them on a comparable basis.

Consider the following example:

Cost of finance = 10%

Initial outlay = £15,000

Project life = 2 years

The annual cash flow required to recover £15,000 over two years and just meet the 10 per cent required return is:

$$= \frac{£15,000}{1.735} = £8,645$$

(1.735 is the 2 year annuity factor for 10%)

The actual cash flows are £8,000 in Year 1 and £10,000 in Year 2. The present value of this stream is:

$$\text{Present value} = \frac{£8,000}{(1.1)} + \frac{£10,000}{(1.21)} = (£7,273 + £8,265) = £15,538$$

This is equivalent to an annuity of

$$\frac{£15,538}{1.735} = £8,956$$

As this exceeds the required annual cash flow of £8,645, the project is worthwhile.

The annuity method is sometimes used when project lifetimes differ and when the capital expenditures are different as it is a way of comparing projects on an equivalent basis.

Internal rate of return (IRR)

The IRR is the rate of discount at which the NPV = 0. The decision rule is to accept the project if the IRR exceeds the minimum required rate of return, i.e. the cost of finance. It will always give the same answer as the NPV method to the accept/reject decision. The IRR is the highest rate of discount at which the project is viable, in effect the highest financing cost a firm can afford before the project ceases to be viable. In this sense, it specifies a break-even financing cost.

Consider the following project. Outlay in year 0 is £16,000. Expected cash flows in each of years 1 and 2 are £10,000. The firm requires a minimum return of 12 per cent.

The IRR is the solution, R, in the expression:

$$NPV = 0 = \frac{£10,000}{(1+R)} + \frac{£10,000}{(1+R)^2} - £16,000$$

This can be found by trial and error, or by using the IRR function on a spreadsheet package such as Excel. The trial and error approach can be illustrated here quite easily, as the project is an annuity. The IRR is the unknown discount rate in the following NPV expression:

$$NPV = 0 = -£16,000 + [£10,000 \times \text{two-year annuity factor @ } R\%]$$

Hence, the two-year annuity factor = £16,000/£10,000 = £1.600
Consulting the annuity tables, along the two-year row, we find:

@ 16%, the factor is 1.605, and @ 17%, the factor is 1.585.

The answer lies between 16 per cent and 17 per cent but nearer to 16 per cent. As the distance between the two rates is (1.605 – 1.585) = 0.200, the answer is:

16% + [(0.005/0.200) × (17% – 16%)] = 16.25%

This project is therefore returning an equivalent 16.25% p.a. The decision is thus to accept the project as this IRR exceeds the 12 per cent minimum requirement.

The equivalence of NPV and IRR

The two main DCF methods, NPV and IRR, always give the same answer to the question 'Should we accept or reject a project?'. This is simply due to the mathematical relationship between the NPV and the rate of discount – as the discount rate increases, the NPV declines, as shown in Figure 4.1 for the project just examined. This reflects the fact that future cash inflows are less valuable today the higher the discount rate. Eventually, the NPV becomes zero and this locates the IRR – 16.25 per cent in this case. If we discount at 12 per cent to find the NPV of the project, we find it is +£901, indicating acceptability. It follows, therefore, that if, when discounted at the cost of finance, the NPV is positive, the IRR exceeds that cost of finance. The two methods are thus equivalent.

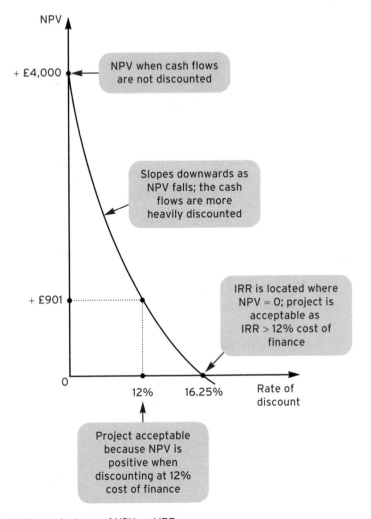

Figure 4.1 The equivalence of NPV and IRR

4.6 Worked example

Mightimeter plc has just developed a new product that monitors the fuel efficiency of cars. The firm is anxious to manufacture the device and has made marketing and feasibility studies to assess probable demand and profit levels. The
following information is available:

● The studies were made and paid for last year at a cost of £350,000.

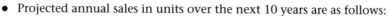

- Projected annual sales in units over the next 10 years are as follows:

Year 1	50,000
Year 2	100,000
Year 3	250,000
Year 4	175,000

- The devices will be sold for £25 each. Unit variable costs are forecast as follows:

Direct materials	£7
Direct labour	£5
Factory overhead	£4
Selling and administrative	£3

- Production and sale of the new device require immediate investment of £2 million. Of this, £500,000 is required to build up materials and finished goods inventories. These stocks will be depleted by the end of four years, allowing Mightimeter to recover its outlay.

- Existing fixed costs of salaries, property maintenance and insurance, to be apportioned to the project, are expected to total £200,000 per year.

- In order to gain rapid entry into the market, Mightimeter will advertise heavily in the early years of product sales. Forecast annual advertising outlays are:

Year 1	£275,000
Year 2	£175,000

Required

(a) Use the net present value method to analyse the proposed investment with a discount rate of 14 per cent, and advise whether Mightimeter should acquire the necessary plant and equipment and produce the monitoring device.

(b) Calculate the payback period.

(c) Calculate the profitability index.

(d) Calculate the internal rate of return.

Answer

The cost of the feasibility study is irrelevant to the decision to proceed or not, as the cost has already been incurred, i.e. it is sunk. The apportioned overheads of £200,000 p.a. are also irrelevant as they reflect existing commitments that will not change whether the project is carried out or not. The relevant cash flows are shown in the following table. The margin is price less relevant unit costs (£25 – £19) = £6 per unit.

(£000)	Year 0	Year 1	Year 2	Year 3	Year 4
Outlay	(2,000)				
Operating cash flow (@ £ margin)		6×50 = 300	6×100 = 600	6×250 = 1,500	6×175 = 1,050
Advertising/ Working capital recovery		(275)	(175)		500
Net cash flow	(2,000)	(25)	425	1,500	1,550
Discount factor @ 14%	1.000	0.8772	0.7695	0.6750	0.5921
Present value	(2,000)	(22)	327	1,013	918

(i) Adding together the individual present value figures shown in the bottom line of the table, yields a total of (−£2,022 + £2,258) = +£236. As the total is positive, i.e. the net present value is positive, the project looks acceptable.

(ii) Payback does not occur until into the fourth year. By the end of Year 3, only £1,925 of the cash outlay of £2,025 has been recovered, requiring a further cash inflow of £100. On a pro rata basis, this would occur (£100/£1,550) = 6% into the year. So we can say that payback occurs after about three years and a month or so. If we treat cash flows as flowing at end-year, the answer would be four years. On a discounted payback basis, the corresponding answers for pro rata cash flow and end-year cash flows are 3.75 years and 4 years respectively.

(iii) The PI calculations are:

NPV/Outlay = £236/£2,022 = 0.12, accept since PI > 0

PV/Outlay = £2,258/£2,022 = 1.12, accept since PI > 1.0

Notice that the discounted outlay is used, allowing for the series of negative cash flows in years 0–1.

(iv) NPV is positive @ 14 per cent hence the IRR > 14%.
Trying 16 per cent, NPV = +£111
Trying 18 per cent, NPV = −£3
The IRR is taken to be 18 per cent (in reality, fractionally below this).

Comment

Most investment evaluations are more complex than this in reality. In particular, the firm would have to consider the impact of both inflation and taxation on net cash flows. Moreover, the cash flow figures are only estimates in terms of their amount and their timing – we would have to consider the extent to which they may vary over the lifetime of the project and the impact of these variations. Finally, we have built in only a four-year lifespan which may be unduly cautious even for a new product exposed to developing competition, and have ignored any terminal value for the equipment. Allowing for all these (and other) factors may well change the picture.

> ## Self-assessment activity 4.10
>
> Now that you know the mechanics of these methods, find out what techniques are used to evaluate new investment proposals in your organisation or in one that you are familiar with.

4.7 Problems with DCF methods

Although the DCF methods remedy the main problems with alternative approaches, certain other problems emerge, especially with the IRR.

(i) The IRR can yield more than one solution when there are multiple sign changes in the cash flow profile.

For example, the following cash flow profile over four periods

$$- \qquad + \qquad + \qquad -$$

exhibits two sign changes and may generate two positive solutions to the IRR calculation.

The 'rogue' negative might arise when there is a warranty charge after completion of a project, or some sort of legally required environmental 'clean-up'. For the technically minded, the problem occurs because the equation for the IRR is a polynomial equation, i.e. one possessing several solutions but usually (where there is only one sign change) only one positive one. In this situation, it is better to use the NPV.

(ii) In the case of mutually exclusive projects of different sizes, the NPV and IRR can give conflicting signals.

For example, consider these two projects, both of which have a one-year life.

Project	Year 0 outlay £m	Year 1 cash flow £m	NPV @ 10% £m	Internal rate of return
A	100	125	+14	25%
B	50	65	+9	30%
(A – B)	(100 – 50) = 50	(125 – 65) = 60	= –50 + 60/(1.1) = +5	20%

IRR says 'do B' and NPV says 'do A'. The ranking of the two projects is totally inconsistent, so which should be undertaken? The IRR should not be relied upon in this and similar cases. This 'ranking problem' arises because the IRR ignores the scale of the two projects and thus the relative magnitude of the benefits. This can be illustrated by a simple device. Scaling down project B to just 1 per cent of the original size would not affect its IRR, but the NPV would become minuscule, yet the rankings would not change. Is there still a case for doing B? A huge percentage return on a minuscule outlay may well be less attractive than a more modest percentage return on a large outlay. Most of us would prefer a 20% return on £1000 rather than 100% on £1!

Incremental analysis

A good way of reconciling the two methods is to use an incremental analysis, that is, by looking at the difference between the two projects. This is shown on the bottom line of the above table. Project A, the bigger of the two, requires an extra £50 million of outlay, an additional cash flow of £60 million, and thus offers a positive NPV. The IRR on the incremental expenditure is 20 per cent, which is well above the required return of 10 per cent. This shows that project A offers everything that project B does plus a worthwhile incremental return. The message is clear: do project A. *As it happens, the recommendation given by the incremental approach always coincides with that of the NPV.*

In such situations, decision makers are therefore recommended to use the NPV method as it signifies how much wealth is created by the project (which is the object of the exercise). IRR does not signify the amount of wealth created by a project, merely its percentage return.

4.8 Assessment of the methods

When assessing the respective advantages and disadvantages of the various methods, it is useful to first contrast the non-discounting methods with those that do involve discounting cash flows, then to make a direct comparison between the two main DCF methods, NPV and IRR, before undertaking a general assessment.

Discounting *vs.* non discounting methods

The key thing to appreciate is that the DCF methods remedy all the major drawbacks of the other methods. In particular:

- they focus on cash flows rather than accounting profits, avoiding the arbitrariness of methods like the ARR

- they also consider all the cash flows over the expected lifetime of the project

- most importantly, they allow for the time value of money, thus recognising that £1 received today is worth more than the same £1 received next year because it can be invested, i.e. put to work earlier.

NPV *vs.* IRR

However:

- DCF methods, especially the IRR, are not totally problem free. There are problems with mutually exclusive projects and multiple solutions.

- IRR yields a break-even discount rate – the maximum discount rate which the project can tolerate. This also gives a useful indicator of risk – the difference between the required return and the IRR can be seen as a safety margin, i.e. scope for tolerance of adverse outcomes. People often say something like, 'If the IRR is 25 per cent and we require a 10 per cent return, a lot can go wrong before the project loses money'.

- IRR is useful when it is difficult to identify the required return on a project, or when it is changing rapidly. With the IRR, this cut-off rate can be applied *after* the calculation, whereas NPV requires a discount rate *prior* to the calculation.

- Conversely, while NPV can cope with a set of different annual discount rates, the IRR, by definition, is unique (except where cash flows are abnormal).

- NPV is the best available method because of its clear signal regarding wealth creation, but IRR remains popular with business people who often prefer to work in percentage terms.

A general assessment

- In reality, firms often use a combination of methods – commonly, payback is used to 'screen' projects, then NPV or IRR is used for a more rigorous appraisal.

- ARR is the least popular primary appraisal method, but it does have a role in firms that are concerned about the effect of a project on accounting measures of performance, i.e. the profit and loss account and the balance sheet.

- All methods are heavily reliant on the quantity and quality of data input.

- Information is not cost-free. Sometimes, firms may economise on data collection and rely on less rigorous methods. Data collection also takes time – the more detailed the data required, the longer the time taken by the overall investment appraisal and decision process, increasing the danger of missing a market opportunity.

- Finally, there is no evidence that use of allegedly 'sophisticated' evaluation methods like DCF is associated with superior company performance (although a study by Susan Haka (1987) showed that failing firms that introduced DCF subsequently improved their performance). This suggests that quality and speed of project identification, development and operation are more important than the rigour of the evaluation method itself. (It is noteworthy that many organisations that have introduced a balanced scorecard scheme of performance metrics often include 'time to market' to indicate success in new product development.) However, this lack of concrete proof in itself does not constitute an argument for avoiding systematic scrutiny of investment proposals.

4.9 Summary

This chapter has looked at the nature and importance of investment decisions and how investment proposals may be evaluated. It stresses the importance of access to plentiful information, without which investment decisions are often 'shots in the dark'. The next chapter will examine three key problem areas of project appraisal where decision makers often make mistakes – the ways in which inflation, corporate taxation and risk are treated.

References

Textbooks

Arnold – chs 2, 3 and 4.
Brealey & Myers – chs 5 and 6.

Pike & Neale – chs 3 and 5.
Samuels, Wilkes & Brayshaw – chs 4 and 5.
Watson & Head – chs 3 and 4.

Other

Haka, S F (1987) 'Capital budgeting and firm-specific contingencies: a correlational approach', *Accounting, Organisation & Society*, Vol. 12, No. 1, pp. 31–48.
Hirst, I. (2001) Investment appraisal for Shareholder Value (FT/Prentice Hall).
Lumijarvi, O P (1991) 'The selling of capital investment projects to management', *Management Accounting Research*, Vol. 2, No. 3, September, pp. 171–88.

Questions and mini-case study

1 Boothroyd Stationery plc has collected the following financial data for a project manufacturing gel pens from bought-in components. The demand for these pens is expected to last for three years.

(i) Sales in the first year of 100,000 units, increasing by 5 per cent p.a. Each unit will be sold at £1 throughout the project.

(ii) Purchases of components will be paid for in cash at 50p for each pen. Purchases of components in any year will be made as required to cover sales during that year plus closing stock requirements.

(iii) In any year, enough components will be purchased to ensure that closing stock is equal to 10 per cent of the next year's unit sales.

(iv) There is no initial opening stock of components and there will be no closing stock in the final year.

(v) Other annual costs include £10,000 leasing cost (payable in advance) and other fixed costs of £9,000.

(vi) Equipment required to manufacture the pens will cost £30,000. It is expected that the residual value of this equipment at the end of the project will be £6,000.

Required

(a) Using the above information, identify the cash flows of this project.

(b) Using the cash flows in part (a), calculate:

- the payback period
- the net present value using a required return of 10 per cent
- the internal rate of return.

(c) Calculate the accounting rate of return for this investment based on the cost of the initial investment.

(d) Based on your results, what decision would you recommend? Give reasons.

2 Sean's Shavers plc ('The shaver you can trust') has been a long-established manufacturer of men's and women's razors. The company has a policy of constantly redesigning its razors and bringing these new products onto the market. It has recently spent £70,000 on the design of a new razor, the Mark III. The company's management accounting department has produced the following budgeted information concerning the production and marketing of the new razor.

	Year 1 £	Year 2 £	Year 3 £	Year 4 £
Sales revenue	750,000	820,000	700,000	650,000
Less related costs				
Materials	440,000	480,000	420,000	400,000
Advertising	20,000	20,000	15,000	10,000
Salaries & wages	80,000	90,000	80,000	78,000
Depreciation	100,000	100,000	100,000	100,000
Design & development	70,000			
Dividend payments	4,000	4,000	4,000	4,000
Total operating costs	714,000	694,000	619,000	592,000
Profit	36,000	126,000	81,000	58,000

The following information is available concerning the costs and capital expenditure:

(i) Additional plant and machinery to the value of £900,000 will have to be purchased on the first day in the life of the project and it is anticipated that all equipment will be sold at the end of the project for its net book value of £500,000. The company uses the straight-line method of depreciation which has given rise to the depreciation charge.

(ii) The company has decided on a 'prudent policy' of charging all the design and development expenditure to the first year of the project.

(iii) The expenditure on materials and advertising is directly linked to the project and would be avoided should the project not be undertaken.

(iv) The expenditure on salaries and wages includes £10,000 each year which is an allocation of a portion of the salaries of the company's senior management team. All projects suffer a similar charge as part of the company's overhead recovery policy.

(v) The dividend payments represent additional dividend payments the company intends to make out of the profits generated by this project.

(vi) The company requires a rate of return of 15 per cent on this particular project.

(vii) All operating cash flows occur at the end of each year except for the capital expenditure previously mentioned.

(viii) Inflation can be ignored.

Required

(a) Sean's Shavers plc calculates its accounting rate of return for projects by expressing the average annual operating profit as a percentage of the average capital employed over the life of the project. Perform this calculation for the above project.

(b) Calculate whether or not the project is beneficial to Sean's Shavers plc in net present value terms.

(c) Imagine the information detailed for the above project related not to the production of a razor by the company but to the production of a sports car, in an attempt by the company to diversify into the vehicle industry. What additional concerns would you express to management when advising on the viability of the project?

3 Gustaffson plc is a soft-furnishing manufacturer and is considering investing in a project to manufacture a new range of cuddly toys, the Meany Mineys. With sufficient marketing, Gustaffson hopes to establish the brand as a highly fashionable collector's item, particularly among the 8–12 age group. For planning purposes, the company expects this project to generate sales for 3 years. As a result of some market research costing £40,000, the company expects to sell 1 million cuddly toys in the first year, 2 million in the second, and 1 million in the third and final year. Gustaffson will produce enough each year to meet the demand for each year, and to provide a closing stock equal to 10 per cent of the expected sales units in the following year (the company will not budget for any closing stock at the end of Year 3).

(i) Manufacturing costs for each cuddly toy are estimated to be:
Material: 50 pence
Labour: 15 pence

(ii) In projecting the annual profit, Gustaffson's accountant has allocated £500,000 of overheads per annum to the production of Meany Mineys, of which 50 per cent are estimated to be incremental costs arising from the project itself.

(iii) The project will require the rental of a warehouse at £100,000 p.a, payable in advance.

(iv) The company is buying six machines at £40,000 each to meet the production requirements of Meany Mineys. After the three years, it is estimated that these machines can be sold at £15,000 each.

To meet the increased production requirement in Year 2, the company will utilise five machines that it owns that are currently used elsewhere in the factory.

It will transfer these five machines to Meany Miney production to Year 2 only. The transfer of these machines will require the company to out-source some of its production to a small local company and a total cost of £25,000 has been agreed for this arrangement.

(v) Each Meany Miney will sell for 99p.

(vi) The company requires a return of 15 per cent p.a. on this particular project.

Required

(a) Using the above information, calculate the net present value of this project (assume all cash flows, apart from the warehouse rental, occur at the year-end). Based upon your calculation, what is your advice to the company regarding this project?

(b) How might you qualify the decision that you have made in part (a)?

Mini-case study – Eni

In January 2000, the 35 per cent state-owned Italian energy combine Eni announced a programme of technical and financial investments totalling €40 billion to be undertaken over the next four years. Of this, €24 billion was to be invested upstream to increase by 50 per cent its production in equivalent barrels of oil, and €6 billion in gas, transport and distribution. Seventy per cent was to be invested outside of Italy. Part of the programme would involve cost-cutting exercises of €1 billion p.a.

Factored into the programme was a fall in the price of selling gas in Italy to reflect greater competition. The company was also threatened by Italy's competition authority's proposal to cap Eni's share of the domestic gas market at 60 per cent, compared with its then 98 per cent. In the oil sector, as well as worrying about the world price of crude, Eni had to contend with increasing state intervention into its hitherto protected markets. The Italian government, as major shareholder, clearly had an ambivalent role in this situation.

As it happened, Eni's planning difficulties were considerably lessened by the surge in the price of oil in late 1999 and 2000, suggesting that chairman Gianni Maria Gros-Pietro's lamentations about state interference were probably mainly for public consumption.

Required

(a) Identify the stakeholders involved in Eni's investment planning.

(b) What information inputs did Eni require in order to make a coherent evaluation?

Self-assessment answers

4.1 and 4.2
Your call.

4.3
The opportunity costs are what the firm gives up now – £1 million (a non-cash cost) – plus the repair costs of £500,000 (a cash cost), offset by the (reduced) future resale value.

The PV of the costs involved in this decision is:

Costs of [£1m + £0.5m] now offset by £0.2m in five years

The future cash inflow has a PV of $[£0.2m/(1.12)^5]$
$$= (£0.2m \times 0.567) = £0.113.$$

Overall, the PV is (£1.5m – £0.113m) = £1.387 million.

4.4
(i) Not true, as some relevant opportunity costs do not involve a cash outlay, although they can be measured in monetary terms.

(ii) True, because investment decision making involves analysing future costs and benefits. Note that it is untrue to say that all future costs are relevant, e.g. the firm may yet have to settle a contractual obligation such as market research study.

(iii) False, if a firm builds a new factory whose expected operating costs are split into fixed and variable components, all these costs are incremental as of now, the decision point.

4.5
Discounted cash flows over three years are:

$$£350,000/(1.1) + £350,000/(1.1)^2 + £350,000/(1.1)^3$$
$$= (£318,182 + £289,256 + £262,960) = £870,398$$

Allowing for the time value of money, the project fails to pay back quickly enough, although *before* discounting it would pay back within three years.

4.6
In order to advance your career, you want to make a name for yourself by 'championing' a successful project. To maximise its chance of acceptance, you might be tempted to present the figures in the most flattering light, which means using the definition of ARR based on the lowest possible denominator of capital expenditure, average capital in this case. Of course, you now have to deliver!

4.7

Item/Year	0	1	2	3	4	Total
Impact on cash flow (£)	−12,000	–	–	–	–	−12,000
Impact on reported profit (£)		−3,000	−3,000	−3,000	−3,000	−12,000

4.8

$$\text{Share price} = P_0 = \frac{D_0(1+g)}{(k_e - g)}$$

$$= \frac{40\text{p}(1 + 5\%)}{(12\% - 5\%)} = \frac{42\text{p}}{0.07} = £6$$

4.9

PV of annuity of £2m @ 12% = (£2m × 4.564) = £9.13m

NPV = −£10m + £9.13m = −£0.87m

NPV/Outlay = −£0.87m/£10m = −0.087, i.e. reject as PI < 0

PV/Outlay = £9.13m/£10m = 0.913, i.e. reject as PI < 1.0

4.10

Over to you.

5

PROJECT APPRAISAL II: THE TRICKY BITS

Missing the target

In 1998, the Confederation of British Industry (CBI) reported the results of a survey on investment appraisal practices among 326 firms, all with turnover exceeding £20 million. Many results seemed to reflect irrational behaviour, at least across the overall sample.

Firms in general tended to set much higher target rates of return than warranted by prevailing conditions such as risk and inflation, and failed to adjust target rates in the light of changing inflation rates. The study found that, on average, firms were demanding a real rate of return on new investment little different from that revealed in a previous survey in 1994 when inflation was considerably higher.

Moreover, within the overall sample, the firms that used the IRR method in terms looked for an average real (i.e. net of inflation) rate of 17.6 per cent, while among those who used nominal (i.e. including inflation) rates, the average target was 16.5 per cent. A similar perverse relationship was found among users of the NPV method.

Source: Target Practice – How companies approach their key capital investment decisions, CBI, 1998

Objectives:

This chapter aims to examine some of the main methods for treating the following problem areas in project appraisal:

- dealing with inflation
- dealing with taxation and depreciation allowances
- dealing with risk and uncertainty.

5.1   Introduction

The Mightimeter example in the previous chapter mentioned several problem areas in evaluating investment projects, namely the tricky areas of inflation, taxation and risk. The task of this chapter is to examine each of these issues and suggest ways of incorporating them into project appraisal. These are wide areas that we cannot do full justice to in the space available. However, they are very real practical issues that are found in virtually every investment decision problem. Moreover, as the CBI study showed, firms do not always get these things right.

5.2   Allowing for inflation in project appraisal

A common misconception is that the case for discounting cash flows is to offset inflation. This is only part of the truth. A rational decision maker would still discount in the absence of inflation because of time preference. Inflation merely underlines the case for discounting but, nevertheless, it can pose severe problems.

Inflation is the upward movement in the price level over time, as measured by a representative price index. In the UK, the Retail Prices Index (RPI) purports to show how inflation reduces the purchasing power of the monetary unit.

Under inflation, shareholders expect managers to at least maintain the real value of their investment and the purchasing power of their income. This means achieving an overall rate of return that fully compensates for inflation. The purchasing power of future project cash flows must be no less than with stationary prices.

For example, consider a two-year project with cash flows of £100 in each year. Without inflation, the purchasing power of each cash flow is £100 in the year received (although the present values differ due to discounting for the time value of money). However, with, say, 10 per cent compound inflation, future purchasing power falls exponentially. A newspaper that now costs £1.00 will cost £1.00(1.1) = £1.10 in one year's time and a £1 coin will buy only (100/110) = 0.91 of a newspaper after one year. Thus, after one year of 10 per cent inflation, the purchasing power of every £1 is only 100/110 = 91% of its value a year earlier. As the figures below indicate, the effect is also a compound one:

Year 1:

$$\text{Purchasing power of }£100 = \frac{100}{\text{Year 1 Price index}} = \frac{100}{110} = £90.9$$

Year 2:

$$\text{Purchasing power of } \pounds100 = \frac{100}{\text{Year 2 Price index}} = \frac{100}{121} = \pounds82.6, \text{ etc}$$

Thus, future cash flows should be adjusted, i.e. reduced, for two reasons: for the time value of money in the normal way, and also for inflation. If shareholders require a real, i.e. net of inflation, return, r, of 12 per cent, the real present values (RPVs) are found by discounting the above figures again:

$$\text{Year 1: RPV} = \frac{\pounds100}{(1.12)(1.10)} = \frac{\pounds90.9}{(1.12)}$$

$$= \pounds81.2$$

$$\text{Year 2: RPV} = \frac{\pounds100}{(1.12)^2(1.10)^2} = \frac{\pounds82.6}{(1.12)^2}$$

$$= \pounds65.9, \text{ etc}$$

The discount rate, that defines the investor's required rate of return, adjusted for inflation at the rate p, is found by compounding the real return and the inflation rate together, viz:

$$m = (1 + r)(1 + p) - 1 = (1.12)(1.10) - 1 = (1.232 - 1) = 23.2\%$$

This is known as the *nominal* or *money cost of capital* and denoted as m. This is the cost of finance expressed in terms which incorporate expected inflation. It can be approximated by adding together the two elements r and p, i.e. $m = r + p$. This is only a short-cut and may be misleading for high values of r and p.

Self-assessment activity 5.1

To illustrate these relationships, suppose today's bank base rate is 7.0 per cent and the current rate of inflation is 2.5 per cent. What is the rate of return required by lenders in real terms?
(answer at end of chapter)

The general point here is that under inflation, firms need to achieve a higher nominal return to meet shareholder requirements. Because people often get this wrong (remember the cameo!), we will look at it another way for emphasis.

Say expected inflation over the next year is 10 per cent. A rational investor will require at least this rate of return simply to maintain the real value of his investment. Any return in excess of 10 per cent is a real return. If our investor seeks a 12 per cent real return over and above inflation, he will want to see a total annual cash return on an investment of, say, £100, as follows:

Initial investment	£100.0
Compensation for inflation	£10.0
Total	£110.0
12% real return	£13.2
Total cash return	£123.2

This reflects an overall money return of 23.2 per cent on the initial investment. This return covers inflation and generates a real return of 12 per cent on top.

Self-assessment activity 5.2

I expect to receive a legacy of £500 in three years' time. I am expecting inflation to run at an average of 3 per cent p.a. over the next three years, and in real terms I require a return on my investments of at least 8 per cent.

(i) In terms of today's purchasing power, what is the value of the legacy?

(ii) What is the real present value of the legacy?
(answer at end of chapter)

Types of inflation

Inflation can occur in various ways. It is useful to distinguish between:

- *general inflation*, the average rate that occurs throughout the whole economy, as measured by a price index such as the RPI, and

- *project-specific inflation*.

Not all prices inflate at the same rate. The revenues from the project could inflate by more than general inflation (which is beneficial for the company) or the costs could overshoot the general rate. Even when the *rates* of inflation are equivalent, different items may adjust in price at different times. For example, firms often produce price lists at the start of the year and stay with these figures, although their costs may inflate during the year. This is *unsynchronised inflation*.
Inflation could benefit an investment project when:

- the rate of inflation of the product's selling price and hence revenue inflation exceeds the rate of cost inflation

- revenue inflation occurs in advance of cost inflation

- both of the above apply.

Should we ignore inflation?

It is often tempting to ignore inflation on the grounds that it is too difficult to forecast and that, on balance, the effect will be neutral. This is dangerous – projects can be devastated by imbalances in inflation rates and vice versa. So clearly the answer to the question is 'no'.

Sometimes, companies simply add the expected inflation rate to the current cost of capital and then discount cash flows at the resulting higher rate. But this is incorrect since the current cost of finance, i.e. today's prevailing money cost, will already include an allowance for inflation, simply because rational lenders attempt to anticipate future inflation when offering funds to the market. Simply to 'bolt on' the firm's inflation expectations to the current nominal rate would thus involve double counting for inflation, resulting in too high a discount rate.

So how should firms deal with inflation in project appraisal.

The two correct ways of dealing with inflation

There are two (equally valid) correct ways of tackling inflation in project appraisal, both of which give the same answer.

1	**discount money cash flows** (including future inflation i.e. at current year prices)	**at**	**the money cost of capital** (current capital market rate incorporating inflation)
		OR	
2	**discount real cash flows** (at constant prices)	**at**	**the real cost of capital** (net of inflation)

To illustrate the equivalence of these approaches, consider a simple example.

● In the absence of inflation, shareholders want a real return of 10 per cent.

● The project's cash flows are expected to inflate in line with general inflation of 10 per cent.

● A single cash flow of £1,500 is expected, as measured in today's prices, receivable at the end of one year. This is the real-terms cash flow, i.e. expressed in constant prices.

● The initial outlay is £1,000.

Calculation

Money cash flow, incorporating inflation = £1,500 (1.1) = £1,650
Money cost of capital: $m = (1 + 10\%)(1 + 10\%) - 1$ = 21%

- Method 1: $NPV = -£1,000 + \dfrac{£1.650}{(1.21)} = +£364$

- Method 2: $NPV = -£1,000 + \dfrac{£1,500}{(1.1)} = +£364$

What firms do in practice

The CBI survey found that 35 per cent of firms projected cash flows in nominal terms, i.e. incorporated inflation, and adjusted the cut-off rate accordingly, 52 per cent conducted the analysis in real terms, and 13 per cent ignored inflation totally.

The majority of firms that either ignored inflation or made projections in today's prices, i.e. in real terms, were thus failing to allow for differential inflation (possibly due to difficulties of prediction).

5.3 Allowing for taxation in DCF

Allowing for taxation is essential. It is necessary because the measures of profitability and value which really matter to shareholders hinge on what remains after the tax authorities have taken their cut. However, it can be tedious because of the intricacies of the tax regulations. These vary from country to country, so yours may well be different from those discussed here. Fortunately, the UK corporate tax system has been overhauled and simplified as it affects investment appraisal.

Relevant features of the UK tax system for 2003–4 were:

- The rate of corporation tax (CT) imposed on profits was 30 per cent, although a lower rate applies for certain small firms.

- Companies pay CT quarterly. For simplicity, however, we will assume all tax payments are paid in one chunk at the end of each year of operation of the project.

 - Investment allowances are **tax breaks** designed to offer tax-allowable depreciation to investing companies. The main one is the 25 per cent writing-down (or annual) allowance (WDA). This enables a company to set 25 per cent of the written-down value (historic cost less tax-allowable depreciation) against profit for tax purposes. This applies on a reducing balance basis. Adjustment may also be necessary when an asset is sold (see below).

The impact of CT

It is fruitful to show the treatment of tax by using a building-block approach. We will look at three versions of a simple project:

1 in the absence of CT

2 allowing for CT, paid at year-ends

3 allowing for tax and the 25 per cent WDA.

The project details

Outlay = £8m	Discount rate = 10%
Lifespan = 3 years	Tax rate = 30%
Scrap value = 0	WDA 25% p.a. (Reducing balance)
Product price = £1,000	Variable cost = £400 per unit
Incremental overheads = £1m p.a.	Output volume = 10,000 units p.a.

The analysis

1 With no corporate taxation
In the simplest case, the NPV is found by evaluating a three-year annuity, viz:

Pre-tax cash flows (£):

Year	0	1	2	3
Outlay	(8m)			
Revenues		10m	10m	10m
Variable costs		(4m)	(4m)	(4m)
Fixed costs		(1m)	(1m)	(1m)
Pre-tax cash flows	(8m)	5m	5m	5m

$$\text{NPV} = -£8m + £5m\,(\text{PVIFA}_{3/10}) = -£8m + £5m\,(2.487) = £4.43m$$

The project appears worthwhile.

2 Allowing for corporation tax @ 30 per cent

We assume that CT is paid at the end of the year in which the profit is earned. Note that introducing CT creates a 3-year annuity outflow of (30 per cent × £5m) = £1.5 million p.a., reducing the NPV to:

$$NPV = +£4.43m - £1.5m \ (2.487) = +£4.43m - £3.73m = +£0.7m$$

This calculation recognises that incomes are taxable and expenses are tax allowable, i.e. expenses save tax because they are set off against revenue, thus reducing the amount subject to tax. The project is still worth doing but its profitability is severely impaired. Note that no tax adjustment to the initial outlay is made in this case. We will incorporate tax relief on the initial outlay in case 3.

3 Allowing for tax and the 25 per cent WDA

The WDA reduces the taxable profit by 25 per cent of the net book value of the asset on a declining balance basis and thus reduces the tax bill in each year. It helps first to set out the tax-allowable depreciation profile, for the outlay of £8 million, and the effect on the book value of the asset.

Year of project	Written-down value (WDV) at start of year (£)	Tax-allowable depreciation (£)	End-year WDV
1	8m	25% × 8m	6m
2	6m	25% × 6m = 1.5m	4.5m
3	4.5m	(8m – 2m – 1.5m) = 4.5m	0

Two further comments are pertinent here. First, the project ceases in Year 3 and so the remaining WDV can be set against tax so as to write it down to zero for tax purposes. This is called a *balancing allowance* (BA). If the resale value was, say, £2 million, the BA would have been (£4.5m – £2m) = £2.5 million.

Self-assessment activity 5.3

You now know what a balancing allowance is. What do you think a balancing charge is?
(answer at end of chapter)

The second point concerns the timing of the firm's access to the tax break. It is usually assumed that tax relief is taken from the first year of the project. Exactly when the tax relief does occur in practice depends on when tax is paid on the profit of the accounting year in which the asset is acquired. Tax is saved when tax is paid in this case.

In reality, the tax relief may 'kick in' earlier. If the company has sufficient profits from other operations, it may claim the WDA in Year 0, i.e. in the year immediately before the project begins and set it off against other taxible income. In tax matters, a day can make quite a difference! For simplicity, we will assume that the WDA claimable conforms to the table above, although it would be useful for you to project the NPV for the alternative case.

£	Year	0	1	2	3
1 Pre-tax cash flow	(8m)	+5m	+5m	+5m	
2 WDA (= reduction in taxable profit)		(2m)	(1.5m)	(4.5m)	
3 WDV (end-year)		6m	4.5m	0	
4 Taxable profit (1) – (2)		3m	3.5m	0.5m	
5 Tax @ 30%		(0.9m)	(1.05m)	(0.15m)	
6 Post-tax cash flows (1) – (5)	(8m)	4.10m	3.95m	4.85m	
PV @ 10%	(8m)	3.73m	3.26m	3.64m	

NPV = −8m + 10.63m = +£2.63m

Another way of looking at this is to note that for each year of the project, the tax saving is the tax payable in case 2 less the tax payable in case 3, i.e.:

Year 1: (£1.5m – £0.9m) = £0.6m

Year 2: (£1.5m – £1.05m) = £0.45m

Year 3: (£1.5m – £0.15m) = £1.35m

In each year, the tax saving is equal to the tax rate times the WDA applicable for that year, i.e.:

Year 1: (30% × £2m) = £0.6m

Year 2: (30% × £1.5m) = £0.45m

Year 3: (30% × £4.5m) = £1.35m

It is sometimes easier to show these tax savings directly rather than to compute taxable profits and the resulting post-tax cash flows as in the table for case 3.

The NPV of the project rises sharply compared with the 'tax-only' case, i.e. by

£1.93 million. By implication, this is the present value of the tax savings generated by the writing-down allowance. The total tax reliefs amount to (£8 million × 25%) = £2.4 million but, of course, these are spread out over time and thus have a lower present value. The quicker a company can exploit tax relief, the better. A temporarily unprofitable company would have to carry forward the tax relief, thus reducing its present value – you can't save tax unless you pay tax.

What firms do in practice

In the CBI survey, only a bare majority of respondents (52 per cent) based their calculations on post-tax cash flows in the way suggested in the preceding theory. Overall, 32 per cent of firms analysed projects using pre-tax cash flows and then adjusted the cut-off rate accordingly, 16 per cent made no specific allowance for tax. Seventy-two per cent of the smaller firms surveyed seemed to work on pre-tax figures or to ignore tax totally.

5.4   Risk and uncertainty in project appraisal

Previous discussion of investment appraisal has assumed that all future cash flows are known for certain. In reality, this is rarely true. Future returns cannot usually be predicted with total accuracy. We now examine ways to modify the appraisal to take account of this reality. We concentrate on two methods of dealing with risk: **sensitivity analysis** and use of probabilities.

We will examine the following key issues:

- What is meant by project risk?

- What are the sources of risk?

- How can we measure risk?

- How can we control risk?

- How can we choose between alternative projects under risk?

We first examine the terms *risk* and *uncertainty*.

The meaning of risk and uncertainty

No investment project is totally safe. Many have the capacity to inflict great damage on the company if they go wrong. Not infrequently, companies have been effectively ruined by the big project (often a takeover) that went wrong. Often, the capacity for disaster can be reduced by careful planning. However, much of the problem stems from the sheer unpredictability of the future state of the economic and political environment and hence the size of cash flows.

Self-assessment activity 5.5

Imagine you are responsible for investigating the feasibility of building a new petro-chemical plant. Try listing all the things that could conceivably go wrong with the investment.
(answer at end of chapter)

However, excessive attention on the downside way carries the danger of talking ourselves out of doing perhaps a potentially worthwhile project. It is worth bearing in mind that risk is a two-sided phenomenon – sometimes, things turn out *better* than expected.

So, a sensible way of looking at risk is as 'the likelihood that things will turn out differently from what we expect'. This definition covers both the 'downside risk' and the 'upside potential'. Figure 5.1 may clarify this idea.

However, although the term risk is generally used to indicate the likelihood of things not going to plan, true risk situations are quite rare. In principle, there is a technical difference between conditions of risk and the far more common state of knowledge of uncertainty.

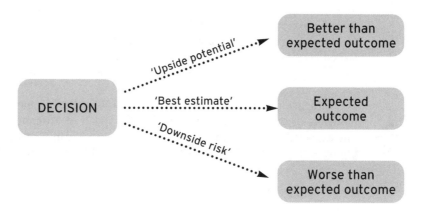

Figure 5.1 The two-sided nature of risk

- *Risk* relates to repetitive phenomena where we have compiled sufficient information about past outcomes to enable us to use the relative frequencies of past occurrences as assessments of the future probability of the same things happening again. For example, when dealing with equipment replacement, our past experience of input and cost levels should help in cash flow prediction.

- *Uncertainty* is where the event in question is unique and there is no objective basis for formulating probabilities. Most investment projects, apart from routine replacements, tend to involve uncertainty. Think about the information gaps involved in planning and developing a new project. However, some people are prepared to use their insight, experience and judgement to make shrewd assessments about the relative likelihood of different outcomes. These 'guesses' have no objective basis – we call them *subjective probabilities*. But they may have a useful role to play if people accept them as rough-and-ready guides to decision making in particular situations. If so, people are effectively treating uncertainty as if it were risk. In reality, the two terms tend to be used interchangeably, and when people talk about 'risk', they often mean 'uncertainty'.

5.5   Expected NPVs and probabilities

One way of dealing with the risk/uncertainty of future cash flows is to assign subjective probabilities to them. For example, a firm may reckon that a project's NPV might vary with the state of the market as shown below.

Outcome	NPV (X_i)	Probability (P_i)
Growth market	£8m	30%
Stable market	£5m	50%
Market in recession	(£3m)	20%

One dimension of this project is its *expected value*, which is a measure of central tendency of the outcome, analogous to the mean of a frequency distribution. The expected value of a project's NPV – the ENPV – can be calculated by multiplying each possible NPV by its associated probability and summing, viz:

$$\sum_{i=1}^{N} X_i P_i = \text{ENPV}$$

Applied to the figures in the table, we obtain in £m:

$$[(8 \times 30\%) + (5 \times 50\%) + (-3 \times 20\%)] = \text{£4.3m}$$

The concept of the ENPV requires explanation. The ENPV is simply a *weighted average*; each possible outcome is weighted by its probability of occurrence. In statistical theory, the ENPV would be the average outcome over many repetitions. This poses a conceptual problem because relatively few investment projects are ever repeated. However, the ENPV is a useful conceptual device for guiding decisions.

Regarding the example, if you can invest in this project only once, although the bias is towards a positive NPV, there is still a risk that it might end up negative. However, if it were possible to do the project many times, the average NPV per project would tend towards £4.3 million, that is, the negative NPVs would be more than outweighed by the positive ones.

Knowing the ENPV does not make the decision for you. The ENPV only summarises information about possible outcomes. But we can use the concept of the expected NPV to help us describe the riskiness of the project. The actual decision then depends on the attitude to risk of the individual or company.

Describing risk: another example

The risk characteristics of an investment project can be described by the probability distribution of future possible outcomes thus:

£m NPV outcomes (X_i)	Probability (P_i)
10	0.10
20	0.20
30	0.40
40	0.20
50	0.10
	1.00

Self-assessment activity 5.6

First, you should verify that the ENPV is £30 million.
(answer at end of chapter)

In this example, the distribution of potential outcomes is perfectly symmetrical or normal. In a normal probability distribution, the expected value is also the most likely value, i.e. £30m (and it coincides with the arithmetic mean). Now we consider the project's degree of risk. This can be assessed by calculating a measure of dispersion such as the standard deviation. When dealing with probabilities, the formula for calculating standard deviation is:

$$\sum_{i=1}^{N} [P_i (X_i - \text{ENPV})^2]$$

Self-assessment activity 5.7

Complete the entries in the following table to calculate the standard deviation.
(answer at end of chapter)

£Outcome (X_i)	P_i	(X_i − ENPV)	(X_i − ENPV)^2	P_i(X_i − ENPV)^2
10	0.10			
20	0.20			
30	0.40			
40	0.20			
50	0.10			

Applying the formula step by step, you will derive a standard deviation of:

$$\sqrt{120} = 10.95, \text{ or } £10.95m$$

But what does this mean?

To answer this question, recall that we are dealing here with a *normal* distribution. The normal distribution has some useful properties including the '4-in-6' rule, illustrated in Figure 5.2. In a normal distribution, roughly 4-in-6 (but exactly 68 per cent) of observations locate in the range ENPV ± one standard deviation, i.e. £30m plus or minus £11m.

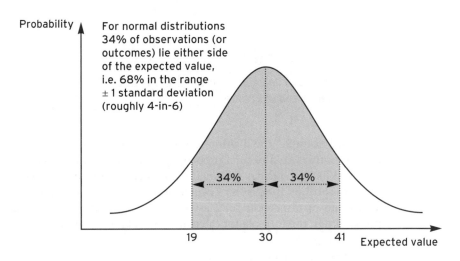

Figure 5.2 The '4-in-6' rule

This suggests there is a 68 per cent chance of an outcome between £19 million and £41 million, a 16 per cent (1-in-6) chance of an outcome less than £19 million, and a 16 per cent chance of getting more than £41 million.

However, continuous normal distributions are usually found only in textbooks. When dealing with uncertainty, people generally pinpoint only a limited number of focus outcomes and assign 'gut feeling' estimates of possibility to them. Given the uncertainties, it is not surprising that decision makers tend to focus more strongly on the 'downside potential' or the likelihood of getting outcomes less than the expected values and the consequences for the company.

There are other problems with using probability data. For example, consider the decision problem in Table 5.1 that shows the ENPV and standard deviations for three choice situations. How would you choose between the three pairs of projects? (*Hint:* recall the concept of risk aversion you met earlier.)

Table 5.1 Choosing between risky investment projects

(Figures in £m)		ENPV	St. Deviation
Choice A	X	100	20
	Y	100	40
Choice B	X	100	20
	Z	200	20
Choice C	X	100	20
	W	200	60

Choice A is easy. For the same expected value, most people would opt for the choice with the lowest risk, i.e. X. Choice B is also easy. For the same risk, most people would go for the option with the highest ENPV, namely Z.

Choice C is more complex – W is both more rewarding and riskier. Risk averse investors are prepared to take on risk but only if suitably compensated. The question is whether the extra £100 million offered by W is worth the extra risk (£60 million rather than £20 million). Would you be prepared to treble the risk for double the return? Probably not, which points to choosing X.

The coefficient of variation

Our intuitive result in this activity is an application of the *coefficient of variation*. This is given by:

$$\frac{\text{Risk}}{\text{ENPV}} = \frac{20}{100} = 0.2 \text{ for X}, \quad \text{and} \quad = 0.3 \text{ for W}$$

This reflects the amount of risk you have to bear per unit of return. Risk averse investors would want to minimise risk per £ of return and would therefore select the option with the lowest coefficient, i.e. project X.

Understandably, most managers are reluctant to use probabilities because they are so difficult to assign. The most popular method of allowing for risk in practice is sensitivity analysis.

5.6 Sensitivity analysis

This involves varying the key input values of a project appraisal to determine how sensitive the NPV outcome is to specified variations in them. If we also determine how far a variable can alter before wiping out the project's NPV, we can calculate the break-even value of key variables. The value of this approach is that, having identified the critical factors we can arrange to focus resources in that area in order to try to engineer a favourable outturn. Consider the following project:

	Year 0	Year 1	Year 2
Outlay	(£1,000)		
Revenue		£1,200	£1,200
Operating costs	_____	(£500)	(£500)
Net cash flow	(£1,000)	£700	£700
PV @ 12%	(£1,000)	£625	£558
NPV =	−£1,000 + £1,183 = +£183		

With the above cash flows, the NPV = +£183, so the project is worth doing. At what NPV does doing the project become a matter of indifference to the company? This occurs if the NPV = 0, where the project offers the same return as the cost of finance. This is the point at which the project just breaks even. One aim of sensitivity analysis is to find the break-even values of each variable. Consider the initial outlay.

One question may be: 'By how much could the outlay increase before the project merely breaks even?' You should realise that since the cost of the outlay is already expressed in present value terms, any increase will directly reduce the NPV. Therefore the outlay can increase by a maximum of £183, i.e. £183/£1,000 = 18.3%, before jeopardising the viability of the project.

(answer at end of chapter)

Self-assessment activity 5.8

Now repeat the analysis for all the other input variables.
(answer at end of chapter)

5.7 Worked example: Boeman plc

Determine the break-even values of the key variables in the following example and thus the highest percentage adverse change tolerable for each variable. Draw a graph of NPV against maximum tolerable adverse percentage change. Which variable is most critical in determining the outcome of the project's NPV?

Boeman plc is contemplating an investment project in a sector totally different from its current operations. It therefore has no basis for undertaking a probability analysis but is nevertheless concerned about the riskiness of the proposal. Consequently, it decides to undertake a sensitivity analysis. (*Hint:* the cash flows are annuities. There are several short-cuts available by using annuity tables.)

The details of the project are:

Required expenditure 'up front'	= £3m
Expected volume of output	= 200,000 units p.a.
Expected selling price	= £20/unit
Expected labour cost	= £8/unit
Expected material cost	= £6/unit
Cost of finance	= 10%
Project lifetime	= 4 years
4 year Annuity factor @ 10% (PVIFA)	= 3.17

Answer

1 The basic NPV is:

$$= -£3m + (200,000 \times [£20 - £8 - £6]) \times (3.17)$$
$$= -£3m + [£1.2m \times (3.17)] = +£0.8m$$

2 Sample sensitivity calculation:
To find the break-even volume (*V*), i.e. where NPV = 0, we solve the expression:

$$0 = -£3m + [V \times £6 \times 3.17]$$

V is given by:

$$V = £3m/[£6 \times 3.17] = 157,728 \text{ units}$$

This represents a volume reduction of about 21 per cent, i.e. the maximum tolerable fall in volume below the expected level is 21 per cent.

Self-assessment activity 5.9

Now repeat for material costs, labour costs, price, outlay, and discount rate.
(answer at end of chapter)

You will find that the critical variable is price (see Figure 5.3, where price and volume are shown). The flatter the sensitivity profile, the more sensitive the NPV is to changes in that variable. This suggests that managers should attempt to

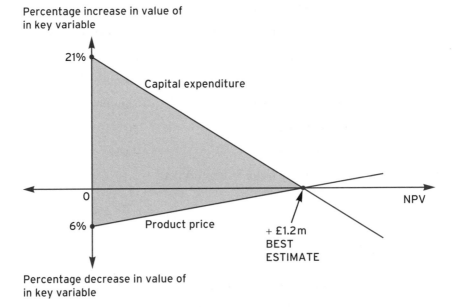

Figure 5.3 The Bowman plc sensitivity analysis

follow policies designed to support the price, for example, by advertising and promotions expenditure.

⊙ 5.8 Limitations of sensitivity analysis

While sensitivity analysis is very popular in practice – for one thing, it involves quite simple calculations – it does suffer from a number of problems, including the following:

- It deals with changes in isolation, and tends to ignore interactions between variables. For example, advertising may alter the volume of output as well as influencing price because price and volume are usually related. More sophisticated approaches attempt to model the implications of simultaneous changes in several variables under different states of the economy or 'scenarios'. The oil major Shell Group plc is well-known as an accomplished exponent of this technique. (e.g. see Leemhuis, 1985)

- It assumes that specified changes persist throughout the project lifetime, for example, a suggested 10 per cent change in volume is projected for each year of operation. In reality, variations in key factors tend to fluctuate randomly and hence unpredictably.

- It may reveal as critical, factors over which managers have no control, thus offering no guide to action. Nonetheless, it may still help to clarify the risks to which the project is exposed.

- No decision rule is provided – it does not indicate the maximum acceptable levels of sensitivity. This is an issue of management judgement and attitude to risk.

- It gives no indication of the likelihood of the variations under consideration. Variations in a factor which are potentially devastating but which have a minimal chance of occurring provide little cause for concern.

What firms do in practice

The CBI study revealed a number of variations on sensitivity analysis applied by respondents. The most common approach (58 per cent) was to specify low, high and middling estimates of selected key variables, e.g. sales, volume, capital costs, and then to compute the resulting NPV or IRR. A less sophisticated approach was to specify high, low and middling estimates for overall net cash flows (41 per cent). Less than 10 per cent engaged in formal scenario modelling, about the same proportion as those which undertook no risk analysis at all.

5.9   Guarding against project risk

Up to this point, we have looked at ways of *evaluating* projects in order to allow for risk. An alternative approach is to consider ways in which project risk can be reduced by astute management, for example by altering the structure of the project and the timing of cash flows and inflows in order to minimise the adverse impact of untoward contingencies. This is the province of *project management*.

Listed below are some ways of managing a project in order to minimise its potential to cause damage to the firm.

1 Invest in more information – market research, etc.

2 Obtain cover via commercial insurance.

3 Obtain more control over the market via forward integration or long-term sales contracts.

4 Control the source and price of supplies via backward integration.

5 Sub-contract critical steps in development.

6 Modify the project's nature, size (scale it down), timing (delay it), etc.

7 Modify the project financing, for example engage in (cancellable) lease contracts.

8 Maintain a financial cushion, e.g. by holding liquid assets and keeping open lines of credit to cope with contingencies.

9 Diversify – spread risk across a wider range of activities.

However, many of the above risk-reducing tactics have a downside. These might include the following:

1 Cost and reliability of research.

2 Cost of insurance; some risks cannot be covered.

3 and 4 Long-term commitment of resources, for example investment in distribution facilities.

5 Releasing an element of the project plus possible loss of control over quality (although penalty clauses can be inserted).

6 Lower scale means smaller returns (even if technically feasible); delays mean lower NPV.

7 Leasing involves financing costs, i.e. rentals.

8 There may be arrangement fees.

9 It is difficult to find activities whose returns do not move together – this may involve moving away from areas of core competence.

In the final analysis, it really depends on how critical the risks are and whether the benefits of greater peace of mind exceed the costs. It is important to realise that none of these methods of risk analysis represents the whole solution. They are simply ways of trying to explore the risk characteristics of a project to understand more clearly its dynamics. If we know what can go wrong and the likelihood of this happening, we are more able to take the sort of evasive actions that we identified under project management.

5.10   Summary

This chapter has focused on the mechanics of investment appraisal methods and extended the analysis to include treatment of inflation and taxation, before looking at possible ways of handling imperfect information in investment decisions. The next chapter will begin to examine another of the three key decision areas of financial management, the financing decision, beginning with an examination of the return which shareholders require when financing business investments. From now on, we assume a thorough understanding of investment appraisal methods.

References and further reading

Textbooks

Arnold – chs 5 and 6.
Pike & Neale – chs 6 and 9.
Samuels, Wilkes & Brayshaw – ch 7.
Watson & Head – ch 4.

Other

Barker, K, McKelvey, K and Waites, C (1998) *Target Practice* (Confederation of British Industry/Association of Consulting Actuaries).

Hull, J C (1980) *The Evaluation of Risk in Business Investment* (Pergamon Press).

Leemhuis, J P (1985) 'Using scenarios to develop strategies', *Long Range Palanning*, Vol 18, April, pp. 30–37.

Lock, D (2003) *Project Management* (Gower Publishing Company).

Project Management (Harvard Business Review Paperback, 1991).

Questions and mini-case studies

1 Howden plc is contemplating investment in an additional production line to produce its range of compact discs. A market research study, undertaken by a well-known firm of consultants, has revealed scope to sell an additional output of 400,000 units p.a. The study cost £100,000 but the account has not yet been settled.

The price and cost structure of a typical disc (net of royalties), is as follows:

	£	£
Price per unit		12.00
Costs per unit of output:		
Material cost per unit	(1.50)	
Direct labour cost per unit	(0.50)	
Variable overhead cost per unit	(0.50)	
Fixed overhead cost per unit	(1.50)	(4.00)
Profit		8.00

The fixed overhead represents apportionment of central annual administrative and marketing costs although these are expected to rise by £500,000 as a result of undertaking this project. The production line is expected to operate for five years and require total cash outlay of £11 million, including £500,000 of materials stocks. The equipment will have a residual value of £2 million. Stocks on hand at the start of the final year will also be £500,000.

The production line will be located in a currently empty building for which an offer of £2 million has recently been received from another company. If Howden keeps the building, it is expected that property price inflation will increase its value to £3 million after five years.

While the precise rates of price and cost inflation are uncertain, economists in Howden's corporate planning department make the following forecasts for the average annual rates of inflation relevant to the project:

Retail Price Index	6% p.a.
Disc prices	5% p.a.
Material prices	3% p.a.
Direct labour wage rates	7% p.a.
Variable overhead costs	7% p.a.
Other overhead costs	5% p.a.

Required

Use the NPV method to assess the financial viability of this proposal. (Howden's shareholders require a real return of 8.5 per cent for projects with this degree of risk.)

Source: ACCA June 1994, question 6

2 Blackwater plc, a manufacturer of speciality chemicals, has been reported to the anti-pollution authorities on several occasions in recent years and fined substantial amounts for making excessive toxic discharges into local rivers. Both the environmental lobby and Blackwater's shareholders demand that it clean up its operations. It is estimated that the total fines it may incur over the next four years can be summarised by the following probability distribution (all figures in present values):

Level of fine	Probability
£0.5m	0.3
£1.4m	0.5
£2.0m	0.2

Filta & Strayne Ltd (FSL), a firm of environmental consultants, has advised that new equipment costing £12 million can be installed to virtually eliminate illegal discharges. Unlike fines, expenditure on pollution control equipment is tax-allowable via a 25 per cent writing-down allowance (reducing balance). The rate of corporate tax is 30 per cent. The equipment will have no resale value after its expected four-year working life, but can be in full working order immediately prior to Blackwater's next financial year.

A European Union Common Pollution Policy grant of 25 per cent of gross expenditure is available, with payment delayed by a year. Immediately on receipt of the grant from the EU, Blackwater will pay 20 per cent of this to FSL as commission. These transactions have no tax implications for Blackwater.

A disadvantage of the new equipment is that it will raise production costs by £30 per tonne over its operating life. Current production is 10,000 tonnes per annum but is expected to grow by 5 per cent per annum compound. It can be assumed that unit production costs and product price will be constant over the next four years. No change in working capital is envisaged. Blackwater applies a discount rate of 12 per cent after all taxes to investment projects of this nature. All cash inflows and outflows occur at year-ends.

Required

(a) Calculate the expected net present value of the investment assuming a four-year operating period. Briefly comment on your results.

(b) Write a memorandum to Blackwater's management as to the desirability of the project, taking into account both financial and non-financial criteria.

Source: ACCA December 1997, question 3

3 Milles Ltd is a small company manufacturing and supplying wooden fish decoys bought by anglers and by collectors as a home decoration. The company is considering expanding its range and is investigating whether or not to manufacture and sell a Canada goose decoy.

In order to manufacture this new decoy, Milles will need to invest in a variety of modern lathe equipment to cut and shape the wood. The total cost of this required capital expenditure is estimated to be £290,000. This expenditure will be eligible for capital allowances at the rate of 25 per cent reducing balance. After three years, Milles expects to be able to sell the equipment for £50,000.

Costs for the product have been estimated by the production department as:

Labour £15 per unit

Material £10 per unit

Fixed costs (including the depreciation of the equipment) £30,000 p.a.

The marketing department has estimated that by selling through mail order catalogues, specialist sports shops and the internet, sales of this new decoy are likely to be 25,000 units p.a. at a selling price of £40 each. At this stage, the company intends only to manufacture and sell this decoy for the next three years. Annual production will be 25,000 units just to meet the sales requirement for each year.

The company's current cost of capital is 10 per cent which it sees as an appropriate discount rate for this proposed venture.

The company pays corporation tax at the small business rate of 20 per cent. Tax payments on operating profit can be lagged by one year although the tax saving on the first year capital allowance will not benefit the company until two years after the purchase of the equipment. All cash flows apart from the purchase of the equipment can be assumed to occur at the end of the year.

Required

(a) Calculate the net present value of the proposed investment in the Canada goose decoy.

(b) How sensitive is the NPV just calculated to:

    (i) a change in the material cost per decoy?

    (ii) a change in the discount rate?

(c) Discuss the advantages and disadvantages of this type of sensitivity analysis.

4 Victory Bikes plc manufactures high-performance motorcycles. In a bid to raise its profile, and therefore sales, in its chosen market segment it is investigating a project to enter a racing team in the British Motorcycle Racing series, for a period of four years. If the financial assessment proves satisfactory the project will start immediately. However, as the first year of the project will be dedicated to developing and testing the racing bikes, no additional sales are expected as a result of the project during its first year.

Shown below is the projected financial data for the project, produced by the company's accounting department.

Motorsport project

	Year 1 £	Year 2 £	Year 3 £	Year 4 £
Additional sales revenue	–	350,000	390,000	410,000
Operating costs				
Materials and components	–50,000	–65,000	–55,000	–50,000
Salaries and wages	–70,000	–80,000	–85,000	–85,000
Depreciation	–45,000	–45,000	–45,000	–45,000
Advertising	–25,000	–25,000	–25,000	–25,000
Overheads	–10,000	–10,000	–15,000	–15,000
Profit	–200,000	125,000	165,000	190,000

Capital expenditure:

Machinery and equipment – initial cost:	£300,000
Machinery and equipment – disposal proceeds:	£120,000

The following information is also available:

1 The capital expenditure on machinery and equipment of £300,000 will be incurred on the first day of the project and this equipment is expected to be sold for £120,000 on the last day of the fourth year.

2 The expenditure on materials, advertising, and salaries and wages is all directly linked to the project and would be avoided should the project not be undertaken.

3 The depreciation charge arises from the company's use of the straight-line method of depreciation.

4 All the overheads included in the costs are a fair allocation of head office costs, which are not expected to show any significant increase as a result of the project.

5 The cost of capital for this type of investment is 15 per cent and the directors set a target accounting rate of return on investment of 15 per cent and a payback period of three years or less for all projects.

6 The company assumes that all its operating cash flows occur at the end of each year with the exception of the capital expenditure involved.

7 The rate of corporation tax is 30 per cent.

 8 **Capital allowances** of 25 per cent (calculated on a reducing balance basis) are available for the purchase of the machinery and equipment; any proceeds greater or less than the tax written-down value of this machinery will result in a balancing charge or allowance respectively.

9 Tax charges or rebates are subject to a one-year delay.

Ignore inflation.

Required

(a) Calculate the NPV of the project.

(b) Calculate the accounting rate of return of the project and the cash payback period for the project. In addition, with reference to these calculations and the results of your calculations in (a), advise the company on the suitability of the project.

(c) A major concern in the assessment of many projects is the uncertainty involved in forecasting the future sales and costs, etc. Suggest where the main uncertainties lie in this project.

Self-assessment answers

5.1

The real rate of return is *approximately* (7.0% – 2.5%) = 4.5%.

More accurately, it is found by using the key relationship noted above for m, and hence for r, and inserting our figures:

$$\text{We obtain } (1+r) = \frac{1+m}{1+p} = \frac{1.07}{1.025} = 1.044,$$

$$\text{so } r = (1.044 - 1) = 4.4\%.$$

Thus the return that rational lenders require net of inflation is 4.4 per cent.

5.2

(i) In purchasing power terms, the £500 will buy only $£500/(1.03)^3 = £458$ worth of goods and services when I receive it.

(ii) The real PV of the legacy is the £458 discounted further at 8 per cent p.a., i.e. $£458/(1.08)^3 = £363$.

5.3

A balancing charge applies when the asset is sold for more than its written-down value for tax purposes. For example, if after two years, it were sold for £5.5 million, there would be tax payable on the difference – at 30 per cent, the tax charge would be 30% × (£5.5m – £4.5m) = £0.3 million.

5.4

The PV of the tax savings is simply the difference between the NPVs in cases 2 and 3, i.e. with and without the WDA, viz:

PV of tax savings = (£2.63m – £0.7m) = £1.93 million.

5.5

Many things could go wrong. Some firms arrange these according to the degree of control that project managers can exert over these factors, e.g.:

- *project-specific* – problems with labour, raw materials prices, machinery breakdowns

- *firm-specific* – new strategic direction, new performance standards
- *industry-specific* – new entrants appear, a rival makes a technological breakthrough
- *Economy-specific* – changes in interest rates, exchange rates, new employment legislation.

5.6

$$\text{ENPV} = (0.1 \times 10) + (0.2 \times 20) + (0.4 \times 30) + (0.2 \times 40) + (0.1 \times 50)$$
$$= (1 + 4 + 12 + 8 + 5) = £30$$

5.7

Outcome (X_i)	P_i	(X_i – ENPV)	(X_i – ENPV)^2	$P_i(X_i$ – ENPV)^2
10	0.1	−20	400	40
20	0.2	−10	100	20
30	0.4			
40	0.2	+10	100	20
50	0.1	+20	400	40
			Total	120

The standard deviation is the square root of 120 = 10.95, say 11.

5.8

The other key variables are revenue, operating costs and discount rate.
Revenue (R): the break-even value of R is the solution to the following NPV equation:

$$0 = \text{NPV} = [R - £500] \times (\text{2-year annuity factor}) - £1,000$$
$$£1,000 = 1.69R - £845$$
$$R = £1,845/1.69 = £1,091$$

Operating costs (C): the break-even value of C is the solution to the following NPV equation:

$$0 = \text{NPV} = [£1,200 - C] \times (\text{2-year annuity factor}) - £1,000$$
$$£1,000 = £2,028 - 1.69C$$
$$C = £1,028/1.69 = £608$$

Discount rate: the break-even discount rate is simply the IRR. Roughly, the IRR has the annuity factor fitting this equation:

$$\text{NPV} = -£1,000 + £700 \times (\text{2-year annuity factor @ } R\%)$$
$$\text{Annuity factor} = £1,000/£700 = 1.4286$$

The tables show: 1.4400 for 25 per cent (too low)
1.4235 for 26 per cent (too high)

The IRR is thus (114/165) of the way between 25 per cent and 26 per cent, about 25.7 per cent.

5.9
Using the same approach as self-assessment activity 5.8, you should find these answers:

- Increase in outlay: £0.8 million (27 per cent).
- Reduction in price: down to £18.85, a reduction of about 6 per cent.
- Increase in labour costs: to £9.3 (16 per cent increase).
- Increase in material costs: up to £7.3 (21 per cent increase).
- Discount rate: the IRR is about 19 per cent (90 per cent increase).

Case study: Virgin's West Coast railway project

This case study outlines the contract struck between Virgin Rail, the railway service operator, and Railtrack, the firm responsible for the operation and upkeep of the UK railway system, in the upgrading of the West Coast main-line railway route, until it went into liquidation in 2002. It traces the early problems with the project – technical, weather, safety – that culminated in Railtrack going into administration in 2002. Key issues here are project planning and development, and risk analysis and management.

This project started as a long-overdue improvement to the West Coast main line but became one of the biggest corporate disasters in project management Britain had ever seen.

The contract

In October 1997, Railtrack and Virgin Rail agreed a £2.1 billion upgrade of Britain's busiest railway line, the 440-mile route from London through the Midlands to Manchester and on to Glasgow. The upgrade was to double the capacity on the line (in terms of the number of trains) and reduce travel time from London to Glasgow by $1\frac{1}{2}$ hours to 3 hours 50 minutes.

The deal involved a revenue-sharing arrangement between Railtrack, which was responsible for track and station maintenance, and Virgin Rail. Under this deal, Railtrack could forfeit up to £160 million p.a. in track charges if infrastructure problems caused train delays. The contract imposed tight specifications for Railtrack to meet regarding track improvements and upgrades. However, Railtrack could earn a similar amount if passenger numbers increased sufficiently. At the time, 75 per cent of the delays on the run-down West Coast line were due to infrastructural problems – a figure unacceptable to Virgin and the reason it was offering Railtrack incentives to improve. Virgin was forecasting an increase in passenger numbers from 23 million to 50 million when the upgrade was finished. The deal required the approval of the regulator, Ofrail, to ensure that other train operators were not being unfairly penalised, but this was largely a formality.

The project – early hopes

This type of deal would not have been possible when the railway network was owned and managed by British Rail, a public corporation. Railtrack had originally anticipated spending £1.5 billion on the line to allow trains to travel at 140 mph by 2005, but the cost to Railtrack was cut to £600 million under the revenue-sharing agreement, in line with Railtrack's ten-year investment plan. The line had had little money spent on it since its electrification in the 1960s and 1970s. Railtrack intended to finance this investment from its own resources. Railtrack's shares fell by 27.5p to 892.5p on the announcement of the project. However, within a month, its share price had risen to over £10. Soon after, the company announced pre-tax profits of £400 million.

'This project will end railway's period of decline,' said Will Whitehorn, Virgin Rail director. 'This will be the first time in two generations that railways have taken back market share from air and the roads.' Virgin was to spend £550 million on trains that would tilt into bends, allowing the faster speed. British Rail had tried this in the 1980s but had failed.

As a train operator, Virgin was facing declining government subsidies (£192 million in 1997–8) to be followed by costly charges (£231 million by 2011–12) for using the network. It intended to finance its purchase of trains and rolling stock by leasing (paralleling the £2.5 billion leasing arrangement which Virgin Atlantic negotiated for its aircraft in 1997). Any deal hinges on getting the forecast passenger numbers right. 'Our numbers are conservative enough to make them easily financeable,' said Whitehorn. 'Passenger revenues must increase by four-fold to £1 billion if this business plan is to be met. Maintenance by the rolling stock suppliers will be included in any lease package.'

The emphasis was to be on keeping trains in service. Thus, more maintenance would take place at night rather than in daytime, and records of train unit reliability would be kept. The contracts brought new suppliers to the UK railway, including Fiat from Italy and Bombardier from Canada. Both would assemble trains at their UK factories. Ivor Warburton, Director of the Virgin Rail Group and Chairman of the Association of Train Operating Companies, was confident of the robustness of the project. 'Long-term contracts agreeing subsidies and private finance should mean that railways are no longer subject to short-term investment pressures,' he said. 'The company intends to revolutionise aspects of rail travel, including the introduction of tilting trains, internet ticket sales and on-train entertainment.'

In addition, Virgin was upgrading its trains on its cross-country Manchester–Plymouth and Birmingham–Newcastle routes. Again, this upgrade imposed commitments on Railtrack. By this time, Railtrack was using the project as an entrée into other big projects, such as the London Underground Jubilee Line, the Channel Tunnel high-speed link as well as an extensive modernisation programme for rail stations as it was raising its profile as a fast-growing FTSE 100 company.

Soon after negotiating the deal, Virgin plugged a gap in its management by appointing a board-level director to deal with train operations. Railtrack, on the other hand, found it difficult to obtain and retain skilled financial managers to take control of these risky yet potentially lucrative infrastructure projects. Moreover, Railtrack had no engineering department at its Euston head office in London. Indeed, most of its engineering work was outsourced.

How it developed

By the end of 1999, the first signs of cost increases started to appear. The overall cost of the upgrade had risen to an estimated £5.1 billion, with Railtrack demanding a taxpayer subsidy increase of £1 billion p.a. to cover all spending plans across the network (partly propelled by an overall increase in customers). Indeed, Virgin announced that since the project had started, passenger numbers on the West Coast service had increased by 30 per cent, and it anticipated a similar increase during the first three years of the millennium.

By mid-2000, some of the technological advances began to be downgraded. The major cause of this was the withdrawal of the plan to introduce sophisticated electronic signalling because Railtrack could not guarantee that it would work properly, the technology being brand new and as yet untested. This failure caused major delays in meeting the original targets and resulted in Railtrack paying Virgin £1 billion in compensation.

October 2000 saw the Hatfield rail crash in which four passengers were killed. As there were fears that the crash had been caused by a faulty rail, speed limits were imposed throughout the rail network. The situation was aggravated by the widespread flooding that occurred throughout the winter. However, by July 2001, Virgin had introduced 53 new tilting trains, involving an investment of £600 million. By allowing a 20 per cent increase in speeds around bends, these trains would be able to achieve maximum speeds of 140 mph. The original plan envisaged these trains operating at this speed from May 2003.

The impact of Hatfield and the unremitting problems and delays and spiralling costs that Railtrack was facing in maintaining the network led to its collapse in October 2001 when the government placed the company in administration. This was a controversial move as many argued that it was still financially viable. By this time, the cost of the West Coast upgrade had risen to £7 billion. Virgin was insisting that its original contracts with Railtrack be honoured.

By early 2002, it was announced that the speed of the tilting trains would be cut from 140 mph to 125 mph and that the service would not operate until May 2005. The cost had risen to £13 billion. Railtrack argued that the work to improve existing infrastructure had been carried out – the problems were with the upgrades, particularly with untested technology.

From the outset, Railtrack was out-negotiated by Virgin in terms of contract specification. Top managers at Railtrack had come from a public-sector background and found it difficult to assess and effectively manage risk. In addition, the company had little understanding of the poor state of its essentially 1960s vintage railway line, and the logistics of improving and upgrading it. One manager said it was like trying to rebuild the M6 at rush hour – but without a contra-flow. Railtrack had a dizzy turnover of managers and project consultants, and a chronic lack of leadership.

The saga continued. A 25-mile stretch of the main line was closed for maintenance every weekend from August until Christmas 2002, triggering huge disruption and another £50 million in compensation for Virgin. Relations between Railtrack and the train operators were now rock bottom, poisoned by mutual mistrust and lack of confidence.

Required

(a) Identify the main stakeholders in this episode and analyse the part that they played following the announcement of the project.

(b) In particular, assess what each stakeholder group stood to gain from this project, and which assumptions were revealed as unfounded as the project progressed.

(c) Discuss how you might have assessed the risks inherent in this project.

6

THE RATE OF RETURN REQUIRED BY OWNERS

Equities on top - who cares about the short-term?

By the end of 2002, world equity markets had fallen 50 per cent from their December 1999 peak. Two thousand and two was a desperate year for equity investors, with the major markets all experiencing substantial falls in their benchmark indices. Wall Street fell 21 per cent, slightly better than London's 25 per cent decline, while Tokyo fell 17 per cent to stand over 70 per cent lower than its peak in 1989. In real terms, Frankfurt sported a return of minus 41 per cent.

Nevertheless, the bear market was only the third worst on record - UK equities fell 71 per cent during the 1973-4 bear market and US equities fell by over 80 per cent in the Wall Street Crash of 1929-32. Conversely, in 2002, bonds offered attractive *positive* real returns in most markets, e.g. 15 per cent in New York, 13 per cent in Switzerland, 11 per cent in Japan, 8 per cent in Germany and 7 per cent in London.

So why invest in equities? The simple answer is that over time, equities have returned significant premium returns over bond yields. Taking the 103 years 1900-2002, the main markets gave the following average annual *real* equity premia: Japan 5.3 per cent, USA 4.4 per cent, Germany 4.9 per cent, UK 3.9 per cent. Australian equities gave the best return among developed nations at 6 per cent.

Source: ABN AMRO Bank, *Global Investment Returns Yearbook* (2003)

Objectives:

The objectives of this chapter are:

- to explain the concept of the shareholders' required return (SRR)

- to explain how the dividend valuation model can be used to assess the SRR

- to distinguish between market, or systematic, risk and firm-specific risk

- to show how the Capital Asset Pricing Model can be used to calculate the equity risk premium and hence the cost of equity

- to determine the discount rate that should be applied to an all-equity-financed new investment.

6.1 Introduction

Historical evidence is comforting to those investors nursing severe dents in the values of their investment holdings following the collapse of world equity markets from the peaks of December 1999. The data collected by ABN AMRO shows that, despite short-term disappointments, investing in equities has beaten investment in government stock in the past. But a perennial problem facing corporate financial managers is how to specify the rate of return required by investors looking forward, and hence how to evaluate (i.e. place a value on) an investment project.

The value of individual investment projects and whole businesses is essentially driven by two things – the expected future cash flows and the degree of risk. Different activities carry different degrees of risk, and thus people expect different rates of return to compensate for the risks they face in making their investments. In this chapter, taking the case of the all-equity-financed firm, we ask: 'What rate of return should the managers achieve on behalf of owners?' Knowledge of this rate is critical to assessing the net present value of a new project and understanding how investors value the whole business.

As a first approximation, the return offered to shareholders should at least match what they could expect to achieve elsewhere. This is because they incur an opportunity cost when entrusting their money to the company, as it could be applied to some other investment opportunity. This is why the shareholders' required return is often called the *equity cost of capital* (**cost of equity**) – it measures the owners' (or equity holders') opportunity cost. However, this observation merely identifies the required return relative to other investments. Our real goal is to discover what determines the *absolute* level of the required return.

All rational investors require a return to compensate for three things:

- *The 'pure' time value of money* – this is the return required to satisfy the owners' time preference. This rate will reward investors simply for waiting for future returns. This is the same as the real rate of interest that people demand net of inflation, i.e. with inflation stripped out. The amount of the required return will usually differ among investors according to their relative preferences as between consumption now and consumption in the future, depending in turn on factors such as their ages and wealth levels.

● *Inflation* – as we saw in Chapter 5, expected inflation has the effect of raising the return required by investors as they seek compensation for the expected erosion of the future purchasing power of their returns.

● *Risk* – most investment projects carry the risk of fluctuations in future returns and possibly, in a hostile environment, the risk of getting no returns at all. In return for bearing these risks, investors require a premium, linked to the degree of risk of the activity in question. This is commonly known as the '**equity premium**', past examples of which are shown in the cameo for different countries.

Self-assessment activity 6.1

(i) A check question! If the prevailing nominal interest rate in the money market is 6 per cent and people expect a future rate of inflation of 2.7 per cent, what is the real rate of interest?

(ii) If the prevailing market rate of interest (i.e. already incorporating inflationary expectations) is 6 per cent and equities have generated a risk premium on average in the past of 5 per cent p.a., what rate of return is required on a new investment of average risk to match past performance?
(answer at end of chapter)

In this chapter, we assume that expected inflation is built into the ruling benchmark market rate of interest. In an earlier chapter, we called this the risk-free rate of interest. This is usually measured by the yield on short-term government securities, such as Treasury Bills in the UK, or its close relation, LIBOR, the London Inter Bank Offered Rate, the interest rate at which the London banks lend to each other on a very short-term basis. The critical issue is, what risk premium should investors require (and managers seek to achieve) over and above this risk-free rate of interest for activities of different risks?

Before directly addressing this issue, we examine a method popular among investment analysts for assessing the shareholders' required return.

6.2 The Dividend Valuation Model (DVM)

A common way of assessing the shareholders' required return is to use the Dividend Valuation Model. The DVM is based on the premise that the value of an ordinary share is the sum of all discounted returns from holding it, i.e. all future dividends. In other words, it assumes that the share price is the present value of all future dividends. The discount rate that equates the present value of these future expected dividends to the present market price of the share is the rate of return that investors apparently require from holding the share.

If we observe how the market values a company, we can infer the rate of return that shareholders are seeking from it, i.e. the rate of discount that the market implicitly uses to discount future dividends (denoted by k_e). In other words, we take the current market price and work backwards to deduce what discount rate has been used in setting that market price, i.e. we are deducing the market's required return from a particular share by scrutinising how the market values the share.

The market price of a listed share itself is readily available. An assumption about the future flow of dividends will now provide the key to identifying the shareholders' required return from investing in that share.

Starting from the premise that the share price is determined by the present value of the series of future dividend payments, and assuming a constant rate of growth in dividends over time, the DVM formula for today's share price (P_0) is:

$$P_0 = \text{share price} = \frac{D_0(1+g)}{k_e - g} = \frac{D_1}{k_e - g}$$

where D_0 = the latest dividend paid (net of tax)

D_1 = next year's dividend

g = expected annual dividend growth rate

k_e = rate of discount applied to future dividends

By implication, k_e is the cost of equity. Rearranging this formula, it converts to:

$$k_e = \frac{D_1}{P_0} + g$$

Thus, the formula tells us that the return required by shareholders is a compound of two elements:

- the prospective dividend yield on the shares, i.e. next year's dividend expressed as a percentage return on today's share price, and

- the rate of growth of the dividend.

The share price is assumed to be ex-dividend, so that the next expected dividend payment is in about a year's time. Much of this information is known at any point in time:

- We know today's share price.

- We know the *latest* dividend.

- We can work out the dividend growth rate by looking at the last few years' dividends.

These information requirements, and how to obtain them, are highlighted in Figure 6.1. A numerical example is also given to illustrate the approach.

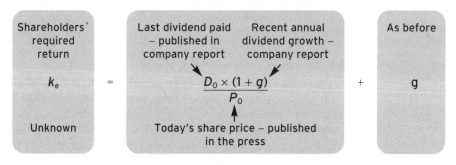

Figure 6.1 Using the DVM to find the shareholders' required return

Example – XYZ plc

The share price of XYZ plc is now £2.80. Last week, it paid a dividend of 15p per share (net of tax). Over the past few years, dividends have grown at an average rate of 8 per cent. What is the apparent rate of discount applied by the market when pricing XYZ's ordinary shares?

Solution

Clearly, £2.80 is the ex-dividend price.

Given
$$P_0 = \frac{D_1}{k_e - g}$$

and
$$k_e = \frac{D_1}{P_0} + g$$

Substituting:
$$k_e = \frac{15p(1.08)}{£2.80} + 0.08 = (5.8\% + 8\%) = 13.8\%$$

By implication, 13.8 per cent is the cost of equity, the rate of return required by investors.

Self-assessment activity 6.2

The price of ABC plc ordinary shares is 117p. Recently, ABC paid a dividend of 5p per share (net of tax). Over the past few years, dividends have grown at an average rate of 3.5 per cent. Use the DVM to find the implied rate of discount applied by the market when valuing ABC's ordinary shares. (answer at end of chapter)

There are several problems with the DVM as a model, and hence, this whole approach to assessing the required return. For example, the DVM works only when $k_e > g$, so it may not apply when firms are going through exceptionally high growth spurts. To check this, recalculate the share price in the XYZ example for the case where $g = 15\%$.

Other problems involved in using the DVM

- It assumes that today's share price can be relied upon to reflect the market's 'true' assessment of the value of the shares, i.e. the share price is assumed to be set by an efficient capital market.

- The model is based on the ex-dividend share price, that is, it assumes that the next dividend is payable in a year's time. The arithmetic is made more complex if we are between ex-dividend dates because this means that the next dividend payable will be due in less than one year.

- The figure obtained for the equity cost depends on which day we do the calculation because share prices fluctuate on a daily basis.

- It implies a constant rate of future dividend growth.

- It assumes that recent past dividend growth is a good indicator of future growth.

- It works only for quoted companies, i.e. those actually having a market price, although surrogate companies can be used.

- It does not work when the company pays no dividend, or a historically low one, as in a recovery situation, when investors expect much higher future dividends. Dell Computers in the USA has never paid a dividend, and International Power in the UK has decided to stop paying dividends in future as a matter of policy. Neither firm has a zero value.

One further problem with the DVM is that it yields a figure for the SRR that is applicable only at the level of the whole company. It is a 'blanket' figure of limited use for evaluating the cash flows generated by individual projects with degrees of risk that differ from those of the firm as a whole. For evaluating most projects, we need to 'tailor-make' a discount rate to reflect the risk of the project in question. For this, the Capital Asset Pricing Model (CAPM) can be used.

6.3 The Capital Asset Pricing Model

The **CAPM** is the cornerstone of much of modern finance theory and research. As its title implies, it is a device for explaining how markets price capital assets, i.e. it explains how an efficient capital market sets a price on individual securities by taking into account their respective risks and the expected returns from holding them. A full treatment of the model is beyond our scope here – we will concentrate on what it tells us regarding the determination of the rate of return that rational investors should require on different securities.

Types of risk

The starting point in the CAPM is the notion that investors require compensation for two burdens that they bear:

- Having to wait for returns on their investment. The compensation is the *price of time* – reflected in the going market interest rate on low- or no-risk securities (which will also anticipate future inflation, as explained in Chapter 5, section 2).

- Having to expose their capital to the risk of fluctuation in returns received. The compensation required is the *price of risk*, or risk premium that is applicable to the risk of the particular activity in which they have invested.

The key question remains, however: 'How do we assess the size of the risk premium?' The answer hinges on what we mean by risk. Here we find the particular contribution of the CAPM is to clarify our understanding of risk. It does this by breaking down the overall risk into two separate components. These are as follows (note the various, interchangeable names):

- *Firm-specific or unique risk* is the variability in the returns from holding the shares of a company resulting from factors unique to that company; for example, vagaries of the markets in which the firm sells its product, any labour problems it has and progress with its R&D programmes. As these aspects are specific to the individual firm, they can be diversified away by forming a portfolio of securities from different industries. In a well-diversified portfolio, when some companies in the portfolio do badly, the effects are usually counterbalanced by others that are doing well. This is due to lack of correlation in the returns from individual firms. The old adage about not putting all your eggs in one basket is highly relevant here – risk is spread out across a range of investments. This source of risk is also called **unsystematic** or **diversifiable** risk.

- *Systematic or* **relevant risk** relates to variability in returns stemming from macro factors, both political and economic, which impact on the fortunes of all firms, such as interest and exchange rate changes. Because such factors impact on the stock market as a whole, they will be reflected in movements of the market index (or **market portfolio**). Their impact cannot be diversified by portfolio formation, although the extent of the impact may vary between companies. All firms whose shares are quoted on the market are subject to this risk, which is why it is also called *market risk*. Unlike firm-specific risk, this cannot normally be diversified away.

A rational investor will want to lower risk as far as possible without jeopardising expected returns. This can be achieved by building a **portfolio** of shares, i.e. combining investments in the shares of a variety of firms. The overall risk of the portfolio reduces because the returns on different securities are not perfectly correlated. Even if one security is performing badly, it is likely to be compensated by relatively good performance in other holdings, thus moderating the overall fluctuation in returns. A simple example will illustrate this.

Example

Imagine two investments are available, A and B. Their returns vary inversely as follows:

- When A yields a return of 15 per cent, B yields 5 per cent.

- When A yields a return of 5 per cent, B yields 15 per cent.

If both outcomes are equally likely, then a portfolio weighted equally in A and B will always generate an overall return of 10 per cent. Returns are either:

$$(50\% \times 15\% \text{ return on A}) + (50\% \times 5\% \text{ return on B}) = 7.5\% + 2.5\% = 10\%$$

$$(50\% \times 5\% \text{ return on A}) + (50\% \times 15\% \text{ return on B}) = 2.5\% + 7.5\% = 10\%$$

Effectively the portfolio is risk-free – diversification has eliminated *all* the risk of the individual components. The standard deviation of the returns on the portfolio is zero.

In this extreme example, the investor is assisted by the existence of perfect negative correlation between the returns from the two securities. In practice, any degree of negative correlation is rare, but it can be shown that so long as the degree of correlation is less than perfectly positive, it is possible to benefit from diversifying.

Thus, as an investor includes more and more securities in his/her portfolio, the overall risk (measured, for example, by the standard deviation of returns) diminishes because specific risk is eroded. Market risk cannot be removed except by diversifying into the stock markets of other countries (see next section). It is suggested that an investor needs 25 or so securities, spread across a variety of industrial sectors, in order to exploit the major part of the risk-reducing potential of diversification. The behaviour of the two types of risk is shown in Figure 6.2.

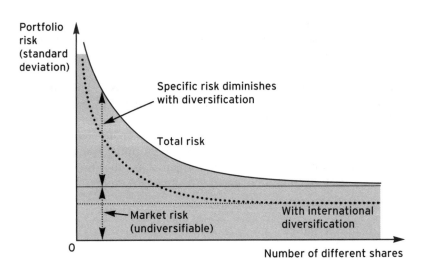

Figure 6.2 How diversification lowers portfolio risk

The total risk of the portfolio is measured by the variability of the return on the portfolio, i.e. the standard deviation. As the number of securities incorporated in the portfolio increases, the total risk declines until reaching an effective floor, where virtually all specific risk has been removed. The remaining risk is due to factors which influence the returns on all shares and which cannot be diversified away. It is thus worth adding securities to a portfolio so long as there is scope for eliminating specific risk. However, specific risk can be totally eliminated only when the investor holds every component in the whole market, the so-called market portfolio, although to achieve this degree of diversification is beyond the resources of most investors. The so-called *tracker funds* which aim to replicate a major stock market index get quite close to this, hence their popularity among rational investors.

Self-assessment activity 6.3

How could you eliminate *all* of the specific risk?
(answer at end of chapter)

6.4 **International diversification**

Investors tend to prefer investing in their own national stock markets, although this is changing. Their past insularity stems from a mixture of their lack of information and their perceptions of greater risk. Common reasons for avoiding foreign investment are:

- scarcity of analysts' research into overseas markets and firms

- transactions costs, especially connected with foreign exchange

- exposure to foreign exchange risk

- legal and institutional restrictions, e.g. custody regulations

- political risk.

Several studies have shown that international diversification can generate greater portfolio benefits than investing only in domestic shares. The reason for portfolio risk reducing as the number of component shares increases is the less than perfect correlation between international markets and hence investment vehicles traded on them, enabling investors to reduce specific risks. In this case, the relevant correlation is between individual stock markets. Even though foreign investments carry greater risks, when foreign stock markets are less than perfectly correlated with the domestic market, relevant risk can be lowered below the level of market risk relating to purely domestic investment.

Studies pioneered by Solnik (1974) have shown that international markets are not all closely correlated. Kaplanis (1997), for example, showed that between 1990 and 1994, the London market had the following cross-national correlation coefficients:

USA	+0.7
Germany	+0.4
Italy	+0.2
Japan	+0.3
Australia	+0.5

However, European markets tended to have higher inter-correlations, e.g. Germany/France (0.7) and Netherlands/Germany (0.7), probably resulting from ever-closer European integration.

Astute investors could exploit these imperfect correlations by combining investments in two or more markets, thus achieving a bodily shift downwards in the risk profile. The effect is shown by the two dotted lines in Figure 6.2.

However, these opportunities seem to be receding. By the mid-1990s, the correlation between changes in US and European share price movements was estimated at around +0.4 – Wall Street movements would 'explain' 40 per cent of movement in the main European indices. But Brooks and Catao (2000) showed that rapid technical and institutional change had raised the correlation to 0.8 by 2000.

They suggested several reasons for this convergence:

- removal of controls on capital movements

- more efficient trading systems

- greater cross-border trading volumes

- more large companies obtaining listings on several markets

- more cross-border mergers and acquisitions, resulting in firms' foreign activities accounting for higher proportions of profits (e.g. it has been estimated that over 50% of the revenue of UK FTSE-100 companies now comes from overseas)

- easier access to information on foreign firms via the internet.

Owing to these developments, equity markets have become more integrated. Nowadays, it seems that changes in prices in one market are more easily and quickly transmitted to others, e.g. good news for US telecoms shares is increasingly likely to lead to higher share prices for telecoms shares across the world. Conversely, if Nokia announces poor trading results, the adverse market reaction will overspill into the US stock market, i.e. Motorola shares are likely to suffer 'in sympathy'. This means that industry membership rather than location has become a more important determinant of market value. In other words, investors should diversify more by industry than by country to achieve optimal diversification benefits.

Brooks and Catao also showed that the most important factor explaining increased inter-market correlation was developments in information technology. They found an overall correlation between European IT stocks and US IT stocks at May 2000 of 0.85, but for non-IT stocks it was only 0.54. This implies that high-tech stocks now form a channel whereby shocks in one market are disseminated throughout the world. In 2001, for example, the information announced in the USA about the reduced prospects and the stock write-downs by Cisco Systems, the internet technology supplier, had a rapid impact not just on US technology shares but throughout the world stock markets.

① 6.5 **The risk of individual securities**

So far we have considered only the risk of a well-diversified portfolio, but what of individual securities? The CAPM teaches that due to imperfect correlation of returns, not all of the risk of an individual security is relevant for assessing its risk premium because some of this can be diversified away. For single securities, the relevant risk is the systematic, market-related risk. An efficient capital market does not reward people for bearing the unsystematic, company-specific risk that rational investors would eliminate by portfolio diversification. Only the market-related risk is relevant.

The market risk of a single security is measured by its **Beta** value, which reflects the extent to which the percentage return (including both dividend and capital appreciation) on the security varies in response to, or in association with, variations in the overall market returns. Observations are made of variations in both stock and market returns over a period of time and a regression line is fitted to the resulting scatter of points. The slope of the line best fitting that scatter is called the Beta coefficient or simply Beta.

An example is given in Figure 6.3. The line of best fit – called the characteristics line – is found by the statistical technique of linear regression. Here, it slopes upwards from left to right, indicating that, as the return on the whole market increases, the return on the particular stock increases also. Notice that the strength of this relationship will vary between shares, e.g. a steep line would suggest that the return on the share in question would move in quite a pronounced way, possibly by more than the market itself.

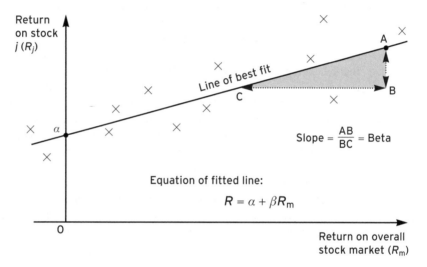

Figure 6.3 Finding the value of Beta

A share that moved in parallel with the market would have a characteristics line at 45 degrees to the origin, i.e. a slope of one. The intercept term α indicates the return on a particular stock, say, stock j, when the market return is zero, i.e. the average return expected independently of market movements. There is no reason why this is necessarily positive. In theory, it will diminish the longer the time period examined, as random influences are cancelled out, and security prices adjust to their equilibrium relationships.

Worked example

By plotting the following pairs of observations on a graph, determine the line of best fit and hence the Beta value. (You can do this by geometry or by using regression.)

Return on shares of XYZ	Return on whole stock market
12%	10%
5%	6%
30%	24%
24%	20%

Solution – the significance of the Beta value

You should find that the fitted line is a perfect fit with slope of 1.20; this is the beta of the share. The slope of a straight line, of course, indicates the rate of change of one variable (the supposedly dependent variable) with respect to changes in another one (the independent variable).

A Beta of 1.20 means that when the stock market offers a return of, say, 10 per cent, this security offers a return of 12 per cent, or when the return on the overall market changes by 10 per cent, the return on this security changes by 12 per cent. Hence, movements in the return on this stock exaggerate movements in the return on the market (in both directions!). When the Beta exceeds 1.0, such a stock is said to be **aggressive**. A **defensive** stock has a Beta of less than one. In this example, because every observation lies on the line of best fit, the variation in the return on share j is perfectly explained by market-related risk factors. Variations in the market return due to factors that affect all firms perfectly explain variations in the return on the company in question. In other words, all variation in returns is attributable to **systematic risk**. This is shown by Figure 6.4. Such a graph will occur when measuring the relationship between the market index and a unit trust, which will have diversified away all specific company risk.

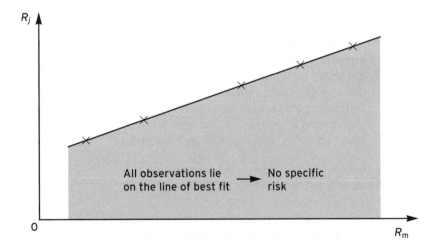

Figure 6.4 The case of no specific risk (unit trusts)

Variation due to specific risk

Variability in returns due to factors unique to the individual firm is shown by Figure 6.5. This sort of scatter of observations lying around the line of best fit results from sources of risk specific to the individual company operating alongside market risk factors. Points above the line, such as point A, represent times when the return on the company's shares exceeded their 'normal' return and there was an excess return resulting from some development particularly advantageous to the company in question. The reverse interpretation applies to points like B that lie beneath the line – bad news has depressed returns on the share.

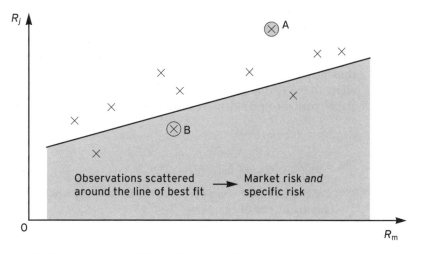

Figure 6.5 Security returns with specific risk (individual shares)

The distinction between specific risk and market risk is crucial. The CAPM assumes that investors are rational and will thus build efficiently diversified portfolios. As a result, they are unconcerned by, and therefore do not expect rewards for bearing, this specific risk. Their only concern is with the undiversifiable market risk, and in particular the extent to which the return on their investment is likely to vary with overall market returns. The size of the risk premium they require depends on how risky the shares they hold are relative to the market. This explains why market risk is also called relevant risk.

Self-assessment activity 6.5

Fill in the gaps in the table below.

FTSE 100 share market index	Share price of firm with Beta = 1.5	Share price of firm with Beta = 0.5
Today = 4,000	£2.00	£2.00
With a 10% rise to ??	??% rise/fall to ??	??% rise/fall to ??
With a 5% fall to ??	??% rise/fall to ??	??% rise/fall to ??

(answer at end of chapter)

Betas in practice

Several organisations, including the London Business School (LBS), calculate Beta values on a regular basis. The LBS publishes a quarterly *Risk Measurement Service* which gives the Beta values of all companies in the UK FT All Share Index. These Betas are based on monthly observations over the preceding five years and thus give 60 data points. An extract is shown in Table 6.1. The Betas shown apply to the FT Index of 30 leading ordinary shares. The Betas tend to be quite stable, period-to-period, as 57 observations are retained for each updating.

Self-assessment activity 6.6

What value would you expect for the Beta of the whole stock market?
(answer at end of chapter)

Notice that for these large companies, the Betas tend to cluster around 1.0, although the range is wide, extending from a low of 0.45 (Cadbury-Schweppes) to a high of 1.50 (Granada). Why do we observe this clustering?

The overall market has a Beta of 1.0 (because it is perfectly correlated with itself) and these large companies make up a significant part of the market index itself. In addition, many of these firms are usually well diversified in themselves – they tend to have eliminated a major part of their respective specific risks.

Table 6.1 LBS Beta values

Constituents of FT 30 SHARE

Company	Sector	Market value	Beta
Allied Domecq Holdings	BevDstVn	4,761	0.66
BAE Systems	Defence	10,227	1.07
BG Group	Oil Intg	10,077	0.61
BOC Group	ChemCom	5,065	0.76
Boots Co	Ret Dept	5,709	0.56
BP	Oil Intg	123,770	0.82
xBritish Airways	Air + Tran	2,017	1.48
BT Group	Telcomfx	21,850	1.24
Cadbury-Schweppes	FoodProc	10,104	0.45
Compass Group	Bus Supp	8,884	0.93
Diageo	BevDstVn	27,702	0.65
EMI Group	PublPrnt	1,964	1.27
GKN	AutoPrts	2,243	1.18
GlaxoSmithKline	Pharmact	86,101	0.53
Granada	Broadcst	3,087	1.50
Imperial Chemical Industries	ChemSpec	3,799	1.34
Invensys	Electrnc	3,115	1.42
Lloyds TSB group	Banks	36,456	1.30
Logica	Comp Svs	897	1.21
Marconi	TeleEqpt	112	1.43
Marks & Spencer Group	Ret Dept	8,602	0.68
Peninsular & Oriental 'Dfd'	Shipport	1,644	1.25
Prudential	Life Ass	11,974	0.94
xReuters Group	PublPrnt	4,984	1.30
xRoyal Bank of Scotland	Banks	53,708	1.09
Royal & Sun Alliance Ins Grp	InsNonLf	3,470	1.33
Scottish Power	Electric	6,537	0.54
Tate & Lyle	FoodProc	1,691	0.90
Tesco	FdrugRet	16,729	0.58
Vodafone Group	Telcomob	61,336	0.96

London Business School　　　　　　　　　　　　　　　July–September 2002

Source: London Business School Risk Measurement Service (2002)

6.6　The core of the CAPM: Security Market Line (SML)

We have discovered that Beta is an indicator of risk, in terms of the relative variability of the returns on a particular share in relation to the whole market. Firms with a Beta of one have a degree of risk identical to that of the market as a whole, i.e. they have average levels of risk and people would expect them to deliver returns over time similar to that of the market as a whole. However, there inevitably will be year-by-year variations as specific risk factors operate. But what of above- and below-average-risk shares?

The CAPM postulates a key condition for the equilibrium in an efficient capital market: all securities will plot along a linear relationship which is called the **Security Market Line** linking risk with return. This tells us two important things:

- the rate of return investors should require from securities of differing risks, and hence

- how large a risk premium (the return above the risk-free rate) should investors require of any share.

All financial markets exhibit a trade-off between risk and return – the higher the risk of the security, the higher the return required by investors. Taking Beta as the indicator of systematic risk, we expect to see the required return increasing as Beta rises. This relationship is traced out by the Security Market Line. Its equation is:

$$ER_j = R_f + \beta_j[ER_m - R_f]$$

where

ER_j = the rate of return that investors require on security j
R_f = return on a risk-free asset, such as government stock
ER_m = expected return on the overall market
β_j = Beta coefficient for security j

This tells us that the required return on the shares of a particular firm, firm j, is made up of two components, the risk-free rate and a risk premium. The risk

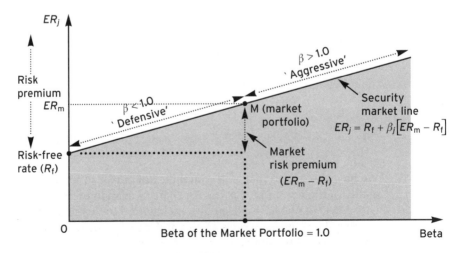

Figure 6.6 The Security Market Line (SML)

premium is made up of the Beta value of the share and the risk premium on the market as a whole. Notice that the content of the bracket is the risk premium on the overall market, i.e. the difference between the expected return on the market and the risk-free rate – it is not the overall market return.

The SML is shown in Figure 6.6. Notice that it originates from the return on the risk-free asset and passes through the benchmark market portfolio, M, which, of course, has a Beta of one. Securities with higher Betas are the aggressive ones and those lying to the left of the market portfolio are the defensive ones. The required return on aggressive securities will be higher than that for the market as a whole and vice versa for defensive securities.

Self-assessment activity 6.7

Delete as appropriate:

(i) For securities riskier than the whole market, the risk premium will be:
less than/the same as/more than that of the market.

(ii) For securities as risky as the whole market, the risk premium will be:
less than/the same as/more than that of the market.

(iii) For securities less risky than the whole market, the risk premium will be:
less than/the same as/more than that of the market.

(answer at end of chapter)

The key conclusions of the CAPM

We can now pinpoint the key lessons of the CAPM:

- Only the systematic risk of any share is relevant for assessing the rate of return required by shareholders – efficient markets do not offer a reward for bearing specific risk, since this can be diversified away by holding a portfolio of shares.

- The required return on a security depends on its relationship (as indicated by the Beta) with the return on the whole market. Securities that are relatively immune from general macro-economic factors have low Betas and thus command relatively low required rates of return, and conversely for those whose returns are more closely geared to these factors.

◎ 6.7 **Application - finding the required return**

To determine the return that people require from investing in a particular ordinary share, we need to know the following:

(i) Its Beta value.

(ii) The risk-free rate, usually taken to be the return on very short-dated government stock such as UK Treasury Bills. These pay no rate of interest as such, but are issued at a discount to their face values to financial institutions. They are repaid in full at maturity, the difference between the issue price and the amount repaid reflecting the 'profit' obtained from which a rate of return or yield can be calculated.

(iii) The expected return on the whole stock market. Generally, the historical return has been taken for this purpose, although the investor may prefer to take a (necessarily subjective) view on the future course of the market. Various studies have shown that this premium is remarkably similar from country to country, and over time. Notice that this is the premium above the risk-free return and that the results of the studies quoted report its value in net-of-inflation terms. In real terms, one might expect a risk premium above the risk-free rate of around 3–4 per cent. Many 'experts' even expected this to fall further during the early 2000s.

The interplay of these data is shown schematically in Figure 6.7.

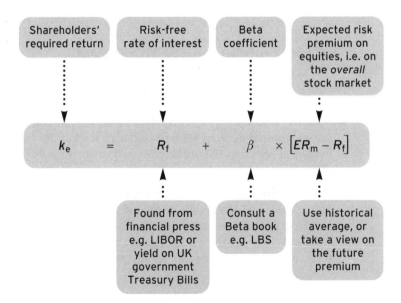

Figure 6.7 Using the CAPM to find the shareholders' required return

To illustrate the use of the LBS Beta tables from Table 6.1, let us select a firm, say Invensys, the electronic control systems group. Its Beta is shown as 1.42, indicating that the shares have above-average risk, i.e. they are more risky than the overall market. Obviously, the date of our calculation is important as both the Beta and risk-free rate may vary, but during the period to which these Beta data relate, the benchmark rate of interest in the London money market was 4 per cent, presumably with inflationary expectations built in.

The final piece of information required is the equity risk premium, i.e. the risk premium on the overall market. We could adopt a forward-looking perspective, indeed, that is what the CAPM requires, but it is usual to side-step the problem of estimation by taking the past risk premium. As shown in the cameo, the ABN AMRO data reveal this to have been 3.9 per cent for the London market.

Inserting these data into the CAPM formula, we obtain:

$$ER_j = R_f + \beta_j[ER_m - R_f] = 4\% + 1.42[3.9\%]$$

$$= (4\% + 5.4\%) = 9.4\%$$

Based partly on past experience at least, Invensys shareholders should require a rate of return of 9.4 per cent. Hence, this is the rate at which Invensys's managers should discount the cash flows from an all-equity-financed investment project with a degree of risk comparable to existing activities. (A qualification here is that we have assumed there is no debt in Invensys's capital structure so that the relatively high Beta of 1.42 reflects its relatively high activity risk rather than any financial risk.)

Projects that offer an IRR below 9.4 per cent will destroy value while those offering above this cut-off rate are wealth-creating.

Self-assessment activity 6.8

Fill in the gaps.

	Shareholders' required return	Risk-free rate	Beta	Equity premium
1	?	6%	1.2	7%
2	11.5%	?	1.3	5%
3	8.8%	3.4%	?	6%
4	12%	5%	1.0	?

(answer at end of chapter)

6.8 Tailoring the Beta value for new projects of varying risks

The calculation in the previous section is appropriate for finding the discount rate for evaluating cash flows from activities whose risk parallels the existing (systematic) risk of the company. For activities of differing degrees of risk, the Beta of a comparable company operating in the area of intended investment can be used. This is known as a *surrogate Beta*. If, for example, Invensys wanted to diversify into electricity generation, it might look at the Betas for firms such as Scottish Power that already operate in the relevant area. Scottish Power's Beta is 0.54, i.e. it is a defensive stock, very much less risky than the market as a whole. Using the CAPM formula again, we obtain:

$$ER_j = R_f + \beta_j[ER_m - R_f] = 4\% + 0.54[3.9\%]$$

$$= (4\% + 2.1\%) = 6.1\%$$

This calculation assumes that Invensys's putative electricity generation project carries the same degree of (systematic) risk as that of the whole of Scottish Power's business, and that the latter's own Beta is not influenced by gearing and financial risk.

In principle, firms should attempt to adjust the required return at which project cash flows are discounted by using a Beta value appropriate for each activity, rather than using a uniform discount rate for all projects. Doing the latter can generate serious errors that may lead to failure to maximise investor wealth. To demonstrate this, consider Figure 6.8 for a company with an assumed beta of 1.30.

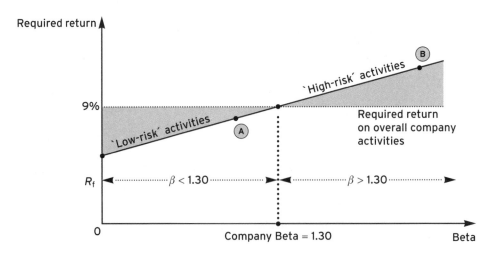

Figure 6.8 'Tailoring' the Beta value for particular activities

The firms' investment opportunities are arranged according to their systematic risk as indicated by the relevant Beta coefficients. The upward-sloping line parallels the SML found in the stock market. Notice that investment projects are separated into 'low-risk' and 'high-risk' categories using the firm's existing average risk, with Beta = 1.30 as the benchmark. Applying the Beta of 1.30, to the above CAPM formula gives a resulting required return on the shares of the firm of 9 per cent.

Consider now the projects indicated by points A and B, which refer to low-risk and high-risk projects respectively. If the average 9 per cent discount rate were applied, project A would be rejected as it offers a return below the standard, while B would be accepted as it offers an abnormal return, i.e. above the standard 9 per cent. But is this decision correct?

Looking at project B, this offers a rate of return above 9 per cent, but in view of its level of risk it should be offering rather more than this. The reverse argument applies to project A – it would be rejected, but it does offer a return compatible with its Beta. It therefore looks as if A might be acceptable. However, it can be argued that the firm has no business in undertaking low-risk activities such as A – if shareholders wanted this low exposure to risk, they could have bought the shares of firms that already operate in this area (although in reality, companies are likely to be invested in projects of different risks).

In summary, using a uniform discount rate might lead to mistakes in project selection. Projects in the right-hand shaded area, lying above the risk–return line, might be wrongly accepted, while those in the left-hand shaded area, lying below the line, might be wrongly rejected. The steeper the line, the greater the scope for error because these areas become larger.

The firm as a collection of activities

The previous section shows that different activities are likely to have different Betas. As a result, the Beta of the overall firm, that is the Beta of its shares, assuming it is all-equity financed, is a composite Beta, made up of the Betas of the component activities (i.e. its different investments). The firm's overall Beta is derived from a weighted average of the individual Betas of its component activities, with the weights reflecting the relative importance of each activity to the overall enterprise. In principle, market value weights should be used, but as there is no market for the shares of the firm's individual activities, some proxy measure of size has to be used, for example the book value of assets, or sales revenue.

The concept of the company Beta as a weighted average is brought out in the following worked example.

6.9 Worked example

Tieko plc is a diversified conglomerate that is financed entirely by equity. Its five activities and their respective shares of corporate assets are shown in the table below. Also shown are the Beta coefficients of very similar surrogate firms operating in the same markets as the Tieko divisions.

Division	% Share of book value of Tieko assets	Beta of a close substitute
Electronics	30	1.40
Property	20	0.70
Defence equipment	30	0.20
Durables	20	1.10

The yield on short-term government stock is currently 6 per cent, and people expect the stock market portfolio to deliver an average annual return of 12 per cent in future years.

Required

In each of the following (separate) cases, determine Tieko's company Beta and the return required by shareholders:

(i)   Now.

(ii) If Tieko sells the defence division for book value and returns the cash proceeds to shareholders as a special dividend.

(iii) If Tieko sells the defence division for book value and places the cash proceeds on deposit (assume this has a beta of zero).

(iv) If Tieko acquires a telecommunications firm that has a Beta of 1.60 and total assets equal in size to the defence division.

Solution

In each case, the Beta value is a weighted average of the Betas of the component activities, with each division's share of total assets providing the weights.

(i)   At present, the Beta is:

$$(0.3 \times 1.40) + (0.20 \times 0.70) + (0.30 \times 0.20) + (0.20 \times 1.05)$$
$$= (0.42 + 0.14 + 0.06 + 0.21) = 0.83$$

Using the CAPM formula, the required return is thus:

$$6\% + 0.83[12\% - 6\%] = (6\% + 5\%) = 11\%$$

(ii) If Tieko 'downsizes' to 70 per cent of its previous size, the weightings for the three remaining divisions become:

Electronics $\quad$ 3/7 = 0.429
Property $\quad$ 2/7 = 0.285
Durables $\quad$ 2/7 = 0.285

The overall Beta becomes:

$$(0.429 \times 1.40) + (0.285 \times 0.70) + (0.285 \times 1.05)$$
$$= (0.60 + 0.20 + 0.30) = 1.10$$

Clearly, Tieko has become more risky, and the required return increases to:

$$6\% + 1.10[12\% - 6\%] = 6\% + 6.6\% = 12.6\%$$

(iii) If it retains the cash, the total assets remain unchanged but the Beta will alter as the Beta of cash is zero – it is uncorrelated with the risky securities quoted on the stock market.
The overall Beta becomes:

$$(0.3 \times 1.40) + (0.20 \times 0.70) + (0.30 \times 0) + (0.20 \times 1.05)$$
$$= (0.42 + 0.14 + 0 + 0.21) = 0.77$$

Having disposed of its least risky division and replaced it with risk-free cash, Tieko has become much less risky. As a result, its overall required return decreases to:

$$6\% + 0.77[12\% - 6\%] = (6\% + 4.6\%) = 10.6\%$$

(iv) If Tieko expands by adding another division of equal size to the electronics arm, i.e. a 30 per cent expansion, the new weightings are:

Electronics $\quad$ 3/13 = 0.230
Property $\quad$ 2/13 = 0.154
Defence $\quad$ 3/13 = 0.230
Durables $\quad$ 2/13 = 0.154
Telecoms $\quad$ 3/13 = 0.230

The overall Beta becomes:

$$(0.230 \times 1.40) + (0.154 \times 0.70) + (0.230 \times 0.20) + (0.154 \times 1.05) + (0.230 \times 1.60)$$
$$= (0.322 + 0.108 + 0.046 + 0.162 + 0.368) = 1.006$$

The required return increases to:

$$6\% + 1.006[12\% - 6\%] = (6\% + 6\%) = 12\%$$

After this expansion, Tieko has a Beta very similar to that of the market portfolio (1.0). It has thus managed to diversify itself into a portfolio of activities of virtually average risk.

6.10 The equity premium in practice

Like the ABN AMRO/London Business School collaboration mentioned in the introductory cameo, Barclays Capital (www.barcap.com), the investment banking arm of Barclays Bank, also publishes an annual study of equity and gilt-edged returns for various time periods. The Barclays Capital data show real investment returns on both **equities** and on gilt-edged securities (government stock), and hence the equity premium being the difference between the two.

Like many observers, Barclays Capital suggests that, as the world economy moved from the low-growth/high-inflation phase of the 1970s and 1980s to the high-growth/low-inflation experienced more recently, equity returns were untypically high in the 1990s. One reason for expecting lower future returns is technological progress in general, and the information revolution in particular, resulting in shorter competitive advantage periods. Firms typically have less time to exploit a first mover's advantage before competitors arrive, i.e. entry barriers are lower. Another likely depressant is the increased openness of the world economy due to the influence of the World Trade Organisation.

Table 6.2 Equity versus **gilts**: relative returns

	UK			USA		
Period	Equities	Gilts	Equity premium	Equities	Gilts	Equity premium
1925–2001	6.3	1.9	4.4	7.2	2.2	5.0
1925–1946	6.0	5.7	0.3	5.0	3.5	1.5
1946– 91	5.9	–1.2	7.1	7.7	0.7	7.0
92	6.1	–0.8	6.9	7.7	0.8	6.9
93	6.5	–0.3	6.8	7.7	1.1	6.6
94	6.2	–0.6	6.8	7.5	0.9	6.6
95	6.4	–0.3	6.7	8.0	1.3	6.7
96	6.6	0.1	6.7	8.5	1.5	7.0
97	6.8	0.1	6.7	8.5	1.5	7.0
98	6.9	0.5	6.4	8.7	1.6	7.1
99	7.1	0.3	6.8	9.0	1.4	7.6
2000	6.8	0.4	6.4	8.5	1.6	6.9
2001	6.4	0.5	5.9	8.1	1.7	6.4

Source: Barclays Capital (www.barcap.com)

The Barclays Capital website carries an interactive facility that allows users to calculate average annual returns for specified periods for the UK markets for any period over 1919 to date, and from 1925 to date for the USA. Table 6.2 shows some sample calculations for long periods and a year-by-year analysis from 1946 through to the 1990s and early 2000s for both countries. The data are *real* geometric average annualised returns, i.e. they exclude the effect of inflation. Note the remarkable similarity between UK and US premia.

The data suggest that, in latter years, equity premia in both countries have been high in relation to longer-term outcomes and are tending to fall due to the bear markets of 2000–2001. One might conclude that although 2000 and 2001 were poor years, pulling down the rolling average, there appears to be little solid evidence in these data of a sea-change in the equity risk premium. However, conventional wisdom is that the risk premium for equities, i.e. the risk premium of the overall market portfolio, will be lower in future years.

The ABN AMRO data largely corroborate these figures for the equity risk premium for 16 countries, over a full century (1900–2002). They suggest that some earlier studies might have overestimated the equity premium by excluding the First World War era when equity returns were poor, and by confining the study to performance of surviving firms, thus excluding relatively poor performers that expired.

The ABN AMRO study found:

- the average global real return on equity was 4.6 per cent

- Australia had offered the highest risk premium at 6.0 per cent

- Denmark offered the lowest risk premium at just 1.6 per cent

- in the USA, for every 20-year period examined, equities outperformed bonds

- only four countries – German, the Netherlands, Sweden and Switzerland – exhibited any 20-year periods over which bonds outperformed equities.

It is reasonable to expect a lower equity premium in the UK in the future. The ABN authors put this at 3 per cent p.a. Legions of investors throughout the world are hoping this is unduly pessimistic.

6.11 Summary

This chapter has examined two approaches to assessing the shareholders' required return, namely the Dividend Valuation Model and the Capital Asset Pricing Model. The former looks at the equity cost facing the firm as a whole, as does the CAPM itself, but the CAPM is also capable of specifying risk premia for specific activities. The chapter has also presented evidence regarding the behaviour of the equity premium over time. Chapter 9 will examine how the required return may be affected when the firm uses a mixture of financing methods.

References

Textbooks

Arnold – ch 8.
Bearley & Myers – chs 7 & 9.
Pike & Neale – chs 10, 11, 12.
Samuel, Wilkes & Brayshaw – ch 11.
Watson & Head – ch 9.

Other

ABN AMRO (2003) Global Investment Returns Yearbook.
Brooks, R and Catao, I (2000) 'The New Economy and Global Stock Returns', IMF
    Working Paper 216, December.
Dimson, E, Marsh, P and Staunton, M *Triumph of the Optimists* (Princeton University Press).
Kaplanis, E (1997) 'Benefits and costs of international portfolio investments', in *Financial
    Times Mastering Finance* (FT/Pitman Publishing).
Risk Measurement Service, London Business School, published quarterly.
Solnik, B H (1974) 'Why not diversify internationally rather than domestically?',
    Financial Analysts Journal, July/August, pp. 48–54.

Questions

1 (a) The following information is given to you about the stock market and the
        shares of Hedman plc.

The average stock market return on equity	13%
The risk-free rate of return	6%
Dividend yield	2.9%
Share price rise (capital gain)	15%
Current dividend per share	10p
Expected growth of future dividends	10% p.a.

Required
Calculate:

(i)   The market required return for Hedman plc's shares using the CAPM.

(ii) An estimate of the current share price of Hedman plc according to the
      dividend growth model, incorporating information from the above
      table and your answer to question (i).

(b) Magnus has just inherited £50,000 and he wants to invest £40,000 in the stock market. He has decided to put his money in the following three shares in the following proportions:

Share	β	Proportion of funds to be invested
Hedman plc	your answer to (a)(i) above	50%
James	1.0	25%
Seaman	0.7	25%

Using the information given above, and in part (a) as appropriate:

(i)   Calculate the β of Magnus's portfolio.

(ii) Calculate the expected return of this portfolio.

(iii) Advise Magnus about the way he intends to invest his inheritance.

2 Mr Hartson currently invests 50 per cent of his savings in a risk-free investment and 50 per cent in the following four shares as detailed below:

Share	Expected return	β of share	Invested in share
A	7.6%	0.2	10%
B	12.4%	0.8	10%
C	15.6%	1.2	10%
D	18.8%	1.6	20%

Required

(a) Using the Capital Asset Pricing Model and assuming that all of the above shares are on the Security Market Line, calculate:
- the risk-free rate of return
- the return on the market
- the current β of Hartson's total portfolio
- the expected return on his portfolio.

(b) Assume Hartson seeks an expected return of 12 per cent and intends to obtain it by selling some of the risk-free investment and using the proceeds to invest in the market portfolio. What proportions must be invested in the risk-free asset and the market portfolio to earn a 12 per cent return, assuming that the investment in shares A, B, C and D remain unaltered?

(c) Discuss how useful the Capital Asset Pricing Model is in practice for investors such as Mr Hartson. In particular, what are its possible limitations?

3 (a) 'Unit trusts offer the investor a diversified portfolio so that he can avoid the risk of investing in just one share.'
Discuss this statement in the context of portfolio theory and the CAPM.

(b) Mr Chippo currently invests 50 per cent of his savings in risk-free government securities and 50 per cent in the following two unit trusts:

Unit trust	Expected return	β of unit trust	Invested in trust
A	13%	1.0	25%
B	16.5%	1.5	25%

Using the Capital Asset Pricing Model and assuming that each of these trusts are on the Security Market Line, calculate:
- the risk-free rate of return
- the return on the market
- the current β of Mr Chippo's total portfolio
- the expected return on his total portfolio.

(c) 'Last year I bought some shares. The returns have not been as predicted by the CAPM.' Give reasons why this is likely to be the case. Does this mean that the CAPM has no value?

4 Comment on each of the following statements:

(i) 'Unsystematic risk is irrelevant to investors'.

(ii) 'Beta is the only factor influencing returns'.

(iii) 'The risk of an individual share will tend to be higher than the risk of the market as a whole'.

Self-assessment answers

6.1
(i) The real rate of interest is given by the formula encountered in Chapter 5, viz:

$$R = [(1+m)/(1+p)] - 1 = [(1+6\%)/(1+2.7\%)] - 1 = 1.032 - 1, \text{ i.e. } 3.2\%$$

(ii) To match past performance, investors would look for a return of (6% + 5%) = 11% to cover the time value of money (3.2 per cent), inflation (2.7 per cent) and the equity risk premium of 5 per cent. Strictly, the answer is found by compounding, i.e.

$$(1.06)(1.05) - 1 = 1.113 - 1 = 0.113 \quad \text{i.e. } 11.3\%$$

6.2

Assuming 117p is the ex-dividend price.

$$\text{Substituting:}\quad k_e = \frac{5p(1.035)}{117p} + 0.035 = (4.4\% + 3.5\%) = 7.9\%$$

By implication, 7.9 per cent is the cost of equity, the rate of return required by investors.

6.3

To eliminate all of the specific risk, the investor would have to hold every stock quoted on the market, which is infeasible for the major markets, at least. To capture the 'lion's share' (90 per cent +) of the benefits of diversification, it is thought that holding 25–30 stocks, drawn from a variety of industrial sectors, is sufficient.

6.4

This would signify that the fluctuations in returns stemmed from two sources – variation along the line resulting from market-related factors (systematic risk), and variations around the line resulting from factors specific to the firm in question.

6.5

FTSE 100 share market index	Share price of firm with Beta = 1.5	Share price of firm with Beta = 0.5
Today = 4,000	£2.00	£2.00
With 10% rise to 4,400	15% rise to £2.30	5% rise to £2.10
With 5% fall to 3,800	7.5% fall to £1.85	2.5% fall to £1.95

6.6

The overall market has a Beta of 1.0 because it is perfectly correlated with itself.

6.7

(i)   more than

(ii) the same as

(iii) less than

6.8

1 14.4%

2 5%

3 0.9

4 7%

7

WORKING CAPITAL MANAGEMENT

Objectives:
By the end of this chapter, you should be able to:

- understand what working capital is, and why firms require it

- understand the principles of working capital management

- understand different strategies for investing in working capital assets

- understand different strategies for financing working capital

- investigate the role of working capital management in financial planning

- analyse the key components of the cash operating cycle and how to manage them.

As with some earlier chapters, the self-assessment activities make reference to the accounts of the 'company of your choice' – it will be useful to have its report and accounts to hand.

 ## 7.1 Introduction

The impact of higher liquidity on value is brought out clearly in the cameo. Alcatel was forced to turn its attention away from long-term planning to repair the previous neglect of another important determinant of value – effective working capital management.

You will remember that two of the key decision areas of financial management – and hence the fundamental drivers of value – are *investment decisions* and *financing decisions*. These decisions involve deciding what to spend and how to pay for it. So far, we have focused on long-term investments. Our attention in this chapter now shifts towards investment in short-term assets – cash, stock and debtors – and how to finance them. We will also explore the relationship between long-term and short-term financing and stress the role of efficient working capital management in pursuit of shareholder value.

In many firms, working capital management is a part of the overall function of the treasury department, which exercises responsibility for managing the cash inflows and outflows of the whole enterprise. While working capital management and treasury management are not totally synonymous, it will be useful to outline the role of the treasury to see how working capital management can contribute to sound treasury management. But first, we need to define working capital.

7.2 What is working capital?

The term working capital, and its location on a balance sheet, will be familiar to readers who have followed a course in accounting. Essentially, working capital refers to the items required to keep the firm working on a daily basis and, in monetary terms, the investment required to obtain these items.

It will help to give some more definitions.

Gross working capital = current assets

(Net) working capital = current assets less current liabilities
= net current assets

Current assets (also known as short-term assets or liquid assets)
= assets expected to be converted into cash within a year

Current liabilities (often shown in a balance sheet under the heading 'creditors due for payment within one year')
= financial obligations expected to be settled within a year

The main components of current assets and current liabilities are as follows:

Current assets	Current liabilities
Inventories/stocks:	Trade creditors/accounts payable
– raw materials	Taxation payable
– work-in-progress	Proposed dividends
– finished goods	**Bank overdraft**
Debtors/accounts receivable	Other short-term loans
Prepayments	Accrued expenses
Short-term investments	
Cash/bank balances	

Self-assessment activity 7.1

Consult the report and accounts of your chosen company. Identify the current assets and liabilities, and hence net current assets, and also examine the composition of both current assets and current liabilities. How much money is tied up in the company's working capital?

Why do firms invest in working capital?

On the asset side, there are usually sound reasons for investing in working capital. In particular:

- cash provides liquidity
- stock (of raw materials and finished goods) gives the ability to meet orders
- giving credit to customers (who then become debtors) encourages demand.

Self-assessment activity 7.2

A language question! Find out what the Americans call stock, debtors and creditors.
(answer at end of chapter)

However, each of these investments has an opportunity cost – investing in these items ties up resources that could be used elsewhere. Sound working capital management needs to balance the benefits of this investment with its cost. This tension between the benefits of investment and the costs of financing is a recurrent theme in the study of working capital management. Recognising the amount of money tied up in working capital items, cash-conscious firms regard working capital as an active decision area, one with implications for value creation. Having too much working capital investment impairs the ability to create value, and having too little may jeopardise the survival of the business.

We examine investment in each of the main items of working capital investment. We will also look at the case of trade creditors which represents *negative* investment in working capital. As we will see, movements in all of these items impact on the firm's cash position, i.e. its liquidity. It is, therefore, appropriate to examine cash management in general before looking at its components.

 ## 7.3 Investment in cash

Why should businesses invest in cash?

The great economist J M Keynes identified three main reasons why firms (and individuals) need to hold cash, what he called the 'demand for money':

(a) *The transactions motive* – cash is required for day-to-day business transactions

(b) *The precautionary motive* – a certain amount of cash needs to be kept as 'just in case' money, i.e. to meet any unforeseen contingencies.

(c) *The speculative motive* – a business holds cash balances in case attractive business opportunities arise. Sir Arnold Weinstock, when chairman of GEC (now Marconi) in the UK, used to maintain a £2 billion cash balance, well above the level required for regular business transactions, for precisely this reason. This may also be a reason why Microsoft is so liquid, holding over $40 billion cash and short-term investments on its balance sheet in early 2003.

Cash provides a pool of liquidity to smooth the sequence of business payments and receipts that occur unevenly over time. For example, cash is required to meet payments while the business is awaiting receipts. It is critical for businesses always to have sufficient cash (or access to cash) in order to meet payments as they arise. If a business cannot pay a creditor when the money is due, the creditor may seek legal redress which may lead to the business being wound up, however 'profitable' that business is. Many profitable businesses go into liquidation through a lack of cash.

We can state the balance of cost and risk regarding cash as follows:

The opportunity cost of too much cash occurs when the

investment in cash earns less interest than the firm's overall cost of finance

The risk of too little cash, however, is clear:

illiquidity can destroy even a profitable business.

Cash management systems

Because the management of cash flow is so critical, firms employ cash budgets and other methods to help them plan the amount and the timing of future cash inflows and outflows. Cash needs for the upcoming year can be assessed by compiling an overall cash budget from the sales, production, administration and capital expenditure budgets within the firm.

Essentially, cash is obtained from operating activities subject to the vagaries of customer payment and supplier settlement schedules. If there is a shortfall between internal cash generation and cash needs, the firm has to utilise the financial markets to plug the gap.

Cash budgets enable businesses to plan and anticipate:

(i)   surpluses which can be invested short term

and/or

(ii) strategies to improve cash flow

and/or

(iii) deficits which need to be financed.

(i) Investment of surpluses

Surpluses can be invested to earn interest rather than being kept in the form of cash balances in call accounts that typically pay minimal interest. Possible short-term investments include:

- investment in bank deposits
- investment in short-, medium- and long-term government securities

- investment in commercial securities (such as commercial paper and certificates of deposit).

However, there are important factors to consider when investing cash for the short term:

- **Matching** – businesses must ensure that the time period of the investment matches the time when the cash is required.

- *Yield curve* – this curve shows the term structure of interest rates and is used to anticipate future interest rates. As we will see later in the chapter, this is likely to influence decisions such as whether to invest in (or borrow using) fixed or variable interest rate securities.

- *Risk* – different investments carry different risks. It is probably not advisable to save for next year's summer holiday by investing all your savings in ordinary shares.

- *Transaction costs* – investing often incurs transaction costs, particularly when purchasing securities. This will deter small investments in securities where the cash available is swallowed up in charges.

- *Liquidity* – businesses must ensure that cash is not tied up in an investment that cannot be redeemed when the cash is required.

(ii) Strategies to improve cash flow

If a deficit is looming, the immediate reaction of most businesses is to try to 'rearrange' future cash flows. In particular, can revenues be collected earlier or, perhaps more likely, can expenditures be deferred?

(iii) Financing deficits

If future short-term deficits are still expected despite rearranging cash flows as far as possible, the firm should plan for the financing of this deficit. Drawing up a budget allows this to be done well in advance of the deficit actually occurring. If the business waits until the last minute, it risks being unable to find the necessary finance, with potentially terminal consequences. Some possible sources of short-term finance include:

- *Bank* **overdraft**: many businesses arrange an overdraft facility with their banks, up to certain agreed limits.

- **Trade credit**: most business purchases are on credit terms.

- **Operating leases**: these are usually short-term leases which allow businesses to lease assets rather than buy them.

- *Hire purchase*: this is a way of spreading out the cost of equipment purchase over time.

- **Factoring** *and* **invoice discounting**: this is a way of turning debtors into cash by selling them to a factor, usually a subsidiary of a commercial bank.

- *Commercial paper*: large companies can sell commercial paper (effectively, IOUs) to financial institutions as a means of short-term borrowing.

Effective cash management can enhance the business in many ways. In the following example, a leading computer chip maker added value to the firm by reducing the rate at which it was using up cash.

State of the Arc

The share price of Arc International plc was boosted in December 2002 after the UK-based chip design group announced that it would return £50 million to shareholders, stating that it expected full-year performance to be in line with expectation. Analysts' consensus estimates were for a loss of £20 million on sales of £12 million, according to Multex Global Estimates.

Arc International, forced earlier into issuing two profits warnings and a change of management after being hit by the semi-conductor industry downturn, said it was making 'meaningful progress' towards achieving break-even before interest, tax, depreciation and amortisation, although it did not give a date for reaching this target.

The decision to return funds to shareholders during 2003 followed a strategic review at the company, which found that Arc had 'more than sufficient working capital funding to bring the group to profitability on the basis of reasonably prudent assumptions'.

At the end of the third quarter, Arc had £108 million net cash, and a cash-burn rate of only £4 million a quarter, meaning it would have had enough cash for the next seven years even without reaching profitability.

Returning part of the cash, Arc said, would improve the company's capital structure and enhance shareholders' potential for future returns.

Source: Information from Arc International Investor Update 2002

The corporate treasury

Treasury management encompasses the management of all cash transactions and is an important and well-paid job in many organisations. Firms realise that cash flow needs careful management and is a necessary (but not sufficient) requirement for survival. In valuing businesses, the market will look carefully at cash flow as it is difficult to manipulate.

Many companies now operate a dedicated treasury department that reports to the finance director. The range of functions will vary between companies, but typically treasury functions cover the following areas:

- *Cash and liquidity management* – forecasting the firm's cash inflows and outflows, and arranging to invest any temporary surpluses in appropriate ways or to secure additional funds if necessary.

- *Credit management* – the scrutiny of the creditworthiness of both old and new customers, domestic and national, and adoption of methods to secure quick and predictable payment to benefit cash flow.

- *Managing banking relationships* – arranging credit limits and generally ensuring that lines of credit are available as required.

- *Corporate finance* – raising short and long-term funds, bearing in mind the firm's overall profile of assets and liabilities. Most firms try to achieve a match between the life span of assets and the maturity of liabilities.

- *Interest rate risk management* – to avoid being caught out by unexpected increases in the costs of borrowing, firms use a variety of devices, including derivative products.

- *Foreign exchange risk management* – unexpected adverse foreign exchange rate movements have the capacity to inflict great losses on companies, but there are many devices available to restrict, if not eliminate, the downside.

- *Tax planning* – tax avoidance is not illegal – companies and individuals are entitled to arrange their financial affairs in order to minimise their tax obligations. Some UK taxes, such as employees' income tax, are paid to the Inland Revenue weekly or monthly, but other obligations, like value added tax and corporation tax, are paid quarterly or annually. To meet these obligations clearly requires liquidity.

Treasury management in practice

Viridian plc (formerly Northern Ireland Electricity plc) operates a dedicated treasury department. The following extract gives a clear indication of the work of this unit.

'As the Group has developed, treasury management has become more complex and diversified. The primary role of the Group's centralised Treasury operations is to manage liquidity, funding, investment and the Group's financial risk from volatility in currency and interest rates and counterparty credit risk. The Treasury operation is not a profit centre and its objective is to manage risk at optimum cost. It operates within policies and procedures approved by the Board and controlled by the Group Finance Director.

> The Treasury operation employs a continuous forecasting and
> monitoring process to ensure that the Group complies with its
> banking and other financial covenants. All Treasury operations and
> future planned activities are identified in a monthly Treasury report
> to the Group Finance Director.'
>
> *Source*: Viridian plc annual report 2001/2002 (www.viridiangroup.co.uk)

The case for centralised cash management

Treasuries are centralised cash management units. Because of the increasing recognition of the importance of measuring cash flow, most big companies now choose to centralise their cash management as a more efficient alternative than operating a decentralised system. Particular advantages of a centralised system include better management via the ability to take an overview of the whole firm's liquidity, more flexible management, obtaining better terms from banks when borrowing or lending, and the ability to operate at lower cash levels than might otherwise be the case, hence reducing the opportunity cost of cash to the business. It also tends to improve communication within the company. Data accuracy is vital so that everyone knows, for example, whether or not a customer has paid a particular account. Reports on such things as customer payment histories, the speed of collection and the level of bad debts can improve future working capital management.

Some firms have chosen to outsource several treasury functions to specialist institutions that can mobilise more concentrated expertise and relationships. Two institutions that offer specialist services are the Chase Manhattan Bank with Chase Treasury Solutions which, in 2000, took over the global cash management operations of Japanese motor manufacturer Nissan; and the Dutch bank ING's specialist unit ING Barings Treasury Consultancy Desk, operating in Amsterdam. Increasingly, such specialised units are offering internet-based systems to simplify and speed up clients' cash management.

Regardless of whether the firm has a dedicated treasury department or outsources its cash management, there is no question that efficient cash flow management is a major ingredient of working capital management, and thus enhances value, not to mention the firm's ability to survive.

7.4 Investment in stock

Why should businesses invest in stock (USA : 'inventory')?

Quite simply, stock allows businesses to meet customer orders rapidly. For this reason, businesses can carry stocks of raw materials, partly manufactured goods (work-in-progress) and finished goods. The level of investment in stock depends on anticipated demand and/or production schedules and the reliability of supply.

Like all areas of working capital management, stock control is a question of balancing the costs of holding stock against the benefits. The benefits are obvious – without stocks, it is difficult to make sales. The costs of holding high levels of stocks include the interest lost in tying up capital in such assets, the costs of storing, insuring, managing and protecting stock from theft and deterioration, and obsolescence. Stock is the least liquid current asset.

Against this, there are costs involved in holding low levels of stocks or running out of stock, or *stock-outs*:

- loss of goodwill from failure to deliver by the date specified by customers

- lost production and disruption due to unavailability of essential items

- more frequent re-order costs (buyer's and storekeeper's time, telephone, postage, invoice-processing costs, etc).

Stock management systems

A coherent stock control policy should specify, for important items, the appropriate timing for stock replenishments, re-order quantities, levels of safety (or 'buffer') stock and the implications of being out of stock. One of the simplest ways of managing stock is the *ABC system*. This divides a company's inventory into three groups according to the item's importance to sales value. Category A items are selected for closest attention in the form of regular forecasting and monitoring and holding of generous levels of safety stock. The approach to Category B items would be less intense, with looser monitoring, while for Category C items more risks might be taken.

Computer systems to monitor stock balances

As with cash, computers can be widely employed in stock control. For example, they can be used to monitor ABC systems. Computerised stock control can be seen in action at supermarkets as purchases are passed over bar-code reading machines. These machines not only produce the bill, they also inform the store management of what stock is being sold which will trigger replenishment on the shelves, and new orders from suppliers.

A more sophisticated approach is to construct a model of stock management which gives clear decision recommendations regarding stockholding periods, timing of replenishments and appropriate re-order quantities. One of these is the **Economic order quantity (EOQ) model**.

In its simplest form, it assumes a single item of stock, immediate stock replenishment when required, and a constant rate of usage. The model calculates the amount of stock that should be ordered at any time that will minimise the holding costs (such as storage and insurance) and the costs of ordering (especially the cost of administration). For example, where storage costs are high (such as specialised chemicals), it is likely to be better to order small amounts on a frequent basis. Conversely, if ordering costs are expensive, the advice may be to order large amounts infrequently. The following formula calculates the EOQ from these variables:

$$EOQ = \sqrt{\frac{2CD}{H}}$$

where D = annual demand
            C = fixed cost of an order
            H = holding cost of one unit p.a.

To illustrate how the model works, consider the following example. XYZ plc uses 2,000 units of a particular component each year. The interest and storage costs of holding a single unit for a year are £2, and the cost of placing each order is £45.
     The optimal order size, Q is:

$$Q = \sqrt{\frac{2 \times 2,000 \times £45}{£2}} = \sqrt{90,000} = 300 \text{ units}$$

The conclusion of the EOQ model is that efficient stock control involves ordering 300 units each time an order is placed. This requires placing (2,000/300) = 6.66 orders per calendar year, or one order about every 55 days.

Self-assessment activity 7.3

What is the EOQ when:

Annual demand = 10,000 units; holding cost = 25p per unit; order cost = £50 per order?
(answer at end of chapter)

Managing the risk of stock-outs

Two weaknesses of the EOQ model are, first, its assumption of constant demand and hence usage, and second, its failure to quantify the loss of goodwill in a stock-out. In the example, the company uses 2,000 units a year, or 8 per working day, assuming a working year of (50 weeks × 5 days per week) = 250 days. If the 'lead time' (the average time suppliers take from the day of the order to supply the business) averages 10 days, this company could re-order its EOQ of 300 units when its existing stock levels fall to 80. On average, in the 10 days before the supplies arrive, the firm will use 80 units and will replenish stock just as the level falls to zero.

However, this is a risky strategy. If daily usage averages more than 8, or if the supplier takes more than 10 days, the firm will run out of stock with all of the accompanying costs. As a result, companies in this position should hold a **safety stock** and re-order when stock falls to the safety stock level. How much safety stock to hold depends on the holding costs of the extra stock compared with the reduced risk and the costs of a stock-out.

Another way of avoiding stock-outs is to develop an intimate relationship with suppliers, known as a **just-in-time (JIT)** agreement. The main purpose of JIT purchasing is to compress as far as physically possible the time period elapsing between delivery and use of materials and components. In extreme cases, this can involve new deliveries being transferred direct to the production line from the receiving bay. The concept is not new, having been applied, for example, in the delivery of building materials (such as ready-mixed concrete) for many years. However, JIT has increasingly been applied in recent years to a wider range of manufacturing, assembly and retail activities.

The essence of JIT is close co-operation between user and supplier. The supplier is required to guarantee product quality and reliability of delivery while the user offers the assurance of firmer long-term sales and contracts. Firms tend to concentrate their purchasing on fewer suppliers (and perhaps only a single one), thus enabling the latter to achieve greater scale economies and efficiency in production planning.

The user would expect to achieve savings in materials handling, inventory investment and store-keeping costs since (ideally) supplies will now move directly from unloading bay to the production line. If JIT operates efficiently, it effectively precludes the need for stock control, although the receiving company must ensure efficiency in receipt and handling of supplies, as well as prompt payment to suppliers in order to retain their goodwill.

Nissan, the Japanese car manufacturer, objected to the proposed development of a new football stadium for Sunderland FC in the north-east of England because it would require rerouting of a road, adding to the time it would take for supplies to reach its factory. Nissan's objection was accepted – Nissan is a large employer in the area – and the football club had to look for an alternative site.

Stock management at Amazon

Amazon.com has changed its approach to stock since its early development as a dotcom star in the early 1990s. Its original business model involved the company holding zero stock as orders from the site were met directly from the stocks of the various book and CD suppliers that it used. However, in 1999, in order to improve the speed of distribution, Amazon spent $300 million on 12 warehouses throughout the USA and a huge 750,000 sq ft warehouse in Milton Keynes in central England.

> However, this new strategy for stock hit problems quite quickly. Dazzled by the dotcom share ramp of the late 1990s, fuelling unrealistically high expectations of future growth, Amazon had overstocked, requiring a $39 million stock write-off. Adoption of more traditional stockholding strategies brought with it the more traditional stockholding problems.

7.5 Investment in debtors

Why should businesses invest in debtors (USA : 'accounts receivable')?

Quite simply, offering credit encourages customers. Indeed, many businesses compete for customers with the ease and the amount of credit they are willing to offer – interest-free periods or 'nothing to pay' periods are common, particularly for large purchases such as furniture.

Debtor management systems

Once again, there is a balance – between having high investment in debtors to encourage sales and profit, and the catch that debtors inflict opportunity costs. Debtors represent tied-up funds unavailable for investment elsewhere in the business. Investment in debtors also introduces an added risk – that the customers may fail to pay, thus becoming 'bad debtors.' This imposes an obvious cost.

Most firms operate various debtor management procedures that determine both the terms of sale – amount of cash discount, period of credit given, amount of credit given – and the control of credit via their collection policy.

Offering customers credit adds to costs and to risk. However, it is important to remember that financial management, including debtor management, is concerned with adding value, not minimising risk. If offering credit gives the prospect of more sales and higher cash flows, this must be set against the extra costs and dangers.

Cost-benefit analysis of credit policies

Credit policies balance the cost of the policy (such as the cost of credit, including discounts) with the extra cash flow from the extra sales attracted by the credit offering. We will look at two simple credit policies commonly adopted by firms to demonstrate this trade-off – **cash discounts** and **longer credit periods**.

1 Offering a cash discount

A firm has annual credit sales of £365,000 (i.e. £1,000 per day) and average debtors of £20,000. Hence, its debtors take an average 20 days to pay. The formula to measure this *average debtor collection period* is:

$$\frac{\text{Closing debtor figure}}{\text{Average daily sales}} = \frac{£20,000}{(£365,000 \div 365)} = 20 \text{ days}$$

The calculation can also be used to work out the average debtor collection in weeks or in months, using weekly or monthly sales respectively instead of daily sales.

If a 5 per cent cash discount is now offered for payment within ten days, and half of the firm's customers take advantage of this, this will reduce the level of debtors to:

$$\left(\tfrac{1}{2} \times \frac{£365,000}{365} \times 10 \text{ days}\right) + \left(\tfrac{1}{2} \times \frac{£365,000}{365} \times 20 \text{ days}\right)$$

$$= (£5,000 + £10,000) = £15,000 \text{ (i.e. a cut of £5,000)}$$

This reduction in debtors does not in itself affect the overall value of the business – one would expect the reduction in the debtors to be matched by an increase in cash. However, a significant benefit ensues – the company can now invest this extra £5,000 and earn a return. If the company can invest at 6 per cent p.a., this £5,000 can earn £300 p.a.

That is the upside. However, the cost of the discount itself must now be matched against this benefit.

$$\text{Annual cost of discount} = 5\% \times (\tfrac{1}{2} \times £365,000) = £9,125$$

Since this is greater than the benefit of £300, this policy would apparently not be recommended on profitability grounds.

However, there could be two further benefits to consider – a more generous discount might attract customers, and by getting customers to pay earlier, the amount of bad debts could fall.

Self-assessment activity 7.4

What is the interest saving if a firm manages to cut its debtor days from 90 to 65 on annual sales of £2 million? It can borrow at 12 per cent p.a. (answer at end of chapter)

2 Extending the credit period

Consider a firm with the following characteristics:

Annual sales:	£520,000
Contribution to profit:	60% gross profit margin
Average collection period	7 weeks
Cost of finance	12%

It now introduces an extended credit policy giving customers longer to pay. The average debtor collection period is expected to rise to nine weeks. No discounts are offered. As a result, sales are expected to increase by 10 per cent, but bad debts will occur at the rate of 1 per cent of sales revenue.

Financial benefits
Increase in sales = (10% × £520,000) = £52,000
Increase in contribution @ 60% = £31,200

Financial costs
The level of debtors will increase. At present, the average is seven weeks' collection, i.e. debtors are equivalent to seven weeks' sales. By value of sales, this is:

$$7 \times \frac{£520,000}{52} = (7 \times £10,000) = £70,000$$

If debtors rise to nine weeks' worth of the new weekly sales level (£520,000 plus 10%) = £572,000, the average amount invested in debtors rises to:

$$9 \times \frac{£572,000}{52} = (9 \times £11,000) = £99,000$$

Thus, debtors increase by £29,000. The extra annual cost of financing debtors is:

$$(£29,000 \times 12\%) = £3,480$$

The cost of bad debts is (1% × £572,000) = £5,720.
 The net benefit is:

Extra profit from the increase in sales		£31,200
Costs:		
Financing cost of higher level of debtors	(£3,480)	
Cost of bad debts	(£5,720)	
		(£9,200)
Net benefit		£22,000

This policy is clearly worthwhile.

The elements of credit control

Application for credit

Whenever anyone applies for credit or a credit facility such as a credit card, the provider will carry out some form of financial analysis to assure themselves that the borrower will be able to repay any loans. The same applies when a business asks another for credit. The main variables determining whether credit will be granted are:

- the past financial record of the credit seeker

- the current financial position, e.g. the accounts for a business

- references from credit agencies or banks.

Lenders will apply some form of numerical credit scoring system to determine the type and amount of credit to extend. Assessment of future prospects often lies behind decisions to give credit. After all, one bad debt can wipe out the profit earned from many customers who do pay on time. Giving credit to attract customers makes sense when the prospect of the good customers continuing to buy is there. A bad debt will cost money only once; good customers may provide profit over their many repeat orders.

Collection policy

Once credit is given, accounts need to be closely monitored. A structured approach to eventual collection is required. This approach is likely to include:

- sending regular statements of account

- sending letters if any payment time is missed

- phone calls enquiring about any overdue amounts

- personal visits if the outstanding debt is becoming a cause for concern

- legal action, or use of a collection agency, if recovery proves difficult.

Companies must concentrate on the dangerous accounts. Part of this monitoring may involve adjusting the amount of credit given – in extreme cases, all new credit facilities could be withdrawn. Lenders will not seek legal redress as soon as a payment period is missed – often, even in extreme cases, the lender's best option is to allow the business to continue in the hope that this will allow repayment in the future.

Liquidating a company may yield too few assets to cover all the outstanding debts. However, most liquidations are instigated by banks when they decide there is no reasonable prospect of loans being repaid out of future revenues and that their best interests (and those of the other creditors) lie in winding up the business.

Using a factor

Factors provide two types of service – factoring and invoice discounting. Companies obtain different benefits from each, although both are methods for obtaining speedier payment from customers.

Factoring is the service provided by a financial institution which lends the firm up to around 80 per cent of the value of its debtors. The factor will then administer the sales accounts and undertake the collection of the debts. A service charge of between 0.5 per cent and 2.5 per cent of turnover will also be applied, and the interest charge will typically be in the range of 1–3 per cent above base rate. There is a distinction between *non-recourse* factoring, whereby bad debts are the responsibility of the factor, and *with-recourse* factoring, under which bad debts remain the liability of the client company. An additional fee, typically 0.5 per cent of turnover, will be required for the factor to provide insurance protection against bad debts.

Sometimes, for reasons of goodwill, a company needing to quicken its cash flow may not wish to reveal that it is using a factor, preferring to retain the role as debt collector. In this case it may use invoice discounting, a less comprehensive service that involves the financial institution purchasing selected invoices from the client at a discount. The interest cost of this provision of finance is reflected in the discount. The administration of the customer accounts remains with the company, which settles the debt to the invoice discounter out of the payments duly collected from its customers.

Factors may thus save the business substantial administrative costs. The factor, perhaps by utilising information about customers obtained from operating the sales accounts of other firms, may also be a more efficient collector of debt than the client company, although there may be adverse goodwill implications. Customers may resent the intervention of a (possibly heavy-handed) third party, and the knowledge that the firm is using a factor may suggest that it is suffering from liquidity problems.

7.6 'Investment' in creditors

Creditors (USA : 'accounts payable') are firms and individuals that are owed money. Why should businesses allow creditors, representing unpaid invoices, to build up? Again, this is an easy question to answer. Trade credit allows businesses a period of free credit (historically, to allow time for the stock to be sold). In this case, creditors save a business the requirement to make immediate payments so that the cash can remain in the business to invest and earn a return.

Trade creditors usually represent the major component of current liabilities, the amounts owed by the company which have to be repaid within the next accounting period. Not only is it usually 'free', it is also readily available. Whereas current assets are an investment of resources, creditors as a current liability represent a form of short-term financing for any business. Because trade credit represents temporary borrowing from suppliers until invoices are paid, it becomes an important method of financing the firm's investment in current assets.

The particular attraction of this source of short-term finance is its low cost, i.e. interest is not generally charged. In this respect, businesses should take advantage of any free credit available since this frees cash for profitable investment elsewhere. However, it is important that this facility is not abused. Any business that fails to pay creditors when the amount is due is liable to upset the suppliers concerned, which may, of course, make the suppliers reluctant to provide credit in the future, which may impact significantly on the defaulting business.

The length of the trade credit period depends partly on competitive relationships among suppliers and partly on the firm's working capital policy.

Creditor management systems

As with working capital assets, creditors need to be managed effectively to ensure that suppliers are paid at the most advantageous time. In financial terms, this usually means paying at a time which allows any cash discount to be taken. Cash discounts, you will recall, are given if payment is made within a certain time period. Although they may look small, they represent a significant annual rate of saving. For example, if you buy from a supplier that offers the credit terms '3/10, net 30', this means that if payment is made within ten days, the business can deduct 3 per cent from the invoice total. If the purchaser chooses not to pay within ten days, it must pay within 30 days, during which time they must pay the invoice net, i.e. with no discount.

Thus the business has the following choices:

Pay £97 on day 10 (in order to maximise the discount period)

versus

Pay £100 on day 30 (in order to maximise the credit period)

Notice that paying £97 on day 10 saves paying £100 on day 30. This represents a return (saving) of £3 on £97 over 20 days, i.e. $3/97 = 3.09\%$. As there are $(365/20) = 18.25$ twenty-day periods in a full year, paying early represents an annual return of roughly:

$$(3.09\% \times 18.25) = 56.4\%$$

(or more precisely $[(1.0309)^{18.25}] - 1 = 1.743 - 1 = 0.743$, i.e. 74.3%)

This analysis implies that it would be worth borrowing money at a cost of up to 56 per cent p.a. (strictly 74.3 per cent) in order to pay these debts after ten days and access the cash discount.

As well as monitoring creditor payments, good creditor management involves negotiating the most favourable terms possible.

Self-assessment activity 7.5

What is the effective interest rate paid where a firm delays payment to the very last day of the credit period, despite facing terms of '2/20, net 40'?

(answer at end of chapter)

7.7   The cash conversion cycle

The analysis of working capital management has shown the important position of cash and cash flow. The effects on cash flow of the different working capital management strategies can be brought together by analysing how they affect the *cash conversion cycle* (or working capital cycle). This is the length of time elapsing between parting with cash and getting it back from customers. To measure it, we need to compute the three key working capital holding ratios:

- Stocks   Average stockholding period = closing stock ÷ average daily purchases

- Debtors   Average collection period = debtors ÷ average daily credit sales

- Trade creditors   Average payment period = trade creditor ÷ average daily credit purchases

Creditor and stockholding days should be calculated from the figure for trade purchases, but this figure is not always given in the accounts. Otherwise, the figure for cost of sales is used, recognising that this is likely to exceed purchases since it will include such items as direct wages.

Self-assessment activity 7.6

If, by default, the cost of sales figure is used rather than purchases, will this over or understate the relevant ratios?

(answer at end of chapter)

We can use the three holding periods to obtain the cash conversion cycle, given by:

Stock period + debtor days – creditor days

The following example shows how the cash cycle can be calculated for a business:

Annual sales: £1 million
Annual purchases of stock   £400,000

At year end, it has the following balances:

Debtors: £191,781
Creditors: £38,356
Stock: £93,151

Each holding period can now be calculated and then inserted into the formula to find the cash cycle:

Stockholding period   = £93,151/(£400,000 ÷ 365)   = 85 days
Debtor collection period   = £191,781/(£1m ÷ 365)   = 70 days
Creditor payment period   = £38,356/(£400,000 ÷ 365)   = 35 days

Using this formula, the cash conversion cycle time is:

Stock period + debtor days – creditor days = 85 + 70 – 35 = 120 days

This is shown in Figure 7.1.

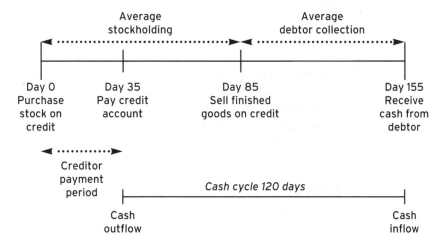

Figure 7.1 The cash conversion cycle

Self-assessment activity 7.7

What sense do you make of the case where the overall cycle time is *negative*?
(answer at end of chapter)

This analysis identifies the following key points:

- It makes sense to minimise the cash conversion cycle, the period elapsing between laying out cash to support production and sales, and recouping it (and more) via debtor collection. The shorter the cycle, the faster the cash flow and the more easily the firm can settle its debts and purchase more inputs, and make more goods and sell them.

- The shorter the cycle, the lower is the firm's reliance on external supplies of finance, for example costly bank overdrafts.

- The longer the working capital or cash conversion cycle, the more capital is required to finance it.

- The cash conversion cycle will be affected by, among other things, the type of business. Companies which have long manufacturing cycles will tend to have long stockholding periods which will lengthen the cycle. Supermarkets, on the other hand, have predominantly cash sales so that their cycles are often negative.

Self-assessment activity 7.8

Look at the accounts of your selected company and calculate the length of its cash cycle.

Shortening the cash conversion cycle

Improvements in the cash conversion cycle, i.e. by making it shorter, will lower risk and raise profitability. Money trapped in working capital cannot be used to add value elsewhere in the business. A reduction in the cash conversion cycle can be achieved by:

- speeding up collection from debtors
- slowing down payment to creditors
- shortening the stockholding period.

As in most areas of financial management, there are arguments for and against each of these actions. Let us look at the options.

Speeding up debtor collection

The quicker debtors pay, the quicker the cash cycle. The two main ways of improving the cash flow from debtors that we have already examined are the use of discounts to encourage early payment and the use of factors to provide cash against debtor balances. Both methods are effective, but can be costly. Although discounts are expensive, withdrawing them might drive away customers to competitors who continue to offer them.

Slowing down payment to creditors

As Figure 7.1 suggests, the longer a business takes to pay its creditors, the shorter is the cash cycle. It is tempting to extend this period for as long as possible. In addition, having a debtors' collection period shorter than the trade collection period may be taken as a sign of efficient working capital management. However, there are dangers in exploiting trade creditors too much:

● First, by delaying payment of accounts due, the company may be passing up valuable discounts, thus effectively increasing the cost of goods sold.

● Second, excessive delay in settling invoices can undermine the business in a number of ways. Suppliers may be unwilling to extend more credit until existing accounts are settled, they may begin to attach a lower priority to future orders placed, they may raise prices in the future or simply not supply at all. In addition, if the firm acquires a reputation among the business community as a bad payer, its relationships with other suppliers may be soured.

Reducing the stockholding period

The shorter the stockholding period, the shorter the cash cycle. This is usually achieved by increasing the stock turnover within the business. The most radical approach to achieve this is by JIT. However, the main risk is that of a stock-out with its many ensuing costs, including the effect on goodwill. Hence, a balance has to be drawn between the opportunity cost of investing in stock and the risk of running out of stock and incurring the associated costs.

Thus, none of the three options to reduce the cash conversion cycle is without risk. Nevertheless, the model is simple to operate and does focus management attention on the key areas concerned.

7.8 Putting it all together – strategic working capital management

We have now examined the four main components of working capital: cash, debtors, stock and creditors. Working capital is clearly the lifeblood of the firm; the essential oil to lubricate the business. Without investment in working capital, the firm is unable to pursue its strategic aims. However, there are different types of working capital strategies that a firm might pursue, depending on how it sees the answers to the following key questions.

- How much investment should there be in current assets? We have seen that investment in working capital assets imposes an opportunity cost. However, if there is insufficient investment in working capital assets, the business is likely to suffer, or even fail. The overall level of investment in working capital depends on the volatility of cash flows. The more uncertain they are, the more the firm is likely to invest in cash and in stocks. Aerospace companies usually have high levels of investment in working capital, whereas food and drug companies tend to have low levels.

- How much use should be made of short-term sources of finance in financing working capital assets, and indeed the business as a whole? This question also requires the business to decide the amount of short-term finance used relative to longer-term finance (such as bank loans or share issues) in the overall financing of the business.

These are now examined in turn.

Investment in working capital items

Working capital requirements increase with level of activity. Most companies exhibit growth at some stage of their development. Some grow at a steady pace and others grow in fits and starts depending on how closely their activities are affected by the overall economy. Growing firms face the need to finance both higher levels of fixed assets and working capital requirements. Fixed capital needs tend to be 'lumpy' – firms buy plant and equipment in discrete chunks (although replacement investment to remedy wear and tear may have a smoother profile). Working capital requirements tend to vary with seasonal factors and with changes in policy towards debtors and creditors.

The business can adopt one of three stances to support an increase in activity:

1 *Aggressive.* Actively try to reduce the percentage increase in the investment in working capital. This recognises that increased working capital investment imposes opportunity costs. The relevant asset holding periods will shorten and the creditor days will lengthen.

2 *Moderate*. Maintain working capital at a constant proportion of activity and thus maintain the holding periods.

3 *Relaxed*. Increase the holding periods as business activity increases and thus the percentage of working capital to activity level.

These three policies are illustrated in Figure 7.2.

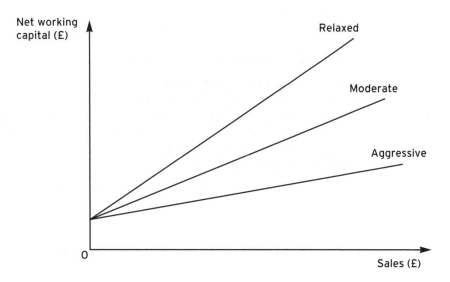

Figure 7.2 Alternative working capital stances

The aggressive working capital policy attempts to minimise investment in working capital assets. With limited resources, this policy will push the business to invest in fixed assets (which add value) rather than in working capital (which has an opportunity cost). By focusing on the fixed assets that usually add more value, and by minimising the opportunity cost of investing in working capital items, this approach is potentially very profitable. It is also extremely risky. By minimising investment in working capital assets the firm risks:

● running out of stock

● driving customers away because of uncompetitive credit terms

● driving the company into illiquidity and failure by not keeping sufficient cash balances

● antagonising suppliers.

Thus, an aggressive policy for investing in assets is relatively profitable but risky. An aggressive stance might be adopted in an environment of relatively high certainty over future cash flows that permits working capital to be held at low levels without fear of any sudden changes in activity levels. Minimal stocks would be held, customers would be pressed for early payment, while settlement of trade creditors would be delayed until they objected.

At the other extreme, we see a far more relaxed stance, reflecting large cash balances, more generous trade credit for customers, and higher stocks, with probably quicker payment to suppliers. This might be applicable to a firm in a relatively uncertain environment where safety levels of stock are required, with customers demanding longer credit and suppliers requiring quick settlement.

In between these two extremes lie many intermediate possibilities.

Gillette shaves working capital investment

James Kilts, the new CEO of Gillette, a consumer products company, found a very conservative level of working capital. On appointment in February 2001, he went to work. He extended the time taken to pay bills and shortened collections on accounts receivable. The changes added up, and in the first nine months of 2002, working capital improvements produced savings of $1.2 billion in cash.

Source: Figures from Gillette earnings press release, October 2002

Financing investment in working capital

The extra investment in both working capital and fixed assets as a firm grows needs to be financed, and whether to use short-term or long-term finance is a key decision. Businesses may well be tempted to use mainly short-term finance, including bank overdrafts as well as trade credit from suppliers, for the most basic reason that it is likely to be cheaper than long-term finance. In particular:

- short-term interest rates are usually cheaper than long-term rates

- with short-term borrowing, you pay only for the finance you use.

Businesses that finance their operations, including fixed assets, using mainly short-term financing are said to follow an *aggressive* financing policy. However, this approach goes against one of the golden rules of finance. It is generally considered prudent to *match* the maturity of the finance raised to the lifetime of the assets acquired with it. This simply means financing long-term assets with long-term funds such as equity or long-term debt, and financing short-term assets such as stock and debtors with short-term methods of finance like bank overdraft and trade creditors. The rationale of this policy is that it is dangerous to finance long-term assets with short-term finance which can be withdrawn, because it may be difficult to liquidate rapidly the assets acquired with that finance.

On the other hand, financing a variable amount of short-term assets with fixed, long-term capital may be wasteful, as there may be periods when not all the capital is required, yet it must still be serviced, i.e. interest and dividends paid on it. Firms following such a *conservative* policy tend to finance their businesses predominantly with long-term finance.

There are four issues likely to influence this decision regarding the relative reliance on short- and long-term borrowing:

- relative risk

- managers' attitudes to risk

- flexibility

- cost.

Relative risk

From the firm's perspective, short-term borrowing, e.g. on overdraft, is inherently more risky for several reasons:

- the risk of an overdraft being called in at short notice

- the risk of an overdraft not being renewed

- exposure to fluctuations in interest rates.

 Firms that are unable to roll forward their short-term borrowing may have to sell assets to meet their liabilities, one of the symptoms of **financial distress**. Extensive use of trade credit also carries similar risks of non-renewal.

Managers' attitudes to risk

Risk-averse managers are likely to use a higher proportion of long-term debt even though it may reduce profitability. Notice the importance of agency issues here. Shareholders may have a far more relaxed attitude to risk than managers. This is because they are likely, if they are rational, to have invested across a portfolio of securities which enables them to diversify away much of the risk they would otherwise face when investing in single stocks. Managers, conversely, for reasons of job security, may focus only on the likelihood of the one firm they manage encountering financial distress, and try to limit this by undertaking only modest levels of borrowing.

Flexibility

Using short-term debt tends to offer more flexibility to financial decision making.

1 If working capital requirements fluctuate, it might be advisable to avoid extensive long-term debt financing as this could involve overcapitalisation (i.e. paying for long-term finance which is not required).

2 When interest rates are 'high' and expected to fall, it may be better to borrow short and refinance long at lower rates in the future.

This last observation prompts the question of forecasting. Generally, forecasting interest rates, like forecasting exchange rates, is notoriously hazardous due to the uncertainties involved. However, some clues can be obtained by studying the so-called term structure of interest rates (TSIR).

The term structure of interest rates (TSIR)

The **term structure of interest rates** shows how yields offered in the financial markets for loans of different maturities vary as the term of the loan increases. It is most easily explained in relation to government stock. The TSIR, illustrated in Figure 7.3, shows how the rate of return expected by investors to maturity varies with the length of time to maturity or redemption, i.e. when the stock will be repaid by the government. The line linking these different returns over time is called the **yield curve**, which is normally upward sloping.

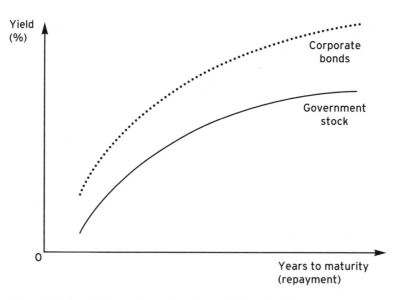

Figure 7.3 The yield curve (term structure of interest rates)

> ## Self-assessment activity 7.9
>
> Look in the FT for details of available yields to maturity. What shape of yield curve is implied? (The Saturday issue often carries a diagram showing this.)
> (The FT website is at www.ft.com)

How firms can use the yield curve

The yield curve offers useful information to managers wanting to borrow money. Although it is based on the structure of yields on government securities, the curve implies the terms under which corporate borrowers can access the financial markets. Corporate borrowers have a higher default risk than governments so markets require higher yields on corporate bonds. However, the market for government stock dictates the shape of the yield curve. The position of the curve will simply be different, i.e. higher, for corporate bonds. This is shown by the dotted line in Figure 7.3. The distance between the two lines represents the premium for risk required on corporate securities.

Today's yield curve therefore incorporates how people expect interest rates to move in the future. An upward-sloping yield curve reflects people's expectations of higher future interest rates, and vice versa. The managerial action points are clear:

1 A rising yield curve suggests higher future interest rates. This provides a case for borrowing long term now and for avoiding variable interest rate loans which will of course rise if the yield curve predicts correctly.

2 A falling yield curve suggests lower future interest rates. This provides a case for borrowing short term now, and preferably at a variable interest rate.

Of course, the yield curve should only used as an *estimate* of future rates of interest. Political and economic events may produce an entirely different future reality.

Cost

Finally, the normal shape of the yield curve gives the lie to the common misapprehension that short-term debt is more expensive than long-term debt. This misconception is presumably based on personal experiences with credit cards and other forms of consumer finance. However, for secured company loans, long-term debt is usually more expensive, as implied by the *normal* yield curve. Nevertheless, short-term interest rates do tend to be more volatile than long-term ones. It has been known at times of economic crisis for short-term rates to be in excess of 100 per cent equivalent p.a.

In summary, the different policies which a business may follow to finance growth are:

- aggressive – borrow short term rather than long term
- moderate – balance short-term with long-term financing
- relaxed – use predominantly long-term finance.

The aggressive financing policy is potentially more profitable but riskier.

Combining financing and investment strategies – aggressive and conservative businesses

Businesses can be aggressive both in their investment policy and in the financing of their investments. At one extreme, they may invest predominantly in fixed assets rather than working capital, and finance this investment with short-term finance, an aggressive strategy that is potentially profitable but risky. An aggressive stance may suit a business that is fast growing, has insufficient finance, and any finance that is used tends to be short term.

Such a firm is said to be **overtrading**. It is also said to be *undercapitalised* in the sense that it has an insufficient platform of long-term finance on which to build its business. Pushing short-term financing, for example, bank overdrafts and trade credit, to the limits of creditors' tolerance may lead to inability to meet financial obligations and thus insolvency.

At the other end of the spectrum, **overcapitalised** businesses have substantial long-term finance and copious levels of working capital and liquidity. This policy is safe (there is little chance of running out of any working capital assets such as cash or stock) but is relatively unprofitable. First, the investment in working capital has a high opportunity cost, and second, the policy is costly because the large amount of long-term financing requires servicing, i.e. payment of interest or dividends, even when the capital is not needed.

Overtrading is so common and potentially so devastating a phenomenon that it merits closer examination.

7.9 Overtrading

An overtrading firm typically increases its turnover rapidly without having sufficient long-term capital backing. To fuel its growth, it may extend too much credit to customers or invest too heavily in stocks (in order to meet the rapidly increasing demand) so that cash flows in too slowly to meet financial obligations.

The term is thus commonly associated with inadequate working capital to sustain a sales expansion. Further growth has to be financed by more intensive use of existing working capital and extending what short-term finance facilities are available, such as bank overdrafts and trade creditors. In practice, this means paying suppliers more slowly, attempting to collect more quickly from customers and trying to speed up stock movements.

Overtrading companies have probably raised insufficient long-term finance in the past, hence the term 'undercapitalisation' that is often applied to such firms. In the past, a company might have been unwilling to raise long-term capital, and by the time its growing pains begin to bite, it may look less attractive to providers of long-term finance. The only alternative is heavy reliance on short-term sources. Overtrading is thus characterised by rising short-term borrowing and declining liquidity.

Debtors usually increase sharply as the company follows a more generous credit policy in order to win sales. At the same time, overtrading companies are likely to give away a lot of their profit margin to customers by offering them high discounts to encourage them to pay early. An overtrading company is thus likely to sacrifice profit for cash flow. Stocks may increase as the company attempts to produce at a faster rate ahead of increases in demand. Output increases are obtained by more intensive utilisation of existing fixed assets (since it does not have the cash to buy more).

A checklist of common symptoms of overtrading is as follows:

- rapid sales growth

- sharp fall in cash balances/increase in overdraft, i.e. reduced liquidity

- static long-term finance (although retentions may increase)

- sharp increase in trade creditors and/or creditor days

- sharp increase in gearing, especially from short-term borrowing

- sharp change in stocks: either falls or increases could indicate overtrading – an increase could represent stocking up in advance of an expected sales increase, while a decrease could reflect inability to satisfy demand out of current production

- sharp fall in profit margins (resulting from cut-price offers to fuel growth, rising operating costs and discounts allowed to improve cash flow)

- sharp increase in fixed assets–turnover ratio (sales/fixed assets)

- sharp increase in debtors and/or debtor days, although tempered by cash discounts given.

These are symptoms typical of a business that is following an 'aggressive' financing policy (i.e. short-term financing rather than long-term, with a declining percentage of assets financed by long-term finance) and adopting an 'aggressive' asset structure (i.e. focusing scarce resources on value-adding fixed assets resulting in insufficient working capital).

Remedies

Companies that fail through overtrading represent great financial tragedies. Often, they are profitable businesses brought down by a lack of cash flow. Yet if the business has strengths, the solutions are relatively simple. Overtrading businesses urgently need to increase their long-term finance. This enables them to focus on earning profit rather than chasing cash. The treadmill of 'robbing Peter to pay Paul' is replaced by a fund of finance which is in place for the long term. This is the same logic used by a house-buyer taking out a mortgage to buy a property. The mortgage is likely to be for 25 years or so, not six months!

Overtrading businesses may also need to control their growth. In the early days of a business, it is tempting to accept all offers of work. However, it will become apparent that some contracts are more profitable than others, and that if all are taken on, resources become stretched and corners are cut. It may be advantageous for the business to turn away less profitable business and business in areas where resources and/or expertise is stretched. This will allow it to establish itself at being good at everything it does.

If both of these remedies are followed, the business can establish more appropriate working capital management. This is likely to include maintaining enough liquidity, having 'profitable' credit policies in place for its debtors, having enough stock on hand and not abusing creditor payment terms. All of this will compare favourably with the aggressive and risky policies of overtrading businesses.

◉ 7.10 Worked example

Ewden plc is a medium-sized company producing a range of engineering products which it sells to wholesale distributors. Recently, its sales have begun to rise rapidly following a general recovery in the economy as a whole. However, it is concerned about its liquidity position and is contemplating ways of improving cash flow. It can borrow at 12 per cent p.a. on overdraft.

Ewden's accounts for the past two years are summarised below.

Profit and loss account for the year ended 31 December

	2002 (£000)	2003 (£000)
Sales	12,000	16,000
Cost of sales*	(7,000)	(9,000)
Operating profit	5,000	7,000
Interest payable	(200)	(400)
Profit before tax	4,800	6,600
Taxation	(1,000)	(1,600)
Profit after tax	3,800	5,000
Dividends	(1,500)	(2,000)
Retained profit	2,300	3,000

*Purchases are 50% of cost of sales

Balance sheet as at 31 December

		2002 (£000)		2003 (£000)
Fixed assets (net)		9,000		12,000
Current assets:				
Stock	1,400		2,200	
Debtors	1,600		2,600	
Cash	1,500	4,500	100	4,900
Current liabilities:				
Overdraft	–		(200)	
Trade creditors	(500)		(1,000)	
Other creditors	(1,500)	(2,000)	(1,200)	(2,400)
10% Loan stock		(2,000)		(2,000)
Net assets		9,500		12,500
Ordinary shares (50p)		3,000		3,000
Profit and loss account		6,500		9,500
Shareholders' funds		9,500		12,500

Required

Identify the reasons for the sharp decline in Ewden's liquidity and assess the extent to which the company appears to exhibit 'overtrading' symptoms.

Source: ACCA Managerial Finance Exam, June 1994, Question 5

Answer

An overtrading firm is expanding too fast on a limited platform of long-term capital. Without raising further long-term finance, its working capital becomes overstretched, even to the extent that investment in the fixed assets that are required to support growth are financed by short-term sources of finance.

A year-on-year (YOY) analysis of Ewden's two balance sheets reveals a sharp fall in liquidity – cash has fallen by £1.4m in 2002, and coupled with the opening of an overdraft of £0.2m, net cash funds have fallen by (£1.4m + £0.2m) = £1.6m. Meanwhile, considerable funds have been re-invested in capital equipment – net fixed assets increase by £3m, presumably the net result of Ewden reinvesting its £3m retained earnings plus an unspecified amount of depreciation provisions.

As Ewden has recovered from recession, it has recorded a sound increase in profits – operating profits rise by 40% from £5,000 to £7,000. Quite simply, it has

run down its liquidity to finance the acquisition of assets required to enable growth in production and sales. Its strong cash position (£1.5m cash = 12.5% of sales) in 2002 might simply have been built up to support this expansion in 2003.

However, as well as increasing its fixed assets, Ewden invested a further £0.8m in stocks and £1.0m in debtors, a working capital investment of £1.8m, only partly offset by increased trade creditors. It has issued neither new shares nor new long-term debt, leaving cash flow and existing liquid resources to bear the brunt of supporting the growth programme.

Checking Ewden's figures against the common symptoms of overtrading, suggests:

- *Rapid increase in turnover?* Ewden's sales increase 33% year-on-year.

- *Increase in short-term borrowing and a decline in cash balances?* Clearly, this has happened.

- *Sharp fall in liquidity?* Ewden still displays quite sound, albeit falling, liquidity ratios. The current ratio declined slightly from (£4,500/£2,000) = 2.25 : 1 to (£4,900/£2,400) = 2.04 : 1, although the decline in the quick ratio, i.e. excluding stocks, from 1.55 : 1 to 1.13 : 1, gives more cause for concern, especially as most of the quick assets (96%) are debtors.

- *Increase in gearing?* Using the ratio of long- *and* short-term debt-to-equity (end-year), i.e. interest-bearing debt, gearing actually falls from 21% to 18% despite the emergence of the overdraft, reflecting the increased equity in the form of reserves.

- *Pressure on working capital?*
  Stock days. This measure rises from (£1,400/£7,000) = 73 days (stock turnover of 5 times) to (£2,200/£9,000) = 89 days (stock turnover of just over 4 times). An overtrading firm would tend to speed up stock turnover.
  Debtor days. Accounts receivable rise as a percentage of sales from 13% (49 days) to 16% (59 days) – this may reflect looser control over collections and/or an overt attempt to 'buy' sales with extended credit. It might be instructive also to examine the age profile of debtors and whether the full Profit & Loss account shows an increase in bad debt provisions and write-offs.
  Credit period. Purchases rise from £3,500 to £4,500, as might be expected, reflecting the increased activity, but its accounts payable increase more quickly. The trade credit period considerably lengthens from (£500/£3,500) = 52 days to (£1,000/£4,500) = 81 days, suggesting that Ewden is exploiting its suppliers to enhance sales.

- *Asset utilisation?* The sales/fixed assets ratio remains steady at 1.33 because the production and sales increase is supported by higher fixed assets, suggesting the output increase was well-planned.

- *Profit margins?* The operating profit margin increases slightly from (£5,000/£12,000) = 42% to (£7,000/£16,000) = 44%, This suggests that

Ewden has not used aggressive price discounting to promote sales. However, cost of sales here includes all costs, direct and indirect – a separate breakdown into gross and net margins might reveal otherwise.

Overall

On balance, Ewden seems not to be overtrading. Its liquidity is under pressure but it does not display all the classic symptoms of overtrading. It should consider raising further long-term finance if it expects a further sales expansion. If no further sales increase is expected, and hence no more investment in fixed assets is required, the recent capacity increase would suffice to produce the current output level, and liquidity can to be restored from future cash flow.

Source: modified from ACCA solution

7.11 Summary

This chapter has set out the nature and purpose of working capital management and some of the ways in which it can be managed to add value. The main elements of such management are:

- the investment decision for each working capital asset, and the total investment in working capital

- the amount of short-term financing and its relationship with long-term finance in the business.

The main ingredients in strategic working capital management have been seen to be the development of policies for:

- cash flow (including the use of the cash conversion cycle) and cash budgeting

- the level of debtors and credit control for debtor collection

- the level of stock

- the use of creditors and their payment.

Companies that successfully manage working capital reinforce value-adding activity in this area by incentivising managers based upon the appropriate working capital ratios. Such companies often use sophisticated data collection methods to assist communication throughout the organisation.

The next chapter looks at ways of raising long-term finance.

References and further reading

Textbooks

Arnold – chs 7 and 8.
Brealey & Myers – chs 30 and 31.
Pike & Neale – chs 14 and 15.
Samuels, Wilkes & Brayshaw – chs 20, 22 and 23.
Watson & Head – ch 10.

Questions and mini-case studies

1 **Campbell Soup**
   In 1999–2000, US firm Campbell Soup ruthlessly cut back its investment in order to free up cash flow. It then used some of the extra funds generated to buy back company shares.

   Required
   Discuss the possible rationale of this strategy.

2 **Dell Computers**
   Dell Computers manufactures very few of the parts used in the production of its computers. Instead, it relies on other suppliers to manufacture parts and hold stocks. In fact, Dell has been said to hold only six days' worth of various items of stock compared with the normal 60 days among its competitors.

   Required
   What are the advantages and the possible dangers of such a policy?

3 The treasurer of Ripley plc, a listed company, contemplates a change in financial policy. At present, Ripley's balance sheet shows that fixed assets are equal in value to the total of long-term debt and equity financing. It is proposed to take advantage of a recent fall in interest rates by replacing the long-term debt capital with an overdraft. In addition, the treasurer wants to speed up debt collection by offering early payment discounts to customers and also to slow down payment to creditors.

   Required
   Write a memorandum to other board members explaining the rationales of the old and new policies and pinpointing the factors to be considered in making such a switch of policy.

   Source: ACCA

4 The final accounts for Eustane & Co, a small trading firm, reveal the following:

P&L	30 Nov 2000		30 Nov 1999	
	£		£	
Sales		3,860		2,000
Opening stock	200		100	
Purchases	2,700		1,000	
Closing stock	(400)		(100)	
Cost of sales		(2,500)		(1,000)
Gross profit		1,360		1,000
Operating and financial expenses		(800)		(400)
Net profit		560		600
Balance sheet				
Fixed assets		1,312		600
Current assets:				
Stock	400		100	
Debtors	220		150	
Cash	10		30	
		630		80
Current liabilities:				
Creditors	(350)		(110)	
Bank overdraft	(380)		(50)	
		(730)		(160)
Long-term liabilities:				
Bank loan		(250)		(225)
Net assets		962		495

Required

(a) Calculate the cash cycle for Eustane for 1999 and 2000. Comment on your findings.

(b) What strategies might Eustane take to reduce the cash cycle? What are the potential problems for each one?

5 Boateng Ltd is a family-run clothing manufacturer specialising in leisurewear. The family owns 70 per cent of the 5.5 million shares in issue. Two years ago, the company decided to move into sportswear as a related high-growth, high-market area. In particular, the company saw opportunities in marketing sportswear relating to the 2002 Football World Cup, and, as a consequence, has negotiated a number of lucrative contracts in this area. These are estimated to increase profits by £200,000 in 2001 and also in 2002.

One of the family directors is now urging the company to go public and have a share issue, as she perceives some signs of the business overtrading. Soundings taken among analysts have suggested that this business will need to generate an annual return of around 20 per cent to satisfy investors, based upon the nature of its activities.

Further information

(i) Because of changing fashions, 15 per cent of the current stock level is considered to be obsolete.

(ii) Three per cent of current debtors are expected to default.

Required

(a) From an analysis of the attached accounts, would you agree with this director that Boateng is exhibiting signs of overtrading?

(b) What advice would you give to a company that is overtrading?

Summarised profit and loss accounts for the year to 30 April (£000)

	2000	1999	1998
Sales	25,137	17,955	13,300
Operating profit	4,776	4,489	4,300
Interest	(410)	(320)	(280)
Other expenses	(2,430)	(2,025)	(1,620)
Taxable profit	1,936	2,144	2,400
Taxation	(620)	(705)	(840)
Profit	1,316	1,439	1,560
Dividends	(658)	(719)	(780)
Retained profits	658	720	780

Summarised balance sheet as at 30 April

	2000	1999	1998
Fixed assets	11,730	10,200	8,500
Current assets:			
Stock	4,514	3,980	3,600
Debtors	4,696	3,612	2,800
Cash	85	90	100
Total	9,295	7,682	6,500
Current liabilities:			
Bank overdraft	(2,764)	(1,960)	(1,400)
Trade creditors	(4,586)	(3,400)	(2,500)
Total	(7,350)	(5,360)	(3,900)
Net current assets	(1,945)	(2,322)	(2,600)
Long-term liabilities:			
Bank Loan	(1,400)	(1,400)	(1,400)
Net Assets	12,275	11,122	9,700

6   WCM Ltd is a private company that sells a wide range of specialist electrical and manual tools to professional builders through a trade catalogue.

The company is considering the improvement of its working capital management in order to reduce its current overdraft. Most customers are required to pay cash when they place an order and thus there is little that can be done to reduce debtors. The focus of the board's attention is therefore on creditors and stock.

The working capital position at 30 April 2002 was as follows:

	$	$
Stock	300,000	
Trade debtors	50,000	
		350,00
Trade creditors	(150,000)	
Overdraft	(550,000)	
	(700,000)	
Net current liabilities		(350,000)

Creditors
WCM Ltd has two major suppliers, INT plc and GRN Ltd.

INT plc supplies electrical tools and is one of the largest companies in the industry, with international operations. GRN Ltd is a small, local manufacturer of manual tools of good quality. WCM Ltd is one of its major customers.

Deliveries from both suppliers are currently made monthly, and are constant throughout the year. Delivery and invoicing both occur in the last week of each month. Details of the credit terms offered by suppliers are as follows:

Supplier	Normal credit period	Cash discount	Average monthly purchases
INT plc	40 days	2% for settlement in 10 days	$100,000
GRN Ltd	30 days	none	$50,000

WCM Ltd always takes advantage of the cash discount from INT plc and pays GRN Ltd after 30 days.

Stock
The company aims to have the equivalent of two months' cost of sales (equal to two months' purchases) in stock immediately after a delivery has been received.

New working capital policy

At a meeting of the board of directors, it was decided that, from 1 May 2002, all payments would be based upon taking the full credit period of 40 days from INT plc, and similarly taking 40 days before paying GRN Ltd.

A review of stocks is also to be commissioned to assess the level of safety stocks held. In particular, it would examine the feasibility of a just-in-time stock management system. Meanwhile, it was decided to make no purchases in May in order to reduce stock levels.

While most of the board supported these changes, the *purchasing manager* disagreed, arguing that working capital would be even worse after the changes.

Required

(a) Calculate the annual rate of interest implied in the cash discount offered by INT plc. Assume a 365-day year.

(b) Calculate the anticipated current ratio of WCM Ltd at 31 May 2002, assuming that the changes in creditor payment policy take place, and that there are no stock purchases during May 2002.

Assume for this purpose that, in the absence of any change to creditor policy, the overdraft would have remained at its 30 April 2002 level.

Clearly state any assumptions made.

(c) As a management accountant of WCM Ltd, write a memorandum to the directors that evaluates:
   (i) the proposed changes to the creditor payment policy
   (ii) the proposed policy to introduce a just-in-time system for stock management.

Source: CIMA (IFIN) May 2002, question 4

7 PRT Ltd is a rapidly growing printing company that uses the latest technology to operate a quick and efficient service to other businesses and to private individuals. Some printing is undertaken to order, while other work, such as posters, is held in stock until sold. Sales to business customers are on credit, while sales to individuals are for cash.

Expansion has been rapid, as indicated by the number of print shops owned at each financial year ended 31 March:

Year	1998	1999	2000	2001	2002
Number of print shops	8	12	18	27	40

While expansion has been very rapid, concerns have arisen regarding the increasing overdraft, which is now approaching the limit of $1 million set by the bank. The company has used equity and debt finance to expand in recent years, but is unlikely to be able to raise further finance from these sources in the immediate future.

Extracts from the financial statements for the years ended 31 March are as follows:

	2001 $000	2002 $000
Raw material stocks	55	80
Finished goods stocks	185	185
Purchases of raw materials	600	850
Cost of sales	1,570	1,830
Administrative expenses	45	65
Sales	1,684	1,996
Trade debtors	114	200
Trade creditors	50	70
Overdraft	400	950
Additions to fixed assets	700	900

Cost of sales includes all relevant production costs including manufacturing overheads and labour.

Required

(a) Calculate the length in days of PRT Ltd's operating cycle, for the year ended 31 March 2002.

(b) So far as the information permits, calculate the cash generated from operating activities for PRT Ltd for the year ended 31 March 2002. State any relevant assumptions.

(b) As PRT Ltd's management accountant, write a memorandum to the board that analyses the company's cash and working capital position, recommending appropriate actions.

Indicate any additional information that would be needed to make a fuller assessment.

Source: CIMA (IFIN) May 2002, question 6

Mini-case study - Too much of a good thing?

In 2001, UK corporate liquidity was the highest among major European economies, with far too much working capital tied up in firms, according to a survey by REL consultants that compared the working capital efficiency of Europe's top 1,000 companies.

REL calculated a figure for excess working capital by focusing on three items: accounts receivable, accounts payable, and inventories. Each company was benchmarked against its peer group, the 'excess' figure being the extra working capital used by a company compared with the top quartile of its sector. On this basis, the amount of excess working capital in UK companies rose from €101 billion to €115 billion between 2000 and 2001. That represented 34 per cent of the total working capital tied up in UK businesses, itself up from 28 per cent at the end of 2000. The worst performing sectors in this sense were information and online services, retailers, brewers, tobacco and aerospace, each of which exhibited 40 per cent excess working capital.

REL argued that the excess capital figure measures the inefficiency of the corporate sector. Across Europe, almost €600 billion of capital was tied up in this way, equivalent to 44 per cent of the sector's net debt. Eliminating excess working capital would substantially lower financing charges and boost profits, the consultancy said. The increase in UK firms' liquidity over the year was greater than all EU countries except Ireland.

By contrast, companies in Germany, France and Spain managed to reduce their excess working capital by some €38 billion over the year. In general, Eurozone companies produced a far better performance than firms located outside the Euro area.

'It is true to say that the Eurozone economy is closer to recession than the UK economy so they may be looking at working capital more closely,' said Alexander Bielenberg of REL. But he added: 'UK business might be at a competitive disadvantage because its prices are not easily comparable with the competition.'

Buying goods from UK companies is more complicated for Eurozone customers, who may also pay less promptly due to currency risk.

Required

Can you suggest possible reasons why UK firms might carry more working capital than their European competitors?

Source: UK is Europe's worst in corporate liquidity, *Financial Times*, 6 November 2002

Mini-case study – Xerox

In 1999, Xerox was a highly profitable company whose name was synonymous with photocopiers, but the arrival of a clutch of low-cost competitors rapidly changed its position at the top of the pile. One of the cost-cutting measures the company introduced was to centralise its billing and debtor control function. It saved money through releasing sraff as a result. Unfortunately for the company, the move turned out to be a false economy. Billing queries from customers rose and it was the sales force that started to take the complaints, commonly taking the brunt of incorrect billing and statements. This affected their ability to sell, and many gave up the cause and left. As a result, the debtors figure started to rise because of the delays in properly billing them. Bad debts almost inevitably started to increase. This impacted negatively on the company's cash flow at a time when it was finding it much more difficult to sell machines.

As a sign of difficulty, in December 2000 the company reported that it had used up a $7 billion line of bank credit. It might now have to rely on asset sales to generate cash flow.

Required

What lessons can be learned from Xerox's experience of introducing a new system of credit control?

Source: John Hechinger and Laura Johannes 'Xerox considers a major revamping', *Wall Street Journal*, 20 October 2000.

Mini-case study – Ford and GM

Ford and General Motors have taken JIT a stage further than most firms. In effect, they have set up online auction sites on which suppliers can bid to supply the manufacturers. This is a huge undertaking for both companies. For example, Ford deals with 30,000 suppliers and orders $300 billion of supplies p.a. The car firms have estimated that they will save millions of dollars in ordering and purchasing costs, GM estimating that its order-processing costs will fall from $100 to $10 an order. In total, GM estimates that by dealing directly with suppliers the company can save around $3,000 costs per $22,000 car. As one executive is said to have remarked: 'Anyone who is a middleman is toast.' In addition, by linking supply and production requirements to customer orders, flexibility and speed of production are greatly improved.

Required

What are the potential problems that companies like Ford and GM face when using the internet for stock management?

Sources: Automotive Intelligence News, 24 March 2000;
Business Week, 28 February 2000; 'Ford e-business strategy'
presentation by Ed Davis and Brandt Aallen 10 May 2000

Mini-case study - European telecoms

In 2003, Europe's heavily indebted companies are still some way from leaving their burdens behind them. Yet the turnaround has begun, with telecoms companies and some car-makers starting to generate significant amounts of cash. Morgan Stanley credit strategists calculate that BT, Telecom Italia, KPN and Deutsche Telecom between them generated €5.2 billion of free cash flow in the third quarter of 2002, even after dividend payments. If they could keep up this pace, the four could produce enough cash to eliminate their net debt within five years.

This, of course, is unlikely. Much of the improvement in cash flow comes from a reduction in working capital. This improvement may not be reversed – some companies have taken inventory management measures that should yield sustainable gains – but it is also unlikely to be repeated. Dividend cuts, too, are not readily repeatable. And although capital expenditure can be kept down, it will be hard to combine low capital expenditure with high margins – a trick several telecoms companies managed in the third quarter – for long.

Source: Cash flow, Lex column, *Financial Times* 3 December 2002

Required

(a) Identify the three main ways these companies have improved their cash flow.

(b) This improvement in cash flow has followed a tough period for European telecoms companies, in trouble from overborrowing and investing in loss-making projects. What would you advise these companies to do with the cash surpluses that they are now generating? Consider the market reaction to your suggestions.

Self-assessment answers

7.1
Over to you.

7.2
In the USA, stocks = inventory, debtors = accounts receivable, creditors = accounts payable.

7.3

$$EOQ = \sqrt{\frac{2 \times 10{,}000 \times £50}{0.25}} = \sqrt{4m} = 2{,}000 \text{ units}$$

This EOQ thus requires five orders p.a., about one every 73 days.

7.4
Debtors fall by 25 days, i.e. to $(25/365 \times £2m) = £136{,}986$ by value, say £137,000. Interest savings are $(12\% \times £137{,}000) = £16{,}440$ (before tax).

7.5
With these terms, the firm is neglecting a 2 per cent discount in order to take an extra 20 days' credit on 98 per cent of the invoiced amount. It is paying interest of $2/98\%) = 2.041\%$ every 20 days, or roughly $(2.041\% \times 365/20) = 37.25\%$ p.a. More correctly, the answer is $(1.0241)^{18.25} - 1 = 54.44\%$ p.a.

7.6
Cost of sales will generally exceed purchases as it might include elements of labour and other costs, e.g. depreciation and overheads in a manufacturing situation. This will increase the denominator in the relevant calculation, thus decreasing the calculated days. This will make the resulting days look shorter than they really are.

7.7
A negative cash cycle is the ultimate in efficient working capital management. It means that the firm is receiving money quicker than it is paying it out, resulting in a permanent cash surplus that it can invest elsewhere, thus increasing profits. An enviable situation!

7.8 and 7.9
Your call.

Case study: Sodexho - Drilling for gold

It is often said that cash is the lifeblood of a business. Chapter 7 has explained how effective working capital management can help improve the rate of cash flow on an ongoing basis, and thus improve the liquidity position of the firm at a point in time. This case examines a firm where attention was distracted by grander strategic events from the more mundane requirements of managing cash flow on an everyday basis. It reports how major improvements can be achieved with quite modest adjustments in operating procedures.

Introduction

While managing a business on a balance sheet basis may not be as exciting as managing for profits, some companies have little choice but to shift their focus. Thanks to the bursting of the internet bubble, accounting irregularities and corporate governance issues, the world has come full circle – it's now 'back to basics'. 'You really need to take a step backwards, because you have to drill down to understand what's behind the numbers on a balance sheet: inventories, payables and receivables, and also what's in the cash numbers,' says Susan Griffiths, a partner at Global Cash Management Ltd.

Industry benchmarks are often of little use in this exercise, so Griffiths recommends getting right down to the operational level to understand what is going on. 'It really does require quite a bit of time to drill down and understand your internal benchmark,' she says. She adds that, 'You can't just look at a number such as the debtor collection period without understanding what it really means. Benchmarks are highly influenced by the country where companies are operating, regulatory requirements and a host of other variables.'

But a successful 'drilling' programme takes more than a sole prospector to discover the mother lode. While treasury can take up the challenge to find ways to improve working capital and set meaningful benchmarks, a team approach will realise better results and give treasury an improved feel for what's going on. Griffiths says that a team approach is the ideal way to achieve improved results and is used by the most successful companies.

On the gold trail

One such company is the US unit of worldwide food and facilities management services company Sodexho. Kevin Nolan, vice president of finance and corporate treasury, says that when he joined the treasury department, the company had just completed a large spin-off and a merger. In the aftermath, it had taken its eye off the ball when it came to working capital management, and cash flow was deteriorating.

One of the first things his company did to turn things around was to prioritise working capital management. 'Creating this visibility, and saying that increasing our cash flow is one of the six most important things we can do, really helped our management team and people understand its significance and importance,' said Nolan. 'So when we talk about increasing cash flow it's just as important as growing our business, satisfying our customers and communicating with our people.' He said that shift in thinking made his job a lot easier, but improvements did not happen overnight.

Three years ago, Nolan realised that more effective accounts receivable management held the biggest potential to improve working capital. So, he set out to reduce day sales outstanding (DSO) that were then in the high thirties. The first task was to reduce the time it took to deliver invoices to customers. Historically, they were not being received until 21 days after the end of the month. 'Today, we've automated that process,' said Nolan. 'The invoices are still generated centrally, but they're generated electronically and transmitted to our on-site manager.' From there, Sodexho managers hand deliver invoices to the client. The streamlined process has cut the delivery time in half and resulted in other indirect benefits to shorten the payment cycle. 'When a manager hand delivers the invoice, it affords us the opportunity to sit down with the client and review the invoice; if there are any problems, we can usually get an answer right on site,' said Nolan.

The other issue was communication. Many managers thought treasury was responsible for collecting receivables. Meanwhile, treasury thought it was part of the on-site manager's job. 'That sounds pretty simple and you might say what a fly-by: how could a $5 billion company let something like that happen?' Nolan commented. 'For me it was a real eye-opener because it said, hey, this is an easy thing to fix.' The next step involved ensuring that all managers were trained in receivable collection techniques. Even with an 80 per cent retention rate, Nolan needed a mechanism to train people efficiently on an ongoing basis. A self-study manual proved to be an inexpensive way to reach Sodexho employees and was in such demand that the company soon ran out of materials.

Lastly, Nolan created a centralised credit and collections team to put greater emphasis on credit granting and to help with collections.

The pot of gold

Nolan says he set out to reduce the debtor collection period by seven days, but ultimately achieved an 11-day reduction. 'We saw a continuous reduction in this period and never had a month where it wasn't lower than the same month last year,' he said. 'That was a measure that the board wanted.'

There was a lot of resistance to some of the changes he proposed, but eventually the culture changed. 'You can have a lot of great ideas and provide training and tools, but it's not going to work unless the organisation embraces it and believes it. You have to make it work for them,' said Nolan.

He said that improving cash flow was a task that never ended. Treasurers needed to fully understand their business so that they spent time on things that would actually work – and help the business. There was very little treasury could do on its own: 'It's the people in the field who are going to make it happen.'

Required

(a) What financial and other benefits did Sodexho achieve through reducing its debtor balances?

(b) What were the main problems the company encountered in introducing this policy of lower receivables?

(c) What are the possible risks to the company in introducing this policy?

Source: this case is based on an article by Richard Ketchen, www.treasurypoint.com. See also website: www.sodexohousa.com

8

RAISING LONG-TERM FINANCE

The record breakers – telephone number borrowing

In May 2001, the ill-starred WorldCom Inc, the US number two long-distance telephone company, sold $11.9 billion worth of bonds, the largest ever issue conducted by a US firm. The proceeds were expected to enable refinancing of $3.1 billion of debt shortly due for repayment, to repay around $6 billion of short-term money market borrowings and to finance expansion. WorldCom was taking advantage of the Federal Reserve's recent cuts in interest rates which had created a favourable climate for the bond market.

As well as setting a record for the largest ever bond sale conducted by a US firm, it included a US dollar component of $10.1 billion, also a record for dollar-denominated borrowing. The remainder was raised in euros and sterling.

The full composition of the issue was as follows:

- $1.5 billion of 6.5 per cent three-year notes yielding 6.6 per cent

- $4 billion of 7.5 per cent ten-year notes yielding 7.7 per cent

- $4.6 billion in 30-year bonds yielding 8.4 per cent

- $1.1 billion seven-year floating rate notes in euros

- $710 million in sterling seven-year floating rate notes.

Ford Motor Co held the previous record for a bond sale by a US firm at a mere $8.6 billion in July 1999, while the previous record for a dollar-denominated bond sale was held by British Telecom which raised $10 billion in December 2000.

But even the WorldCom figures were put in the shade by the giant bond sales made by Deutsche Telekom, that raised the equivalent of $14.6 billion in June 2000, and by France Telecom, that raised the equivalent of $16.4 billion in March 2001.

Objectives:

This chapter aims to:

- examine the general issues involved in selecting long-term finance

- examine the characteristics of equity finance

- examine the characteristics of debt finance

- analyse the gearing phenomenon

- distinguish between operating gearing and financial gearing

- examine hybrid forms of finance.

8.1   Introduction

The main tasks of any finance manager include advising on how to finance the company's operations and then implementing the financing decision. This chapter describes the main ways in which a company can raise long-term capital, that is, capital likely to remain on the balance sheet for several time periods. It is important to understand the advantages and disadvantages of different types of finance in order to understand when to utilise them. Consequently, the emphasis here is not only on the characteristics of different forms of finance but also on understanding the appropriateness of each in particular situations.

Long-term finance is 'core' finance. According to the 'Golden Rule', it should be used to finance acquisition of long-term assets that stay on the balance sheet for the long haul. It thus represents a permanent obligation to pay interest (on debt) or dividends (on equity), and in the case of debt, eventually to repay the principal. Mistakes in raising long-term finance can take years to erase. For example, too high a level of borrowing imposes a permanent prior charge against profits which has to be met year in, year out, good or bad.

Yet borrowing does offer major benefits. Recall the concept of the risk–return trade-off introduced in Chapter 2. Because debt imposes a fixed obligation on the borrower, it is inherently more risky for the firm than equity – the firm must pay interest on debt, come what may, whereas it has discretion over how much, if any, dividend to pay. But remember also that risk is two-sided. Whereas debt is risky for the firm, lending carries relatively little risk for the lender, while the reverse is true for equity. Equity is low-risk capital for the firm but it is highly risky for the investor, which explains why risk-averse investors seek higher returns from equities.

Once again several of the self-assessment activities in this chapter relate to the 'company of your choice' – you will find it helpful to have the report and accounts to hand as you read through the chapter and attempt the activities.

8.2 **The strategic issues**

When raising long-term finance, companies essentially face the choice between borrowing, i.e. debt finance, in its various forms, and equity, i.e. retained profits or issuing shares. In recent times, the distinction between debt and equity has become less clear with the emergence of different forms of 'hybrid' securities, such as convertible debt, which contain elements of both debt and equity, as explained later.

Choosing the appropriate method of long-term finance has a strategic dimension – if done wrongly, it can limit future strategic options. The major European telecommunications firms Deutsche Telekom and BT, in particular, favoured large-scale borrowing for financing strategic investment. They borrowed so heavily to finance foreign joint ventures and R&D into third-generation telephony that their debt was downgraded severely by the US credit rating agencies. As well as the signal flashed to the world about their financial stability, this resulted in their borrowing costs rising – in BT's case, by a full percentage point, which lowered its pre-tax profits by around £300 million p.a.

So what factors should a firm consider in its financing decision? There are four key issues to consider:

- risk
- ownership and control
- duration
- debt capacity.

We now look at these in turn.

Risk

How uncertain is the environment in which a firm operates? How sensitive is it to fluctuations in the economy? Some firms have a very high level of fixed costs which have to be met whatever their level of activity. These types of firm are relatively vulnerable to variations in economic activity, and move quite quickly into and out of loss-making situations. If the firm has a relatively inflexible operating cost structure, it is dangerous to rely on inflexible methods of finance, such as debt, that impose permanent interest obligations. Similarly firms will prefer to finance high risk projects with equity rather than debt (on which interest has to be paid regardless of success).

Ownership and control

Major injections of equity capital by new shareholders can dilute the ownership and control exercised by the present owners. Smaller firms, still perhaps under the control of the original founder members or their families, may prefer to borrow in order to retain that control.

Against this, it is often desirable to bring in new management talent, preferably accompanied by an injection of capital. This combination is called a **management buy-in (MBI)**. Firms that undertake an initial public offering have to relinquish a degree of control to obtain the benefits of a stock market listing, which often causes extensive heart-searching. It is becoming increasingly common for firms to reverse their status by de-listing from the stock market when directors feel that outside scrutiny and the requirement to disclose information is excessive in relation to the benefits of a listing, such as access to a wider pool of finance.

Duration

The finance should ideally correspond to the use to which it is put, as we saw in the last chapter with the matching principle. If the firm requires finance for an investment in which no profits are anticipated in the early years, it might be desirable to raise capital that imposes little, if any, demand on cash flow in these years. This was the principle applied in the financing of many dotcom companies which used equity or mezzanine finance.

Conversely, it would be unwise to raise long-term finance if the projects to be funded have a relatively brief life span. This may result in overcapitalisation and possible inability to generate sufficient returns to service the finance raised.

Debt capacity

Firms with little or no borrowing to date look relatively good prospects to potential lenders. However, a firm's debt-raising capacity depends also on the type of industry in which it operates, the nature and quality of the security it can offer, and the variability of its expected profits and cash flow – remember that interest and dividends are paid *out of* profits but *with* cash.

Before we begin detailed examination of financing options, it may be useful to review your knowledge of investor ratios and equity finance-related terms. The glossary in the appendix to this chapter should help.

Self-assessment activity 8.1

Locate 'your' company in the share price listings of the *Financial Times* and identify as many of the items detailed in the appendix to this chapter as you can that relate to it.

8.3 Equity financing

When looking at a company's balance sheet, you will find that its equity capital is divided into:

- issued share capital
- various kinds of reserves.

Issued share capital

This represents ordinary shares sold to investors, each of which carries the right to vote at company meetings. In most countries (the USA is an exception), ordinary shares carry a *par*, or *nominal, value* which is usually the price at which the shares were first sold (although, sometimes, shares are issued above the par value at the time of launch). For subsequent issues, as the firm grows its asset base and earning power, further shares can be sold above the par value. It is illegal in the UK to sell new shares *below* the par value.

The higher the selling price, the fewer the number of shares that have to be issued to raise a given sum, and hence the less severe the impact on voting control, given that each new share carries a right to vote. However, most companies first offer new shares to existing shareholders in a **rights issue** (see below), although shareholders may waive their rights regarding the sale of a limited number of shares. When not sold to existing shareholders, new shares are likely to be sold to (or **placed** with) friendly financial institutions, such as investment banks.

Before looking at new share issues, we will look at the main form of reserve, profits retained in the business.

Retentions

Retentions, or **retained earnings**, are represented in the balance sheet as part of reserves, often (confusingly) labelled 'profit and loss account'. This signifies their origin – retentions have been introduced as a result of previous years' profitable trading. In the balance sheet, therefore, they represent *past* profits, which have already been ploughed back into the company.

Readers aware of the difference between cash and profits will appreciate that balance sheet reserves are totally different from cash – in balance sheet terms, cash is an asset and the reserve is a 'liability', i.e. a method of financing. Reserves do not therefore represent a source of new finance for investment – new finance can only come from future cash inflows from whatever source. Retentions on the balance sheet represent funds already invested using previous inflows of cash. Any funding from this source will come from *future* profitability (to the extent that it has a cash counterpart).

It may be tempting to regard retentions as 'free' finance, but this is misleading. True, retentions cost nothing by way of issue costs but they impose an opportunity cost on shareholders, who could have invested the funds in other ways, had they received them. Retentions represent funds that could have been distributed as dividends to shareholders. By not paying a dividend, the company is incurring an obligation to achieve a return on reinvested profits at least as great as shareholders could otherwise achieve. Failure to do this destroys shareholder wealth.

Self-assessment activity 8.2

Look at the accounts – and the attached notes – of 'your' company and identify:

(i) the number of issued ordinary shares and their par value

(ii) the balance sheet value of this issued capital

(iii) the value, and description of, its reserves.

Rights issues

A rights issue is an issue of new shares offered initially to existing shareholders on a pro rata basis, based on their existing holdings. For example, in a '1-for-4' issue, the company offers investors the right to buy one share for every four already held. The shares are always offered at a discount, partly to make them look attractive, but mainly to insure against a fall in the market price during the offer period. If the market price fell below the offer price, no rational investor would take up the issue (unless they sought an increase in control).

However, to ensure that the shares are sold and the required funds are realised, a rights issue is usually underwritten by various financial institutions. For a fee, **underwriters** pledge to buy up any shares not taken up by existing shareholders. The underwriting fees, together with the firm's administration costs, will usually account for 2–3 per cent of the funds raised. Discounting the price also helps avoid having to rely on the underwriters to salvage the issue, which is considered bad for the issuer's image.

The discount has the effect of diluting the earnings of each existing share, i.e. until the funds raised are invested and generate profits, EPS falls, pushing down share price. This is partly offset by the value of the greater cash holding by the company – remember that cash has a value. This effect is explained in Table 8.1.

Table 8.1 The arithmetic of a rights issue

Before the issue	After the issue
Share price = £4	Extra shares dilute earnings,
	BUT:
Company makes 1-for-4 offer	
Offer price = £2	Now, the company holds more cash
A shareholder holding 4 shares	Shareholder holds 5 shares
plus cash of £2 has assets of	Value per share is: $\dfrac{£18}{5} = £3.60$
$(£4 \times 4) + £2 = £18$	= theoretical ex-rights price (TERP)

A shareholder who fails to act appears to lose 40p per share, i.e. for the four-share parcel, a total of $(4 \times 40p) = £1.60$. However, he can sell the right to buy new shares on the market. Each right carries an option to buy for £2 a share which will theoretically be worth £3.60 and is thus worth $(£3.60 – £2.00) = £1.60$. This is called the **nil paid rights price**. Rational shareholders should be indifferent between exercising rights and selling them in the market. The discount is an illusion and so is the fall in share price due to earnings dilution. Theoretically, shareholders are no worse or better off.

But notice that £3.60 is only the *theoretical* ex-rights price (TERP). The initial presumption is that the firm will neither create nor destroy wealth with the money raised, i.e. the NPV of the activity financed by the new funding is zero, implying that the cash raised is valued at its face value. Against this, a company with a sound investment proposition and with a good track record may see its ex-rights price rise well above the theoretical ex-rights price – and vice versa. The effect in practice depends crucially on what additional information the firm releases along with the rights issue announcement for the market to take a view on how profitably the company will spend the new money.

Self-assessment activity 8.3

ABC plc ordinary shares have a market price of £6.50. It plans a '1-for-3' rights issue at an offer price of £5.50. What is the TERP?
(answer at end of chapter)

Although, in principle, an investor may be no worse off, and perhaps better off, as a result of a rights issue, the picture is clouded by the need to meet dealing fees if the rights are sold, the sheer inconvenience of having to decide what to do, and the unplanned and possibly unwanted disruption to the investor's portfolio should the rights be taken up.

It is therefore important that a firm making a rights issue should explain the reasons for raising money. If it does not, investors may be inclined to mark down the shares out of concern that the company is desperate for cash, especially if the issue is '**deeply' discounted** (as in our example). A 'normal' or typical discount might be in the region of 15–20 per cent.

Self-assessment activity 8.4

Look out for an example of a firm making a rights issue. Observe under what terms the issue is made, the reaction of the market, and what commentators say about it.

The share premium account

Increasing capital by a rights issue will also create a reserve. Remember that ordinary shares are recorded in the balance sheet at their par value. If shares are issued above par value, as is usual, the excess is entered in the balance sheet as another reserve. Otherwise, the amount by which assets are increased (i.e. the cash received from the issue) would exceed the increase in capital.

For example, if a company issues 1 million new shares of par value 25 pence at a price of £5, the cash received is (1 million shares × £5) = £5 million, but the increase in issued share capital is only (£1 million × 25p) = £250,000.

The discrepancy of (£5m – £0.25m) = £4.75m is recorded as a **share premium account (SPA)**. To appreciate that this reserve is not the same as cash, consider what happens as the cash raised is duly spent on machinery and other assets. As the £5 million cash balance declines and is replaced by other assets, the SPA remains intact. Once again, we see that cash is an asset and reserves represent financing.

Another type of reserve

Before leaving equity finance, it may help to explain the nature and origin of another type of reserve which you might have observed for 'your' company, the revaluation reserve. As the term suggests, a revaluation reserve is created when a company revalues its assets, usually property. Land, in particular, rises in value over time, causing a divergence between its book value and its market value.

While it is generally regarded as prudent not to anticipate a profit until it is realised, if asset values seriously understate their market values, then the accounts no longer offer a 'true and fair view' of the company's financial position, hence the need to revise asset values. While asset revaluation raises the fixed asset total shown on the balance sheet, no new finance is raised. To ensure the balance sheet continues to balance, a new reserve is created as part of shareholders' funds. This cannot be distributed to shareholders except in a liquidation.

8.4 Borrowing

A company unwilling to cut dividends or to make a rights issue really has only two other alternatives if it wants to raise finance: it can sell assets, for example via a sale-and-leaseback, or it can borrow.

Borrowing has a major drawback – if the firm fails to deliver the annual interest payment, the creditors can appoint a receiver to liquidate the company in order to force repayment of their principal. A heavily indebted company is thus running the risk that, in a bad trading year, it may be forced into insolvency.

The downside of debt

Viatel is a US-based telecommunications operator, set up in the mid-1990s and listed on NASDAQ. It operates a 10,000 km fibre optic network linking 59 European cities.

In 2000–1, Viatel's trading was severely hit by a fall in demand for bandwidth from internet service providers and application service providers, leaving substantial spare capacity and severe downward price pressure as operators desperately sought to bring in cash to service loans.

In April 2001, Viatel announced that it would suspend $20 million of interest and dividend payments to give it and its advisers more time to explore 'strategic combinations'. It faced a mounting debt pile of over $2.1 billion and had already put its capital spending on hold, cash and other liquid assets having fallen from $440 million at December 2000 to below $200 million in just three months.

Viatel posted full-year net losses of $1.57 billion, triple what analysts were expecting, albeit boosted by restructuring charges and other exceptional items. Revenues were $750 million. Net interest charges were £181 million.

Viatel shares, already 99 per cent below their 52-week high of $44.63, closed down a further 55 per cent at $0.39. The company looked a certain candidate for insolvency if it could not somehow line up additional finance or restructure its debts in some way.

However, the experience of Viatel and similar headline cases in the technology, media and telecommunications sector notwithstanding, there are major benefits with borrowing which astute financial managers can exploit.

- It is relatively cheap to raise. Unlike a rights issue, underwriting is not normally required. The loan can be syndicated among several banks and other lenders who, by spreading their risks, can offer lower interest rates.

- Interest payments are tax-allowable (although this is of value only to the tax-paying company). The ability to set interest payments against profits for tax purposes creates a **tax shelter** or **tax shield**, measured by the tax savings generated via the ability to set off interest payments against profits for tax purposes.

- Use of debt finance also imparts a gearing effect (hence the name) to shareholder profits, under which an increase in activity and thus sales revenue of a given proportion will have a more than proportional impact. This is explained in detail in the next section.

- A rights issue risks altering the balance of voting control, e.g. if shares are acquired by the underwriters. Debt carries no voting rights. Therefore, the only diminution in control is imposed by the incorporation of restrictive *covenants* in the loan agreement. Examples of these include stipulations of minimum liquidity levels or maximum dividend pay-out ratios, and restrictions on further borrowing. All of these are designed to safeguard the interests of existing creditors (see the Corus Group mini-case below).

Self-assessment activity 8.5

DEF plc borrows £100 million at an interest rate of 7 per cent nominal. Assume its profits are £30 million. What is the annual tax saving if the tax rate is 30 per cent?
(answer at end of chapter)

8.5 Borrowing and the gearing phenomenon

Incorporating debt finance into a firm's capital structure is often referred to as 'gearing up the balance sheet'. The reason for this terminology is brought out by the following example.

Merch plc

Merch plc makes sales of £100 million and applies a 100 per cent mark-up on costs in setting price. Half its costs are fixed and half are variable. Its borrowings require debt interest payments of £20 million. The interest rate is fixed and no further borrowing is planned. To illustrate the gearing effect, let us examine the impact of doubling sales, say, as a result of expansion in the economy. Examine Table 8.2.

Table 8.2 The gearing phenomenon

£million	Before	After
Sales	100	200
Cost of sales		
Fixed	(25)	(25)
Variable	(25)	(50)
Profit before interest and tax (PBIT)	50	125
Interest on debt	(20)	(20)
Taxable profit	30	105
Tax @ 30%	(9)	(31.5)
Profit available for shareholders		
(Profit after tax)	21	73.5

There are several important things to note in this example:

● The percentage increase in shareholder profit resulting from the doubled activity is (£73.5/£21) = 250%. This reflects a *gearing factor* of (250%/100%) = 2.5 – sales have doubled, while shareholder profits have more than trebled.

● If the process works in reverse, i.e. if sales fall from £200 million to £100 million, there is also a gearing effect, but it is negative. The percentage fall in shareholder profits by £52.5 to £73.5 would be 71 per cent, reflecting a multiplier of (71%/50%) = 1.42 – when sales halve, shareholder profits fall by 142 per cent as much.

● Use of debt is excellent for shareholders when companies expand – a given increase in sales feeds through in a higher proportion into shareholder earnings, but the reverse applies in adverse trading conditions. Use of debt is good news in booms but can have dire consequences in recessions. Highly geared companies are prone to insolvency in recessions, which explains why firms strive to reduce their borrowings when trading conditions 'turn south'.

Another way of putting this is to say that use of debt finance raises the break-even point, i.e. the volume of output (or percentage of capacity utilisation) required to enable the firm to avoid making a loss. To explain this point, we need to examine the concept of operating gearing.

Operating gearing

Gearing is a more subtle process than suggested above. Even firms with no bor-rowings are geared via their methods of production and operation, i.e. via the technology they use. This determines the balance between their variable costs and the fixed costs that they have to meet to stay in business in the long term.

Whereas capital gearing refers to the proportion of the firm's capital structure comprised by borrowing, **operating gearing** refers to the proportion of the firm's costs which are fixed. Firms with high proportions of fixed costs will gen-erally have high break-even points. It is usually argued that such firms should not borrow to any great extent.

To break even, a firm must earn sufficient gross profits (or *contribution*) to cover its fixed costs. Contribution is the excess of revenue over variable costs. A firm's break-even volume (V) of output is found by dividing the fixed cost by the contribution generated by each unit of output, i.e. price less variable cost per unit:

$$V = \frac{FC}{P - AVC}$$

For example, to break even, a firm which incurs fixed costs of £20 million, selling its output at a price of £100 per unit with a variable cost per unit of £50, would have to produce the following amount:

$$V = \frac{£20m}{£100 - £50} = 400,000 \text{ units}$$

Introducing borrowings of £10 million at an interest rate of 10 per cent adds a further fixed charge of £1 million. This raises the break-even point by (£1m/£50) = 20,000 units to 420,000. Clearly, the greater the interest charge that must be met, the higher is the overall break-even volume.

This observation explains why companies in highly capital-intensive activi-ties like steel and chemicals should be especially concerned about their levels of both operating and financial gearing. Such companies operate in highly cyclical industries, producing basic products whose demand tends to fluctuate to a greater degree than the overall economy. Steel, for example, usually leads the economy into recession and is one of the last sectors to recover.

Capital-intensive firms with high operating gearing are especially exposed to oscillations in the business cycle. As their output volumes decrease, their earn-ings before interest and tax decline sharply and vice versa. As a result, they are regarded as relatively risky and the stock market attaches low P : E ratios to their earnings. In other words, investors tend to seek relatively high returns from their shares to compensate for the greater variability in earnings and the potential loss.

Adding a second tier of risk in the form of financial gearing accentuates the risk of inability to meet prior charges. As noted, given the need to meet these interest charges, the effect of financial gearing is to raise the break-even point. Generally, companies with high operating gearing should not over-rely on debt finance.

Self-assessment activity 8.6

Now return to the Merch example of Table 8.2.
How much of the overall gearing of 250 per cent is due to operating gearing, and how much is due to financial gearing?
(answer at end of chapter)

Measuring financial gearing

Financial gearing is introduced via financial policy. It can be measured in various ways. There are two types of financial gearing:

- **capital gearing** indicates the extent to which the firm uses borrowed capital, hence it is also called **balance sheet gearing**

- **income gearing** refers to the company's ability to meet ongoing interest charges out of its operating profit, i.e. profit before interest and tax. This is obtained from the Profit and Loss Account.

Capital gearing

The most common measure of capital gearing is:

$$\frac{\text{Long-term debt}}{\text{Net assets}}$$

Net assets, or shareholders' funds, can be measured using book values, i.e. the figures in the accounts, or at market values, i.e. market capitalisation. Some people prefer the latter because it is more up to date, although others prefer to use book values out of prudence – in times of financial distress, firms which need to sell assets to repay debts are unlikely to achieve what they thought was market value. In addition, until you try to sell, you do not know the market value.

Some prefer to include short-term borrowing on the basis that this also imposes obligatory interest payments. This seems sensible for companies that make extensive use of overdrafts. Against this, it seems 'fair' to allow for cash holdings which offset the impact of short-term borrowing. Increasingly common is the **net debt** measure of financial gearing:

$$\frac{\text{Long-term debt} + \text{Short-term debt } less \text{ Cash}}{\text{Net assets}}$$

Net debt can be expressed as a ratio (as here) or as an absolute amount. For a cash-rich company, the measure could record net cash rather than net debt.

The capital gearing measure, being derived from the balance sheet, purports to indicate the company's ability to repay debts by selling assets should the need arise, since capital is the counterpart of assets. However, the 'first line of defence', i.e. where the strain of borrowing is first revealed, is on the Profit and Loss Account, or income statement.

Income gearing

This is most commonly measured in terms of *interest cover*, or *'times interest earned'*, using EBIT (profit or earnings before interest and tax), i.e:

$$\frac{\text{EBIT}}{\text{Interest charges}}$$

From the safety perspective, the greater the number of times the firm is able to make its interest payments from profit before interest and tax, the better, i.e. its profits have 'room' to fall further and interest rates have 'room' to rise. Alternatively, income gearing can be expressed by inverting the expression for interest cover, viz:

$$\frac{\text{Interest charges}}{\text{EBIT}}$$

This signifies the *percentage* of EBIT which is pre-empted or 'spoken for' as a prior interest charge.

Self-assessment activity 8.7

Look at 'your' company's accounts and identify both its capital gearing and its income gearing.
Does it disclose its net debt in the summary statistics? If not, calculate it.

8.6 Types of long-term debt

Forms of long-term debt can be divided into two types: non-traded debt, and debt that can be bought and sold.

Non-traded debt

This originates as, and remains, a contract between a financial institution and its customer, with a specified interest and repayment profile. It is provided by a bank or similar financial institution. Banks offer both short-term advances and longer-term facilities. The shortest term of advance is the overdraft, which is technically repayable on demand and carries the risk of fluctuating interest rates. But it does possess the advantage that the borrower pays interest only on the balance of the overdraft outstanding at any one time.

A term loan can be offered for periods extending to 15 years or even longer for top-quality borrowers. The repayment profile is typically a matter of negotiation between the lender and the borrower. Interest is charged on the initial amount of the loan regardless of ongoing repayments of capital, which means that the effective interest rate is considerably higher – frequently about double – than the quoted rate. When the interest rate on the term loans is fixed, the borrower has the advantage of more certain cash flow planning, knowing in advance the precise profile of interest and capital repayments.

Revolving credit facilities ('revolvers')

A term loan generally specifies an agreed payment profile and amounts repaid cannot normally be reborrowed. Revolvers allow borrowers to borrow, repay and reborrow over the life of the loan facility, rather like a continuous overdraft. Like an overdraft, it is frequently secured on the borrower's working capital, e.g. using debtors and stocks as collateral, although very large firms may not be asked for any security. The advantage of revolvers is the enhanced flexibility provided, i.e. funds can be re-used in a continuous credit line. The commitment by the bank thus 'revolves' – the borrower can continue to ask for loans, subject to giving suitable notice, so long as the committed total is not exceeded. The fees charged include:

- a front-end, or facility, fee for setting up the loan
- a commitment fee to compensate the bank for having to commit some of its loan capacity by setting aside reserve assets to meet capital adequacy rules
- the interest cost, usually expressed as so many basis points (one bp = 0.01%) above LIBOR, the London Inter-Bank Offered Rate, the rate at which London-based banks lend to each other.

Marconi

In May 2001, the soon-to-be-disgraced electronics and advanced tele-coms equipment firm Marconi plc announced a new syndicated revolving credit facility of €3 billion. This was designed to consolidate two existing facilities, a €6 billion revolving credit (€1.3 billion already drawn down) dating from 1998, and a further €2.5 billion revolver signed in 1999. The new facility had a 12-month term with a margin of 40 bp above LIBOR with a commitment fee of 12.5 bp. When drawings exceeded 50 per cent of the facility, a 5 bp utilisation fee would become payable.

Self-assessment activity 8.8

Try to discover what loan facilities your local banks extend to corporate borrowers and on what terms.

Market debt

Market debt is issued in the form of a security, known as a bond, a security that can be traded on a financial market. There are many types of bond.

Debentures

Legally, a **debenture** is any loan agreement, but the term is usually applied to *secured loan stock issues*. If the firm defaults on payment of interest or capital, lenders can force the sale of company assets to obtain repayment from the sale proceeds. Debentures can be secured on specific assets (a **fixed charge**) or on assets in general (a **floating charge**). With a fixed charge, the management is unable to dispose of the asset(s) without the agreement of creditors. These are often called *mortgage debentures*, being secured on high-quality assets such as land and buildings.

Debentures normally carry a fixed rate of interest expressed as a percentage (the **coupon rate**) of the par value of the stock. They are commonly issued in £100 units. The interest is a prior charge on profits, payable before shareholders receive a dividend and indeed before taxation is assessed, i.e. the interest qualifies for tax relief.

Almost invariably, they have a fixed term to redemption (i.e. repayment), although rare cases of perpetual bond issues occur, e.g. the permanent interest bearing bonds (PIBS) issued by some building societies and inherited by their demutalised successors, such as HBOS plc (Halifax Bank of Scotland).

Not all corporate bonds are redeemable!

In December 2000, the Dutch insurance company Aegon launched a €450 million perpetual subordinated cumulative bond in order to repay outstanding short-term debt. The bonds had a coupon of 6.875 per cent, and Aegon retained a **call option**, giving it the right to redeem the bonds at par after five years, and every year thereafter. Aegon also reserved the right, under certain circumstances, to defer interest payments.

During the lifetime of the bond, its market value fluctuates with variations in the going rate of interest in the market on debt of a comparable risk. Specifically, if interest rates increase, the values of existing securities fall, and vice versa. They usually carry restrictions on management freedom of action, called *covenants*, which can take various forms, designed to protect the interests of the lenders, viz:

- restrictions on the size of dividend payouts
- restrictions on permissible levels of key financial ratios, e.g. minimum levels of liquidity
- restrictions on permissible amounts of further borrowing
- provision of a regular flow of financial performance data.

Unsecured loan stock

The word unsecured is something of a misnomer – although the loan is not secured on assets as such, it is backed by people's faith in the company's ongoing ability to meet the required interest payments. In that sense, the loan is secured on the firm's future expected earning power. By definition, these are relatively high-risk securities ranking behind secured loan stock for payment, i.e. they are *junior stock* or *subordinated stock*. Accordingly, they carry relatively high interest rates.

The unsecured loan stock of companies which operate in high-risk areas or which have a limited track record is rated by agencies such as Moody's as below investment grade or quite simply 'junk'. The stock of even some very large and well-known companies can come into this category.

Self-assessment activity 8.9

Now look at 'your' company's long-term borrowing and its composition by type of security and by time to maturity – you will find this in the notes to the accounts.

Asset-backed securities (ABSs) – a new development

In recent years, some companies, and even individuals, have issued a new breed of security, backed not by physical assets but by a reliable long-term stream of future earnings. A category of assets commonly utilised has been intellectual property represented by patents and copyrights. Like most security issues, Asset-backed securities (ABSs) are sold essentially to raise cash for investment in other activities.

Organisations effectively capitalise their future income into a single lump sum and sell it on the financial markets to generate immediate cash. The firm's financial advisers set up a special purpose vehicle (SPV), effectively a 'bank' into which the designated income stream is paid and from which is paid the stream of interest payments needed to service the borrowing.

This process of converting non-tradable claims into tradable ones is called securitisation. Like most financial innovations, securitisation originated in the USA. Banks began to parcel up mortgage commitments made by house purchasers into bundles of mortgages and sold them as interest-bearing securities. Having both liquidity and a bank's guarantee, these could be offered at a lower interest rate than that charged on the underlying mortgages, the difference representing profit for the bank. This practice is now widespread in Europe.

The following examples of the ABS principle demonstrate its flexibility and versatility:

- Holland's De Nationale Investeringsbank NV (DNIB) is a major player. Its ABS issue in March 1999, worth €290 million, was its fourth inside two years.

- In 1992, Disney Corporation issued $400 million in seven-year notes with a variable rate of interest to be paid from royalties receivable from its portfolio of film copyrights, a path followed also by News Corporation in 1996.

- Calvin Klein, GE Capital and Nestlé have all issued ABSs secured on trademarks.

- In 1997, the rock star David Bowie raised $55 million by selling bonds backed by his music copyright portfolio, with an average bond life of ten years.

- This tactic was also adopted in 1998 by Rod Stewart and Michael Jackson, using similar security.

8.7 **Hybrids**

Hybrid finance exhibits features of both debt and equity – it is neither totally one nor the other. Hybrids are particularly important in financial planning as they offer flexibility to both firms and investors. For this reason, hybrids are often favoured by risky new ventures, like the dotcom firms. We discuss the two most common forms, preference shares and convertibles, and also warrants.

Preference shares

Under current UK accounting regulations, preference shares count as part of shareholders' funds, although they often bear a strong resemblance to debt finance. They normally carry no voting rights – abnormal circumstances include when the firm faces a takeover bid – but they have preferential rights over ordinary shares in the distribution of profits after tax and in the return of capital in a liquidation.

The preferred dividend is thus a prior charge before ordinary dividends can be paid, usually expressed as a fixed percentage of the par value of the share. HBOS plc preference shares pay a dividend of 6.125 per cent as a percentage of the par value of £1, thus yielding a gross return of 6.125p, and actual cash returns after 10 per cent dividend tax of 5.51p per share. However, there is no legal obligation to pay a dividend – in a bad year, directors may decide not to pay at all.

Significant use of preference shares is rare nowadays, largely because they are not tax-efficient compared with debt securities on which the interest payment qualifies for tax relief. An exception is Tomkins plc which uses preference share capital quite extensively – its 2002 accounts gave an indication of the variety of types of preference share that companies might issue. Under Capital & Reserves, it disclosed:

- convertible cumulative preference shares: £337 million

- redeemable convertible cumulative preference shares: £386 million.

(The former pays a dividend at 5.56 per cent of par value, and the latter pays 4.34 per cent.)

This terminology needs explanation:

- Convertible means that the shares can be converted into ordinary shares usually at some specified date (although Tomkins' preference shares are *perpetual*, i.e. convertible at any time at the holder's option).

- *Cumulative* means that if, in any year, the dividend is not paid, it will be carried forward to a future year. When this happens, preference shareholders assume voting rights as they now have no advantage over ordinary shareholders.

- Redeemable means that they may be repaid either at the option of the company or of its preference shareholders.

Two other varieties (not applicable to Tomkins) are participating preference shares and floating rate preference shares. Holders of the former may participate in profits in addition to the otherwise fixed dividend in a particularly profitable year at the discretion of the directors. An example of floating rate preferred shares was the non-cumulative redeemable shares issued by Six Continents plc (formerly Bass plc) which, until their redemption at their (unusual) par value of

95.5p in April 2000, entitled holders to receive a net dividend at the rate of 75 per cent of the London Inter-Bank Offered Rate.

These examples show how it is possible to combine several attributes of preference shares in the same security. You can also see why preference shares are regarded as hybrids. But are they more like equity or debt? Arguably:

- convertibles look more like equity than debt
- redeemables look more like debt
- cumulative ones look a little more like debt
- participating ones look more like equity
- floating rate shares look more like debt.

Thus, a convertible, irredeemable, non-cumulative, participating preference share would have strong equity characteristics, and vice versa for a non-convertible, redeemable, cumulative, non-participating share. Varieties with some other combinations of attributes are more difficult to place along the spectrum between pure equity and pure debt. Many observers almost automatically classify preferences shares as debt, but it is usually worth a closer look to see how justifiable it is to do this.

Self-assessment activity 8.10

How much preference dividend is Tomkins plc committed to paying each year?
(answer at end of chapter)

Convertibles

A convertible begins life as a form of debt, but carries the right, at the holder's option, to convert into ordinary shares at some specified date in the future and on specified terms, e.g. how many new ordinary shares can be obtained on conversion per unit of convertible stock.

Firms that issue convertibles have higher gearing ratios and may be viewed as being relatively risky. Yet the greater risk is not reflected in a higher coupon rate. Because there is a prospect of making a capital gain should the share price market perform strongly, convertibles can usually be issued at a lower rate of interest than straight or 'plain vanilla' debt. Until the date of conversion, the holder receives a fixed rate of interest and is a long-term creditor of the company.

Convertibles are particularly suitable for companies facing relatively high business risks but strong potential growth because they offer investors the possibility of participating in future prosperity. This explains the ease with which dotcom companies were able to issue so much convertible debt. The downside for companies is that payment of interest, although tax-deductible, must be paid every year, good or bad, and the principal requires repayment if holders do not convert.

The downside for shareholders is the prospect of dilution of their equity as and when conversion occurs. Dilution is especially damaging if the conversion terms are misjudged, e.g. if growth is a lot stronger than expected, the conversion terms may be overgenerous to convertible holders. It often makes sense for existing shareholders to hedge against this risk by acquiring the convertibles themselves. Indeed, convertibles may be issued initially to owners in a rights issue.

Convertible conversion terms can be complex. As well as a specified conversion date (or range of dates), the security will carry a *conversion rate*. This is stated either as a *conversion price* – the nominal value that can be converted into one ordinary share – or as a *conversion ratio* – the number of ordinary shares that will be obtained from one unit of loan stock.

Conversion value is the market value of ordinary shares into which a unit of convertible loan stock can be converted. This is equal to the conversion ratio times the current market price per ordinary share. The *conversion premium* is the difference between the market price of the convertible and its conversion value. The *rights premium* is the difference between the market value of the convertible and its value as straight debt. Each of these last two terms can be expressed as an absolute value or per share.

An example will clarify this plethora of terms.

Example: Cannon plc

Cannon plc's balance sheet shows 10 per cent convertible loan stock, redeemable at par in seven years, which can be converted at any time in the next three years into 20 ordinary shares. The debenture currently trades at £117, interest has just been paid and the current share price is £3.60. The ex-interest market price of the stock of a company of similar risk is £109.

> The current conversion value = (20 × £3.60) = £72
> The current conversion premium = (£117 – £72) = £45
> > (or £2.25 per share)
> The current rights premium = (£117 – £109) = £8
> > (or £0.40 per share)

At the initial date of issue, the conversion value will be less than the issue price. Investors hope that as the conversion date nears, and as the market price of the underlying shares increases, the conversion value will rise accordingly, i.e. conversion becomes more attractive to investors. The conversion premium is proportional to the time remaining before conversion occurs. As conversion approaches, the market value and the conversion value converge until the conversion premium disappears. With no conversion premium, the value of the convertible is simply its value as straight debt with a similar coupon and maturity.

The value of the convertible on the market thus depends on the current conversion value, the time remaining to conversion, the market's expectations regarding the expected returns, and the degree of risk of the underlying ordinary shares.

The year 2000 accounts of Arcadia plc, the stores group, showed a convertible issue of 4.75 per cent convertible unsecured bonds. Holders of this stock had the right in 2001 to convert their stock into ordinary shares at a price of £2.34 per share. Beyond this date, Arcadia could redeem the stock at par on giving 30 days' notice to investors.

Warrants

Warrants are coupons attached to other securities that give the holder the option to buy new shares, and unlike convertibles, they bring in new finance when the option is exercised. They are usually linked to debt issues, although some companies attach them to equity or, like Eurotunnel plc, issue them directly to ordinary shareholders as *equity sweeteners*. The warrant holder is entitled to buy a stated number of shares at a specified price up to a specified date. Each warrant states the number of shares the holder may purchase and the time limit beyond which the option cannot be exercised (unless it is a *perpetual warrant*).

Like convertibles, warrants confer flexibility. If attached to loan stock, they offer the holder the opportunity to participate in the future growth and prosperity of the firm. As with convertibles, they may allow debt financing at lower interest rates since they offer a potentially valuable option. They may be issued by new and expanding companies to attract investors, or as part of the purchase consideration in an acquisition. Whether or not the option is taken up, and whether in turn, it raises additional finance, depends on the future trading success of the firm and on the market price of its ordinary shares compared with the exercise price.

Like convertibles, warrants carry a hidden kick. When they are exercised, they can dilute the earnings of each existing share and thus lower share price. An example should clarify this.

Defoe plc

In 2000, when its ordinary shares had a market price of £4.00, Defoe issued loan stock with one warrant attached giving the right to buy one ordinary share at a price of £5.00 in 2007. Rational investors would exercise the right to buy in 2007 if the market price exceeded £5.00. If, at the exercise date, the share price on the market was £7.00, investors would make a capital gain of £2.00. The diluting effect, which is calculated in the same way as in a rights issue of ordinary shares, would moderate this gain. Existing investors who do not exercise their warrants thus see their ownership diluted and their wealth reduced as the company effectively gives away £2.00 per new share.

Warrants can be traded on the market separately from the securities to which they are initially attached, and can offer spectacular gains. For example, if in 2003 Defoe plc shares trade at £5.50, the warrants will be worth 50p each as they carry the right to buy for £5.00 something now worth £5.50. If the price of the ordinary share rises to £6.00, i.e. by 9 per cent, the value of each warrant will double to £1.00. For this reason, they are described as *'geared plays'*.

Self-assessment activity 8.11

(i)   Does your company use any hybrid finance?

(ii) If so, what characteristics does it exhibit?

(iii) Do you think these securities are more like debt or equity for your company?

(iv) What difference to the gearing ratio does it make whether you classify these as debt or equity?

8.8 Worked example

The following Bardsey plc study is an ACCA Managerial Finance exam question (June 1997, question 1). It provides an opportunity for you to apply many of the above ideas. The solution also brings in a few more additional issues, e.g. sale-and-leaseback (SAL) as a method of financing.

Bardsey plc

Bardsey plc operates a chain of city centre furniture stores. It is 60 per cent owned by the original family founders. Annual sales growth in real terms over the past decade has averaged 3 per cent and sales even fell during a recent recession. No real growth is expected from existing operations in the next few years despite plans to continue to offer generous credit to customers.

To achieve faster growth, Bardsey is considering developing a number of 'out-of-town' sites, adjacent to giant supermarkets and DIY stores. During 200Y, this will involve capital outlay of £50 million plus extra working capital requirements of £20 million to finance stock-building. In recent years, Bardsey's capital expenditure (mainly store refurbishment and vehicle replacement) has averaged £20 million per annum and has been financed entirely from depreciation provisions.

The stock market currently applies a price : earnings ratio of 11 : 1 to Bardsey's shares compared to the sector average of 14 : 1. Bank base rate is 8 per cent.

Exhibit A gives information on key financial indicators for the stores sector (listed companies only), and Bardsey's accounting statements for 200X are summarised in Exhibits B and C.

Required

As Bardsey's chief accountant, you are instructed to:

1 Calculate Bardsey's expected net cash flow in 200Y without the new investment, assuming no changes in the level of net working capital.

2 Prepare a report which:
   (i) discusses Bardsey's financial performance and health as compared with the stores sector as a whole
   (ii) advises the board of Bardsey as to how the proposed investment programme might be financed.

Exhibit A Selected ratios for the stores sector

Return on (long-term) capital employed	14.3% (pre-tax)
Return on equity	12.3% (post-tax)
Operating profit margin	26.2%
Gearing (total debt/equity)	42.0%
Stock period	180 days
Interest cover	3.2 times
Dividend cover	2.1 times
Fixed asset turnover (sales/fixed assets)	1.2 times

Exhibit B Bardsey's Profit & Loss Account for year ended 31 December 200X

	£m
Turnover	150.0
Cost of sales	(90.0)
Operating profit	60.0
Interest paid	(15.0)
Pre-tax profit	45.0
Corporation tax	(12.0)
Profits after tax	33.0
Dividends	(20.0)
Retained earnings	13.0

Exhibit C Bardsey's balance sheet as at 31 December 200X

Assets employed	£m	£m	£m
Fixed (net):			
Land and premises	200		
Fixtures and fittings	50		
Vehicles	<u>50</u>		300
Current assets:			
Stocks	60		
Debtors	100		
Cash	<u>40</u>	200	
Current liabilities:			
Trade creditors	(85)		
Dividends payable	(20)		
Tax payable	<u>(12)</u>	<u>(117)</u>	
Net current assets			<u>83</u>
Total assets less current liabilities			383
15% debentures 2015–16			<u>(100)</u>
Net assets			283
Financed by:			
Issued share capital (par value 25p):			100
Revaluation reserve			60
Profit and loss account			<u>123</u>
Shareholders' funds			283

Source: ACCA Managerial Finance Exam, June 1997, question 1

Answer

1 Cash flow forecast

Bardsey is currently more than able to finance routine investment requirements from its positive cash inflows. Neither the depreciation provision nor the regular investment expenditure is specified, but, being equal in amount, they are offsetting. With unchanged operating activities and no net change in its working capital position, its expected cash inflow for 200Y is:

	£m
Operating Profit	60
+ depreciation	unspecified
Working Capital	–
Cash Flow from operations	60
Less:	
Investment expenditure	(unspecified)
Interest for 200Y	(15)
Taxation due from 200X	(12)
Dividends due from 200X	(20)
Net Cash Flow	13

2 (i) Report on Bardsey plc's financial health and performance

Comments on financial indicators

Benchmarking Bardsey's ratios against the industry average, we find:

1. Bardsey's ROCE is (£60m/[£283m + £100m]) = 15.7%, in line with the industry average. However, because the measured ROCE is depressed by the recent asset revaluation, it may reflect above average performance if other firms have not themselves re-valued.

2. Bardsey's ROE is (£33m/£283m) = 11.7%, well short of the industry average, probably reflecting the higher post-revaluation equity. However, this could also be due to the lower than average gearing ratio, assuming that competitors face interest rates below their ROEs.

3. Bardsey's operating profit margin is (£60m/£150m) = 40%, well above the industry average. This may suggest that Bardsey operates more efficiently than competitors, or that it charges higher prices, possibly competing on service quality of service. It may even serve a different market segment that is willing to pay more for higher quality products.

4. The fixed asset-to-turnover ratio indicates the productivity of a firm's fixed assets. Bardsey fares relatively poorly on this measure – each pound of fixed assets generates sales of only (£150m/£300m) = £0.5 against the industry average of 1.2, reflecting Bardsey' s fixed asset revaluation.

5. Lengthy stock holding periods are common among furniture retailers, needing to hold high value items for display. Based on stocks/cost of sales, Bardsey turns over stock every (£60m/£90m) × 365 = 243 days, compared to the industry figure of 180 days, although if Bardsey does serve an up-market segment, such a disparity would be expected.

6. Bardsey's capital gearing of (£100m/£283m) = 35% using book values, is less than the sector average, although the latter includes short-term debt which Bardsey does not utilise. However, a high proportion of fixed-to-total costs in the stores sector makes for high operating gearing in this sector. If Bardsey's operating gearing is greater than the sector as a whole, it may be obliged to use relatively less borrowed finance.

7. Bardsey's interest cover is a seemingly safe (£60m/£15m) = 4 times, against the sector average of 3.2. Its operating profits could fall substantially without threatening difficulty in meeting interest charges.

8. Bardsey's dividend cover – (£33m/£20m) = 1.65 times – is low. This could reflect pressure from the dominant shareholders to pay high dividends. Equally, the cover could be deflated by temporarily low post-tax profits as Bardsey emerges from recession. Bardsey has no difficulty in financing a high payout with its substantial cash holdings and its strong cash flow.

9   Finally, although no industry comparators are given, the liquidity ratios appear satisfactory. The current ratio is (£200m/£117m) = 1.71 times, and the quick ratio is (£140m/£117m) = 1.20 times. Looking at the composition of the current assets, debtors at £100m (67% of sales) appear high, probably reflecting lengthy interest-free credit periods, a typical marketing ploy in this sector.

Overall Assessment

Bardsey's performance is solid, if not spectacular. Despite operating in a mature market for retailing quality products, currently emerging from recession, Bardsey generates adequate profitability and sound cash flow. The relatively low P : E ratio suggests the market is not expecting substantial growth from Bardsey. The existing highly-concentrated, share-holding structure, makes it an unlikely take-over target. Bardsey at present appears to be over-capitalised, suggesting a case for paying rather higher dividends.

2 (ii) Financing the new investment programme

Bardsey needs additional finance of (£50m + £20m) = £70m for new developments. Operations can provide £13m of this, leaving a substantial net external financing requirement of (£70m – £13m) = £57m. Possible financing alternatives are:

Run down cash balances

Bardsey is highly liquid with cash balances of £40m. These would largely cover the additional financing needs. However, some degree of liquidity – 5% of sales is not unusual – is desirable as a buffer against adverse contingencies. Although there are no 'rules' governing optimal liquidity levels, a cushion of highly liquid assets, say £5 to 10m, held in cash and interest-earning investments, would be prudent. A further consideration is the low return on cash, depressing the ROE – moreover, interest rates are expected to fall further.

Rights issue

With its present over-capitalisation, selling more shares seems pointless, especially as it would further weaken the ROE. Moreover, Bardsey's already relatively low P : E ratio, implying a modest stock market rating, would be damaged by a rights issue.

Borrowing

1   *Short-term*: The 'Golden Rule of Finance' advises firms to match the maturity of their financing with the life of their assets. Following this advice, Bardsey would use short-term financing for its extra working capital requirements. Overdrafts are cheaper than equity, especially in view of the tax relief on debt interest. With its strong asset backing, a modest increase in gearing carries little additional risk. Even excluding the cash and profit returns from the new ventures, borrowing perhaps £15m at say, 2% above base rate i.e. 10%, thus imposing extra interest charges of (10% × £15m) = £1.5m, would lower interest cover only to £60m/[£15m + £1.5m] = 3.87 from its present 4.00.

2   *Long-term*: With such strong asset backing, especially land and premises of
£200m, Bardsey should have little trouble raising long-term debt gearing.
However, as interest rates are expected to fall, variable rate borrowing
looks more appropriate, although usually a little costlier than fixed rate
borrowing. Failing this, it may be cheaper to use short-term debt until
interest rates fall, and then to re-finance long-term. There also seems a
case for repaying the existing long-term debt (if permitted) that costs 15%
pre-tax to finance.

Bardsey will also need to consider why the market expects a cut in
interest rates. If the money market is efficient, it might be argued that
expected lower rates are *already* factored, at least in part, into the existing
term structure of interest rates.

Lower future rates provide an opportunity for fixed-rate long-term borrowing to lock into historically low interest rates. Meanwhile, variable
rate short-term financing is good insurance against falling interest rates.

Sale-and-leaseback (SAL)

SAL involves selling good quality assets (usually property) to a financial institution but retaining the right of continued occupation. (An example was the
£465 million sale by Center Parcs, the leisure resort firm, of properties to Sun
Capital, a private equity group, on a 15–48 year rental basis). With its city-
centre location, many of Bardsey's assets might qualify. SAL has a neutral
impact on the balance sheet. The assets sold remain on the balance sheet as
they are held for the long-term, a liability is created in relation to future rental
payments, and the cash raised is used to acquire more assets.

Conclusion

Assuming, Bardsey does not raise the dividend, a safe financing package would
involve utilising say, £30m of its cash balances, short-term financing to cover
the working capital requirements, plus a SAL.

Source: modified from ACCA solution

8.9   Summary

In this chapter, we have described the general issues that a firm should consider
when raising long-term finance. Especially important is the strategic aspect, as
an inappropriate decision can limit the firm's options in the future. The internal
and external ways of raising new equity were contrasted and various methods of
borrowing and quasi-borrowing, using hybrid financing instruments, were
analysed.

Particular attention was given to the phenomenon of gearing, in both its operating and financial dimensions. The chapter rounded off with a worked example which applied much of the material in the chapter as well as drawing upon your prior knowledge in the field of ratio analysis.

The next chapter will focus on two core issues – what percentage rate of return a firm should seek to achieve on its invested capital, and how this might be influenced by its choice of financing method.

References

Textbooks

Arnold – chs 10 and 11.
Brealey & Myers – chs 15, 23 and 24.
Pike & Neale – ch 18.
Samuels, Wilkes & Brayshaw – chs 12, 14 and 15.
Watson & Head – chs 5 and 6.

Questions and mini-case studies

1   Carbonari plc is an engineering company operating in the UK. It has recently won a new contract from abroad which will entail a lot of new investment. After much consideration, the company has decided to raise the extra finance by means of a rights issue. At the moment the company has 50 million shares in issue and the latest share price is 846p. The company requires £150 million extra finance for the new contract although it will also need to cover the £10 million cost of the rights issue.

Required
(a) Advise the company on the terms of the rights issue that it should make (there are lots of possible permutations available for you to choose from). Give reasons for your advice.
(b) Using your answer to (a):

   (i)   What will be the theoretical ex-rights price?
   (ii) What options are open to a shareholder who owns 1,000 shares in the company? Calculate the financial outcome for each option. In your answer give reasons for a shareholder choosing between these options.
   (iii) Discuss the possible reasons behind the company's decision to obtain the extra finance by means of a rights issue rather than debt.

2 Hughes plc is a relatively young company specialising in the manufacture of digital components. The Hughes family still has a substantial stake in the company. The company operates in a fast-moving business where there are frequent changes in technology. However, it has benefited from the growth in the economy over the last few years fuelled by strong consumer spending on products that it is involved in, such as DVD players. Indeed, the company has recently stated that it wants to increase dividend per share by 10 per cent p.a. over the next few years.

The latest accounts for the company are as follows (all figures in £m):

Balance sheet as at 31 March 2002

Fixed assets			
Land	15.3		
Buildings	13.7		
Equipment (net)	18.7		
			47.7
Current assets			
Stock	7.3		
Debtors	12.6		
Cash	1.8		
		21.7	
Current liabilities			
Trade creditors	(4.3)		
Bank overdraft	(3.9)		
		(8.2)	
Net current assets			13.5
Total assets less current liabilities			61.2
Less creditors amounts falling due after one year			
Bank loan		(12.6)	
8% debentures		(27.8)	
			(40.4)
Net assets			20.8
Capital and reserves			
25p ordinary shares	10.0		
Reserves	10.8		
			20.8

Profit and loss account year ending 31 March 2002

Sales	118.6
Operating profit	14.6
Interest	(5.9)
Profit before tax	8.7
Corporation tax	(2.7)
Profit after tax	6.0
Dividends	(4.3)
Retained profits	1.7

Hughes has decided to make a significant investment in new manufacturing equipment costing £10 million. As a result of this investment and including normal growth, it is expected that earnings before interest and tax will increase by £3 million per annum in the medium term.

The company has identified two possible sources for the required £10 million finance:

● a rights issue at a 10 per cent discount to the current share price of 200p

● an issue of ten-year debentures at 10 per cent interest per annum.

Issue costs can be ignored. The marginal rate of corporation tax on any increase in profit before tax is 24 per cent. The company's debentures have a current market price of £97 per debenture.

Required
From the information given, write a report to the company advising on the choice between these two sources. Your report should include:

● the projected profit and loss account for next year on the assumption that the investment takes place

● the effect of the decision on existing financiers of the company

● an analysis of the main issues likely to affect the financing decision.

Include in your report any calculations and ratios (with any assumptions) that you think appropriate.

3 DEB plc is a listed company that sells fashion clothes over the internet. Financial markets have criticised the company recently because of the high levels of debt that it has maintained in its balance sheet.

The company's debt consists of $150 million of 8 per cent debentures that are due for repayment by 31 March 2005. Financial markets indicate it would not be possible to issue a new loan under the same conditions. The market value of the debentures is $90 per $100 nominal.

DEB plc's draft balance sheet at 31 March 2002 was as follows:

	$ million
Ordinary shares of $1	100
Reserves	<u>20</u>
	120
8% debentures (at nominal value)	150
	<u>270</u>
Fixed assets	200
Net current assets	<u>70</u>
	<u>270</u>

Fixed assets consist of $150 million of capitalised development costs and $50 million of land and buildings.

The company's share price has fallen consistently over the past two years as follows:

	Price per share
31 March 2000	$20
31 March 2001	$8
31 March 2002	$4

The company intends to make a 1-for-2 rights issue at an issue price of $2.50 on 30 June 2002. It is assuming that the cum-rights price at the issue date will be $4. Immediately thereafter, all the proceeds will be used to redeem debt at its nominal value and thereby reduce its gearing.

Required

(a) Calculate the gearing (that is, debt/equity) of DEB plc at 31 March 2002 using both

   (i)   book values
   (ii) market values.

b) Evaluate

   (i)   the weaknesses
   (ii) the benefits

   of the two methods used to calculate gearing in requirement (a) above.

(c) Calculate the gearing of DEB plc in market value terms, immediately after the rights issue and redemption of debt.

(d) Briefly explain the advantages and disadvantages for DEB plc of redeeming part of its debt using an issue of equity shares.

Source: CIMA Finance (IFIN) May 2002, question 2

Mini-case study – Amazon Inc

Conventional wisdom says that firms can borrow only if they have 'quality' (i.e. highly marketable) assets to use as security to back the debt. If the company defaults, that is, it becomes unable to pay interest or repay the capital, creditors can force the sale of the assets to recover the loan. Firms without a sound asset base are therefore normally obliged to raise finance by equity. Dotcom stocks might appear to fit into the second category – their assets are very largely intangible, often representing a core idea, marketing expertise and little else.

But little was normal about dotcom stocks. Their shares soared in value during 1998–early 2000, inflated by expectations of spectacular growth as new avenues of business-to-consumer (B2C) and business-to-business (B2B) business emerged. Dismal Jeremiahs predicted it would all end in tears – very few of these companies were making profits or generating cash, far from it. Their hunger for cash to set up marketing networks would surely spark a financing crunch.

Several big internet companies had contrived to convince investors to purchase convertible bonds, a form of borrowing. These securities can be converted into ordinary shares at a predetermined 'strike price' above today's market price but, people hope, below the market price at the conversion date. To the investor, the appeal of a convertible is the prospect of a capital gain on conversion, so companies can usually offer a much lower interest rate than on orthodox debt securities. US companies that exploited this opportunity included America Online, which issued $2.6 billion in convertibles, and Amazon with issues of $1.9 billion. In 1999, dotcom companies accounted for around a quarter of all convertibles issued in the USA.

By spring 2000, the bubble in internet stocks on Wall Street had burst. The NASDAQ index, dominated by high-technology stocks, fell 25 per cent in a few days, recalling the famous meltdown of 1987. Much of the glitter of the glamour stocks had faded. As a result, dotcom convertibles were traded so far below their strike price that the prospect of conversion became a mirage. Convertibles effectively became straight debt and, moreover, not very highly rated debt – effectively 'junk bonds'.

In June 2000, Standard & Poor's rated Amazon's convertible debt at

CCC-plus, and Moody's applied a rating two levels lower at Caa3. Both are regarded as low junk grades. A Moody's analyst said: 'It's one of the lowest ratings we have. It's highly speculative. In order for the company to improve its rating, we'd have to see more evidence that it will turn cash-flow positive.' It was widely believed that Amazon would run out of cash within a year and needed 'to pull another financing rabbit out of its rather magical hat', as another analyst put it.

One source of finance now blocked off was income from staff exercising stock options. While the share price was riding high in 1999, employees exercising stock options had generated over $300 million cash. Meanwhile, Amazon needed to find over $100 million p.a. in interest payments and, of course, find the wherewithal to repay the debt itself.

Required

(a) Explain why convertible financing was so attractive to both issuers and purchasers at this time.

(b) Discover what is meant by a 'junk bond'.

Mini-case study – Corus

The notes to the accounts of Corus Group plc, the steel group formed in 1999 from British Steel and the Dutch firm Hoogovens, disclose an item of long-term borrowing labelled '11.5 per cent debenture stock 2016'. This has book value of £150 million, and is repayable at par in the year 2016. Until then, Corus is committed to paying annual interest at 11.5 per cent on this debt.

One of several covenants attached to this loan stipulates a minimum asset backing. It requires that Corus's tangible fixed assets located in the UK shall not fall below £2,000 million.

Required

(a) What is the required asset backing for the debenture?

(b) Why do you think it is so high?

(c) What is the tax shield for Corus?

Mini-case study - Urtica

ABS issues are not restricted to 'sophisticated' financial environments. Urtica is a Polish pharmaceuticals wholesaler and a main supplier of Poland's notoriously slow-paying (state-owned) hospitals. In 1999, it was reported that Urtica would issue 50 million zlotys ($12 million) in three-month commercial paper over the next three years. These securities were backed by monies owing from Urtica's customers and the proceeds would ease Urtica's working capital problems. Non-payment risk was shifted to outside investors, who were paid only when the hospitals paid up. Urtica's bank set up a special company to receive payments from customers and take responsibility for investors receiving their dues.

The securities were overcollateralised. This arrangement enabled investors to buy securities from firms they would normally regard as too risky. Urtica's securities were purchased mostly by Polish corporates having a temporary cash surplus and which would normally invest spare cash in lower-yielding state debt securities. Because of the overcollateralisation, Urtica's ABSs were regarded as less risky than normal corporate debt. Of course, while some of Urtica's customers might default, not all would do so, nor at the same time!

Required

(a) Identify the benefits to Urtica of this arrangement.

(b) What is meant by 'overcollateralisation'?

(c) What are the risks incurred by purchasers of Urtica's bonds?

Appendix

A glossary of equity financing terminology

1 A **gross dividend** is the amount of dividend per share in pence *before deduction* of tax. In the UK, dividends are paid net of 10 per cent tax. If a company pays a **net dividend** of, say, 9.0p per share, this is equivalent to a gross-of-tax payment of 9.0p/[1 – 10%] = 10.0p. The difference of 1.0p is called a tax credit. Until April 1999, this was reclaimable from the tax authorities by non-tax-paying personal investors.

2 The **dividend yield** of a share is the rate of return which shareholders currently earn on their shares, ignoring any capital gain. It is measured by dividing the last annual dividend paid by the current share price. It can be expressed either in net-of-tax terms or, as is more usual, in gross terms, enabling comparison with yields on other securities, in particular, government stock.

3 The **dividend cover** indicates the number of times the company could afford to pay out its net dividend from its post-tax profits. It thus purports to measure the degree of security of the dividend payments by suggesting the extent to which profits can fall before endangering the dividend.

4 The **payout ratio** is simply the inverse of the dividend cover and shows the proportion of a company's post-tax profits paid out as dividends. In other words, it is the dividend per share divided by the earnings per share = DPS/EPS – where EPS is the profit after tax divided by the number of ordinary shares issued.

5 The **price : earnings ratio (P : E ratio)** is the relationship between a company's current market value and its profit after tax, or expressed in per share terms, the market price per share divided by post-tax profit per share. It supposedly indicates the number of years a company would take to earn back its share price, although this assumes constant earnings. A relatively high P : E ratio indicates the market's confidence in the company's earnings growth (or recovery) potential.

6 When a share trades **cum-dividend**, the purchaser will have the right to receive the recently declared dividend. On a specified cut-off day, shares will go **ex-dividend**, signifying that new purchasers will not receive the dividend. Other things being equal, the share price will fall by the amount of the dividend paid.

Self-assessment answers

8.1 and 8.2
Your call.

8.3
Value per three shares prior to issue = (£3 × £6.50) = £19.50
Value per four shares post-issue = (£19.50 + cash of £5.50) = £25.00
TERP = £25.00/4 = £6.25

8.4
Over to you.

8.5

This can be shown by looking at the profit after tax (PAT) with and without the tax relief.

With no relief, DEF will pay tax of (30% × £30m) = £9m.

With tax relief, it pays tax on only (£30m – interest of 7% × £100m) = £23m.

The tax charge becomes (30% × £23m) = £6.9m, a saving of (£9m – £6.9m) = £2.1m.

The tax shield can also be found by the formula (tax rate × interest payments) = (30% × £7m) = £2.1m.

8.6

Operating gearing is the motor behind the 150 per cent increase in operating profits from £50 to £125, reflecting a gearing factor of 150%/100% = 1.50.

Financial gearing drives the further increase in PAT from £21 to £73.5. The separate contribution of financial gearing is found by dividing the overall increase by the portion due to operating gearing, viz: 2.5/1.5 = 1.67.

We *divide* here to unscramble the two effects because the overall process is multiplicative.

8.7, 8.8 and 8.9

Over to you.

8.10

The answer is zero as both stocks are cumulative, meaning that the payment of dividend can be rolled over into future years.

8.11

Over to you.

9

THE REQUIRED RETURN ON INVESTMENT

Improving returns to investors

Tomkins plc, a diversified engineering conglomerate, attaches great importance to sound financial management, in particular, the need to achieve a rate of return that satisfies its various finance providers. Its 2003 annual report stated:

'An accounting measure we monitor closely for all of our businesses is the annualised return on invested capital. Comparison of return on invested capital with the weighted average cost of capital gives an indication as to the extent to which a business is covering its cost of capital over time. Return on invested capital represents the after-tax operating profit in the business expressed as a percentage of the average invested capital in the business including all goodwill associated with acquisitions made in the past.

The annualised return on invested capital for the Group, before operating exceptional items and goodwill amortisation, was 9.7 per cent compared with 8 per cent for the period to December 2001. The improvement in the period is due to improved operating performance and the effect of the lower rate of tax ... We use an internal estimate of weighted average cost of capital of 9 per cent.'

Source: Tomkins plc report and accounts 2003

Objectives:

This chapter aims to:

- demonstrate how to calculate the cost of debt finance, before and after corporate taxation
- show the impact on the required return of using debt finance
- examine the impact of gearing up the capital structure on the value of the whole company
- discuss some of the limiting factors on a company's ability to raise debt.

9.1 Introduction

A central problem in financial management is identifying the rate of return that should be achieved by the firm on both its existing operations and on new investment projects. If managers cannot achieve a return at least as great as the minimum required by the firm's owners, then shareholders are likely to ask some searching questions. Either managers restructure company operations to achieve greater efficiency, or they step aside to make way for a more dynamic management team. Knowledge of this required return is needed both for valuing the company as it stands and for assessing the value of any new operations, which should enhance the value of the corporate whole. More specifically, the required return dictates the discount rate applicable to cash flows anticipated from new investments.

 Most firms are financed partly by debt – lenders also require a return to compensate for the opportunity costs they incur in making their capital available. Thus *all* types of capital carry a cost which firms must cover. Having already looked at the cost of equity in Chapter 6, in this chapter we now examine the cost of debt, and then the concept of the weighted average cost of capital (WACC), applicable when different types of capital are used in tandem. Broadly speaking, the WACC is the minimum rate of return required to satisfy all providers of capital, including both shareholders and lenders. As we will see, the WACC depends on the amount of debt in the capital structure

9.2 The cost of debt

 The cost of any form of finance is the return that the firm has to offer in order to attract and retain investors. As a very rough approximation, the cost of debt is the interest rate payable on it. For example, consider Campbell plc which issued an irredeemable £10 million debenture in units of £100 par value with a coupon rate of 8 per cent – the coupon rate gives the annual interest that will be paid out on this debenture = coupon rate × par value = 8% × £100 = £8 p.a.

Now that an investor knows how much interest he will receive on this debenture, the price he will be willing to pay for it depends on the percentage return he requires. This will largely be decided by the return he can obtain elsewhere in the market on another debenture of similar risk.

The market value of debt capital varies inversely with changes in interest rates. For irredeemable debt, the simplest case, the formula is:

$$\text{Market value} = \text{Par value} \times \frac{\text{coupon rate}}{\text{market rate}}$$

To examine the interaction between bond values and market interest rates, imagine the going rate set by the bond market for securities of the same degree of risk as Campbell's debt rises to 10 per cent. This would make the Campbell's debenture look bad value if it were still traded at par, yielding just 8 per cent, when newly issued securities would be offering a yield of 10 per cent. People would be unwilling to buy the old debenture unless its price fell to equalise its yield with the market rate. This price would be:

$$£100 \times \frac{8\%}{10\%} = £80$$

$$\text{At this price, the yield} = \frac{8\% \times £100}{£80} = 10\%$$

The fall in price is the market's way of telling Campbell that it faces a marginal cost of debt of 10 per cent. If it wanted to raise further debt capital, it would have to offer the going interest rate of 10 per cent.

The cost of debt: redeemable bonds

However, our formula works accurately only for irredeemable or very long-term bonds – very few firms can issue such long-dated bonds (although 18m did issue 100-year bonds – century bonds – in 1998). Redeemable bonds have a specific repayment date – usually, they will be repaid in full, i.e. at par value. When working out the yield on limited life debt, we have to allow for the eventual repayment of the principal.

With redeemable bonds, the arithmetic is complicated by having to build this capital repayment into the calculation – like the interest payment, it represents a valuable cash flow for the investor. The nearer the bond is to maturity, i.e. its repayment date, the more its value is dictated by the final lump sum payable (usually the fixed par value) rather than the annual interest.

When the market assesses the price of a bond, investors will look at the amount and timing of all future payments, both interest and principal, anticipated from holding the bond, in relation to the rate of return deemed appropriate. The cost of debt is simply the rate of return or yield built into the current market price.

Strictly, the cost to the firm is found by solving the **internal rate of return** equation:

Market value = Σ discounted payments up to redemption date

For a £100 bond with two years' life to redemption, the expression is:

$$\text{Market value} = \frac{I_1}{(1+R)} + \frac{I_2}{(1+R)^2} + \frac{P_2}{(1+R)^2}$$

where I = annual interest payment (paid in Years 1 and 2)
P = repayment of principal (paid at the end of Year 2)

Initially, look at this from the firm's point of view. It knows the amount and timing of interest payments and capital and also can observe the market price. The cost of debt is found by working out what yield is implied by the current market price, i.e. it can work backwards from the market price to infer the cost of debt imposed by the market. This is brought out by the following activity.

Self-assessment activity 9.1

For limited life bonds, calculating the yield involves more awkward arithmetic than for irredeemables (although spreadsheet functions include an IRR facility). To get a feel for the approach, work out the yield on the following bond:

Market value = £98.26 (ex-interest); coupon rate = 9%; interest paid at year-ends, redeemable in exactly two years.

(*Hint*: start discounting at 11%.)
(answer at end of chapter)

So far, so good. However, there is a further aspect to consider – yields and rates of return on corporate debt are not symmetrical as between lender and borrower. Because of the tax relief available to firms on debt interest, the effective cost of debt to the firm is usually less than the yield that the investor gets from holding the same security. We need next to introduce tax relief on corporate debt.

Allowing for taxation - an approximation

The previous calculation took no account of the tax-deductibility of debt interest. Interest can be set against profits for tax purposes, assuming the company has sufficient *taxable capacity*, i.e. profits. This means that the cost of debt for firms is generally less than the nominal cost, or coupon rate. If, for example, the company can borrow at 10 per cent before tax, the after-tax cost, with tax paid at 30 per cent, is 10% (1 – 30%) = 7%. To appreciate this, work through self-assessment activity 9.2.

Self-assessment activity 9.2

Calculate the post-tax profits with and without tax relief on debt interest. You should discover a tax saving of £0.3 million which reduces the effective interest cost from 10 per cent to 7 per cent.

(£m)	With no tax relief	With tax relief @ 30%
Operating profit	£10m	
Interest on £10m debt @ 10% interest		
Taxable profit		
Tax at 30%		
Post-tax profits		
Tax saving	–	

(answer at end of chapter)

Because the tax bill falls from £1 million to £700,000, giving a tax saving of £300,000, the after-tax cost of servicing this loan falls from a nominal 10 per cent to just 7 per cent.

Allowing for taxation – fixed-term loans

In the absence of tax, the cost of debt would simply be the going market rate of 10 per cent. However, tax relief on interest payments reduces the cost to the firm to roughly 10 per cent $(1 - T)$, where T = the rate of taxation applied to company profits. However, this simple formula works only for non-redeemable debt. For redeemable debt, the correct cost of debt to the firm is found by solving another internal rate of return equation that now includes the tax impact, viz:

Market value = Σ discounted after-tax payments up to redemption date

Remembering that the capital repayment is not tax-allowable, for a £100 bond with two years' life to redemption, the expression is:

$$\text{Market value} = \frac{I_1(1-T)}{(1+R)} + \frac{I_2(1-T)+£100}{(1+R)^2}$$

where I = annual interest payment

Example

Let us demonstrate this by computing the cost of debt in relation to the two-year bond examined in self-assessment activity 9.1. Recall that the market price was £98.26 and the coupon rate was 9 per cent. With tax relief at 30 per cent, the annual interest cost before tax of £9 per £100 of stock reduces to £9(1 − 30%) = £6.3.

The yield is the discount rate which satisfies the expression used above, i.e.:

$$£98.26 = \frac{£6.3}{(1+R)} + \frac{£6.3}{(1+R)^2} + \frac{£100}{(1+R)^2}$$

The solution for R is 6.3 per cent (found by interpolating between the result when discounting at 6 per cent and that found when discounting at 7 per cent – verify this). When you do this by trial and error, you may appreciate the case for working with irredeemable bonds whenever possible!

Self-assessment activity 9.3

Now repeat this analysis for this example, assuming a three-year life for the following bond:

Market value = £80.00 (ex-interest); coupon rate = 8%, interest paid at year-ends.

Redeemable at par in exactly three years; rate of corporate taxation = 30%.
(answer at end of chapter)

9.3 The required rate of return when equity and debt are combined

Previously, we have looked at the costs of debt and equity in isolation. The issue now arises of what happens when companies mix debt and equity. Does this affect the required return on investment? If so, how? We will examine this issue by looking at the case where a firm borrows to finance a new project, thus adding a layer of debt finance to an existing equity base. This will enable us to consider the question of what rate of return it should seek before and after the issue of debt. The before-and-after situations are referred to as Cases 1 and 2 respectively.

How gearing affects the required return - the WACC

Consider the two cases below, before and after the firm raises debt finance.

Case 1

Initially, the firm has zero gearing.

- Book value of shareholders' funds = £100 million (par value of shares = £1).
- This comprises 50 million £1 shares and £50 million in reserves.
- Share price = £4.
- Shareholders require a return of 20 per cent.
- The firm now borrows £25 million at 10 per cent interest.

Case 2

Now the firm borrows £25m to finance a project.

- Shareholders' funds = £100 million.
- Long-term debt = £25 million. (Assume this is very long-term.)
- Gearing (debt/equity) is now (£25m/£100m) = 25%.
- Interest rate on debt = 10% (before tax).

With these figures, how does use of debt affect the required return on investment on the new project? It is tempting but wrong to regard the cost of the new finance (10 per cent before tax, 7 per cent after tax) as the appropriate cost. Why is this wrong?

Looking ahead in time, as the capital structure of the company is expected to stay the same, some future projects will be financed by loan capital and some by equity. The choice between the two at any particular point in time will be determined by various factors such as prevailing market conditions. At times, it may be easier to raise finance by borrowing, and on other occasions, by equity.

If the cost of the specific source of finance was used as the relevant discount rate for a project, it could lead to bizarre decisions. For example, assume that the company has decided to invest in two projects, A and B, and that Project A is financed by loan capital at a cost of 7 per cent and Project B is financed by equity at 20 per cent. Assume that the IRR for project A is 8 per cent and for project B 15%. If the specific cost of finance is used in each case, Project A would be accepted and Project B would be rejected even though project B looks the better project. If a balanced or weighted average cost is used, this type of discrepancy is avoided. It is thus more appropriate to view the firm on a continuous basis dipping into an ongoing 'pool' of finance, carrying the corresponding weighted finance cost.

Returning to the example, in Case 1, with zero gearing, the firm has to achieve a return of at least 20 per cent on new projects, simply because this is the return that shareholders demand.

In Case 2, assuming its shareholders still want a 20 per cent return, the overall required return becomes a weighted average of the component required returns. Thus the cost of each type of finance is weighted according to its contribution to the overall capital structure. Thus, so long as the firm adheres to 25 per cent gearing, the overall return, or weighted average cost of capital:

$$WACC = (\text{cost of equity} \times \% \text{ of equity}) + (\text{post-tax cost of debt} \times \% \text{ of debt})$$

Remember that reserves form part of equity, and to allow for tax relief on debt interest at 30 per cent. At the debt-to-equity ratio of 25 per cent, the weights are 4/5 equity (£100m/£125m) and 1/5 debt (£25m/£125m), and the WACC is:

$$[20\% \times \tfrac{4}{5}] + [10\%(1 - T) \times \tfrac{1}{5}] = (16\% + 1.4\%) = 17.4\%$$

If the firm achieved a rate of return less than this, it would be unable to satisfy the demands of its investors – 17.4 per cent is thus the minimum rate of return required to keep all its providers of finance happy. As a result, this rate becomes the cut-off rate for investment, assuming that this gearing ratio is maintained. The rationale for using the WACC in this way is explained further in the worked example in section 9.4.

In addition, now that the WACC is less than 20 per cent, it means that a wider range of projects becomes available to the company and there is greater scope for creating value.

Some experts consider that the appropriate weights should be measured at market values. If the share price of £4 is used, the market value of the equity is (£4 × 50m) = £200 million. Taking the debt at face value (e.g. it may not be traded on the market), the weights become (£200/[£200m + £25m]) = 89% for equity and (£25/[£200m + £25m]) = 11% for debt. The WACC increases to:

$$(20\% \times 89\%) + (11\% \times 7\%) = (17.80\% + 0.77\%) = 18.57\%$$

The difference in results arises because the market value of equity is substantially greater than the book value. This suggests that generally it may be better to use market values. A moment's thought should justify this conclusion – book values of assets are based on original costs, i.e. ancient history. When judging the performance of their investments, are rational investors likely to relate current returns to historic costs or to modern-day values?

The validity of the WACC

You should be aware that the WACC is not always the appropriate rate to discount cash flows from new projects. Use of the WACC embodies some key assumptions. Most critical are the following two:

- As noted, the WACC implies that project financing involves no further change in gearing. If the company intends to change its long-term gearing ratio, a new WACC will have to be calculated using the new debt: equity ratio.

- The WACC implies that the new project is in the same risk category as the company's other projects, i.e. the new project is not moving the firm into different fields of activity. Higher risk projects will cause both debt and equity investors to demand higher returns, thereby increasing the WACC.

Two other assumptions are that the project is small in relation to existing activities, so that any 'spillover' effects of an operating or financial nature are minimal, and that the cash flow profiles of the new projects are level perpetuities, as in the underlying cost of capital theory.

So long as these conditions apply, the WACC can be used to appraise new investments.

9.4 Worked example

The worked example below is designed to consolidate and to extend your understanding of the WACC, and in particular when and why it can be used.

Hussain Foods plc

Hussain Foods plc produces a range of processed foods for large supermarket chains. Its existing capital structure is:

	£m
50p ordinary shares	90
Retained profit	150
Long-term loan stock @ 9%	70

Hussain's Board envisages no change in its capital structure in the foreseeable future. The ordinary shares currently trade on the London Stock Exchange at £4.70. Hussain recently paid a cash dividend of 22 pence net of tax. Analysts expect the dividend per share expected to grow at a compound rate of 6 per cent per annum over the next few years. The loan capital issued by the company is irredeemable and has a current market value of £105 per £100 nominal and is trading ex-interest.

The directors are currently considering building a large processing plant, a venture requiring substantial investment. Although Hussain uses DCF methods to appraise new investment projects, the directors cannot agree on the appropriate rate to use in discounting future cash flows:

- Mr Trescothick believes that the appropriate figure is the cost of long-term loan capital, on the basis that, as the funds employed for the venture will be raised in this form, this represents the actual cost of funds used.

- Mr Vaughan suggests that the cost of equity be used, as given by the dividend valuation model.

- Mr Thorpe believes that the overall cost of capital should be used. He argues that the weighted average cost of capital should be used to represent the overall cost of funds used by the company.

- Mr Flintoff believes that the risks associated with the venture are considerably higher than those of the existing business of company and, given the size of the proposed investment and the potential impact of mistakes, a risk-adjusted discount rate should be used. Hussain's Beta coefficient is 0.7.

- Mr Giles argues for using the firm's target return on long-term capital employed (ROCE). Because a ROCE of 15 per cent has been achieved more often than not in the past, this rate should, therefore, be used as this hurdle rate.

The current rate of return on government long-term bonds is 5 per cent and corporate tax is paid at 30 per cent. A leading security analyst expects the FTSE 100 Index to yield an overall average return of 10 per cent in the next decade.

Required:

- Calculate the discount rates proposed by Trescothick, Vaughan, Thorpe and Flintoff and Giles respectively.

- Comment on each of the director's arguments concerning the appropriate discount rate to be used, and recommend a suitable rate.

Answer

Looking at the individual suggestions:

1 **Cost of loan capital – Trescothick**
   The cost of debt is:

$$k_d = \frac{1}{V_d} = \frac{£9(1-30\%)}{£105} \times 100 = 6.0\%$$

This is unsuitable as a discount rate even though project finance may be raised in this form. With Hussain's capital structure expected to stay constant over time, this means that some projects will be financed by loan capital and some by equity capital. The choice between the two at any particular point in time will be determined by various factors, in particular, prevailing financial market conditions. Sometimes, it may be easier to raise debt finance and sometimes, equity.

Using the cost of particular sources of finance as the relevant project discount rate might lead to bizarre decisions. For example, assume Hussain considers investing in two projects A and B; Project A is debt-financed at a cost of 7 per cent and B is financed by equity at 11 per cent. Imagine the IRR for both projects is 9 per cent. If the specific cost of finance is used in each case, Project A would be accepted and Project B rejected even though each promised exactly the same IRR.

2 Cost of equity – Vaughan

The dividend valuation model suggests the cost of equity is:

$$k_e = [D_1/P_o] + g = [22p\ (1.06)]/£4.70 + 6\% = (5\% + 6\%) = 11\%$$

Problems with this method include the following:

- It assumes the share price used in calculation is 'correct', i.e. set by an efficient capital market.

- It suggests that the future annual rate of dividend growth is constant.

- It gives a required rate of return across the firm as a whole, and may not be suitable for evaluating projects with risks different from the overall average.

- Being the cost of equity alone, it neglects other methods of financing that may be used.

3 Weighted average cost of capital – Thorpe

The market value of shares and loan capital are used for establishing the weightings in the capital structure. It is assumed, that with no plans to alter the capital structure, the existing debt-equity ratio is the target ratio.

	Amount	Market value (£m)	Weighting
Ordinary shares	180m @ £4.70	846.0	92%
Loan Finance	£70m @ £105/£100	73.5	8%
Total		919.5	100%

	Cost %	Weights	Weighted cost
Cost of equity	11.0	0.92	10.1%
Cost of debentures	6.0. or 6%(1 - 30%) = 4.2% after tax	0.08	0.3%
WACC			10.4%

The WACC provides an average cost of capital and projects are accepted or rejected according to whether or not they generate a return above this benchmark figure. The WACC assumes that various types of finance enter a common pool of funds, shedding their individual identities. From this pool, the funds required for a particular project are drawn. It is therefore considered inappropriate to associate a particular source of finance with a particular investment project. Instead, the WACC of the pooled funds should be used.

The WACC, however, may not always be appropriate as a discount rate. It is most useful for marginal projects where the project is relatively small in size compared to the business as a whole. The larger the project, the more likely it will have 'spill-over effects', e.g. size-related effects such as distribution and other economies and diseconomies of scale affecting the management of existing operations, and hence the risk/return profile of the whole firm. Where the risk of the new project differs significantly from that of existing activities, using the WACC will be less valid. Also, where project financing differs from the existing capital structure, this affects the overall cost of capital.

4 Risk-adjusted discount rate (CAPM) – Flintoff

The CAPM equation suggests:

$$k_e = \text{risk-free rate} + \text{risk pemium} = 5\% + 0.7\%(10\% - 5\%) = 8.5\%$$

The CAPM calculates a discount rate by adding a risk premium to the risk-free rate of return, which is usually taken from short-term government stock. The risk-adjusted discount rate reflects the fact that shareholders will expect higher returns from projects whose risks are higher. Using a risk-adjusted discount rate implies that risk will increase over time (via the compounding effect on the risk premium). This may not always apply.

Moreover, as with the dividend valuation rate, the CAPM rate is the return required by shareholders – it should be used in conjunction with the cost of debt to calculate the WACC where the firm, or the project, is financed by a mixture of debt and equity.

The new venture is riskier than Hussain's existing activities so the current Beta of 0.7 is probably inappropriate. A 'tailored' beta taken from a surrogate company that already operates in the intended area needs to be identified.

5 Return on capital employed (ROCE) - Giles

The ROCE measures overall return on investment, usually expressed as operating profits to long-term finance, and is widely used by managers in setting target profitability. It may therefore, appear logical to employ a discount rate reflecting the ROCE target. However, ROCE makes no allowance for capital structure, and is usually expressed in pre-tax terms. Although it is easy to adjust to a post-tax basis, the use of a target ROCE as a hurdle rate for investment projects is likely to be inappropriate as it uses the ROCE for purposes for which it is not designed.

The ROCE is rooted in accounting data, and relates accounting profits to the long-term capital invested. Capital expenditure decisions, however, concern cash flows rather than accounting profit. Moreover, the ROCE neglects the cost of funds employed by the business. Where the ROCE exceeds the cost of capital, using it as a discount rate may result in rejecting profitable projects. Conversely, where the ROCE is below the cost of capital, it may result in accepting unprofitable projects.

Assessment

The cost of debt and the ROCE would be highly unsuitable choices as discount rates in most, if not all, circumstances. This leaves the choice between WACC and the risk-adjusted discount rate. However, neither approach is perfect – each has drawbacks. Nevertheless, if Flintoff is correct in stating the new project is in a different risk class than the existing activities of the company, the risk-adjusted rate may be appropriate, although it might be more appropriate to use the Beta of a firm already operating in the sector targeted.

Source: modified from ACCA Managerial
Finance Exam, June 1997, question 1 and solution

9.5 Gearing and company value

As we have seen, for a geared company, the lower WACC opens up a wider vista of attractive wealth-creating opportunities. This suggests a higher company value is achievable. To explore the impact on company value, we will develop the example analysed in section 9.3 in further detail. You should bear in mind that when we talk of the value of a company, we mean the value of its assets, which, by definition, according to the accounting equation, have to correspond to the value of the methods of financing. Put another way, and given that acquisition of assets can be achieved by either debt or equity:

Value of the firm = [value of its equity + the value of its debt]

To explore the issue of how company value relates to financing mix, we will use the device of a share repurchase, which involves borrowing to buy back ordinary shares from owners. This therefore represents a transfer of cash from firm to owners but with no change in the size of firm or in its range of activities or

its operating profitability. It is the same basic firm but with different financial packaging. This device allows us to isolate financing from investment issues, i.e. had we added debt to existing equity, this would have raised the issue of how the new finance would be used, in what projects and with what degree of profitability. Also, for simplicity, it is assumed that all cash flows are perpetual.

The figures in Case 1 relate to the situation *before* the company undertakes the share repurchase, or buy-back.

Case 1

Debt	=	0
Profit before tax (PBT)	=	£57.14
Tax rate = 30%, hence PAT (0.7 × £57.14m)	=	£40m
Shareholders' funds	=	£100m
(£1 ordinary shares = £50m; reserves = £50m)		
Earnings per share = (£40m/50m)	=	80p
Shareholders require a return of 20%		
Share price is EPS discounted at 20% viz. 80p/20%		
using the perpetuity formula)	=	£4
Value of equity = (£4 × 50m shares)	=	£200m

The buy-back

The company borrows £40 million at 10 per cent interest in order to replace ordinary shares. It can thus buy (£40m/£4) = 10 million shares. There are no other changes in either operating or financial policy.

In Case 2, we will examine the two questions:

● What is the effect of the share repurchase on the EPS?

● What is the effect on share price?

Case 2

PBIT	=	£57.14m
Interest = (10% × £40m)	=	(£4.00m)
Taxable profit	=	£53.14m
Tax @ 30%	=	(£15.94m)
Shareholders' earnings	=	£37.20m
EPS = (£37.20m/40m)	=	93p
Share price = (93p/20%)	=	£4.65
Value of equity = (40m × £4.65)	=	£186m
Value of debt	=	£40m
Value of whole firm	=	£226m

Apparently, this exercise in '*financial engineering*' has created value for the benefit of shareholders of £26 million out of nothing. How can this happen? There has been no change in the company's operations – the only thing to have changed is the method of financing and hence the sharing out of the firm's operating income. Why then has its value increased?

There are two main reasons. Firstly, the company has replaced 'expensive' equity finance with cheaper debt finance. The second explanation is the free gift from the government – the opportunity to exploit the tax relief on debt interest. However, some writers argue that this effect is likely to be offset by shareholders seeking a higher return to compensate for the greater financial risk. This question should make us a little suspicious of the claimed benefits of borrowing, or, at least, of the extent of them. This issue is addressed in the next section.

Self-assessment activity 9.4

Calculate the WACC in the preceding situation, before and after the buy-back, and using book values and market values.

(answer at end of chapter)

9.6 Is there an optimal gearing ratio?

The preceding analysis suggests that the higher the gearing, the higher the company value. What an appealing prospect! It suggests that a company can keep raising its value by gearing up the capital structure.

But in reality, there are practical limits to how far a company should push its gearing. However, we conclude that until it reaches these limits, careful use of debt finance can make shareholders better off. One of the financial manager's tasks is to explore the frontiers of permissible gearing until the *critical gearing ratio* – where value is maximised – is discovered. The relationships between gearing, firm value and the cost of finance are shown in Figure 9.1.

Figure 9.1 shows that the costs of equity and of debt are constant over modest gearing ranges up to OG. However, it is likely that investors will respond adversely at some stage to increases in gearing. Both lenders and shareholders will eventually come to question the company's ability to maintain ever-increasing interest payments, which have to be paid whether the firm makes a profit or not and the threat of *insolvency* will begin to loom. As a company approaches and reaches the point of insolvency, it will incur various costs in trying to avert the danger, or if the worst happens, the costs of insolvency itself. These are called *financial distress costs*. The word 'cost' here should be interpreted broadly to include the costs of lost opportunities.

Some theorists argue that shareholders will react *immediately* to any increase in gearing by demanding a higher rate of return so as to neutralise the supposed benefits of gearing. This is really an empirical issue. All we can conclude is that

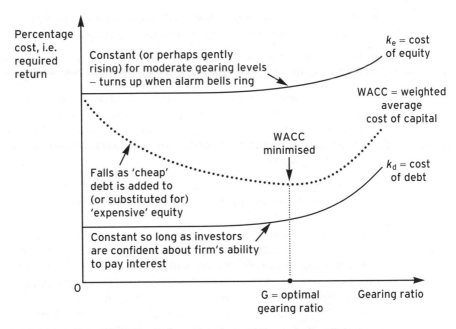

Figure 9.1 The relationships between gearing and the cost of capital

debt can be advantageous so long as shareholders do not 'scare easily', and if they do, there are still the tax advantages of debt to consider. On balance, the WACC probably does fall over some range.

Financial distress

Financial distress costs may be classified into the following:

- *Direct costs*. These are the 'obvious' costs – the legal and administrative expenses and delays of receivership and liquidation if the worst does happen.

- *Indirect costs*. Well before a distressed firm hits the buffers, it will find that its performance and financial health, and hence the prospects of recovery, are hampered by actions it must take to stave off its creditors.

Among the latter are the following:

- Companies in distress suffering a forced sale of assets are likely to be stripped of their established winners, their 'stars', and promising new developments, their more attractive 'question marks'. For example, in 2003, Fiat sold off its Toro Assicurazioni insurance operation and its aerospace division, Fiat Avio, in order to repay debt to restore financial stability to its ailing core automobile business.

- They are forced to cut back both R&D programmes and training programmes, cuts which hinder their longer-term ability to compete effectively.

- They are forced to control working capital more tightly, e.g. by reducing stocks and by giving shorter credit periods, both of which may damage sales.

- Conversely, although they may want to take more credit from suppliers to ease cash flow problems, these are likely to offer less attractive terms as it becomes generally known that the company is in distress. As well as less credit by volume and by duration, this may involve lower discounts/higher prices and lower delivery priority.

- Lower capital expenditure – 'essential' replacements may be delayed and strategic investment programmes may be put on hold.

In distress situations, cash is not just 'King' but also Queen and Jack, and probably the ten as well! The key to survival is generating enough cash to meet ongoing obligations. While investment spending will be curtailed, those projects that do survive are likely to be evaluated on their short-term payback properties, with all the drawbacks that reliance on payback entails.

Possibly, the most severe cost is the diversion of managerial energies away from strategic management into often prolonged and tortuous negotiations with creditors simply 'to keep the ship afloat'. A good example was the protracted and ultimately fruitless parallel negotiations which directors of the South Korean motor manufacturer Daewoo Motors had to undertake during 1999–2000 with bankers on one side and a series of possible rescuers, such as General Motors and Ford, on the other.

Self-assessment activity 9.5

In your regular reading of the financial press, look out for an example of a company in distress and observe what steps it is taking (or, more likely, it is having forced upon it by creditors) in order to relieve its difficulties.

9.7 What factors affect borrowing decisions in practice?

There is no universal optimal gearing ratio – different companies are likely to settle for different levels of gearing which they and their advisers feel are safe or comfortable. Clearly, there is little point in undertaking excessive levels of borrowing which have to be managed so carefully that it diverts management attention away from the 'real' business of finding and exploiting worthwhile investment projects.

One might expect the following factors to impact on borrowing decisions:

- The extent to which sales are expected to fluctuate. This depends both on fluctuations in general levels of economic activity and on the extent to which the firm's sales are linked to the overall economy. The sales of some firms are highly geared to the economic cycle while others are largely immune. Fluctuations in sales lead to fluctuations in operating profits.

- The extent to which operating profit (PBIT), *out of which interest is paid*, is expected to fluctuate. This is linked to sales fluctuations but also to the firm's cost structure via its operating gearing, as we saw in Chapter 8. This is why lenders closely monitor the interest cover of a firm.

- The extent to which the flow of cash, *with which interest is paid*, is expected to fluctuate. This depends both on variations in sales and profit and on the effectiveness of working capital management.

- The extent to which interest rates are expected to vary. If interest rates are expected to rise, now might be a good time to borrow on fixed-rate terms.

- In any walk of life, it takes a certain bravery to deviate from what is regarded as normal or acceptable. Firms must have a sound justification to borrow at a different level of gearing to the industry norm.

- The attitude of lenders – whether, and to what extent, they are prepared to take risks. This depends partly on what other risks they accept, and how well diversified they are. These aspects will be reflected in the type of security they require and the types of covenant imposed.

- The attitude towards risk of the firm's managers. Managers may be more risk-averse than shareholders because they are more exposed to risk than shareholders. If the firm cannot meet financial commitments, then managers' jobs are on the line, while if a well-diversified shareholder has a holding in a firm in financial distress, his exposure to loss is compensated by the success of other firms represented in his portfolio.

- The marketability of the firm's assets. *In extremis*, if a firm has to sell assets to pay off debt, the ability to sell quickly and at a 'full' price is essential – how easily does it expect to sell assets in a distress sale?

Self-assessment activity 9.6

The topic of gearing raises several agency issues, e.g. should managers worry about the risks imposed by gearing, or should they allow share-holders to take their own defensive precautions? When thinking about this, reflect on the information available to shareholders and managers respectively, and what information may be signalled by a firm's borrowing decision.

(answer at end of chapter)

Generally, firms strive hard to avoid reaching the upper levels of gearing where the costs of distress are encountered. Cultural factors also have a part to play. There is evidence in the UK that companies are relatively risk-averse and 'gear up' only to levels that would be regarded as quite conservative in some other countries such as Germany and Japan, where the banks traditionally have had closer links with industry.

9.8 Summary

This chapter has covered the cost of debt and has shown how to combine it with the equity cost in assessing the overall rate of return for a company financed by a mixture of debt and equity – the WACC. This led on to a discussion of some benefits of combining debt and equity, in particular a potentially lower cost of capital and higher equity value. The next chapter, looks more closely at how to value companies that are ungeared and geared respectively.

References and further reading

Textbooks

Arnold – ch 18.
Brealey & Myers – chs 17, 18 and 19.
Pike & Neale – chs 20 and 21.
Samuels, Wilkes & Brayshaw – ch 18.
Watson & Head – ch 8.

Questions

1   Celtor plc is a property development company operating in the London area. The company has the following capital structure:

	£000
£1 ordinary shares	10,000
Retained profit	20,000
9% debentures	12,000
	42,000

The ordinary shares have a current market value of £3.90 per share and the current level of dividend is 20 pence per share. The dividend has been growing at a compound rate of 4 per cent per annum in recent years. The debentures in the company are irredeemable and have a current market value of £80 per £100 nominal. Interest due on the debentures at the year-end has recently been paid.

The company has obtained planning permission to build a new office block in a redevelopment area. It wishes to raise the whole of the finance necessary for the project by the issue of more irredeemable 9 per cent debentures at £80 per £100 nominal. This is in line with a target capital structure set by the company where the amount of debt capital will increase to 70 per cent of equity within the next two years. The rate of corporation tax is 25 per cent.

Required

(a) Explain what is meant by the term 'cost of capital'. Why is it important for a company to calculate its cost of capital correctly?

(b) What are the main factors which determine the cost of capital of a company?

(c) Calculate the weighted average cost of capital of Celtor plc that should be used for future investment decisions.

Source: ACCA Exam Cert Dipl in Financial Management 1996, question 3

2 Strachan plc produces electronic components for car manufacturers. It is now wondering whether to invest in new machinery which would allow it to extend its product range, in particular to supply the military, where Strachan thinks it could win some significant contracts. However, this is a higher risk area for Strachan because it involves investment in more research and more advanced technology.

The following information applies to the company at the moment:

	Strachan
Market value of debt	£200m
Market value of equity	900m
β of the shares	0.8

In addition, while financing this new investment, Strachan also intends to take the opportunity to change the capital structure. The company wants to take advantage of the current low rates of interest to increase its gearing to 30 per cent of the value of its equity (in terms of relative market value).

In bidding for these new contracts, Strachan is likely to be in competition with Nillson plc, an electronics company that concentrates very largely on meeting military contracts to supply electronic components.

Nillson has an equity beta of 1.1, reflecting this company's current business activities.

The risk-free rate is currently 4 per cent p.a. and both companies can borrow at 2 per cent p.a. above the risk-free rate. Both companies pay corporation tax at 30 per cent. The market risk premium is expected to be 6 per cent p.a. above the risk-free rate.

Required

(a) Calculate Strachan's current weighted average cost of capital.

(b) Calculate a more appropriate discount rate for Strachan's proposed investment in the military contracts. Give reasons for any adjustments that you make to your calculation in part (a).

(c) Discuss the reasons for the difference between Strachan's cost of debt and cost of equity.

3 Palmer plc, a construction company, is funded by a mixture of debt and equity capital. The company's debt capital consists of 8 per cent redeemable debentures (with a nominal value of £100) and redeemable at par on 31 December 2003. These debentures have a total book value of £400,000 and a current market price of £98.75 per debenture ex-interest, i.e. the interest for the year to 31 December 1999 has just been paid.

Palmer's issued share capital is made up of 100 million ordinary £1 shares. These shares have a current market price of £2.80 ex-div which reflects the fact that the final dividend for 1999 has just been paid. The company has paid the following dividends per share for each trading year ended 31 December:

1995	1996	1997	1998	1999
10p	11.5p	13p	14p	15p

The directors of Palmer plc expect to maintain the recent history of dividend growth for the foreseeable future. Palmer pays corporation tax at the rate of 30 per cent.

Required

(a) Calculate Palmer's weighted average cost of capital using market prices. (Assume that it is now 31 December 1999.)

(b) Under what circumstances might Palmer usefully use the weighted average cost of capital calculated in part (a) as a discount rate for future projects? (And by implication, under which circumstances should it not be used as a discount rate?)

4 WEB plc operates a low-cost airline and is a listed company. By comparison with its major competitors it is relatively small, but it has expanded significantly in recent years. The shares are held mainly by large financial institutions.

The following are extracts from WEB plc's budgeted balance sheet at 31 May 2002:

	$ million
Ordinary shares of $1	£100
Reserves	50
9% debentures 2005 (at nominal value)	200
	350

Dividends have grown in the past at 3 per cent a year, resulting in an expected dividend of $1 per share to be declared on 31 May 2002. (Assume for simplicity that the dividend will also be paid on this date.) Due to expansion, dividends are expected to grow at 4 per cent a year from 1 June 2002 for the foreseeable future. The price per share is currently $10.40 ex div and this is not expected to change before 31 May 2002.

The existing debentures are due to be redeemed at par on 31 May 2005. The market value of these debentures at 1 June 2002 is expected to be $100.84 (ex-interest) per $100 nominal. Interest is payable annually in arrears on 31 May and is allowable for tax purposes. The corporation tax rate for the foreseeable future is 30 per cent. Assume taxation is payable at the end of the year in which the taxable profits arise.

New finance

The company has now decided to purchase three additional aircraft at a cost of $10 million each. The board has decided that the new aircraft will be financed in full by an 8 per cent bank loan on 1 June 2002.

Required

(a) Calculate the expected weighted average cost of capital of WEB plc at 31 May 2002.

(b) *Without further calculations*, explain the impact of the new bank loan on WEB plc's

   (i)   cost of equity
   (ii)   cost of debt
   (iii) weighted average cost of capital (using the traditional model).

(c) Explain and distinguish

   (i)   debentures and
   (ii)   a bank loan.

In so doing, explain why, in the circumstances of WEB plc, the cost of debt may be different for the two types of security.

Source: CIMA (IFIN) May 2002, question 5

Self-assessment answers

9.1

Discounting at 11%, the PV $= -£98.26 + £9/(1.11) + £109/(1.11)^2$
$= -£98.26 + £8.11 + £88.47 = -£1.68$
Discounting at 10%, PV $= -£98.26 + £8.18 + £90.08 = 0$
Hence, yield to redemption $= 10\%$

9.2

(£m)	With no tax relief	With tax relief @ 30%
Operating profit	£10m	£10m
Interest on £10m debt @ 10% interest	–	(£1m)
Taxable profit	£10m	£9m
Tax at 30%	(£3m)	(£2.7m)
Post-tax profits	£7m	£7.3m
Tax saving	–	£0.3m

9.3

Discounting at 10%, the PV $= -£80 +$ [three-year annuity of £8(1 – 30%)] + [PV of £100 in three years].
PV $= -£80 + £13.93 + £75.10 = -£0.97$
Discounting at 9%, PV $= -£80 + £14.17 + £77.20 = +£1.37$
By interpolation, yield to redemption $= 9.58\%$.

9.4

- Before issue of debt, 'WACC' = cost of equity = 20%.

- After issue, the firm has £90 million equity at book value and £40 million debt.

- Book value weights are: [90/(90 + 40)] = 69% for equity; thus 31% for debt.

- WACC = (20% × 69%) + (10%[1 – 30%] × 31%) = (13.8% + 2.17%) = 15%.

- Market value of equity = (£4.65 × 40m) = £186 million.

- Market value weights are [186/186 + 40)] = 82% for equity and 18% for debt.

- WACC = (82% × 20%) + (10%[1 – 30%] × 18%) = (16.4% + 1.26%) = 17.7%.

9.5

Your call.

9.6

Given the tax and other advantages of debt, there is a case for urging managers to gear up the capital structure, at least until the market starts to transmit alarm signals. The gearing of other, similar firms might provide an indicator of safe levels. Shareholders can diversify away financial risk in the same way as they diversify specific activity risk. Arguably, managers who fail to utilise debt are imposing opportunity costs on shareholders, ostensibly to protect their own job security – low-geared firms are unlikely to go bust because of financial risk. Against this, managers are in possession of fuller information, and are thus better placed to assess the potential dangers of gearing. However, accepting this argument leads to the suggestion that failure to gear up is a way of signalling to the markets that less prosperous times await in the future. So managers are damned if they do, and damned if they don't!

10

HOW TO VALUE COMPANIES

Drinking games

In May 2002, South African Breweries (SAB) agreed to buy Miller Brewing Co, famous for its Miller Lite brand, from tobacco giant Phillip Morris for $5.6 billion, comprising $3.6 billion in shares and $2 billion in assumed debt. The deal would make SAB the number two beer-maker in the world, behind Anheuser-Busch of the USA, pushing Interbrew and Heineken back into third and fourth places respectively.

In addition to increasing global scale, the acquisition was motivated by a desire to diversify away from dependence on South African rand-denominated sales. Analysts suggested that SAB might have difficulties in reviving Miller's 'tired' brands as its expertise lay in emerging markets, like the Czech Republic, where it controlled the Pilsner Urquell brand, rather than mature ones like the USA. Moreover, given that estimated cost savings amounted to only $50 million over three years due to lack of overlapping activities and markets, it seemed that SAB might have paid a 'full' price.

The offered price of $5.6 billion valued Miller's EBITDA at a multiple of 9.4, around the typical multiple of 10 paid for recent brewing deals. However, relating value to volume rather than earnings, SAB was paying $112 per hectolitre for Miller, compared with $289 paid by Interbrew for Brauerei Beck GmbH in Germany, but only $100 paid by Scottish & Newcastle plc for Finland's Hartwall Oyj.

SAB's share price fell by 26p (4.5 per cent) on the announcement. Meanwhile, Phillip Morris was planning to extract nearly $2 billion in cash from the deal and return this to shareholders, thus moving cash out of a corporate entity subject to tobacco litigation.

Sources: Gulf News (UAE)/Bloomberg 31 May 2002; FT (Lex Column) 31 May 2002; FT (Lex Column) 1 June 2002. *Note*: South African Breweries is now called SAB Miller plc

Objectives:
This chapter aims to:

- help you understand why financial managers need to value companies

- remind you how the stock market values ordinary shares

- show how to value a company and its shares using:
  - the net asset value (NAV) method
  - the price : earnings ratio method
  - the discounted cash flow approach

- discuss the limitations of these three methods

- apply the shareholder value analysis (SVA) procedure

- discuss the link between value drivers and shareholder value analysis.

 ## 10.1   Introduction

The primary focus of financial decision making is value creation on behalf of the owners of the firm. Good decisions create value, poor decisions destroy value. Financial managers, therefore, need to have a good understanding of how companies are valued in order to assess the likely impact of their financial decisions on the wealth of shareholders. For example, how will a new investment project affect firm value? What may happen to the share price if the firm announces an increase in dividends? What is the effect of borrowing on company value?

There are many reasons why knowledge of valuation principles is useful:

- valuing other companies for acquisition

- assessing the value of one's own company when reacting to a takeover bid

- valuing a company for stock market flotation, i.e. an initial public offering

- valuing a company for privatisation

- valuing a company for a trade sale, or a management buy-out

- valuing a small company for assessing estate taxes.

This chapter integrates much of your earlier study – it builds upon the expertise you have acquired from previous chapters, allowing you to apply a great deal of the knowledge and skills which you have developed via a series of 'hands-on' activities, culminating in a detailed shareholder value analysis. It is relatively lengthy, reflecting the pivotal importance of valuation, both for managers and for the whole subject of finance. As you will see, the primary focus is on how to use, and appreciate the limitations of, a variety of valuation techniques.

The analysis relies heavily on concepts such as the relationship between risk and return, and the notion of value drivers. You will also see further application of discounting approaches to value measurement, and the impact of capital structure decisions on firm value. Many valuation techniques are used in practice, but our space, and your time, allow us to focus only on the most well known and widely used of these. You will discern a preference for cash-flow-oriented measures of value. As well as being theoretically and conceptually more valid, these are becoming more and more prevalent as guides for corporate financial managers and their advisers. Here, therefore, we see theory and practice converging.

◯ 10.2 **The value of quoted firms**

Valuation may seem relatively straightforward if the company already has a quotation on the stock market. The market price of the shares can be observed daily and if financial managers are prepared to accept the validity of the current market price, end of story! However, not all managers are this sanguine.

The market price of a firm's ordinary shares represents people's best estimate of the likely future profitability, and hence dividend-paying capacity, of the company, taking into account all available information. It is thus a consensus that strikes a balance between those who are *bullish* about the company and those who are *bearish*. However, market prices can only reflect the information made available, and some firms are very 'cagey' in releasing information. Also, there are times when rumour and speculation may predominate, distorting the 'true' picture!

In financial management, we are frequently concerned about the *accuracy* of the stock market valuation or **market efficiency**. What is meant by efficiency and how does an efficient market value a company? This is the province of the Efficient Markets Hypothesis that we encountered in Chapter 2.

Self-assessment activity 10.1

It may be useful to refresh your memory by revisiting the discussion of the EMH in Chapter 2, especially the three forms of market efficiency.

Remember how an efficient market values a company

While opinions differ about the impact of rumour and speculation, there is general agreement that what fundamentally determines the value of shares in a company is the future stream of benefits, in the form of the cash dividends which the company is expected to generate. Some people say earnings are more important than dividends since, ultimately, dividends can only be paid out of earnings. While this is true, it is equally valid to say that future earnings represent future dividends; eventually, even a company with a policy of high retentions will unlock these in the form of dividends. For example, Microsoft, after years of phenomenal growth, has only just started to pay dividends. Its value in previous years has been driven by expectations, now coming to fruition, that it will eventually deliver more value to shareholders in cash form.

Valuation according to future dividends is incorporated in the **dividend valuation model**, which simply states that the value of a share is given by the sum of all future discounted dividends:

If D_1 = dividend in Year 1, etc

k_e = the rate of return required by ordinary shareholders

P_0 = today's share price

$$= \frac{D_1}{(1 + k_e)} + \frac{D_2}{(1 + k_e)^2} + \cdots + \frac{D_n}{(1 + k_e)^n}$$

If D is constant, and the series infinite,

$$P_0 = \frac{D}{k_e}$$

Self-assessment activity 10.2

Value the following company's shares in the following situations, given that the risk-free rate is 5 per cent, people expect an overall return on the market portfolio of 10 per cent, and the Beta of the firm's shares is 1.0.

- Dividend per share £1 p.a., constant over a ten-year period. (Company liquidates after ten years with no resale value.)

- As above, but the shareholder expects to sell after five years.

- Dividends £1 p.a., payments made for ever.

- Dividends initially £1, but growing at 5 per cent p.a. thereafter and for ever.

(answer at end of chapter)

The dividend valuation model is really useful only for valuing part-shares in a firm. The value of the whole firm may often be perceived to exceed the market capitalisation. This is because value is attached to ownership of the firm's whole cash flows. For example, a successful takeover bidder is able to dispose of these cash flows at will, e.g. to pay higher dividends, to invest in growth opportunities to which only it has access. This is why takeover bids are usually completed at a significant premium – on average around 40 per cent – to the pre-bid market price. This premium is called 'the premium for control'.

This suggests that the DVM is not an especially good way of valuing a whole firm (or its equity component), and that even an efficient market cannot fully value a firm. There are different valuations according to who does the valuation and what the purpose of the acquisition might be. Obviously, a firm taken over to successfully exploit synergies with the new parent would be worth more than the same firm chugging along under the existing set of managers.

So, if we suspect that the market is not semi-strong form efficient, or we are in possession of information not generally available to investors, we have to use other approaches to valuation. In this respect, valuation of quoted firms becomes equivalent to valuing firms not listed on a stock market, for which a variety of techniques is available.

10.3 Valuing unquoted companies

By definition, there is no organised market in the shares of unquoted companies, although in some financial centres, off-market deals may be organised outside the main market by market-makers on an *over-the-counter (OTC)* basis, which matches selling and buying orders. Due to the lack of an established market benchmark when valuing such companies, we often have to rely on various valuation techniques. These tend to give different answers, reflecting the subjectivity of the valuation exercise. There is no 'correct' value; for example, in a takeover situation, the final price depends on negotiation. The best you can do is to analyse the situation carefully and make reasoned assumptions in order to arrive at a credible valuation which you then hope is justifiable and acceptable for the intended purpose.

The three main methods

1 (Net) asset value – this focuses on information on the value of assets and liabilities found in the firm's balance sheet.

2 Price : earnings ratio – this focuses on accounting profits and thus on the profit and loss account.

3 **Discounted cash flow** – like the previous method, this is also income-based, but instead of using profits it relies on expected cash flows and the time value of money concept.

Example: BigShark and SmallMinnow

We now apply these methods to the following example. BigShark ('Shark') is a quoted company contemplating a takeover of an unquoted company, Small-Minnow ('Minnow'). Their respective accounts reveal the following information:

	Shark £m	Minnow £m
Fixed assets (net)	12.2	3.5
Current assets	7.3	3.7
Current liabilities	(2.2)	(1.1)
10% long-term loan stock	(3.5)	(0.5)
Net assets	13.8	5.6
Ordinary share capital (par value £1)	10.0	5.0
Share premium	-	0.2
Profit and loss account	3.8	0.4
Shareholders' funds	13.8	5.6
Profit after tax attributable to ordinary shareholders	2.4	1.5
Current market price/share	£2.40	n/a
EPS	24p	30p
P : E ratio	10 : 1	n/a

Notes:

(i) No synergistic benefits are expected (although this is unrealistic in a takeover situation, exploitation of synergies being a major motivation for takeovers. However, this assumption simplifies the arithmetic).

(ii) Minnow's depreciation charge = £200,000 p.a. Minnow's profits include a (non-taxable) exceptional item of £300,000 relating to the profit on the sale of an asset.

Self-assessment activity 10.3

What is the significance of the two items mentioned in note (ii), i.e. how might they affect the valuation?
(answer at end of chapter)

10.4 The net asset value method

In accounting terms, the total value of the company is the book value of all its assets, whatever the method of financing. However, the valuation for a takeover hinges on valuing the equity stake – the value of the owner's stake, net of all liabilities. This is the **net asset value**, usually regarded as the minimum amount that must be offered to persuade the owners to relinquish their control.

However, in order to complete the acquisition, the bidder will also have to make arrangements about the liabilities of the company, e.g. repay them now or some time in the future. Whereas the NAV is the book value of the equity stake, the total asset value (TAV) would be the total cost of acquiring the assets of the company, based on book values, viz:

> TAV = book value of all the assets = book value of financing used

> NAV = book value of owners´ stake = (TAV − book value of liabilities)

The two questions we need to address are:

- What is the total value of the firm?

- What is the net asset value?

The TAV is simply the value of the total assets, i.e. £7.2 million in the case of Minnow above. To obtain ownership of the whole company's assets, Shark would normally have to pay at least this amount.

> Net asset valuation = (total assets *less* total liabilities)

> = (fixed assets + current assets − current liabilities − long-term debt)

> = (£3.5m + £3.7m − £1.1m − £0.5m) = £5.6m

Expressed in terms of value per share, this is $= \dfrac{£5.6m}{5m} = £1.12.$

Shark would have to pay £5.6 million to the owners, but to complete the deal it would also have either to pay off the liabilities of £1.6 million or to assume responsibility for them. Obviously, you cannot normally expect to buy assets worth a total of [£3.5 million + £3.7 million] = £7.2 million for just £5.6 million. It should also be appreciated that, in most cases, the NAV puts a floor to the amount that the owners might settle for – in practice, they are likely to hold out for much more than the NAV.

The difference between the value of the equity and the value of the whole enterprise was shown in the introductory cameo – SAB paid $5.6 billion for the whole firm, of which $3.6 billion was paid to owners.

Two further takeover examples illustrate this distinction. In 1998, the UK engineering group GKN bid a total of $570 million to acquire the US group Sinter Metals of Ohio. The offer was made up of $386 million in cash to acquire the equity and the assumption of $184 million of Sinter debt. In 2002, German water and energy group RWE agreed to buy Innogy Holdings plc, the largest British electricity supplier, for a total of £5 billion, comprising around £3 billion in cash and £2 billion in assumed debt. (In both cases, the amount paid for the equity exceeded the NAV as shown in the accounts.)

Problems with the NAV method

In its simplest form, the NAV is based on taking at face value the figures presented in the accounts, i.e. the book values. In reality, there may be problems involved with values of both assets and liabilities. Among these are the following.

Assets

- Stated fixed asset values are based on historic cost less depreciation. Different depreciation methods result in different values of fixed assets. Whatever the method of depreciation, the book values are unlikely to correspond to market values. Although companies do revalue their assets periodically, this is a subjective exercise, often undertaken by the directors themselves. If we incorporate higher valuations of fixed (and other) assets than those shown in the balance sheet, the NAV becomes the *adjusted NAV*. This gives the value on a *break-up basis*, i.e. the value of the assets when sold piecemeal, as opposed to their value when combined with other assets in an ongoing business operation, the so-called **going concern value**.

- The stated values of stocks may not be reliable, especially if the accounts were prepared some time ago. (They could be up to a year old.) Companies often 'window-dress' their accounts at year-end to make them appear stronger at year-end than is typically the case during the operating year. Stock values in sectors such as high technology and fashion industries are often soon outdated.

- Some accounts receivable may be not collectable – of course, provision should have been made for bad and doubtful debts but the bidder should be wary of the extent of this allowance.

Liabilities

- Some liabilities are 'off-balance sheet', such as guarantees to other companies, for example in a joint venture, warranty obligations and operating lease commitments. Inspection of the notes to the accounts should reveal these. This heading includes contingent liabilities, which may or may not arise, e.g. damages arising from a court case.

- Some other provisions may be inadequate for the purpose intended. A provision is a charge against profits to allow for some anticipated contingency, such as replacement of assets or redundancy payments relating to planned closure of a factory.

To some extent, such factors can be adjusted in order to arrive at an adjusted NAV, but the fundamental problem remains with the NAV method that it views the company merely as a set of assets rather than as an income-generating activity. The NAV ignores the company's earning power which is what really drives value. The NAV is of most help when a company is making losses, or has a collection of assets which have a much greater value when put to some alternative use, for example farming land converted into a housing estate.

Of the valuation approaches which focus on future income, the most commonly-used ones are the price : earnings ratio approach which is based on accounting profits, and discounted cash flow.

10.5 The price : earnings ratio method

This approach involves applying the P : E ratio (PER) of a representative, or surrogate, quoted company to the *maintainable* earnings of the unquoted company which we wish to value. The term maintainable refers to the earnings net of special factors such as gains or losses on disposal of an asset, which usually are noted as 'exceptional items' in the accounts. Obviously, the surrogate should be as close a match to the unquoted company as possible.

Self-assessment activity 10.4

Suggest further examples of items that might be 'exceptional'.
(answer at end of chapter)

The PER is used as a guideline to valuation as it indicates how the market rates a company's prospects. Specifically, it signals how the stock market values each £1 of company earnings. For example, a company with post-tax earnings of 20p per share and share price of £2 has a P : E ratio of £2/20p = 10, or 10 : 1.

Note that it is based on the relationship between today's share price and the most recently reported earnings. Hence, a high PER indicates faith in the potential of a company to grow its earnings. One way to look at this is to say that a P : E ratio, because it is driven by market price, indicates *not how well a company has done in the past, but how well it is expected to perform in the future.*

Valuing Minnow using the PER

The first issue is what PER to use as a benchmark. Assuming Shark is in the same industry, we could use its P : E ratio to value Minnow's earnings. Minnow's profit after tax is £1.5 million, but £0.3 million was due to an exceptional item. Removing this one-off event, we have 'maintainable earnings' of

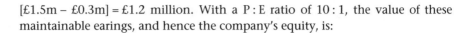

[£1.5m – £0.3m] = £1.2 million. With a P : E ratio of 10 : 1, the value of these maintainable earings, and hence the company's equity, is:

[10 × £1.2m] = £12m, or (£12m/5m) = £2.60 per share.

Problems with the PER approach

- A fundamental flaw is that the method is based on valuing accounting profits rather than cash flows. The earnings figure can be distorted by divergent accounting policies – for example, Shark and Minnow may adopt different depreciation policies.

- The current earnings may be atypically high or low. It may be more appropriate to take an average over the past few years, although this raises the question of how many years to cover.

- We should consider the possible future growth in Minnow's earnings, especially as Shark would presumably exploit its assets more effectively. This suggests that the valuation from the seller's perspective could well fall short of the valuation of the buyer, who in turn will try to hide this from the seller. This reflects the inherent 'game-playing' role of valuation in a takeover situation.

- It is difficult in reality to find close substitutes, that is, companies which produce the same product lines, serve the same markets and have similar management capabilities. These are all factors which help determine the firms' growth potential (which is what the P : E ratio is supposed to reflect).

- Shark and Minnow are not comparable firms in two important respects. Shark is a larger company, and it has a stock market quotation. Investors are usually prepared to pay a premium for size, and especially, marketability, that is, the ability to easily buy and sell their shareholdings. For this reason, it is usual to reduce the P : E ratio, often by as much as half, that is applied to the unquoted company's earnings. But by how much is a question of judgement – and ultimately what the seller will accept. Applying a P : E ratio of say 5, we obtain a value for Minnow of (£1.2m × 5) = £6 million.

- There is an element of circularity in this method. It is based on accepting as valid the PER of the surrogate firm. We are accepting that Shark is correctly valued by the market when adopting its PER. In an important sense, we are saying that the value of Minnow depends on the value of Shark, but how was Shark valued? In this respect, we have only a relative measure of value. This comment is appropriate for any method that uses multiples implicit in the value of particular firms to set a value on another. This point applies to EBITDA, mentioned in the SAB cameo. We cover this next.

EBITDA – a half-way house

As you are well aware, cash flows and profits differ because of the application of accruals accounting principles, and value depends upon cash-generating ability rather than 'profitability'. An intermediate concept currently in vogue is that of EBITDA, an unattractive acronym standing for Earnings Before Interest, Taxes, Depreciation and Amortisation. EBITDA is equivalent to operating profit with depreciation (amortisation generally refers to the writing down of intangible assets) added back. As such, it is a measure of the basic operating cash flow before deduction of taxation, but ignoring working capital movements.

Many companies use EBITDA as a measure of performance, especially when related to capital employed. For example, Eon, the German utility and chemicals group, evaluates the performance of both the whole firm and individual business units by using a measure known as cash flow return on Investment (CFROI). This is essentially a cash-based measure of return on capital employed, which is not influenced by the capital structure. In other words, being expressed before interest and tax, and being based on total assets, it is independent of financing policy, which determines the 'share-out' of the operating profit and cash flow as between interest payments, taxation and profits for shareholders. According to Eon, EBITDA has the merit of being

> 'net of one-off and rare effects, which mainly include book gains from divestments and expenses for restructuring and cost management. EBITDA thus represents the sustainable return on capital employed.'
>
> (Eon annual report, 2000)

However, you should appreciate that EBITDA is essentially a performance measure. It can be used in valuation only if we look at the way in which the market values other companies' EBITDAs. As with the use of P : E ratios, a comparison with other companies is needed as a reference point.

For example, in late 2000, when Coca-Cola was evaluating Quaker as an acquisition candidate, observers noted that Coke was prepared to pay 16 times Quaker's EBITDA, which appeared expensive, being well above recent deals in the US food sector. Attempting to explain this, the *Financial Times* suggested that if the Quaker food division were valued at the then prevailing industry average of ten times EBITDA, the bid price implied an EBITDA multiple of 25 times for the real jewel in Quaker's crown, the fast-growing Gatorade sports drink.

In July 2001, the US oil firm Amerada Hess acquired Triton Energy in order to acquire the upstream capability and exploration skills. The price paid per share was $45 cash, a premium of 50 per cent to Triton's previous share price. Observers commented that it was paying 'top dollar'. Including $500 million of debt, Amerada was laying out nine times 2001 EBITDA, in line with similar deals involving acquisition of proven reserves but ahead of valuations for oil companies oriented more towards downstream activities.

Like a P : E multiple, an EBITDA multiple used in valuation stems from the value which the market attaches to other companies' earnings, which invites the question of how it values those other companies, i.e. the EBITDA multiple is led by the valuation of those companies. Moreover, even when used crudely as a rough and ready comparison of value, one should appreciate that it is still based on accounting earnings. Although gross of depreciation and special items, it is still subject to different accounting practices between firms at the operating level, e.g. stock valuation. Moreover, it ignores a major part of the profit and loss account, the section detailing interest and tax and obligations that need to be settled before shareholders can be paid a dividend. For this reason, it is more a measure of operating performance than an indicator of value creation for the owners.

Continuing to focus on income-generating methods, we now turn to the genuine article, discounted cash flow.

◔ 10.6 The discounted cash flow approach

A DCF valuation has the advantage of focusing not on profits but on cash flows which are less easily distorted by accounting manipulation. Also, of course, DCF uses the investor's required return as the basis for assessing the value of those cash flows. As in the EBITDA approach, we have to add back non-cash items to Minnow's profit after tax, primarily depreciation, viz:

PAT + depreciation = (£1.5m + £0.2m) = £1.7m

In reality, there will also be working capital adjustments to incorporate – these are assumed to be off-setting, which might be more or less accurate over the longer term. In this example, there is also the exceptional item, the profit on the sale of the asset, again a non-cash item, and, here, a one-off item. This apparently yields a sustainable cash flow of:

[£1.7m – £0.3m] = £1.4m

There is yet another adjustment to make. To maintain this cash flow, the company must replace worn-out capital equipment, but at what rate? For simplicity, we may assume that the annual depreciation provision is an accurate reflection of the replacement investment undertaken. (In fact, many companies link investment expenditures to their annual depreciation provisions, often on a one-to-one basis.) With this assumption, the sustainable cash flow is:

[£1.4m – £0.2m] = £1.2m

This is one measure of **free cash flow** (FCF) which means the cash flow free of all obligations including ongoing replacement investment requirements. Thus it is 'free' for disposal by the directors on discretionary strategic investment and/or dividend payments. You should be a little wary of this concept as people define and measure the FCF in different ways. For example, it is common to define FCF as the cash flow remaining after *all* investment expenditures, including strategic investment. However, as there is no discretionary investment to allow for in this example, this complication does not arise (but see the Bafa example below).

There are yet two more elements required before we can complete the DCF appraisal: a discount rate and a time period assumption. For illustration, we assume a 20 per cent return required by shareholders and a ten-year time span. Using these assumptions, the value of the equity is:

$$(\pounds1.2m \times \text{ten-year annuity factor @ 20\%}) = (\pounds1.2m \times 4.192) = \pounds5.0m$$

Self-assessment activity 10.5

Value Minnow incorporating growth of 6 per cent p.a.
(answer at end of chapter)

Note that this calculation assumes no residual value of the company at the end of ten years – this omission will be rectified when we look at the shareholder value approach in the next section. Obviously, other assumptions regarding life span and the discount rate will yield different results.

Problems with the DCF approach

Problems with DCF centre on specifying the key variables involved:

- Can future investment levels be accurately projected? To do this requires detailed knowledge of the firm's growth strategies.

- Most valuations of this type project cash flows over only 5–10 years or so for this reason but build in a residual value to indicate the likely value of the company at the end of the horizon period. This is very largely guesswork, although errors are moderated by the time factor. Here distant cash flows would be more heavily discounted anyway.

- How can we measure the discount rate? When valuing the equity stock, we need to know what rate of return is required by shareholders. If we are dealing with an acquisition, the valuation is effectively an investment appraisal and the return required by the bidders' shareholders should be used in the normal way. However, if the 'project' is to develop a different line of business activity, adjustment should be made for any risk differential.

- Over what time period should we assess value? This depends partly on the size of company – small companies are more exposed to risk and are more likely to have short lives. Market positioning factors are also relevant. Company life cycles often correspond to their project life cycles and the periods over which they enjoy competitive advantages.

● Should we accept the current earnings figure? There are two reasons why we might want to adjust the earnings and hence the cash flow. First, the current figure may be atypically high or low. Taking an average over the past few years may overcome this problem. Second, we may want to build in growth potential. This is easily done as a numerical exercise, but choosing the appropriate rate to incorporate is a problem. One approach is to take a forecast rate of growth of the industrial sector of which the company is a member.

Is there a correct valuation?

One might be tempted to ask which of our several valuations is correct, but this is not an appropriate choice of words. There can never be an *absolutely correct* answer. Two influences are critical to the outcome of the valuation – first, the set of assumptions which we build into the valuation, and second (and closely related to the first), the reason why we want to make a valuation. Obviously, in a takeover, a seller will apply a higher value than a buyer, and each party is likely to apply a different mix of assumptions and perhaps rely on different methods. The final outcome depends on the negotiations – the 'value' is not established until the deal is finalised. Remember, too, that all these methods can be applied to a quoted company if we take exception to the market value, for example if we are not inclined to accept the EMH, or have information not available to the market, such as proposed reorganisation of a takeover victim's assets.

 DCF principles also provide the foundation for a more comprehensive valuation model, shareholder value analysis.

◯ 10.7 Using value drivers - shareholder value analysis

As we saw in Chapter 1, recent years have seen greater appreciation of the need for managers to optimise the interests of shareholders. In general terms, this can be achieved by generating a rate of return on investment which, at the very least, matches their required return on investment, or the cost of equity. Remember that shareholders incur an opportunity cost when subscribing capital for firms to use and managers are then legally obliged to safeguard those funds with all due diligence.

Sometimes, managers feel that 'their' companies are not 'correctly' valued by the stock market – there has been a steady trickle of firms delisting from the main UK market since 1998, largely for this reason. For example, in spring 2003, Dave Whelan, former Blackburn Rovers footballer and the founder of sports goods retailer JJB Sports, which he began as a stall on Wigan market, was reported to be planning to take the firm private at an estimated valuation of about £500 million.

Moreover, share prices overall can swing quite violently in the short term, for example note the 25 per cent fall in the UK FTSE 100 during July–September 1998, its subsequent recovery by December 1998, before marching to its all-time peak in December 1999, followed by one of the severest bear markets in history. In the USA, the NASDAQ rose by nearly 50 per cent in late 1999 and early 2000, then lost all its gains by the autumn of 2000, only to recover sharply in December of the same year, and subsequently collapse. In the early stages of the second Gulf War, London rose by nearly 20 per cent in a few days.

If non-plussed and disillusioned by such gyrations, both managers and shareholders may require a more objective and reliable measure of value than simply the prevailing market price. Such a measure can be provided by the shareholder value approach, propounded by Alfred Rappaport (1986), which draws on the work of Michael Porter (1985).

Rappaport was concerned to identify the drivers of inherent shareholder value (SV), in effect, the fundamental value of the firm to its owners. The SV figure provides a cross-check on the market's current valuation of the company. This may be regarded as a more stable and possibly more reliable indicator of the firm's value that is unaffected by short-term vagaries of the market. Notice that this implies less than total faith in the EMH creed. The following example of Bafa plc is our vehicle for investigating the SV approach. But first, we need to explain the notion of value drivers.

Rappaport developed a simple but powerful model to calculate the fundamental value of a business to its owners by focusing on the key factors that determine firm value. He identified seven value drivers, comprising three cash flow variables and four parameters:

- sales, and its speed of growth
- fixed capital investment
- working capital investment
- operating profit margin
- tax rate on profits
- the planning horizon
- the required rate of return.

In its simplest form, SVA assumes that the last four drivers are constant, and that the first three, the cash flow variables, change at a constant rate. The key to the analysis, as with a budgeting exercise, is the level of sales and the projected rate of increase. From the sales projections, we can programme the operating profits and cash flows over the planning horizon and discount as appropriate to find their present value.

In the full model, the value of the firm comprises three elements: the value of the equity, the value of the debt, and the value of any non-operating assets, such as marketable securities. However, to keep the analysis simple, we focus initially on an all-equity-financed company with no holdings of marketable assets. In addition, we need to explain the treatment of investment expenditure. To maintain and enhance value, firms have to invest, i.e. to generate future cash flows requires preliminary cash outflows. These reduce value in the short term but hopefully generate a more than compensating increase in value via future cash flows.

Categories of investment

Investment in working capital, especially inventories, is required to support a planned increase in sales. Often, companies attempt to apply a roughly constant ratio of working capital to sales, say 5 per cent, so that a 5 per cent sales increase needs an equivalent increase in working capital investment. This is called *incremental working capital investment.*

Replacement investment is undertaken to make good the wear and tear due to equipment use, and thus maintain the capacity to produce. However, there are phasing issues to consider. In reality, it is correct to observe that, in relation to particular items, the actual act of replacement is sporadic, occurring in discrete chunks, whereas depreciation is an annual provision, so that in all but the year of replacement, depreciation will exceed replacement expenditure. However, taken in aggregate over time, replacement may be closely related to depreciation provisions.

New investment in fixed assets has two dimensions. First, if the firm wants to expand sales of existing products, then unless it has spare capacity, it will need to invest in additional capital equipment to support the planned sales increase. Second, new investment may be undertaken to accompany a major strategic venture such as development of a new product, which will also generate an increase in sales. Both types of investment may be undertaken to meet a planned sales increase, although there is likely to be a time lag before strategic investment comes fully 'on stream' and is able to deliver high sales quantities. Any extra investment above replacement is called *incremental fixed capital investment.*

Self-assessment activity 10.6

In practice, is it possible to easily differentiate between replacement and incremental investment?
(answer at end of chapter)

In the following demonstration example of Bafa plc, replacement investment is assumed to equal depreciation provisions (which are treated as part of operating expenses in accounting terms) and both working capital investment and incremental fixed capital investment are made a percentage of any planned sales increase.

10.8   Worked example I: Bafa plc - ungeared version

The board of Bafa plc is concerned about its current stock market value of £100 million, especially as board members hold 40 per cent of the existing 100 million ordinary shares (par value £1) already issued. They are vaguely aware of the SVA concept and have assembled the following data:

- Current sales £100m

- Operating profit margin 20 per cent
  (after depreciation. On average, depreciation provisions match ongoing investment requirements and are fully tax-deductible)

- Estimated rate of sales growth is 5 per cent p.a.

- Rate of corporation tax is 30 per cent (with no delay in payment)

- Long-term debt is zero

- Net book value of assets is £120 million (fixed assets plus net current assets)

- To support the increase in sales, additional investment is required as follows:
  - increased investment in *working capital* will be 8 per cent of any concurrent sales increase
  - increased investment in *fixed capital* will be 10 per cent of any concurrent sales increase.

The risk-free rate of interest is 7.6 per cent, Bafa's Beta coefficient is 0.8 and a consensus view of analysts' expectations regarding the overall return on the market portfolio is 15.6 per cent.

Bafa currently pays out 30 per cent of profit after tax as dividend. The board estimates that Bafa can continue to enjoy its traditional source of competitive advantage as a low-cost provider for a further six years, at the end of which it estimates that the net book value of its assets will be £170 million.

What is the inherent, underlying value of this company?

Answer and comments

First of all, we need to find the return required by the Bafa shareholders. Using the CAPM formula, this is:

$$k_e = R_f + \beta \; [ER_m - R_f] = 7.6\% + 0.8[15.6\% - 7.6\%]$$

$$= 7.6\% + 6.4\% = 14\%$$

To value Bafa on a DCF basis, we will utilise this 14 per cent required return. As there is no debt finance, all operating profits (less tax) are attributable to shareholders. There appears to be no long-term strategic investment programme, and wear-and-tear is made good at a rate roughly corresponding to tax-allowable depreciation provisions. This means that free cash flows are equal to operating profits less tax. The firm enjoys a temporary cost advantage for six years, beyond which cash flows are uncertain (see Table 10.1).

Table 10.1 Cash flow profile for Bafa plc (ungeared)*

(£m)	0	1	2	3	4	5	6 →
				Year			
1 Sales (5% growth)	100	105	110.25	115.76	121.25	127.63	134.00
2 Operating profit margin @ 20%**	20	21	22.05	23.15	24.31	25.53	26.80
3 Taxation @ 30%	(6)	(6.30)	(6.62)	(6.95)	(7.29)	(7.66)	(8.04)
4 Incremental working capital investment @ 8% of sales increase	–	(0.40)	(0.42)	(0.44)	(0.46)	(0.49)	(0.51)
5 Incremental fixed capital investment @ 10% of sales increase	–	(0.50)	(0.53)	(0.55)	(0.58)	(0.61)	(0.64)
6 Free cash flow	–	13.80	14.48	15.21	15.98	16.77	17.61
7 Present value @ 14%	–	11.90	11.14	10.27	9.46	8.71	8.02

* Accuracy of figures influenced by rounding errors.
** These can be taken as cash flows given the assumption that depreciation = replacement investment.

Post-year 6 cash flows can be handled in a number of ways:

1 The year 6 cash flow figure can be assumed to flow indefinitely. This seems quite an optimistic assumption to make both in relation to Bafa plc itself and also more generally, in relation to any firm.

2 A view can be taken on the firm's efforts to restore competitive advantage and some growth assumption can then be incorporated. Again, this can only be speculative, as there is no information on this issue.

3 Perhaps the most prudent assumption to make is that the expected book value of assets at the end of year 6 will approximate to the value of all future cash flows, i.e. the company has no further supernormal earnings capacity. To be more specific, this implies that any subsequent investment has an NPV of zero.

This third possible approach is the one adopted. The value of Bafa is thus:

PV of cash flows during remaining years in which competitive advantage can be enjoyed ('the competitive advantage period')

+

PV of all further cash flows beyond year 6

Valuing Bafa plc

The value created over the competitive advantage period is:

PV of operating cash flows (line 7) =   £59.5m

The PV of the residual value:

= £170m × PV factor = (£170m × 0.4556) =   £77.5m
Shareholder value = £59.5m + £77.5m =   £137m

Self-assessment activity 10.7

Undertake an alternative valuation by treating the post-year 6 cash flows as a level perpetuity equal in value to the year 6 figure.
To perform this calculation, you need to use the formula for the growing perpetuity, as shown in Chapter 4.
(answer at end of chapter)

A note on taxation – two simplifications

You should be aware of how taxation is being handled in this example. All replacement investment is treated as being fully tax-deductible in the year of expenditure. This is a simplification adopted primarily for arithmetic convenience. In reality, the tax relief will be spread out over time as the firm claims the 25 per cent writing-down allowance each year. In addition, we have ignored the tax saving in relation to the 25 per cent WDA on the incremental fixed capital expenditure.

Correcting for the first factor would reduce the valuation simply because delay in taking the tax relief would lower the PV of the stream of tax savings. On the other hand, inclusion of the second set of tax savings would raise the SV figure. We persist with this simplification when we come to examine the geared version of Bafa below. (You may care to calculate the 'true' valuation by allowing for these aspects – you will find a net increase in the valuation.)

We now turn to discuss the actual valuation obtained.

Commentary

Looking at the figures as calculated, we find, rather alarmingly, that a large proportion (57 per cent) of the SV is accounted for by the residual value. Moreover, the SV clearly exceeds market value, itself below the current book value of assets. This seems to imply that the company might be worth more if it were broken up (although this depends on whether the book value of assets would match the market value). It is thus possible that the market could be valuing Bafa for its break-up potential rather than as a going concern.

This raises the obvious question of why the market should place such a low value on Bafa. We can consider some possible reasons for the apparent market undervaluation of Bafa. (See if you can identify which value driver is inherent in each point.)

- The market may currently apply a higher discount rate, for example, seeking a higher reward for risk.

- The growth estimate may be regarded as optimistic.

- The flow of information provided to the market may be inadequate. For example, if Bafa does have its future investment plans, are these generally known and understood?

- Board control – presumably reflecting domination by members of the founding family – may be perceived as excessive. Such enterprises rarely enjoy a good stock market rating because there is often a suspicion that the interests of family members may be allowed to dominate those of 'outside' shareholders.

- The dividend policy may be thought ungenerous – a 30 per cent pay-out ratio is quite low by UK standards, and there appears to be little scope for worthwhile strategic investment. Retentions may simply be going into cash balances.

- There may be doubts about whether Bafa can recover some form of competitive advantage.

- The market may be unimpressed with its present cost advantage-based strategy.

- Its gearing – currently zero – may be thought to be too low, offering no tax shield to exploit.

- The market regards Bafa's current management as an 'off-balance sheet liability'.

Whatever the reason(s), there is plenty for the board to consider.

10.9 Worked example II: Bafa plc - geared version

We will now incorporate debt finance and examine how a geared version of Bafa would be valued. Below are the original and revised versions of Bafa. Notice that we have replaced £20 million equity with £20 million debt. This may well lower the overall required return. To reflect the increased financial risk borne by share-holders, we have adjusted the owners' required return, raising it to 15 per cent.

Table 10.2 Bafa plc: ungeared and geared versions

	Ungeared	Geared
Current sales	£100m	£100m
Operating profit margin	20%	20%
Estimated growth in sales	5% p.a.	5% p.a.
Rate of corporation tax	30%	30%
Book value of equity	£120m	£100m
	(£90m £1 shares	(£70m £1 shares
	+ £30m reserves)	+ £30m reserves)
Book value of debt	–	£20m
Interest rate on debt	–	7%
Shareholders' required return	14%	15%
Competitive advantage period	6 years	6 years
Residual asset value	£170m	£170m

Valuation of Bafa

In the SVA model, the net operating profits after taxation (NOPAT) are discounted at the WACC to find the enterprise value. The interest payments are not deducted as these are the returns to providers of debt. The enterprise value, of course, is the value of the whole firm without attention to the separate values of equity and debt.

The NOPAT is given by

$$= (\text{Operating profits}) \times (1 - \text{Tax rate})$$

This is numerically the same as the free cash flow figures used in the ungeared version, although it will be appropriated differently, i.e. shared out between owners and debt-holders.

To value the geared version of Bafa, we have to follow these steps:

- Calculate the WACC.

- Discount the NOPATs using the WACC.

- Calculate the PV of the book value of assets, using the WACC.

- Add the PV of the after-tax cash flows to the PV of the book value of assets to obtain the value of the whole company.

- Separate out the equity value from the company value by deducting the value of the debt.

Using the total book value of £120 million, the weights for equity and debt are (£100m/£120m) = 5/6, and (£20m/£120m) = 1/6, respectively. Allowing for tax relief on interest payments, the WACC is:

$$(15\% \times 5/6) + (7\%[1 - 30\%] \times 1/6) = (12.5\% + 0.8\%) = 13.3\%$$

Self-assessment activity 10.8

Now find the PV of the cash flows discounting at 13.3 per cent.
(answer at end of chapter)

The PV of the book value of assets is also found by discounting at 13.3 per cent. The answer is £80.3 million.

The total PV, and hence, the value of the company as a whole, is:

$$(£60.9m + £80.3m) = £141.2m$$

This compares with the lower figure of £137 million in the ungeared version. The increase in value is explained partly by the value of the tax shield and partly by the lower overall cost of finance.

We can now identify the separate values of the equity and the debt, and consider the impact on share value of using debt financing.

Remember that there were 90 million £1 shares in issue in the original (ungeared) version and 70 million in the geared version.

Ungeared: Value per share = Equity/no. of shares

$$= £137.0m/90m = \textbf{£1.52}$$

Geared: Company value = £141.2m

Value of equity = (£141.2m – value of debt)

$$= (£141.2m – £20m) = £121.2m$$

Value per share = £121.2m/70m = **£1.73**

The share value is thus increased by 19p per share, reflecting the advantage of a safe level of cheap debt.

Notice that we have used the book value of debt. When the market value of debt is known, this should be used in preference to the book value, both for calculating the WACC and for distinguishing between the value of the whole company and the value of the equity.

It is often argued that, in an efficient capital market, the cost of equity will increase to exactly offset the beneficial effects of cheap debt. Why should the value change when it is the same basic company, but with a different capital structure? What value has been created? None, according to this argument.

However, there are grounds for expecting a value differential due to the presence of the tax shield. This is the discounted value of all future tax savings stemming from the ability to set interest payments against profits for tax purposes, although this depends on the level of gearing, i.e. how 'safe' investors think it is.

When looking at how safe a level of gearing is involved in Bafa's new capital structure, the easiest test to apply is the interest cover. Bafa is now committed to interest payments of $(8\% \times £20m) = £1.6$ million, and its gross or operating profit is £21 million in the first year. This yields an interest cover of $(£21m/£1.6m) = 13.2$ times which looks far from dangerous. The operating profit can fall by over 90 per cent before the company becomes unable to meet interest payments. Remember also that cash flow and profits are rising through time so interest cover will also increase.

Self-assessment activity 10.9

Some experts argue that cash flow cover is more useful than earnings cover, as indicated by the traditional measure of interest cover. Determine the cash flow cover for Bafa for the first year – use FCF before interest.
(answer at end of chapter)

In addition, we should consider the required profile of debt repayments. Adding the annual interest payments to the required capital repayment would reduce the annual burden on cash flow. For example, if the debt were repayable evenly in £1 million tranches over 20 years, total debt servicing payments would be:

Interest of £1m plus capital of £1.6m = £3.6m

This can be used to express the 'cash flow cost of capital' of $(£3.6m/£20m) = 18\%$. Obviously, the longer the term of the repayment profile, the lower the annual burden imposed on cash flow. Note that if interest is based on the outstanding balance of the loan, the annual interest charge will fall.

Finally, we should examine the asset-backing for the debt. The book value of net assets is currently £120 million, compared with the nominal value of debt of £20 million – the asset backing is thus six times, i.e. the firm could repay its debt six times over, assuming it could realise at least book value in a distress sale. As with the interest cover, this figure is by no means alarming, so it seems that Bafa is well within its practical debt capacity. This provides the underpinning to justify the expectation of an increase in share price on the market.

Assessment of SVA

There are a number of advantages and disadvantages of SVA.

Advantages

- It is quite simple to apply using spreadsheet analysis. This can easily be adapted to assessing the sensitivity of the results to changes in key variables.

- It is applicable to both whole firms and business units. In the latter case, one can ignore financing complexities and focus more clearly on inherent business activity value.

- It derives from, and is compatible with, the DCF method of investment appraisal. It can thus be used to show how a proposed investment will affect firm value.

- It utilises the key value drivers identified by Rappaport. These can be adapted for internal performance measurement and evaluation, e.g. in the area of working capital management.

- It can be used for benchmarking the firm against other companies.

Disadvantages

- Using constant percentage increases is often unrealistic, although sensitivity analysis can be used to examine the implications of variable rates of change.

- It is difficult to apply from an external perspective, when lack of data limits the outsider's ability to value business units.

- It may give a veneer of accuracy which is potentially confusing when the SVA result diverges significantly from the market value. When using SVA, as with any other model, caution is appropriate.

10.10 Summary

This chapter presents a variety of perspectives on the valuation of companies and on shareholder-oriented concepts of value. You should now appreciate that accounting concepts are only a beginning in this tricky but fascinating field. Try to observe cases in the financial press of valuations, for example in takeover situations, which to the outsider seem hard to justify and comprehend. This will not be too difficult.

References and further reading

Textbooks

Arnold – chs 16 and 17.
Brealey & Myers – ch 4.
Pike & Neale – chs 4 and 12.

Other

Porter, M E (1985) *Competitive Advantage* (Free Press).
Rappaport, A (1986) *Creating Shareholder Value – The New Standard for Business Performance* (Free Press).

Questions and mini-case studies

1 David Caldwell is the founder and major shareholder in a successful travel agency. He has decided that he wants to sell the business and retire. The latest accounts show:

Balance sheet as at 31 December 2002

	£	£	£
Fixed assets			
Premises			125,000
Equipment			150,000
Investments			200,000
			475,000
Current assets			
Debtors	120,000		
Bank	25,000	145,000	
Current liabilities			
Creditors		(100,000)	
Net current assets			45,000
Total assets less current liabilities			520,000
Long-term liabilities			
Bank loan			(80,000)
Net assets			440,000
Financed by			
Ordinary shares £1 each			360,000
Reserves			80,000
Shareholders' funds			440,000

The following additional information is available:

	2000	**2001**	**2002**
Net profit before dividend	16,000	29,000	45,000
Dividend	14,400	15,480	17,280

Relevant data relating to three listed companies in the travel agent business are:

	Price : earnings ratio
Company 1	9.2
Company 2	10.6
Company 3	10.8

The current market values of the assets are estimated at:

Premises	£280,000
Equipment	£50,000
Investments	£200,000

Ninety per cent of the debtors are thought likely to pay, and the remaining 10 per cent will be irrecoverable. The risk-adjusted return required by shareholders to invest in this company is 16 per cent.

Required

(a) Prepare valuations for the share capital of this company using three different methods.

(b) Discuss the results found in (a) above and explain to David which is likely to be the most suitable method. Include in your discussion any other relevant factors that need to be taken into account.

(c) Discuss the problems inherent in trying to value 'new economy' businesses such as biotech and dotcom businesses.

2 Candac owns a chain of video rental shops. The company has been approached by PDQ plc, which owns a large chain of petrol stations, with a view to a takeover of Candac. PDQ is prepared to make an offer in cash or a share-for-share exchange. Candac's most recent accounts are shown below. PDQ's accountant estimates Candac's future free cash flows as follows:

	2001	2002	2003	2004	2005-10
£m	4.4	4.6	4.9	5.0	5.4 p.a.

Shareholders require a return of 10 per cent. The rate of corporate tax is 30 per cent.

Candac has recently paid a professional valuer to estimate the current resale value of its assets. His estimates are:

	£m
Freehold land and premises	20.0
Equipment	0.9
Stock	6.0

The current resale values of the remaining assets are considered to be in line with their book values. A company which is listed on the stock exchange and which is broadly in the same business as Candac has a P : E ratio of 11 : 1.

Required

Calculate the value of *a share* in Candac using the following methods:

(i)   net asset value
(ii) P : E ratio
(iii) discounted cash flow.

Candac's latest set of audited accounts are shown below:

Profit and loss account for the year ended 31 December 2000 (£m)

Turnover	25.0
Profit before interest and tax*	7.5
Interest	(0.5)
Profit before taxation	7.0
Corporation tax @ 30 per cent	(2.1)
Net profit after taxation	4.9
Dividend	(2.0)
Retained profit	2.9

* Includes exceptional item (a tax-allowable **loss**) of £0.5m.

Balance sheet as at 31 December 2000

	£m	£m
Fixed assets		
Freehold land and premises at cost	12.0	
Less accumulated depreciation	(1.0)	11.0
Equipment at cost	2.0	
Less accumulated depreciation	(0.8)	1.2
		12.2
Current assets		
Stock at cost	7.0	
Debtors	1.5	
Bank	—	
	8.5	
Creditors due within one year:		
Trade creditors	(6.0)	
Dividends	(2.0)	
Corporation tax	(1.0)	
	(9.0)	
Net current assets		(0.5)
Total assets less current liabilities		11.7
Creditors due beyond one year:		
20% secured loan stock		(2.5)
Net assets		9.2
Share capital and reserves		
Ordinary shares – par value 50p		4.0
Reserves		5.2
Shareholders' funds		9.2

3   The British company Dangara plc is contemplating a takeover bid for another quoted company, Tefor plc. Both companies are in the leisure sector, operating chains of hotels, restaurants and motorway service stations. Tefor's most recent balance sheet shows the following:

	£m	£m
Fixed assets (net)	800	
Net current assets	50	
Long-term debt		
(12% debentures 2012)	(200)	
Net assets		650
Issued share capital (par value 25p)	80	
Revenue reserves	420	
Revaluation reserve	150	
Shareholders' funds		650

Tefor has just reported full-year profits of £200 million after tax.

You are provided with the following further information:

- Dangara's shareholders require a return of 14 per cent p.a.

- Dangara would have to divest certain of Tefor's assets, mainly motorway service stations, to satisfy the competition authorities. These assets have a book value of £100 million, but Dangara thinks they could be sold on to another restaurant chain, Lucky Break plc, for £200 million.

- Tefor's assets were last revalued in 1992, at the bottom of a property market slump.

- Dangara's P : E ratio is 14 : 1, Tefor's is 10 : 1.

- Tefor's earnings have risen by only 2 per cent p.a. on average over the previous five years, while Dangara's have risen by 7 per cent p.a. on average.

- Takeover premiums (i.e. amount paid in excess of pre-bid market values) have recently averaged 20 per cent across all market sectors.

- Many 'experts' believe that a stock market 'correction' is imminent due to the likelihood of a new government being elected. The new government would possibly adopt a more stringent policy on competition issues.

- If a bid is made, there is a possibility that the chairman of Tefor will make a counter-offer to its shareholders to attempt to take the company off the Stock Exchange.

- If the bid succeeds, Tefor's ex-chairman is expected to offer to repurchase a major part of the hotel portfolio.

- Much of Tefor's hotel asset portfolio is rather shabby and requires refurbishment, estimated at about £50 million p.a. for the next five years.

Required

As strategic planning analyst, you are instructed to prepare a briefing report for the main board. This report will:

(i) assess the appropriate value to place on Tefor, using suitable valuation techniques (state clearly any assumptions you make)

(ii) examine the issues to be addressed in deciding whether to bid for Tefor at this time.

Self-assessment answers

10.1
Over to you.

10.2
Using the CAPM, the rate, k_e, at which shareholders will discount future dividends is:

$$= R_f + \beta \times [\text{ER}_m - R_f]$$
$$= 5\% + 1.0[10\% - 5\%] = 10\%$$

- The share price is obtained by discounting the £1 dividend at 10 per cent over ten years, viz: £1 × 10-year annuity factor (6.145) = £6.145.

- Assuming a ready market in these shares, the change of ownership has no effect on share price, which still depends on the future stream of dividends.

- Using the perpetuity formula for constant payments, price = (£1/10%) = £10.

- Using the formula for a growing perpetuity,
  price = [£1(1 + 5%)]/(10% − 5%) = £1.05/5% = £21.

10.3
The depreciation charge is not a cash item so would have to be added back when undertaking a DCF evaluation. The exceptional item is a 'one-off' relating only to the year just ended, i.e. it is not part of returns from ongoing operations and thus will have to be removed when undertaking a valuation of future returns.

10.4
Other examples of 'exceptionals' might be the pay-off to a departing senior executive, the costs of factory closure in a restructuring, settlement of legal costs, the costs of environmental restoration, writing down of asset values such as stock or goodwill acquired in an acquisition. The profit figure can also be distorted by the writing back of provisions made in a previous year that turn out to be over-pessimistic.

10.5
To undertake this valuation, the formula for a growing perpetuity is used.

$$\text{PV} = \text{Cash flow} \times (1 + g)/(k - g) = £1.2m(1 + 6\%)/(20\% - 6\%)$$
$$= £1.272m/14\% = £9.09m$$

This clearly exceeds the non-growth answer. However, to be more realistic we might have to allow for periodic capital expenditures (i.e. negative cash flows) required to purchase the fixed assets to support the growth.

10.6

Pure replacement investment is very rare. Firms rarely replace worn-out equipment on a 'like-for-like' basis, most obviously because they want to take advantage of technological progress. The new equipment is likely to perform the same function more efficiently, or perform a wider range of functions. Either way, the firm's capacity to produce will have increased. Thus what may appear to be 'replacement' investment embodies elements of net investment.

10.7

From Table 10.1, we see the Year 6 cash flow is £17.61 million. Discounting this to perpetuity at 14 per cent:

$$PV = (£17.61m/0.14) = £125.8m$$

As this is an end-of-Year 6 value, we need to discount down to year zero, viz:

$$PV \text{ as at year zero} = (£125.8m \times PV \text{ factor of } 0.4556) = £57.3m$$

This is not radically different from the previous result, and would generate a total SV of (£59.5m + £57.3m) = £126.8m. This similarity in value is *not* a general result – it depends on the figures involved.

10.8

Good calculator practice! You should obtain an answer of £60.9m.

10.9

FCF before interest = £13.80m.
Interest payments = £1.6m.
Cash flow cover = (£13.80m/£1.6m) = 8.6 times, lower than the traditional measure, but still very comfortable.

Case study: easyJet plc

This case was written by Martin Kelly of The Management Institute.

The case study outlines the philosophy behind the establishment of a new concept in the European aviation industry, focused squarely on customer value for money. It explains the values and culture of the organisation that are central to easyJet's strategy. Its rapid early growth is highlighted, culminating in the successful IPO in 2000, when it appeared to have been undervalued.

As the case suggests, things move quickly in Easyworld. Since it was written, founder Stelios Haji-Ioannou has stepped down to concentrate on easyRentacar and other ventures, and the airline has fallen out of favour with the stock market in the wake of the second Gulf War, which has damaged the prospects of most airlines.

'If you want to do something new you have to stop doing something old.'

Peter Drucker

1 Introduction

It took the combined energies of a 33-year-old Irish entrepreneur (Michael O'Leary of Ryanair), who prefers Levi jeans to a suit, and a dynamic Greek Cypriot (Stelios Haji-Ioannou), whose father owns a shipping company, to transform the cost of flying within Europe. They took advantage of the deregulation of the European skies to launch a sustained attack on the cosy cartel of national airlines that hitherto had kept the cost of air travel to Europe out of reach of the cost-sensitive budget traveller. Similar to the deregulation of the US airline industry in the 1980s, the liberalisation of European airways meant that any European carrier could fly to any destination and demand landing slots.

Stelios Haji-Ioannou, the son of a Greek shipping tycoon, founded easyJet in November 1995. Stelios's innovative idea for a European low-cost airline was modelled on the US low-cost operator Southwest Airlines. Southwest operated short-haul travel routes utilising only one type of aircraft, and offered no free meals or drinks onboard.

In five years, Stelios built easyJet into a market leader in the cut-throat low-cost airline industry. Like Richard Branson, Stelios came to personify the brand he created. He strongly believes that his business serves the public good and actively cultivates the image of being champion of

the consumer. More recently, he has applied his considerable entrepreneurial talent and low-cost business philosophy to creating other business
ventures such as easyEverything, easyRentacar, easyValue and easy.com.

2 Welcome to easyLand

It was while flying on Southwest Airlines that Stelios felt he had found the
business concept that he wanted to exploit in Europe. Armed with his idea
for a low-cost airline and a business plan, he borrowed £5 million from his
father. The only issue to be resolved was where to base his new budget
airline. To operate from London's two biggest airports, Heathrow and
Gatwick, was prohibitively expensive and so Stelios settled on Luton
because of its proximity to London (30 minutes by train), and the then
favourable airport charges. Luton airport was to be the headquarters for
easyJet, located in a bright orange shed called 'easyLand'.

With an extensive marketing campaign, backed with the slogan 'Fly to
Scotland for the price of a pair of jeans!', the airline's £29 one-way fare for
a 50-minute flight to Glasgow was full to capacity and cost significantly less
than the price charged by British Airways on the same route. Stelios was
soon to add Edinburgh and Aberdeen to easyJet's list of destinations.
Although Luton was critical to easyJet's initial success, capacity constraints and increased passenger numbers necessitated the opening of two
new 'hubs' at Liverpool and Geneva.

After its first 12 months, easyJet had sold approximately 485,000 seats
and had established a network of six routes with four aircraft. In 1998,
easyJet owned a fleet of six Boeing 737–300s and flew 12 routes in five
countries. However, by July 2000, it owned and/or leased 18 Boeing
737–300s. In March 2000 the airline placed a firm order with Boeing for a
further 17 aircraft, taking the fleet size up to 44 planes by 2004 in order to
meet planned growth in passenger volumes. During the year ended 30
September 2000, easyJet flew 5.6 million passengers (up 84 per cent on
the previous year) and generated profits before tax of £22 million on
revenue of £264 million.

3 Business philosophy

easyJet's business philosophy closely follows the model pioneered by Herb
Kelleher at Southwest Airlines: no frills, quick turnaround times and very
high aircraft utilisation. By stripping away the peripherals, by eliminating
the unnecessary complications of buying a ticket, and making airline travel
more accessible to the budget traveller, Stelios has quite simply changed

the way the British public views flying. In essence, he has made it 'easy to fly'. This concept is encapsulated in the company's mission statement:

> 'To provide our customers with safe, low-cost, good value, point-to-point air services. To offer a consistent and reliable product at fares appealing to leisure and business markets from our bases to a range of domestic and European destinations. To achieve this, we will develop our people and establish lasting partnerships with our suppliers.'

4 Cost advantage

Unlike Southwest Airlines, which derives 60 per cent of its revenue through travel agents, easyJet cut out travel agents completely and relies on direct sales via telephone reservations or direct bookings on the internet, thus making significant cost savings on agents' commission. The airline does not issue tickets, passengers simply turn up, quote their booking number and are given a plastic reusable boarding pass. It is estimated that this saves about £5 per passenger. With a strictly enforced minimum check-in time, passengers can board the planes at either end and sit in any seat on a first-come, first-served basis. There is no business class seating, thus allowing the airline to increase its seating capacity. By not offering a meal service, easyJet is able to pass on savings to customers and save valuable time in getting the aircraft ready for the next flight. Soft drinks and snacks can be purchased from the 'easykiosk' on board the aircraft.

The airline operates a turnaround time of approximately 20 minutes, which enables it to fly its planes for about 11.5 hours per day, instead of six hours, the industry average. Stelios decided to fly only Boeing 737s, utilising their maximum capacity of 148 seats, which meant that maintenance and training costs were kept lower than would be the case if he operated different aircraft.

5 Customer orientation

Increasingly, both business travellers and those managing corporate travel budgets are weary of being used as 'cash cows', paying above the odds for flexible economy tickets or business class on short-haul flights with traditional airlines. The airline has identified cost-conscious niche markets which include both leisure and business travellers. In essence, easyJet's marketing strategy consists of making 'limited promises' but ensuring that it consistently delivers on those promises. Marketing managers at easyJet make great play of the fact that destinations served by the airline are all key airports rather than secondary sites miles from the city centres. Customer satisfaction is a high priority for the company, with Stelios flying on easyJet every week, meeting and listening to passengers. All marketing research at easyJet is carried out internally, thus avoiding the need for expensive advertising agencies.

In 1999, easyJet was voted 'Best No-Frills Airline', and in 2000, it was voted 'Best Low-Cost Airline', both in the *Business Traveller* magazine awards.

The airline operates a 'yield management' system, strictly balancing the number of seats available at each tier of fares according to actual demand. The higher the demand for a particular seat, the higher the fare. Customers who are willing to book early would get a better price and those who wanted flexibility would have to pay more. All fares quoted are one way and have the same restrictions. The cost to change a flight is £10 plus the difference between the two fares.

To buy tickets, customers call a local rate number, which connects them to one of easyJet's reservation agents based at the call centre in Luton. Reservation agents are paid solely on commission at the rate of £0.80 per seat sold, and can sell on average between 60 and 90 seats during an eight-hour shift.

Although easyJet is a low-cost airline, management emphasises that safety is of paramount importance.

6 Sub-contracting operations

When easyJet started up it had limited resources, diseconomies of scale, and out of necessity had to rely on sub-contractors, confining its own role to providing the planes, the pilots and cabin crew, and marketing staff. Sub-contractors handled everything else. The company's ability to be operationally efficient and meet its operational targets such as a 20-minute turnaround and punctuality are crucially dependent on managing the performance of its sub-contractors. Top management has devoted significant time and resources to managing the relationship with outside vendors.

7 Corporate image (orange is the colour)

'The company has a stated intention of being a good employer and strongly believes that work can be performed well and enjoyed within an informal environment by its approachable management style and dress code.'

(Annual report 2000)

Bright orange appears on the aircraft's tail and is carried throughout the airline, its flight attendants' clothing, timetables, advertising, promotional materials and website. The colour was chosen because it was deemed an underutilised colour.

The company has established a strong brand in its important European markets – the UK, the Netherlands and Switzerland. Stelios has undoubtedly contributed to the easyJet brand image, but management believes it is the 'business philosophy' of low cost, keeping it simple, and listening to customers that differentiates easyJet from its competitors. Stelios's well-publicised battles with British Airways, Swissair and, later, Barclays Bank have inevitably raised public awareness of the company.

Another unique way in which easyJet has enabled its brand name to reach the travelling public is through the 'warts and all' documentary series, commissioned by London Weekend Television. The first series attracted around 7.5 million viewers on a Friday night.

8 Culture

At easyLand, the company's headquarters at Luton Airport, everyone is equal and there are no transparent signs of hierarchy. The chairman sits in the same nondescript open-plan office as everyone else. Staff are instructed to dress casually (no ties), as does Stelios. Stelios expects people to work long hours because he also works long hours. There are weekly barbecues at easyLand where staff may socialise and get to know each other better.

Another aspect of the easyJet culture is the 'paperless office' that is also part of the 'keep-it-simple' philosophy. All documents are scanned and placed on the computer system so that those members of staff who need information can access it. There are no secretaries or private offices and full economic use is made of all available space.

Stelios, who constantly shuttles between Luton, Monaco and Greece, can access his desk from anywhere in the world. More prosaically, Luton workers can move from desk to desk and still call up their files. In principle, there is no need for paper anywhere in the office. The management team can easily access data on their screens showing revenue and profitability figures for any flight and the forward booking numbers. The paperless office and efficient internal communications facilitate important decisions on price setting and arrival times.

'As a concrete demonstration of the value generated by staff, almost all employees have received an offer of either a gift of shares or an option over shares, dependent on a future flotation of the company.'

(easyJet plc financial statements September 2000)

9 The internet

The company promotes itself as the 'web's favourite airline' and paints the website address on all its aircraft. In the week ending 3 October 1999, the airline sold more than half of its seats over the internet. In September 2000, this figure reached 78 per cent. easyJet's strategy is to encourage passengers to book flights via the internet, as it is the most cost-effective distribution channel for the company. In March 2000, the airline announced that it had sold 2 million tickets online.

10 Competition

Ryanair

Michael O'Leary took the top job at Ryanair in 1991 when he signed up to a debt-laden family airline business based in Ireland. At the time of writing, the charismatic chief executive was at the helm of an operation which commanded pre-tax profits of £43 million and carried 6 million passengers in 1999. Unlike easyJet, Ryanair chooses to fly in and out of the quieter secondary airports where landing costs are lower and turnaround is easier.

Go

In May 1998, British Airways entered the low-cost market by establishing its own no-frills airline called Go. BA's decision to enter the market provoked an immediate response from easyJet, which expressed concern that BA had formed the new airline to force other low-cost operators out of the marketplace. Stelios organised a competition on easyJet's website in which the first 50 people who came closest to guessing Go's annual losses would be awarded free easyJet tickets. Stelios also entered into a legal battle with BA, claiming the company was unfairly subsidising its low-cost subsidiary. easyJet eventually bought Go for £374m in 2002.

11 Stock market lift-off

On 15 November 2000, despite market volatility and a decline in aviation stocks, easyJet floated on the London Stock Exchange. The offer was restricted to institutions and institutional investors in the USA, with no retail offering. It appeared that the company wanted to avoid the hype associated with dotcom companies that saw massive oversubscription and then a collapsing share price. As well as institutional stockholdings, a further

12 per cent of the shares were earmarked for allocation to management and staff. Proceeds from the flotation were to be used to help finance the ever-expanding fleet of 737–700s on order during the following four years.

The prospectus for the offer listed several risk factors for investors, including:

- strong seasonal nature of the business
- difficulty of managing rapid growth
- fuel price fluctuations
- possibility of not meeting growth targets.

The financial statements (see Appendix 1) disclose that the company made pre-tax profits of £22 million in the year to the end of September, up from £1.3 million in the previous year, on a turnover that increased from £140 million to £263 million.

The offer price for the shares was set at 310p and 63 million shares (25 per cent of the enlarged share capital) were made available. The airline raised approximately £195 million and was valued at £777 million at flotation. The issue attracted strong interest and was just under ten times subscribed. The terms of the offer allowed for a further 9.45 million shares to be issued via an over-allotment option, granted to Credit Suisse First Boston and UBS Warburg, joint sponsors of the flotation. On the first day of trading, shares in easyJet closed up 10 per cent at 342p. On 1 December, proceeds of the flotation were enhanced when the over-allotment option was exercised. This resulted in bringing the total value of the easyJet initial public offering to £225 million. Share price information in the months following the flotation is shown in Appendix 2.

easyJet has been marketed as a growth stock in what many see as a growing industry. At the time of writing it ranks as the second largest low-cost airline, flying 28 routes to 16 destinations, but this still accounts for a low percentage of the overall European aviation market. In the longer term, the airline aims to triple passenger numbers and double its staff, at present 1,400, by 2004. There is no doubt that easyJet's low-cost philosophy has been an outstanding success, as evidenced by market reaction to the flotation, and there is further potential for the airline to expand in Europe. The unanswered question is, how long can it last?

Questions

1 Identify the core competences of easyJet, and the type of competitive advantage that it exploits.

2 Acting as a member of the easyJet flotation team, prepare notes for a presentation to potential institutional investors, which sets out the extent to which you believe the company's vision can provide a sustainable competitive advantage.

3 'Any "brand value" that can be attached to easyJet is inextricably linked to the airline's chairman, Stelios Haji-Ioannou.'
 Critically discuss.

4 Using the information in the case study and subsequent share price movements, consider whether the company was over/undervalued in relation to the financial statements, given in Appendix 1.

5 How would you value an airline?

Source: Website: www.easyjet.com

Appendix 1

easyJet plc

Consolidated profit and loss account for the year to 30 September

	2000 £000	1999 £000
Revenue	263,694	139,789
Cost of sales	(191,291)	(103,848)
Gross profit	**72,403**	**35,941**
Distribution and marketing	(25,868)	(16,165)
Administrative expenses	(17,875)	(10,726)
Operating profit	**28,660**	**9,050**
Share of operating loss of associate	-	(779)
Interest receivable	1,687	664
Interest payable	(8,244)	(7,675)
Profit on ordinary activities		
Before tax	22,103	1,260
Tax on profit on ordinary activities	-	-
Retained profit for the year	**22,103**	**1,260**
Earnings per share	11.9p	0.7p

Consolidated balance sheet at 30 September

	2000		1999	
	£000	£000	£000	£000
Fixed assets				
Intangible assets		3,163		3,327
Tangible assets		202,159		164,233
		205,322		167,560
Current assets				
Debtors	40,959		27,497	
Cash at bank	14,088		29,845	
	55,047		57,342	
Creditors: amounts falling				
due within one year	−84,483		−56,882	
Net current (liabilities)/assets				
		−29,436		460
Total assets less current liabilities		175,886		168,020
Creditors: amounts falling				
due after one year		−108,315		−127,069
Provisions for liabilities and charges		−1,854		−1,463
Net assets		**65,717**		**39,488**
Capital and reserves				
Called up share capital		46,647		-
Other reserves		-		38,314
Profit and loss account		19,070		1,174
Shareholders' funds		**65,717**		**39,488**

Source: easyJet plc Annual Report and Accounts for the year ended
31 December 2001, easyJet plc (2001)

Appendix 2

easyJet plc share price movements six months to April 2001

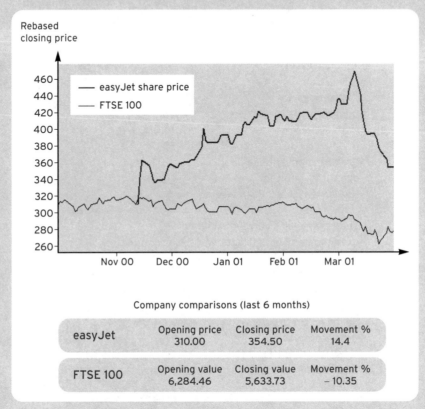

Company comparisons (last 6 months)

easyJet	Opening price 310.00	Closing price 354.50	Movement % 14.4
FTSE 100	Opening value 6,284.46	Closing value 5,633.73	Movement % − 10.35

Source: FT.com

RETURNING VALUE TO OWNERS

Good news comes in threes

In December 1999, General Electric Corporation (GE), the world's second largest company (behind Microsoft) by stock market value, thrilled the markets with a triple announcement.

- First, it announced a 17 per cent increase in the quarterly dividend from 35 to 41 cents per share.

- Second, it promised a 3-for-1 stock split, its third in six years, and the fifth in 17 years, and the ninth in its 107-year history.

- Third, it announced plans to step up its stock repurchase programme by $5 billion, making $22 billion over a five-year span.

The impact on share price was immediate and beneficial – an increase of over $6 to $154 (4 per cent). Accompanying the announcements was a statement that these actions reflected GE's financial strength and the excellent prospects for its diverse array of global businesses ranging from light bulbs through television networks to jet engines, and including one of the world's biggest investment banks, GE Capital.

It certainly looked a juicy package – more dividends, free shares and the rest. But the market's delight really lies in the (not very!) hidden information. Most analysts, who were expecting a 2-for-1 stock split and a lower dividend increase, took all this as an expression of high confidence in the company's future earning capacity, i.e. a way of signalling rapid growth in future profits.

Objectives:
This chapter aims to:

- examine how shareholders can receive their overall returns

- argue the question of why companies pay dividends at all

- evaluate whether a company can manipulate its share price via its dividend pay-out

- identify the key determinants of dividend policy

- explain alternatives to cash dividend payments.

11.1 Introduction

Although we emphasise throughout this book that the focus of financial management is on value *creation*, we have devoted relatively little attention the issue of how to *deliver* this wealth to shareholders. When a company is already profitable and has good future prospects, wealth has been *created*, but how should this wealth be *delivered*? In the form of annual dividends to shareholders or as retentions that should promise further capital appreciation?

There is a dilemma for management in this area. If high dividends are paid, the company may have insufficient capital to finance future growth – although this implies inability of the capital market to supply finance for worthwhile projects. Conversely, too low a level of dividend may starve investors of ready income and may even give the impression that the company is highly risky. High retention and high liquidity may signal that the company expects difficult trading conditions in the future, and wants to build a financial cushion.

You will find that the issue of **signalling** dominates analysis of dividend decisions. For example, if a company raises its dividend, it may convey the information that it is confident that future earnings will be sufficiently bouyant to at least maintain, and hopefully increase, this higher dividend. Why is this? Simply, because few financial managers ever want to *cut* a dividend except under extremely adverse conditions. To cut a dividend is regarded as the ultimate sign of financial incompetence on the part of directors, as well as signalling desperate future prospects for the company.

Hence, to avoid ever having to cut a dividend, the astute financial manager will avoid increasing dividend levels to possibly unsustainable levels. Even in parlous situations, managers often strive to pay dividends, maybe dipping into reserves to do so, i.e. running down retained earnings. This generally requires borrowing to raise the required cash. Remember that dividends are paid *out of* profits – whether from this year or previous years – but *with* cash.

Permeating this introduction is the notion that dividend decisions, like any other financial decision, convey information – they are said to possess an

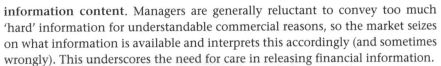

information content. Managers are generally reluctant to convey too much 'hard' information for understandable commercial reasons, so the market seizes on what information is available and interprets this accordingly (and sometimes wrongly). This underscores the need for care in releasing financial information.

You may have read of companies reporting good results to the financial community yet having their share prices savaged. This happened to Abbey National plc in early 1999. It reported higher profits and higher dividends but managed to give the impression that it anticipated difficult future trading conditions by making higher provisions against possible future bad debts. All very cautious and commendable, but its share price fell by 8 per cent.

11.2 Theories of dividend policy: overview

It is tempting to expect an increase in dividends to increase share price. However, the academic world is divided on the relationship between dividend pay-outs and share price. We now review some of the leading theories.

The principal theories of dividend policy are as follows:

- *The residual school*/**dividend irrelevance.** This says that a firm should pay a dividend only after all worthwhile investment opportunities have been financed. Company value is driven by cash flows that result from worthwhile investment, not by dividends per se. Thus, dividend policy itself is irrelevant – what matters is the firm's investment policy.

- *Dividend relevance.* Some people argue that the future dividends expected to be paid out of the cash flows generated by retentions-financed investment are inherently more risky than dividends paid now. Investors might prefer early resolution of uncertainty and thus value today's dividend more highly than future dividends.

- *Pragmatists.* Most people argue that it is too difficult to generalise about a firm's dividend policy – it depends on the particular circumstances of the firm. We can identify the factors that should be taken into account but not all may apply, or they may apply to different firms in varying degrees.

We will look at these three positions in this order.

Self-assessment activity 11.1

Look at the report and accounts of your chosen company. How much is dividend per share? What proportion of profit after tax is the dividend? Does it state its dividend policy?

① 11.3 Dividends as a residual: dividend irrelevance

This line of argument says that a firm should use retained earnings to finance the pool of worthwhile investment, and pay a dividend only if there is an unspent residue of cash. In its most basic form, it implies that the firm has no access to external supplies of capital. The following example will make this clearer.

ABC plc has the following set of projects available. Its shareholders require a return of 20 per cent. How much dividend should it pay? In the year just ended, it achieved earnings, still held as cash, of £100,000. ABC plc has no external access to finance.

Project	Internal rate of return	Outlay required
A	32%	£28,000
B	28%	£12,000
C	24%	£20,000
D	22%	£10,000
E	21%	£10,000
F	15%	£10,000

Notice that ABC *could* finance all these projects internally, but that project F is unattractive. So projects A–E would be recommended, requiring a total outlay of £80,000, leaving £20,000 available for dividend payment. If the IRR on project E was less than 20 per cent, the dividend would be £30,000. Notice that there may be problems in cases where projects are indivisible.

Self-assessment activity 11.2

A firm currently has no access to external finance. Its cost of finance is 15 per cent. It has the following projects available.

Project	Investment required (£ million)	Internal rate of return
A	10	24%
B	8	12%
C	15	20%
D	12	14%
E	10	16%

What investment programme, and what dividend payment, would you recommend if, in the year just ended, earnings are: £35 million? £30 million? £10 million?
(answer at end of chapter)

Financing new investment – internal finance only

Under this view, it may be advisable to reduce the level of expected dividend if worthwhile projects are available. Consider the following case:

- An all-equity financed firm will operate for a further three years only.

- Shareholders seek a 10 per cent return.

- On present policies, its expected end-year cash flows are:
  £100 Year 1   £100 Year 2   £100 Year 3

- All cash flows are usually paid as dividends.

- It now proposes a new venture which involves:
  - total retention of Year 1 earnings
  - investing in a one-year project with a single cash flow of £120 (i.e. internal rate of return = 20 per cent)
  - restoring the 100 per cent pay-out policy in Years 2 and 3.

What is the impact of accepting this project on the value of the company?
Without the project, the value of the company is:

$$V_0 = \frac{£100}{1.1} + \frac{£100}{(1.1)^2} + \frac{£100}{(1.1)^3} = £248$$

After accepting the project, the company's value becomes:

$$V_1 = \frac{0}{1.1} + \frac{[£100 + £120]}{(1.1)^2} + \frac{£100}{(1.1)^3} = £256$$

Company value increases because:

$$\frac{£120}{(1.1)^2} > \frac{£100}{(1.1)}$$

or   £99 > £91

Accepting the project is beneficial because the cash generated by the project in Year 2 more than compensates (even when discounted) for the reduced dividend in Year 1. Quite simply, it is rational to retain earnings for reinvestment because the return on the project concerned exceeds the shareholders' required return. Moreover, it would actually penalise shareholders to pay them a dividend because it would exclude them from participating in a worthwhile venture. Dividends are 'relevant' only in the narrow sense that they may impose an opportunity cost.

Self-assessment activity 11.3

Show that investment in a similar project that offered a cash flow of only £107 in Year 2 would reduce firm value.
(answer at end of chapter)

It might still be argued that earnings retention would penalise shareholders who depend on a steady income stream from dividends, e.g. relatively late-in-life investors and financial institutions. However, it is easy to rebut this argument. If the project is truly worthwhile and is perceived as such by the financial markets, the share price will increase as soon as the relevant information is released to the market (if it is semi-strong efficient). Those shareholders requiring income now can sell off some portion of their shareholding at the higher price and use the proceeds to finance their desired expenditures. Under this view, the people in older age brackets who have relatively short time horizons, i.e. whose time preference leans towards income now rather than in the future, can 'home-make' dividends by selling shares in the market to realise the capital gain generated on their behalf by the investing company.

Allowing for access to external finance

The preceding discussion implies no external access to finance. If external financing is allowed, a company can pay a dividend and still undertake as much investment as it desires. We will now widen the analysis to allow for equity financing via a rights issue. There are now two alternative methods of financing investment:

- cut dividends and finance from retention
- pay the dividend and 'claw back' the required finance via a rights issue.

If we can show that shareholder wealth is the same under each financing option, then dividend policy really is irrelevant.
 Consider the following case:

- An ungeared company has just made earnings, still held as cash, of £100 and expects to earn the same level in future years from existing activities.
- Its shareholders require a return of 10 per cent per annum; normally it would make a 100 per cent pay-out.
- It has available a project requiring an outlay of £100 (this is equal to the dividend which it would normally pay, i.e. 100 per cent of £100), that is expected to generate a perpetual cash flow of £20 per annum.
- What is the value of the company now?

- What is the NPV of the project?
- What is shareholder wealth under each of the financing options identified above?

The value of company before the dividend is paid

$$= \text{Cash} + \text{PV of future cash flows}$$

$$= £100 + \frac{£100}{0.1} = £1,100$$

The project is acceptable because the NPV is positive, viz:

$$= -£100 + \frac{£20}{0.1} = +£100$$

Consider now the two financing alternatives:

(i) *Using retentions*:

Shareholder wealth

$$= \text{Dividend} + \text{PV of cash flows for existing projects}$$
$$+ \text{PV of cash flows from new project}$$

$$= 0 + \frac{£100}{0.1} + \frac{£20}{0.1}$$

$$= 0 + £1,000 + £200 = £1,200$$

The owners' wealth thus increases by the NPV of the project.

(ii) *Using a rights issue*:

Shareholder wealth

$$= \text{Dividend} + \text{PV of cash flows for existing projects}$$
$$+ \text{PV of cash flows from new project}$$
$$- \text{Cost of undertaking project}$$
$$(= \text{Proceeds of rights issue})$$

$$= £100 + \frac{£100}{0.1} + \frac{£20}{0.1} - £100$$

$$= £100 + £1,000 + £200 - £100$$

$$= £1,200, \text{ as in (i)}$$

Since the wealth of shareholders is the same under each alternative, the method of finance, and therefore whether to pay a dividend, is irrelevant.

To many investors, this is a surprising conclusion. Some models of shareholder value, e.g. the dividend valuation model, stress the role of dividends, yet here we seem to be saying that dividends are irrelevant. How can we reconcile these apparently conflicting positions?

11.4 Evaluation of the irrelevance argument: alternative views

Dividends are important – most people would prefer more dividends to fewer, other things being equal. Yet dividends may impose a cost, for example if a worthwhile investment cannot be financed in other ways. What drives company value is thus the investment decision and the resulting cash flows (and their degree of risk) rather than the way that value is delivered. Thus, it is the actual pattern, i.e. the time profile of the dividend flow, that is at issue. In other words, using a famous quotation from two Nobel prize winners in Economics, Merton Miller and Franco Modigliani (MM):

> 'For a company acting in the best interest of its shareholders, dividend policy is a mere detail'.
>
> (Miller and Modigliani, 1961)

Put another way, if in the above example we were to strip out the effect of the investment decision by assuming zero NPV, we would find that the impact of the dividend cut was totally neutral. Any effect on the company value thus comes only through the impact of the investment decision.

Objections to dividend irrelevance

The previous conclusion on dividend irrelevance may sound perfectly logical in theory (it is!), but there are many 'practical' objections that one might level at this notion. Most obviously, there is the information content – the notion that investors may read messages into dividend decisions. If in the past, the company has used the dividend decision to convey information, news of a dividend cut will not be greeted with equanimity.

Four other major issues that merit more detailed information are:

(i)   In reality, investors may be unwilling or unable to 'home-make' dividends.

(ii) Shareholders may, in reality, prefer 'near' dividends to 'distant' dividends.

(iii) Rights issues are not always received favourably by investors.

(iv) Tax implications may drive investors towards a clear preference for or against dividends.

The first three of these issues are now addressed in turn, and the fourth is addressed in section 11.6. As we examine these aspects, we will develop the 'pragmatic' approach (it is hardly a 'theory'), which is that dividends may matter depending on the circumstances. Some factors pull the firm towards higher dividends, and vice versa for others.

(i) Problems with home-making dividends

There are several reasons why investors might object to having to 'home-make' dividends:

- they may incur dealing fees

- decisions to deal involve time and inconvenience

- significant share sales may lower share price. If a large percentage of shareholders are income-dependent, their selling pressure may drive share price down if the market demand for the company's shares is less than perfectly elastic

- having to sell shares to realise a capital gain may trigger a capital gains tax liability. However, this point is country-specific. In the UK for 2003–4, the first £7,900 of capital gain was tax-exempt, and inflation indexation on gains applied up to April 1998. Moreover, husbands and wives had separate allowances. In some countries, for example the Netherlands, at the time of writing, there was no tax on capital gains.

(ii) 'Early resolution of uncertainty' – the Gordon theory

It is plausible that investors may prefer dividends paid now – what Gordon (1959) called 'early resolution of uncertainty'.

This is a more complex issue. Retention of earnings, even if wisely invested, postpones income. Hence, shareholders in a company that pays lower dividends now to finance (albeit worthwhile) investment have to wait longer for the (hopefully) higher dividends to be paid out of the higher future dividends generated. Gordon argued that shareholders will resent having to wait longer, especially due to the higher risk associated with more distant dividends. He argued that people discount more distant dividends more heavily to allow for risk. This implies investors believe risk increases over time.

However, this may not be the case – in many instances, for example oil-drilling and R&D-intensive projects, the risk is 'front-loaded' and may even decline over time. Moreover, even if risk does increase over time, this aspect should have been allowed for already in the discount rate when evaluating the cash flows from the project in the first instance. To further discount the dividends paid out of those cash flows 'to allow for risk' would be to double-count for risk – the higher risk is reflected in the project cash flows, not in the dividend payments.

For this reason, Gordon's argument is usually dismissed as the **bird-in-the-hand fallacy**. Admittedly, if the company has a poor record with reinvestment, it might be logical to look askance at more retention even when managers predict higher future dividends. But this is a reaction to investment policy (or doubts about management competence) rather than dividend policy itself.

(iii) Problems with rights issues

We examined the mechanics of a rights issue in Chapter 8. There are several reasons why investors may resent the announcement of a rights issue.

- A rights issue is always made at a discount to the market price, resulting in earnings dilution and a fall in share price. However, this is a purely technical adjustment and should not damage the shareholder if he/she takes up the rights or sells them in the market. Any 'problem' is purely psychological.

- The rights issue forces the investor to act, thus imposing the costs of time and inconvenience.

- A rights issue can result in 2–3 per cent of the funds raised leaking into advisers' and underwriters' fees, and the company's own administrative costs. This effectively raises the cost of finance.

- If the rights are sold, the investor incurs dealing fees.

- If the rights are taken up, the investor may end up holding rather more of the company's shares than he/she might have wished, thus disrupting the balance of their portfolio.

- A rights issue needs careful timing if the bulk of the shares are not to be left with the underwriters. Despite being paid to bear this risk, underwriters bitterly resent having to perform, and few companies recover their image and credibility after a 'failed' rights issue.

- A rights issue may alarm investors if the reasons for the issue are not made crystal clear. The information content is important here. For example, a rights issue with a deep discount may signal that the company is really anxious to raise cash. If the company has a poor track record with acquisitions, the reaction to a rights issue, if it is intended to finance further acquisitions, may be adverse.

Agency issues

A final consideration in this analysis is whether managers can be trusted to use retentions wisely. Other things being equal, high pay-outs will require companies to seek further finance in the future, which will require managers to give information about future investment plans. In addition if they are tempted to invest in low-yielding projects or to engage in unwarranted diversification, possibly to enhance their personal job security, it seems desirable for owners to demand a high pay-out policy. The mechanism for doing this is problematic, given that the amount of the dividend is set by the board, and although this requires ratification at the AGM, it is rare for board proposals to be voted down. As ever, the 'behind-the-scenes' pressure of institutional investors may play an important part.

 11.5 Alternatives to cash dividends

The distinction between cash dividends and capital gain is not as rigid as it may appear as companies can reward their owners in many other ways. Among these are share dividends (**scrip dividends**), bonus issues and stock splits.

Scrip dividends

Many major companies offer shareholders the opportunity to choose to receive new shares instead of a cash dividend. A shareholder entitled to receive cash dividends of £220, say, from a company whose share price is £10 may instead elect to receive 22 new shares. Like the cash dividend, it counts as income for tax purposes.

In recent years, in the UK, the take-up rate of scrips has been very low, due to taxation factors. However, changes in the tax regime have made scrip issues relatively more attractive, although firms may be wary of releasing too many new voting rights.

Some companies increase or 'enhance' the scrip dividend above its cash equivalent value to make investors an offer difficult to refuse – hence the term enhanced scrip dividend. For example, in 1998, Yorkshire Water plc (now Kelda plc) offered a scrip alternative valued at 110 per cent of the cash alternative.

> ### Self-assessment activity 11.5
>
> Does 'your' company offer a scrip alternative?
> (You may find that, instead, it offers something that glories in the acronym DRIP – if so, find out what this is!)

The advantages of scrip dividends

From the company's point of view, the scrip alternative preserves liquidity, which may be important at a time of cash shortage and/or high borrowing costs, although it may become committed to a higher level of cash outflows in the future if shareholders revert to a preference for cash. However, having issued more shares, the company's reported financial gearing may be lowered, possibly enhancing its borrowing capacity.

This is why, the scrip dividend resembles a rights issue. For example, a company which declares cash dividends of £10 million (net of tax), and half of whose shareholders choose the scrip alternative, would make a £5 million cash saving, and the share capital (issued plus the share premium account) rises by £5 million.

For shareholders who wish to increase their holdings, the scrip is a cheap way into the company as it avoids dealing fees (although it may lock in shareholders who may find themselves holding blocks of shares in sizes awkward to trade). The conversion price used to calculate the number of shares receivable is based on the average share price for several trading days after the 'ex-dividend day'. Should the market price rise above the conversion price before the date at which shareholders have to declare their choice, there is a capital gain, although if the share price appreciation exceeds 15 per cent, any such gain is taxable.

A scrip dividend has no tax advantages for shareholders as it is treated as income for tax purposes. If the capital market is efficient, there is no depressing effect on share price of the scrip dividend through earnings dilution. This is because the scrip simply replaces a cash dividend which would have caused share price to fall anyway due to the 'ex-dividend' effect. In other words, shareholder wealth is unchanged. However, if the additional capital retained is invested wisely, share price may benefit.

Splits, scrip issues and bonus issues

A stock split involves increasing the number of shares in issue without any money changing hands – a sort of free rights issue. Companies like GE (see introductory cameo) give existing shareholders free shares in proportion to their existing holdings. It is not only well-established market giants which do this – the internet portal company Yahoo! Inc also made a stock split in February 2000.

While less common in the UK, US firms have announced between 300 and 400 stock splits annually. Over 1996–8, there were around 2,200 splits in the USA, including 840 in 1998 alone. A major UK company which adopted this tactic was Barclays Bank plc in 2001.

Strictly, a stock split is where a company literally splits one existing share into two or three (or four in Barclays' case), say, and reduces the par value accordingly. For example, if a company has 10 million 50p shares in issue, a 1-for-1 stock split will double the number of shares into 20 million units at a par value of 25p, with no other balance sheet adjustment.

A bonus issue, or scrip issue, also involves increasing the number of shares but without adjusting the par value, the adjustment usually being made via the share premium account, or if there is none, via other reserves. In the USA, this distinction is irrelevant as company stocks do not have par values and hence no share premium accounts.

Because stock splits increase the number of issued shares, they lower share price. In fact, this is deliberate. 'Heavyweight' shares, i.e. with a high price per share (before splitting, GE's stock stood at $148, Yahoo!'s at over $400, and Barclays' at a more modest £24.50), are thought to be unattractive to retail investors. Such shareholders are thought to be more loyal and thus to exert less volatility on share prices. If issued shares are doubled, the share price should halve, but the shares now have greater liquidity – people allegedly become more ready to buy (and sell) them. Some companies will adjust the dividend per share accordingly, e.g. twice as many shares means the dividend per share is halved.

This may all look rather cosmetic but the dividend is often *not* reduced pro rata, yielding an effective dividend increase, thus enhancing share price. Moreover, evidence exists that, with or without an effective dividend increase, a stock split presages a subsequent rise in earnings, that is, it is a signalling device – companies which split their stock generally increase their earnings.

Some US research suggests that stock-splitting companies outperform over the 12 months following the announcement, and often exceed their earnings forecasts. Hence, it seems that although stock splits do not return value in a direct way, this appears to be an effective mechanism for creating value, or at least alerting the market to the true value of a company's stock.

Self-assessment activity 11.6

A firm has issued share capital of £100 million (par value 50p) and reserves of £500 million. The share price is £10.

How many bonus shares should it issue if it wanted to reduce share price to £8? What would happen to reserves?

(answer at end of chapter)

11.6 **Personal taxation**

As suggested earlier, the system of personal taxation can affect people's relative preferences for dividends and capital gain via retention. But precisely how depends on where you live. In the UK, it is generally true to say that high-rate tax-payers prefer retentions, and low- or no-rate taxpayers prefer dividends. Both dividends and capital gains are taxed as income, although the relief and allowances generally favour retentions. For 2003–4 in the UK, dividend income up to £30,500 was taxable at 10 per cent and at 32.5 per cent beyond this threshold.

 Capital gains tax is paid only when the investor realises the gain, whereas income tax on dividend payments is paid automatically at the 10 per cent or 32.5 per cent rate by the firm paying the dividend. For capital gains, tax payable depends on how long the asset is held for. Inflation-indexing is applied to the period 1982 to 1998, when it was replaced by a system of tapering rates – the rate of tax declining as the holding period lengthens. Also, the first £7,900 of gain is exempt from tax, with husbands and wives qualifying for separate allowances. With careful planning, capital gains tax can often be avoided altogether.

Each pound of dividend income carries a tax credit, at the 10 per cent rate, the rate applicable to lower rate tax-payers. Hence, £1 of after-tax income is equivalent to £1/0.90 = £1.11 before tax, yielding a tax credit of £0.11, i.e. 1/11 of the cash dividend paid.

> ### Self-assessment activity 11.7
>
> A firm declares a cash dividend of 12p per share. What is the total tax credit for an investor holding 1,800 shares?
> (answer at end of chapter)

For many years, the tax credit could be reclaimed from the Inland Revenue by non-taxpayers, but this facility was abolished, first, for pension funds in 1997 and then for personal investors in 1999 (but it still applies for investments held within Individual Savings Accounts, or ISAs – tax-free investment plans).

The ability of the pension funds to reclaim tax credits allegedly led to severe pressure on corporate boards to pay out ever-rising levels of dividends, which with the associated tax credits boosted the income of pension funds and thus the apparent performance of pension fund managers. This pressure to distribute rather than reinvest prompted the government to act in the hope that higher retention would lead to higher levels of corporate investment.

11.7 **Dividend policy: key determinants**

If a company had full knowledge of its shareholders' desires and tax positions, it would tailor its dividend policy according to the following:

(i)   The time preference of the shareholders, and thus their relative preferences for income now against future income as governed by factors such as their age profiles.

(ii) The relative tax efficiency of dividends and capital gains – for example, a predominance of non-taxpayers might suggest orientation towards relatively high payouts.

(iii) The perceived information content of dividend decisions. The company would bear in mind that dividend cuts, however justifiable in terms of accessing investment projects, cause severe damage, and dividend increases may encourage unrealistic expectations of even higher future dividends.

(iv) Desired levels of liquidity. This would depend on the upcoming programme of investment and the extent to which the company felt able to use the external capital markets.

(v)   Covenants on debt. It is common for lenders to impose restrictions, called covenants, on borrowers' financial actions in order to protect their interests as prior claimants. One form of covenant is an upper limit on the firm's payout ratio.

The reality is rather different. Although the aim of tailoring dividend decisions to the particular needs of shareholders may be laudable, it is almost impossible to obtain sufficient information about their needs and desires. Shareholders are simply too widely dispersed. Often, a company will consult 'key' shareholders such as the institutional investors but this raises the danger of dividend policy being driven by a small select band of shareholder (albeit the most important ones).

Instead, most companies generally try to follow a *stable* dividend policy involving either a relatively high or low pay-out, but with regular increases in the dividend. This is known as a '*progressive*' dividend policy. In this way, the company attracts a clientele of shareholders for whom its particular dividend policy is appropriate. Shareholders then develop confident expectations about future dividends and can plan their affairs accordingly. 'What you see is what you get' would sum up this approach. This does, of course, underline the need not to abruptly change the dividend policy – people do not like shocks. This would apply to sharp dividend increases as well as decreases. People are not always able to find a home for a sudden increase in liquid assets and besides, such a dividend increase may impose tax penalties.

With such a policy, the dividend would be 'smoothed' and the company would pay regular and steady increases even though earnings per share might fluctuate. This would leave the pay-out ratio to rise and fall with variations in reported earnings.

Alternative policies

Two other possible approaches to dividend payouts are as follows:

- To pay out a fixed percentage of earnings in dividends. As well as being simple, this has the advantage of rewarding shareholders in line with company performance. However, it can lead to variations in amount of dividend over the business cycle and can also leave the firm short of investment capital during the downturn. Moreover, shareholders may perceive their income as subject to creative accounting.

- Zero payout. This would benefit high income-tax-paying individuals, and may well be appropriate for the young, fast-growing company with many attractive investment opportunities. For example, only recently has Microsoft begun to pay dividends, more than 20 years after its formation. Dell Computers and Ryanair, Europe's most valuable airline operator, have never paid dividends.

11.8 Dealing with cash surpluses: special dividends and share buy-backs

Firms periodically accumulate large stockpiles of cash. These companies are looking at ways of utilising these cash surpluses.

To pay out a higher dividend is clearly an option. However, it is important not to encourage unrealistic expectations. This explains why such companies announce these as special dividends and usually pay them at different times from the regular dividends. For example, Porsche, enjoying booming car sales and profits, paid a special dividend in 2002.

Cash-rich US companies have used the technique of share buy-back as a way of returning value to shareholders – repurchasing shares off the stock market. This is not totally tax-efficient in some countries, and illegal in others. It has been practised in the UK since 1983 (following the 1981 Companies Act) when GEC became the first British company to repurchase its own shares. At first glance, this seems an odd tactic as it appears to deliver important negative information – that the firm has no worthwhile investment opportunities.

There are several reasons why firms engage in buy-backs:

- They may be a convenient way of returning surplus cash to shareholders, especially when the interest rate available on short-term deposits is low. Why invest in liquid assets returning, say, 5 per cent when shareholders seek a return of 15 per cent?

- The increased demand for the shares should drive up their price. This might be useful at times of temporary weakness in share price, for example when the company has just reported disappointing results.

- The reduced number of shares will have higher EPS (notwithstanding lost interest income). Higher EPS generally results in higher share price.

- It may be a way of adjusting the capital structure. If it is financed by borrowing, the gearing ratio increases. If cash is used to implement the buy-back, assets fall, but the book value of equity also falls, thus raising the gearing ratio.

- It is a way in which managers can signal to the market that the current share price is cheap. This is why share buy-backs often have the effect of raising the share price It may also be a way of deterring an unwelcome takeover bid by making it more expensive. Also, with fewer shares in issue, it might make the task of the acquiring firm more difficult.

Using cash balances to mount a share buy-back

The following example shows how the increase in EPS (and thus share price) works when a company uses excess cash balances to launch a buy-back.

Market price per share	= £10
Number of shares	= 200m
Trading profit	= £150m
Cash balances	= £260m
Interest income @ 5%	= £13.0m
Taxable profit	= £163.0m
Tax @ 30%	= £48.9m
Profit after tax	= £114.1m
EPS = (£114.1m/200m)	= 57p

The company now repurchases 20 million shares at the market price for an outlay of £200 million, leaving 180 million in issue. The effects are:

- interest earnings fall by (5% × £200m) = £10m, to just £3m

- taxable profit is £153m (£163.0m − £10m)

- tax @ 30% = £45.9m

- profit after tax = £107.1m, and EPS becomes (£107.1m/180m) = 59.5p.

The hope is that the higher EPS should now result in higher share price.

Self-assessment activity 11.8

Buy-backs generally are made at a level above the market price. Rework the above answer assuming a buy-back price at a 20 per cent premium to the market price.
(answer at end of chapter)

Methods of share repurchase

UK companies can repurchase shares in three ways:

- First, a company can purchase shares through the Stock Exchange with the aid of its broker.

- Second, in a tender offer, shareholders are invited to sell their shares back to the company at a price fixed by the company. This allows all shareholders to participate. This is a much more formal and protracted procedure which requires extensive documentation.

- Third, via negotiation with individual shareholders. The capital proceeds (based on current market price) are liable to capital gains tax in the normal way. Receipts above the par value may be treated as a net dividend payment and thus taxable as income.

The following cameo reports a novel way of circumventing adverse tax consequences of a buy-back.

Financial innovation in operation

In June 1999, the nuclear power group British Energy (BE), then the UK's largest power producer, announced an ingenious package for returning £420 million to its owners, in order to reduce its equity base by 10 per cent.

Shareholders were offered the choice, depending on their tax positions.

All would receive 43 new ordinary shares and 48 'A' shares with a nominal value of 60p each for every 48 ordinary shares held. They could then sell the A shares for 60p to BE in August 1999, should they wish to be treated for capital gains tax – the conversion to A shares created a new base for CGT. Alternatively, they could receive a special dividend for the same amount in October 1999 if they wanted to be treated for income tax. The third option was to keep the A shares and receive regular dividends at a rate just below London inter-bank rates.

11.9   Summary

For many people, the ground covered in this chapter represents one of the most fascinating aspects of financial management: having created wealth, how should a company deliver that wealth to its owners?

We focused on the factors which determine whether a company should pay a 'high' or a 'low' or even a reduced dividend. In principle, dividend decisions are linked to the investment decision as too high a dividend may preclude worthwhile investment. However, this link is broken if the company has ready access to external capital markets. In theory, dividends are irrelevant, but in practice there are several important influences on the dividend policy of a company. The safest policy is to develop a clear dividend policy, thus attracting a clientele of investors for whom that policy is suitable, and then adhere to that policy over time.

References and further reading

Textbooks

Arnold – ch 19.
Brealey & Myers – ch 16.
Pike & Neale – ch 19.
Samuels, Wilkes & Brayshaw – ch 17.
Watson & Head – ch 7.

Others

Gordon, M H (1959) 'Dividends, earnings and stock prices', *Review of Economics and Statistics*, Vol. 41, May, pp. 99–105.
Miller, M H and Modigliani, F (1961) 'Dividend policy and the valuation of shares', *Journal of Business*, Vol. 34, October, pp. 411–33.

Questions and mini-case studies

1   Gustaffson plc manufactures compact disc players. Its most popular model is the Gustaffson Supreme. Indeed, the advertising jingle for this model, 'For music that's as clear as a mountain stream, get out and buy the Gustaffson Supreme', had been on everybody's lips a few years ago. However, growth in this market, once very rapid, has begun to slow down significantly. The possible introduction of new music formats, such as enhanced laser discs, digital

cassettes coupled with the ability to download directly from the internet, has also increased the uncertainty of future sales forecasts.

As a result, the directors have decided to reconsider Gustaffson's traditional dividend policy of low payments and have asked the financial director to prepare a paper for discussion. The financial director has identified various options for the directors to consider and has asked you to detail the advantages and disadvantages of each one:

- increase the dividend per share
- repurchase shares
- continue the existing policy.

Required

(a) Prepare a report for the financial director as requested. Make sure that you make the director aware of the possible market implications of each option.

(b) What courses of action may Gustaffson follow to stimulate growth for its products?

2 Carsley plc is an old-established engineering company whose main business for many years has been to produce car bodies for a major car manufacturer. This contract accounts for the majority of Carsley's business, and growth in recent years has been steady rather than spectacular. The management and the production processes within this company are very much focused on this car contract.

However, the company has recently been contacted by another car-maker and has now won a contract to supply custom-built car bodies made from newly developed, lighter materials. As a result, Carsley has invested a considerable amount of money in building a new advanced-technology and computerised production facility. In addition, the company is committed to spending large sums on staff training over the next couple of years.

As a result of these recent changes to the company's activities, the board has decided to review the company's dividend policy. In particular, some members of the board are concerned about whether the company's traditional high-dividend payment policy is still appropriate and that dividends in the future should be set at a lower level.

Required

(a) Discuss some of the possible reasons why companies such as Carsley pay high dividends including the type of shareholder that such a policy might attract.

(b) Discuss reasons why companies (including Carsley) might prefer to reduce dividends in the future.

(c) Discuss the possible risks to a company if it decides to change its policy and become a low-dividend-paying company rather than a high-dividend payer, and suggest strategies that such a company could follow to address these risks.

3 Breene Holdings plc operates a collection of retail outlets for wine and other alcoholic beverages. The latest summarised accounts are as follows (all £000):

	£	£
Net fixed assets		31,500
Current assets:		
Stock	5,250	
Debtors	2,250	
Cash	1,275	
	8,775	
Current liabilities:		
Trade creditors	(2,700)	
Taxation	(675)	
	(3,375)	
Net current assets		5,400
Net assets		36,900
Share capital and reserves:		
Share capital (25p par)		25,000
Profit and loss account		11,900
Shareholders' funds		36,900

At a recent meeting with journalists and investors, there was considerable discussion about dividends. The company announced that it was considering reducing the level of dividend in view of the substantial capital investment required to meet the company's strategic growth targets. Until now, growth has been financed from internal sources, but this investment in growth to meet perceived market opportunities is expected to be the main plank of the company's strategy for the next two or three years. Ultimately, these investments are expected to yield a return significantly above the existing cost of equity capital.

Some of the institutional investors expressed concern at a possible reduction in the level of dividend since, until now, there had been no hint that this year's dividend would not be an increase on last year's total pay-out of £3 million. The directors of Breene were a little concerned at these comments as approximately 37 per cent of shares were in the hands of the institutional investors, so they emphasised that no final decision had yet been made with respect to dividends.

Required

As Breene's financial adviser, prepare a brief report for the directors in which you identify the factors that should be taken into account when trying to determine the company's dividend in any year. As well as recommending a level for this year's dividend, you are required to recommend a dividend strategy for the medium term. Outline and assess the options for future dividend policy available to the company. Refer to the accounts and notes as appropriate in your answer.

4   Discuss the following possible company dividend policies, including their likely effect on shareholders.

  (i)   Company A always pays a dividend equal to 10 per cent of the previous year's profit.
  (ii) Company B pays no dividend, and invests all retained funds in projects.
  (iii) Company C pays no dividend, but has no profitable use for the funds retained.
  (iv) Company D pays out all profits as dividends even if it means forgoing investment opportunities in order to do so.

Mini-case study - Campbell soups

In July 2001, Campbell, the US soup-maker, announced that it would cut its dividend by 30 per cent from 90 cents per share to 63 cents, and that EPS would fall from $1.65 to around $1.60 for the current fiscal year, but forecast a further fall to around $1.30 for 2002.

The reduction in dividend was designed to enable Campbell to increase investment by 50 per cent in 2001-2 to $200 million. The funds released were to be spent on equipment upgrades, R&D, new product development, and increased advertising as well as installation of new technology to improve the quality of the company's soup and snack businesses.

New investments in the soup business would include quality improvements such as better ingredients, the roll-out of easy-open lids for its condensed soup cans, and testing of a new range of 'sipping soups' for the 'away-from-home' market. Doug Conant, Campbell's CEO, said that Campbell urgently needed to rejuvenate its soup business and increase investment in other brands:

'We have stumbled in the marketplace, weakened our connection with consumers and disappointed investors.'

Shares fell 3 per cent on the announcement.

Required

(a) News of higher levels of strategic investment usually leads to an increase in share price. Why did Campbell's share price fall in this case?

(b) Do you think a dividend cut is a good way of financing new investment?

(c) What other alternative methods of finance might Campbell have considered?

Read the following two mini-cases and answer these questions:

(a) Compare and contrast the policies of these two companies regarding dividend declarations in uncertain business environments.

(b) Identify the particular reasons why the share price reaction to both of these dividend announcements was so severe.

(c) What advice would you have offered to each company prior to these announcements in order to 'head off' negative share price reaction?

Mini-case study – Prudential plc

In early 2003, several insurance and other financial companies announced dividend cuts in order to preserve liquidity and help maintain capital ratios at a time of falling share prices. One of the biggest, Prudential plc, gave several assurances that its own twice-yearly dividend was not under threat.

However, in February, the firm lost a fifth of its value when, despite reporting a 2 per cent rise in operating profit, it apparently changed its corporate mind. The CEO, Jonathan Bloomer, said Prudential could not be specific about dividend payment plans until July when the interim results were due. The *Guardian* reported him as saying:

'It is about uncertainty. It is just not prudent to commit to a dividend for the year ahead at this point with the market as it is. We have not said that we will cut the dividend, we have just said that we will not make that decision until we have to in July.'

One institutional shareholder said: 'The manner in which this is being done lacks clarity.' Several others recommended clients to sell. However, other analysts pointed out that Prudential was making 70 per cent of its profits from new business outside the UK, especially in Asia and the USA, so that a dividend cut if it came could be portrayed as a way of injecting more capital into rapidly growing businesses.

Nevertheless, the episode was widely interpreted as signalling a forth-coming dividend cut and the shares were marked down 69p to 324p.

Required

(a) Can you identify the ambiguity in Mr Bloomer's reported statement?

(b) Can you suggest an alternative form of words?

(c) Might there have been a case for a dividend increase?

Mini-case study – Lloyds TSB plc

2002 was not a good year for shares in the financial sector – insurance companies were savaged and banking profits declined as firms made more provisions against bad debts.

In February 2003, with hostilities in the Arabian Gulf looming ever larger, Lloyds was widely expected to report lower profits and to cut its dividend. However, although pre-tax profit fell from £3.16 billion to £2.66 billion (damaged by a 38 per cent increase in provisions against bad debts), and EPS dropped from 34.2p to 33.7p, Lloyds surprised the market by announcing a 'flat' dividend payout. The dividend per share was increased from 33.7 p to 34.2p, a little less than the rate of inflation, yet nevertheless an increase, but to a level uncovered by earnings.

Lloyds chairman Martin van den Bergh, said: 'We have signalled a degree of caution about future growth.' He added that the board had not considered a dividend cut, but that when profits began to recover, shareholders should not expect this to automatically feed through into a higher dividend.

This confusing declaration was met by universal derision, reflected in a fall in the share price by 31p, wiping around £1.7 billion off the bank's capitalisation. Few people could understand why a dividend increase, involving a total cash payout of £1.5 billion, could be construed as 'cautious' in the context of a hostile market and political environment.

Mini-case study - Harvey's Furnishings plc

In October 1998, Harvey's Furnishings, seller of bedding and curtains, bought back £2 million (10 per cent) of its shares, paying between 122p and 127p, after its chairman (whom we shall not name) had warned, in July, of a slow-down in sales. A month or so after the buy-back, the directors issued a profits warning, prompting a 40 per cent slump in the share price to 63p, at which price the shares previously bought back would have cost less than £1 million. Clearly, share buy-backs, if ill-judged, like many other financial innovations, have the capacity to embarrass managers.

Required
Why do you think the company bought back the shares when it did?

Self-assessment answers

11.1
Over to you.

11.2
With a 15 per cent cut-off rate, the acceptable projects are A, C and E (just). To accept all three requires a total outlay of £35 million.

- With earnings of £35 million, accept A + C + E, pay no dividend.
- With earnings of £30 million, accept A + C, pay a dividend of £5 million.
- With earnings of £10 million, accept A, pay no dividend.

11.3
Without the project, the value of the company is £248. After accepting the project, the company value becomes:

$$V_1 = \frac{0}{1.1} + \frac{[£100 + £107]}{(1.1)^2} + \frac{£100}{(1.1)^3} = £246$$

The fall in value occurs because the project's IRR is only 7 per cent.

11.4

Only 95 per cent of the funds raised can be used to finance new investment, although a return must be offered on *all* of the shares issues, including the 'dead money'. Hence, the required return on investment increases to: (20%/95%) = 21.05%.

11.5

Over to you.

11.6

Target share price = £8, i.e. £8/£10 = 80% of existing price.

Number of shares at present = £100m/50p = 200 million, capitalisation = 200m × £10 = £2bn.

It should raise the number of shares to £2bn/£8 = 250 million (i.e., by 50 million). 50 million, par value of (50m × 50p) = £25 million, in a 1-for-4 issue. This will involve writing down reserves by £25 million, probably the share premium account (shares are offered at a negative premium).

11.7

Total dividend paid = (12p × 1,800) = £216.

Tax credit = (£216 × 1/11) = £19.64.

11.8

The outlay is now (£200m × 1.2) = £240 million. The effects are:

- interest earnings fall by (5% × £240m) = £12m, to just £1m

- taxable profit is £151m

- tax @ 30% = £45.3m

- profit after tax = £105.7m and EPS becomes £105.7m/180m = 58.7p.

The effects are thus slightly less advantageous for remaining shareholders.

MANAGING RISK

Managing risk at Microsoft

Many companies formulate comprehensive policies to cope with risk. For example, Microsoft pursues risk strategies for both operational and financial risks it faces.

At the operational level, the company employs legions of temporary staff rather than permanent staff. This gives it a flexible workforce that can quickly be adapted to changing needs, e.g. by employing more temporary staff in shortage areas and releasing those no longer meeting require-ments. Microsoft values flexibility rather than stability in the volatile markets that it inhabits. Volatility can be caused by shifts in demand, changes in technology, increases in competition and changes in regulation. This arrangement can also suit many employees. Although temporary staff find it difficult to integrate into the organisational culture, and may receive fewer rights and benefits, they are often paid premium rates reflecting their temporary positions and the firm's need for them.

At the financial level, rather surprisingly for a company valued in excess of $200 billion, Microsoft uses virtually no debt finance. In addition, it usually carries over $40 billion of cash on the balance sheet. Both of these financial policies have a cost.

Objectives:
The objectives of this chapter are to:

- outline the major sources of risk impacting on business success and shareholder value

- explain how effective risk management can enhance value

- examine some commonly used hedging techniques for managing risk.

12.1 Introduction

In most areas of financial decision making, the main yard-stick of success is value creation. Value creation usually involves balancing risk and returns. As you have seen, value is the sum of all future discounted returns, where the discount rate reflects the riskiness of the activity, and in geared firms, includes an element of financial risk.

The higher the risk, the more heavily discounted the future returns, thus dampening value. Imagine two firms with the same stream of future expected returns – the one whose income stream is less exposed to risk will command a higher value. Which of these options would you prefer: option one, which offers a 10 per cent return every year, or option two, which yields an average 10 per cent over time, but 5 per cent in some years and 15 per cent in other years? Most people would go for option one as the return is more stable and thus is more valuable. If a firm can eliminate sources of risk, or at least manage their potential impact, investors may settle for a lower return and thus value it more highly.

Many firms see effective risk management as an activity capable of adding value by reducing risk, or at least reducing people's perceptions of risk. At the least, it can preserve value by protecting sources of value creation from untoward events. Risk management thus has a dual role: value creation and value protection.

However, it is important to recognise that risk management is not about *minimising* risk; after all, profits stem mainly from taking risks. Instead, risk management is concerned with the management of different risks to maximise the prospects of future profits while minimising the potential for financial distress. It is thus an activity that requires identification of risk areas, and then balancing the potentially higher benefits of risky strategies against their potential to inflict damage.

As a result, risk management may lead to firms shouldering a large proportion of these risks because of the potential for future returns. The cameo gives an example of the operational and financial risks facing Microsoft, and the strategies that the company has adopted to manage them. It suggests it is more aggressive in dealing with operational risk than with financial risk.

12.2 Effective risk management

Many companies emphasise the role of risk management in minimising the damage that adverse contingencies may wreak. All firms suffer setbacks, but to a firm that manages risks carefully, no imaginable setback should be catastrophic.

Effective risk management thus requires:

- identification of areas and activities that are exposed to risk

- appraisal of the likelihood that these exposures will crystallise and cause financial damage in relation to the extra returns that taking the risk may produce

- implementation of policies and procedures designed to maximise expected returns and to minimise the adverse consequences.

In the late 1990s, the Turnbull Committee on Corporate Governance was appointed to lay down best practice of risk management, reflecting the increasing importance of risk management for all businesses. Its report in 1999 placed the responsibility for this firmly onto the board of directors and requires a greater communication to investors and other interested groups of the risk management strategies employed.

Self-assessment activity 12.1

Look at the annual report of 'your' company. What does it have to say about risk management?

A survey by the Economist Intelligence Unit on enterprise risk management (2001) identified the following reasons why companies may follow a risk management strategy:

1 To achieve an understanding of risk in the firm across business functions and units.

2 To provide a competitive advantage via a deeper, better understanding of risk.

3 To safeguard against earnings-related surprises within a framework of managing for shareholder value.

4 To improve the ability to respond effectively to risks.

5 To avoid low-probability risks.

6 To achieve cost savings through better management of internal resources.

12.3 What risk is, and how it can be managed

Firms face a wide variety of risks, and to varying degrees. Risks have a financial dimension if they threaten future cash flows or asset values. In some headline cases, like Nick Leeson's 'rogue trading' at Barings, which was sold for £1, and the spectacular loss in value due to poor investment decisions at Marconi, where shareholders lost all but 1 per cent of their holdings in a firm worth £35 billion at one time, the damage can be well-nigh total. Yet it is easy to be wise after the event and ask why these situations were not foreseen. In reality, a determined miscreant can cover his tracks for years, and a powerful CEO, as at Marconi, can dragoon others to follow reckless policies.

However, more openness and transparency, encouraged by corporate governance initiatives such as the Turnbull Report, is shedding more light on how companies identify and manage the risks they face. Companies are increasingly aware that their ability to manage risk is an important influence on the share price.

There are two main types of risk which businesses can be exposed to:

1 *Exposure to business or operational risk* – 'the risk of loss resulting from inadequate or failed internal processes, people and systems, or external events' (Basel Capital Accord 1999).

   Business risk encompasses many elements that render future operational cash flows uncertain. These include:

   (a) Production risk – such as machine failure or production defects, the risk of inefficiency and poor operations management.

   (b) Input risk – the risk that stock runs out, or the workforce goes on strike; the loss of key staff; the risk of increases in costs.

   (c) Market risk – the risk that demand will change, or that competition will increase, e.g. by the entry of new competitors.

   (d) Regulatory risk – extra regulation usually incurs extra costs to businesses, e.g. changes in legislation affecting health and safety, workers' rights, monopolies, trade agreements, the environment.

   (e) Strategic risk – the risk of poor decision making; the risks involved in expanding into new areas of business, including takeovers – 'synergy risk' is the risk of not being able to deliver the **synergies** promised at the time of acquisition.

   (f) Business interruption risk – risk of IT systems collapsing, such as the 'Millennium Bug'; catastrophic events such as 9/11.

   (g) Reputation risk – the risk of product failure, such as the dispute between Ford and Firestone from August 2000 over the prime responsibility for the overtuning of Ford's sports utility vehicles (SUVs); or of staff being involved in nefarious activities. The reputation of many Wall Street investment banks has been severely damaged by the overpromotion of internet start-ups, many of which were 'rubbished' in private by the promoters.

(h) Political risk – restrictions placed on overseas operations by foreign governments, such as barriers to repatriation of profits and the expropriation of assets.

2 *Exposure to financial risk* – the threat to the cost of finance and even to the viable operation of a company stemming from the way it is financed. Financial risk includes the following:

(a) The risk of insolvency due to the method of financing. Debt is relatively cheap (it is relatively low-risk, and interest is allowable against tax) and is therefore likely to lower the cost of capital. However, debt imposes financial risk on shareholders because of the commitment to pay interest. High gearing adds to the systematic risk of a company's shares as measured by its Beta. The more highly geared the firm, the greater its exposure to insolvency.

(b) It has been argued that geared companies are likely to suffer from higher agency costs as investors monitor the actions (including the risk management strategies) of the managers.

(c) An increase in the cost of finance resulting from a general increase in interest rates, or an increase in the risk of the company which will cause both lenders and shareholders to demand higher returns.

(d) A change in the tax regime, including the rate of corporation tax, the system of capital allowances and the existence of double-taxation agreements for those companies that operate overseas.

(e) A change in macro-economic variables, such as interest rates or exchange rates.

All these factors make the prediction of future cash flows difficult, and often the problem is compounded by the interaction of business and financial risk. For example, a problem facing airlines is their exposure to the risk of increases in the world price of fuel. In fact, for non-US airlines it is not only the price of fuel that is the problem but also the fact that aviation fuel, like most other oil-based fuels, is priced in US dollars. Because of this double-edged risk, British Airways hedges the bulk of its fuel needs, leaving only around 10 per cent exposed to spot fuel prices.

12.4 Integrated risk management (IRM)

So what should firms do about these risks? Should they adopt a 'laid-back' policy and do nothing on the principle that downside risks tend to offset upside risks over time, or actively manage or 'hedge' the identified risks? To assist in the latter option, a variety of techniques for managing risk is available, ranging from internal devices to using external facilities such as insurance and hedging techniques, including the use of sophisticated financial instruments like derivatives. These are designed to neutralise the impact of the adverse contingency on the firm rather than to avoid it.

Many large organisations now operate 'integrated risk management' systems. IRMs involve appraising the risk profile of the whole organisation rather than focusing on individual risks. An overall view facilitates the decision as to which risks to hedge (or insure against) and which will be carried by the firm itself (even though they could be hedged if required). This decision will require analysis of how each risk can affect value, and the effect on future cash flows if the worst happens. The probability and the scale of the impact of the risk factor under alternative scenarios will be carefully modelled.

An integrated approach also allows firms to identify offsetting risk factors. For example, imagine the sales department of a UK company that sells goods denominated in euros fearing a potential strengthening of sterling against the euro. It would make little sense to manage this risk by, say, increasing selling prices (and consequently losing orders) if, simultaneously, the purchasing department was buying materials from the Eurozone. For this department, a stronger pound will reduce the cost of the imports. The risks here are largely 'matched', or self-hedged. However, firms that have a 'lop-sided' selling or buying involvement with Eurozone firms may choose to hedge against changes in the sterling/euro exchange rate.

This integrated approach to risk management often reveals a portfolio of risks that can be lowered in the same way as investment risks are lowered by diversification, e.g. an exporter may diversify its foreign markets and hence the currency of denomination of its income flows. Companies that follow this approach are likely to use financial measurements such as value at risk and economic value added (see Chapter 13) as well as industry benchmarks as comparators.

Because of the fixed costs involved, e.g. in training and setting up specialist departments, integrated risk management systems are found mainly in larger companies. Yet for all firms, risk management has become a higher priority due to a combination of factors. The events of 9/11, and the pervasive threat of world terrorism, the business scandals and collapses such as Enron and WorldCom, and accounting debacles at firms like Ahold, Xerox and MyTravel have led to a greater awareness of risk factors and the need to have contingent arrangements. A joint survey in 2002 by the Institute of Chartered Accountants in England and Wales (ICAEW) and The Risk Advisory Group (TRAG) found that in every risk category identified, companies perceived a higher level of risk than a year previously.

The profile of risk management has also been raised due to its an importance as an element in the corporate governance debate. The Turnbull Report (1999) stated:

'Identifying, evaluating and managing the risks to the achievement of a company's objectives are issues that are now on the agenda of every company that is listed on the London Stock Exchange.'

The guidelines issued by Turnbull require companies to manage their key risks, remedy weaknesses and review all aspects of internal control on a regular basis. To encourage this, the report recommended that the board of all listed companies be responsible for ensuring that measures are in place to manage not only financial but all of the company's principal risks, and that the board should make an annual report to shareholders on such issues.

Two examples of how very different companies have introduced integrated risk management systems are provided by Lloyds TSB plc and BOC plc.

Lloyds TSB Group's Enterprise-Wide Risk Management Programme (EWRMP)

During 2000-1, Lloyds TSB developed the EWRMP which aims to produce a transparent and comprehensive review of risk involving all staff throughout the company. From this will flow appropriate strategies to manage the risks identified. The process consisted of the following key aspects:

- Staff were asked to identify what they saw as the key risks facing their business unit within the organisation.

- All of the risks identified were reported to the appropriate managing director responsible for each unit.

- The company organised a structure to manage risk, consisting of a group risk committee and the creation of risk relationship directors.

- The risk in each business area is assessed against generic risk areas, such as market risk and operational risk. A traffic light system of red-amber-green is used to measure the degree of perceived risk.

Source: Alistair Smith 'Enterprise-wide risk management at Lloyds', *Risk Transfer Magazine*, 25 November 2002.

BOC's risk management strategy

BOC is one of the world's largest industrial gases companies, operating in over 50 countries, generating annual turnover of £5.6 billion and employing 40,000 staff. In an overhaul of its approach to risk management in 2002, it based the reappraisal on shareholder value as the main driver. The process identified key risk factors, aiming to change the culture of risk-taking in the organisation.

The six major risks identified were:

1 possible behaviour of the company's competitors, i.e. strategy changes

2 the political and economic climate in Asia, where much of the company's growth is planned

3 issues in the group's semi-conductor business

4 financial strategy – pricing and profits

5 the impact of macro-economic variables on the company, e.g. assumptions about global growth

6 issues surrounding organisational change within the company.

All these aspects are now routinely monitored.

By involving staff via workshops and meetings, the culture is already changing. Bill Connell, the company's director of risk management, is reported as saying:

'People have become much more comfortable with the risk. They can then take more risks because they understand them and can manage them through.'

Source: Isaac and Connel (2002)

⌀ 12.5 How risk management can add value

It is sometimes argued that much risk management is just guessing the future, and that companies may just as well not bother on the principle that 'some you win, some you lose'. A more sophisticated argument is that there is no point trying to predict future share prices, market levels, oil prices and currency exchange rates because the markets are efficient. The riposte to both of these positions can easily be stated. A systematic analysis of the firm's operations, its risk factors and the likely effects of risky events on future cash flows can provide an informed strategy that, although perhaps not covering every eventuality, does reveal the 'flashpoints' where significant losses may occur.

In a perfect world, hedging would be left to investors who would adjust the level of their risk. Managers could not 'beat the market', so corporate hedging would be pointless. However, there are market imperfections which make risk management a value-adding activity when carried out by managers rather than investors themselves, i.e. managers have a comparative advantage over investors in hedging.

(i) *Effective risk management can reduce the probability of financial distress and failure.* Failure inevitably incurs substantial costs, such as the legal and financial costs of bringing in administrators to find a way out of the financial mire. But even before that stage is reached, signs of financial distress can bring their own costs to an organisation. Customers will be reluctant to buy products from companies that may not be around much longer; neither will suppliers supply, nor will banks lend, to such companies. Management time becomes focused on survival rather than on making strategic decisions to secure the future of the business. Companies must be careful not to enter this vicious circle of distress. All too quickly, distress can descend into outright failure.

Managers are best placed to assess the risk of bankruptcy and other financial distress, and adopt strategies to avert such a dire outcome. There is some evidence that those companies with a higher probability of financial distress, e.g. high gearing, tend to hedge more.

(ii) *Effective risk management can reduce the cost of obtaining finance.* External sources of finance are more costly than internal (e.g. high issuing costs of equity) and may be more difficult to obtain. Hence, managing cash flows through various risk strategies may reduce the volatility of cash flows and ensure there is sufficient internal finance for the business. Fast-growing businesses would benefit from hedging for this reason. In addition, managing the cash flow so that liquidity does not fall below a certain perceived minimum acceptable level will prevent financially attractive investments being rejected because of lack of cash.

In addition, reducing the risk of default via effective risk management can increase a firm's debt capacity and lower the cost of capital.

(iii) *Risk management can mitigate agency problems.* Managers have more to lose than most shareholders if a company fails. Whereas the majority of shareholders hold a portfolio of shares, managers have virtually all their career investment and remuneration tied up in their present position – managers have a lot of undiversified unsystematic risk.

Indeed, companies may reinforce stakeholders' dependence by remunerating managers with share options or investing employee pension funds in their own company. Procter and Gamble had 90 per cent of its employee pension fund invested in the shares of the company – the share price fell 50 per cent in the first six months of 2000. Many Enron shareholders had all of their pension money invested in Enron shares.

The theory is that dependent employees will be reluctant to jeopardise their futures by putting the firm they manage at risk. Shareholders, on the other hand, see their investment in each firm as just one among others in a portfolio. They are likely to find investments in risky projects more acceptable because this is how their investments will produce future returns. The failure of one firm will be balanced by successes elsewhere in their portfolio. For any individual organisation, therefore, risk management must address the tendency towards conservative decision making by managers in order to protect their incomes and job security.

(iv) *Risk management can reduce future tax payments*. This may happen in two ways:

- through income smoothing which reduces taxes in a progressive tax structure
- through increasing the company's ability to borrow (since paying interest reduces the tax liability).

(v) *Informed decision making can add value*. Once risk areas have been identified, assessments can be made of the potential for future rewards relative to the cost of insuring against the risk. In the first instance, areas where risk is high relative to the reward offered should be avoided. But whether those areas that do offer a reward should be insured against depends upon the cost of hedging and the risk attaching to the rewards.

12.6   The importance of communication

By having a well-articulated risk management strategy which is transparent and communicated clearly to the market, a company reduces the costs that the market and investors would otherwise incur in evaluating the company's performance. In many countries, banks and insurance companies have to meet stringent financial benchmarks set by regulatory authorities. This gives the major stakeholders confidence that these companies are safe to do business with. This will add value also by reducing an area of uncertainty.

In particular, companies can use their institutional investors to gauge what they see as the key value drivers that need to be protected. This will give greater insight into how the market is valuing the business, and where to focus risk management. Openness and willingness to communicate with the market will reassure investors that the company is aware of their concerns and has strategies in place to meet them.

This is particularly necessary if the business is affected by a negative event, such as increased regulation. The market will be much more reassured by a company that declares how it will be affected by the new situation along with a strategy to alleviate the negative impacts. The company that says nothing is likely to see its share price fall as a result of market uncertainty, and hence suspicion, as to the likely impact and the firm's strategic response. It is usually best to make a clean breast of bad news.

Sometimes, a company can communicate a higher-risk acceptance to the market by the actions and decisions that it takes. In the late 1980s, the US investment bank Salomon Bros led a consortium to buy the food manufacturer RJR Nabisco, using a leveraged (high borrowing) buy-out. Although the bid failed, the bid signalled to the market that Salomon Bros was now prepared to adopt a much riskier investment strategy than it had done previously. This impacted on the rest of its business. The market reaction to the higher risk was clearly demonstrated when the value of its derivative contracts fell.

Astute managers have always understood the importance of informing the market – it is necessary whenever they require more finance. In these instances companies must justify their investments, including the risk profiles, when appealing for funds (in the same way that elections require politicians to ask the electorate to support their policies). The extra requirement of official protocol such as Turnbull is that companies should report on their risk management in a systematic and structured way, and at regular intervals, to replace the rather ad hoc situation that has prevailed historically.

12.7 Exchange rate risk and interest rate risk

Any risk has financial implications if it is likely to affect future cash flows. There are two specific sources of risk which warrant more discussion, particularly because the market provides sophisticated mechanisms for hedging the future uncertainties in cash flows that each produces.

Exchange rate risk

Exchange rate risk is the risk of loss through adverse movements in exchange rates.

Self-assessment activity 12.2

Use the internet to find a time profile of exchange rate movements – try www.bankofengland.co.uk.

No business expecting to make a payment or receive a receipt in a foreign currency in the future can be sure of the exact amount in its own currency that will be involved. In sterling terms, US$100,000 receivable in three months' time will be worth £66,666 at an exchange rate of £1 = $1.50, but £71,429 at £1 = $1.40. Exchange rates change over time for two main reasons.

(i) Differences in expected inflation between countries

This effect is described by the Purchasing Power Parity (PPP) theorem which incorporates the Law of One Price. In effect, PPP states that a freely traded item (such as a can of Coca-Cola) should cost the same anywhere in the world, after adjusting for exchange rates. Look at the following example assuming a current exchange rate of £1 = $1.45:

	UK	US
Price of traded goods now	£100	$145
Expected inflation rate p.a.	3%	1%
Predicted price in one year	£103.0	$146.45

If the original exchange rate of £1 = $1.45 still held in a year's time despite the differences in inflation, the following would happen:

(a) UK exporters would find it more difficult to sell goods in the USA because at the £1 = $1.45 exchange rate, they would now cost (£103 × $1.45) = $149.35; more expensive than the equivalent American-produced goods.

(b) At the same time, UK consumers would buy US imports because they would be cheaper than UK goods: ($146.45 ÷ 1.45) = £101.

This situation is unsustainable for an open, trading economy. Adjustment of the exchange rate restores the balance. The PPP theorem shows that just as the opening exchange rate ensures that the goods in each country have the same value, this will be true at any time. Thus, at the end of the year, £103 must equal $146.45. This implies an end-year exchange rate of (146.45 ÷ 103) = $1.42 *vs.* £1.

This rate should be reflected in the forward market. This quotes a fixed rate for transactions that are to be settled at specific times in the future. Looking ahead one year, the forward rate =

$$\frac{1 + \text{US inflation}}{1 + \text{UK inflation}} \times \text{current spot rate} = (1.01/1.03 \times 1.45) = 1.42$$

Note how the higher inflation in the UK reduces the value of sterling relative to the US$ – higher relative inflation erodes the value of the currency. More pounds have to be offered to buy each dollar (or each dollar buys more pounds).

Although PPP is not as precise as the above calculation implies, over the long term, the importance of relative rates of inflation as a determinant of exchange rates has been shown to be significant.

(ii) Differences in interest rates between countries

The relationship between interest rates and exchange rates is shown in the Interest Rate Parity theorem (IRP) – equal return for equal risk. Again, an example will demonstrate the main principle involved (again the initial exchange rate is £1 = $1.45).

UK government bond	US government bond	
£100,000	$145,000	1 = $1.45
@ 4% interest	@ 2% interest	
£104,000	$147,900	one-year future value

As before, if the exchange rate does not change, an unsustainable situation arises. In this case, any US investor will buy UK bonds in preference to their own government's because of the higher return they will get, i.e. nobody will buy the

US bonds. In reality, because both bonds are of the same risk (assumed to be zero), they must offer the same return. Thus, the benefit of the higher UK rate of interest must be eliminated by a weaker exchange rate.

Using this information, the markets will set a forward rate as follows:

$$\frac{1 + \text{US interest rate}}{1 + \text{UK interest rate}} \times \text{spot rate} = \$1.45 = (1.04/1.04 \times \$1.45) = \$1.42$$

IRP generally does hold in practice, and underpins the setting of forward rates of exchange.

Self-assessment activity 12.3

Check out the forward rates of exchange in the *Financial Times*. Focus on the US$ *vs.* sterling. Different rates are given for different points in time. What is the trend in the rates quoted? How do you explain this trend? (answer at end of chapter)

Interest rate risk

Interest rates are volatile both in the short term (interest rates on short-term money markets vary by the minute) and in the long term (base rates in the UK have fallen from 15 per cent in 1989 to 3.5 per cent at the time of writing). Of course, any changes in interest rates will affect both savers and borrowers. Most businesses are net borrowers, particularly the highly geared companies. The risk to these companies is even greater if most of the borrowing is in the form of variable interest borrowing rather than fixed interest borrowing.

In his 2003 Budget speech, the Chancellor of the Exchequer, Gordon Brown, identified the predominance of variable interest mortgages as being a significant risk factor in trying to predict total consumer spending in the UK economy. His point was that this made interest rates a particularly sensitive variable in the UK because of its impact on business and consumers.

Interest rate risk is of particular importance to borrowers because they have a continuing commitment to pay interest. Recent economic history provides many examples of companies that failed due to a rise in interest rates increasing their interest expense while also reducing the demand for their products from consumers cutting back on spending in order to meet higher mortgage payments.

Interest rates for any economy are set centrally; by the Federal Reserve in the USA, by the Bank of England Monetary Committee in the UK and by the European Central Bank in Euroland. Commercial rates are linked to these national rates but will be subject to individual negotiation. The rate decided upon will depend on the circumstances of the loan and the risk assessment of the business wanting it. Many contracts in the UK link the interest rate charged to LIBOR.

12.8 Managing exchange rate risk

Movements in exchange rates make the home currency value of future cash flows uncertain. Of course, this is a double-edged sword since it is possible for businesses to gain from such movements as well as lose. However, most businesses value certainty, and, in particular, will want to remove as much 'downside' risk as possible. (Finance managers prefer to sleep at night!) This is why, even though it is possible that businesses *could* benefit from movements in the exchange rate, many hedge future currency transactions to eliminate the danger that profits earned on overseas deals may be lost because of adverse movements in the exchange rate.

There are two broad types of hedge: internal hedges, devised without using the external financial markets, and external ones, which involve using market facilities. Generally, internal hedges are simpler and cheaper to construct.

Internal hedging

Exchange rate risk affects those companies that have future cash payments or inflows likely to be affected by exchange rate movements. A UK company due to receive $100,000 in three months' time from its US customer cannot be sure how much in sterling this US$ amount will convert into. There are a number of 'internal' ways in which the company could hedge this uncertainty:

(a) Ideally, the UK firm would like to invoice the US company in sterling. However, this may deter overseas customers since this will transfer the exchange rate risk to them. As a result, in order to secure the business, the UK company may take on the risk itself and invoice in the currency of the overseas customer.

(b) The UK company could net the future $100,000 receipt against any US$ payments that the company has to make in the future. In other words, instead of converting this amount into sterling, it could use it towards paying a US supplier who is owed this amount.

(c) The UK company could 'match' the future dollar asset by setting up a future equivalent US$ liability, i.e. the company could borrow dollars today (and convert them into pounds at today's spot exchange rate), and in three months' time pay off the dollar loan with the $100,000 receipt. By converting the original dollars borrowed into pounds now, the company is in effect converting a future dollar receipt into sterling today and is no longer concerned about the future exchange rate movements. This is called a 'money market hedge'.

(d) A business that has to make a future payment in an overseas currency could take a view about how the exchange rate is likely to move between now and the time the payment is due to be made. If the home currency is expected to strengthen, it could buy the foreign currency later when more can be bought (this is called 'lagging'). On the other hand, if the home currency is expected to weaken, the foreign currency could be bought now and put on deposit until required ('leading').

Although internal hedging is cheap, it is likely to be more limited in that it will not cover all of the risk that the business is exposed to from both interest rates and exchange rates.

Exchange rate risk management using external financial instruments

There are various financial instruments which can be used to hedge risk. A number of these will be demonstrated using the following example.

Hudson plc

Hudson plc, a UK company, is due to pay US$20,000 to a US supplier in three months' time. The company could of course 'lag', and buy the $20,000 at the spot rate in three months. The concern would be that the company is wrong in its prediction and the pound would weaken against the dollar during the next three months so that Hudson would have to spend more sterling to meet the liability than it would at the moment. As already indicated, this is likely to be of particular concern since it may mean that any profit earned on the overseas transaction is eroded by adverse movements in the exchange rate. Some of the more common hedges against this exchange rate risk will now be examined.

(a) Forward rates of exchange
As well as current or spot rates of exchange between currencies, the market quotes forward rates for the main traded currencies, e.g. the following exchange rates may apply between sterling and the US dollar:

Spot	£1 = $1.59 – $1.61
Three month forward	£1 = $1.62 – £1.65

This means that £1 will buy $1.59 now but it will take $1.61 to buy £1 now; it is easy to remember which rate applies to which transaction since you always get the worst one! The difference between the two rates is the '**spread**' – the commission taken by the currency trader. The forward rate shown in the example shows that the market expects the pound to strengthen against the dollar, i.e. £1 is expected to buy more dollars in the future than at the moment. This is the same as saying that the forward dollar is at a 'discount' to the spot. If the foreign currency is expected to strengthen against the pound, the forward rate for that currency against the pound, it is said to be at a 'premium' to the pound on the spot market.

The forward rate can be seen as the market's best guess about what the spot rate will be in three months' time (based upon, as we have already seen, future expected inflation rates and interest rates in the UK and the USA). However, there is absolutely no guarantee that the market will be right in its prediction (although research tends to show that forward rates are unbiased estimates of future spot rates, i.e. on average they are more or less right).

The three-month forward rates can be agreed today for a transaction in three months' time. Thus, Hudson could agree the rate now for the transaction to take place in 3 months time; in our example it would be £1 = $1.62. When the debt is due to be paid in three months, the company therefore pays ($20,000 ÷ 1.62) = £12,346. It does not matter what the £ : $ spot rate is at the time as the transaction rate has already been agreed. Forward rates provide certainty in an uncertain situation. It may be possible that the future spot rate is $1.65 and the company could have paid fewer pounds to obtain the required $20,000. However, as already suggested, most companies prefer to hedge to prevent losses even though they know they could benefit if they did not.

Using the forward market is a relatively cheap form of hedging that requires no initial payment. It is also flexible in terms of the amounts that can be hedged, and the variety of currencies that can be traded. However, in only the major currencies does the forward market extend much beyond six months.

Self-assessment activity 12.5

Get that *FT* out again and look at the market's forward quotations. For how many currencies is it possible to obtain forward cover for a year?

(b) Options

As the name implies, options provide a choice, a choice that is not available with the forward hedge, namely that if the rate of exchange at the time of the transaction is better than the rate agreed in the option, the option can be discarded. Unlike forward contracts, there is no commitment to transact. Because it is still possible to benefit if the market moves in your favour when you buy an option by not trading on it, options are more expensive than forward hedges.

Currency options are quoted at the Philadelphia Exchange, although most organisations will negotiate these options 'over the counter' at their banks. The banks will then cover their position by trading on the Philadelphia market. Continuing with our example, assume Hudson wants to buy an option to allow it to buy $20,000 at a particular rate of exchange. Imagine it agrees with its bank an option to buy $20,000 at a rate of exchange of £1 : $1.60 at any time over the next three months. The company will have to pay a premium for this option which will be non-refundable in the same way as insurance premiums. In three months' time, Hudson has a choice.

If the spot rate in three months is £1 : $1.65, the company will buy its $20,000 on the market at this spot rate (costing £12,121) and walk away from the option (which is said to be 'out of the money'). But if the spot rate in three months is £1 : $1.55, the company will buy its dollars under the option contract of £1 : $1.60, costing £12,500 – less than if it had to buy the dollars at the market rate (the option is thus 'in the money').

Self-assessment activity 12.6

What if the future spot rate turns out to be £1 = $1.60?
(answer at end of chapter)

Companies buy options to buy or sell currencies at different rates of exchange (the exercise price) over different time periods. The longer you want the option for, the more expensive it will be. Similarly, in the above example, a '£1 buys $1.60' option will be cheaper than a '£1 buys $1.70' option.

Although expensive, options are attractive in that the purchaser does not 'lock into' an exchange rate in the way that it does when it hedges using the forward rate. They are also often used when companies are not sure whether the future cash flow will occur or not. For example, if a UK company tenders for a project in the USA, it may buy options for the purchase or sale of dollars. If the tender is unsuccessful, the company could sell the options or let them lapse – there is no commitment to transact with an option.

(c) Futures

Futures are another financial method that give companies the ability to hedge future exchange rate risk. A futures contract is a binding contract to buy or sell a defined amount of currency with a defined amount of another currency at some point in the future. They are therefore similar to forward contracts. However, with futures contracts, companies are required to deposit what is known as an 'initial margin' of around 2 per cent of the contract amount. As exchange rates move during the period of the futures contract, additional margins will be required to cover adverse movements in the contract; margins can also be rebated if exchange rates move favourably. These margins are calculated as the contract is 'marked to the market' on a regular basis.

When hedging with futures, companies buy and sell futures contracts to cover the exchange rate risk being carried. This risk occurs because the company will not buy and sell the currency it requires until the time of the transaction, so that it accepts the exchange rate risk between now and the transaction. Any loss on exchange rates between the spot rate now and the rate at the time of the transaction is balanced by profits made by buying and selling futures contracts, and vice versa. The future contract is the other side of the see-saw.

Continuing with the example, at the moment Hudson has a three-month commitment to pay $20,000 and the current spot rate for purchasing dollars is £1 : $1.59. If the money were paid today, it would cost Hudson £12,579. This is called the 'target outcome'. However, with a futures contract, Hudson will not buy dollars until required in three months' time. If, by then, the spot rate has moved to £1 : $1.55 – $1.57, Hudson will pay ($20,000 ÷ $1.55) = £12,903, a loss on target of £324.

This prospective loss can be hedged by trading futures. Futures contracts refer to defined amounts of one currency over a period of time. They are priced at an exchange rate likely to be similar to the spot rate at the time. Assume that, at the moment, the £ : $ futures contracts are quoted at £1 : $1.60. Because, in three months' time, Hudson will sell pounds to buy the $20,000 it will need, it sells a sterling future for the same dollar amount, i.e. Hudson will sell two futures contracts (they are denominated in £6,250 units) thereby agreeing to sell £12,500 for $20,000 for delivery some time in the future.

Assume that the futures exchange rate in three months is £1 : $1.54. The company will now net out its sterling commitment by buying a £12,500 sterling futures contract which commits it to pay $19,250. Hudson can now net the two futures contracts. The sterling amounts cancel out, but the company will receive a net $750 over the two contracts. This will provide an income of ($750/1.57) = £478. The profit on the futures in this example is actually more than the loss on target. Futures will rarely give a perfect hedge because futures rates do not move exactly in line with spot rates.

(d) Swaps

Swaps involve firms swapping future cash flows, particularly relating to future interest payments and loan repayments. Currency swaps occur because businesses can usually borrow more cheaply in their own currency than abroad. Thus, if a UK firm wants euros, one possibility is for it to borrow sterling in the UK and swap the currency with a firm in Euroland that has borrowed in euros. All swaps of principal and interest will occur at agreed rates of exchange. Integral to a modern currency swap is an interest rate swap.

12.9 Managing interest rate risk

As with approaches to hedging foreign exchange risk, interest rate hedging techniques can be split into internal and external approaches.

Internal hedging

There are two main ways for companies to manage interest rate risk within the company itself:

(a) Firms may try to balance the amount of variable rate borrowing, the component that carries interest rate risk, with fixed rate borrowing, the component that transfers the risk to the lender. In the latter form of borrowing, the lender charges a premium for taking on the risk – this is the reason why fixing the rate of interest on a loan for a period of time is likely to incur a higher initial rate of interest than on a variable loan.

(b) Firms can match the interest earned on savings with the interest paid on borrowings, including balancing the mix of fixed and variable interest on lending and borrowing. Since most businesses are net borrowers, this is more likely to be relevant to financial service firms that operate with substantial interest-earning assets as well as loan liabilities.

External hedging

Many of the external hedging techniques outlined above for managing foreign exchange rate risk have parallel techniques in managing interest rate risk.

(a) Forward rate agreements (FRAs)

If a company is anticipating raising a two-year loan in six months' time, it faces two risks regarding interest rates:

- interest rates may rise during the next six months

- interest rates may rise during the two-year period of the loan.

An FRA hedges against both of these risks. It involves the company and the bank agreeing now on the rate of interest for the loan over the two years. This is the rate of interest that will then be paid by the company regardless of any changes in the market rate.

(b) Hedging using the money markets

If a company that intends to borrow money in the future is concerned about possible rises in interest rates in the meantime, it could borrow now and put the money on deposit until required. The cost of this is lower interest rates on deposit than on borrowing.

(c) Interest rate futures

These follow the same principles as exchange rate futures. Say a business intends to borrow in the future, it risks interest rates rising in the meantime. This risk is offset by (in this case) selling an interest rate future now and buying it back when the loan is actually taken out. If interest rates have risen, the extra interest cost on the loan will be offset by the profit that will have been earned on the futures contract.

(d) Options

Just as options can be bought and sold on shares, currencies and some commodities, they can be traded on interest rates. Thus an option can be bought to borrow at a particular interest rate at some time in the future. If, on the exercise date, market rates for borrowing are lower, the option need not be exercised. The effect of the option is therefore to effect a maximum rate of interest to pay – this is called an *interest rate cap*. Similarly, minimum interest rates can be assured using options; these are known as *interest rate floors*.

A useful strategy for heavily borrowing companies is to buy a cap and sell a floor. This ensures that their borrowing will be at a rate between the cap and the floor – this strategy establishes an *interest rate collar*. Although the maximum cost may be less than actual market rates, the company is giving up the opportunity to borrow at market rates below the floor.

(e) Swaps

As already outlined with currency swaps, these involve firms swapping their loan and interest repayments. Interest rate swaps in particular can be used to swap a fixed rate interest commitment into a variable rate one. The opportunity for a swap occurs when different companies have different credit ratings for different types of loans. Companies need to borrow where they have the most comparative advantage in order for both parties to benefit in a swap arrangement. Banks often act as intermediaries bringing such companies together.

12.10 Choosing which hedging techniques to use

Choosing which approach to hedging to follow is difficult and not always clear-cut. Internal hedging is cheaper than using external financial instruments, but is also likely to be more limited in which risks it can cover.

Of the external approaches, options have the advantage of allowing businesses to walk away if the market offers a better deal at the time. All of the others lock businesses into an arrangement that does not allow them to benefit if the market moves in their favour.

Futures are generally more expensive and more restrictive to use than the forward market. Forward rate contracts can be for any amount and are available in many different currencies. Futures have to be in standard amount and are available in a limited number of currencies. Futures also require an initial margin, which forward contracts do not. Swaps have the advantage of providing long-term hedges compared with the other methods. Their main problem is the assumption of **counter-party risk** assumed, namely, the risk that if you enter into a swap arrangement with another party and that party fails to meet its commitments, you become liable.

The above review of hedging approaches is by no means complete. Other, more exotic, financial instruments are also available to reduce or eliminate risks, e.g. Disney could buy weather derivatives if it was concerned that income from its theme parks would be significantly affected by bad weather. Of course, this has a cost, and the 'bad weather' cover will cost more for Paris than for Florida. The method used may reflect the risk that the company faces. For example, although interest rate hedging appeals mainly to a highly geared company, it is also likely to be of interest to a company producing a good which could be sensitive to rises in interest rates, such as a car manufacturer, or a builder, both of whose products customers tend to borrow to buy.

The demand for a company's product could also be affected by market or company factors. Thus the demand for penthouse flats, or Ferraris, is probably linked to the size of City bonuses, which will be affected by the level of the stock market. The Ferrari dealer in the City may well hedge this risk by trading on the FTSE 100 index. By selling the index now, the business will cover its losses on sales of cars should the market fall by the profit it makes on the index by buying it back at the lower price. Companies may protect themselves against a fall in their share price by buying puts on their share guaranteeing them a minimum selling price however far the market price itself falls. However, such transactions can become self-fulfilling as the market might see such a transaction as a negative signal.

Sometimes, where the ability to repay the debt has been dependent on the price of a particular commodity, say the price of oil, the debt is denominated in the dependency, i.e. repayments are geared to the price of oil. An extreme example of this was the so-called catastrophe bond issued by the United Services Automobile Association in the USA (1997–8). It sold one-year bonds to the value of $477 million that did not pay out if there was a hurricane during the year.

⏱ 12.11 Managing the future

By definition, nothing is certain in life (apart from death and taxes), so the future is always risky. Organisations, however, must be careful not to stifle risk-taking when making decisions about the future. It is difficult to create a culture that recognises that some decisions will not be successful, one that accepts that it is not always possible to constantly pick winners.

Nevertheless, some bold decisions may turn out right, and may add considerable value to the organisation. The concept of real options can be useful to help map the future. An investment provides real options if it offers possibilities in the future to add value. For example, Disney invested considerable amounts in its cable TV channel, a service rolled out from the mid 1990s, to provide programmes in Spanish for Mexico. This gave the company the option to move into Latin America with relatively little extra investment in programming if the Mexican plan went well.

Real options, of course, do not always materialise. When Concorde was developed and built in the 1960s, it was recognised by all those involved that it would not make money. Its development costs were enormous (£28 billion at today's prices) because it involved new technology, the number of passengers it could carry was small, its noise level provoked environmental resistance, and it was thirsty for fuel. However, those involved in Concorde all had an option to build a bigger, quieter, more fuel-efficient Concorde II that would make them pots of money. Unfortunately, life did not turn out that way, and Concorde II remains only a pipedream. Indeed, in 2003, British Airways announced that Concorde would cease to fly as a commercial airliner. Options do not always come true.

The value of many businesses is embodied mainly in their future prospects rather than in assets owned today. For dotcoms spending on marketing to protect themselves from competitors, and for pharmaceutical companies that spend heavily on research to find a successful drug, it is important that expenditure is targeted in the right areas. The pharmaceutical company Merck uses real options to help target its R&D investment. It spends more money on those projects that have a higher possibility of success and those that have a smaller loss-making potential.

12.12 Summary

Managing for value aims not to minimise risk but to maximise value. Risk is a reality and businesses are now encouraged to recognise this and prepare strategies to manage it. This requires them to set objectives for the strategy based upon identifying and quantifying the exposures that they face. Only then can strategies and techniques be put in place to help the business achieve its objectives. Because this is such a sensitive area, businesses need to be more transparent in their risk management so that markets and investors are informed, can have confidence in what is being attempted, and can take investment decisions accordingly.

References and further reading

Textbooks

Arnold – chs 21 and 22.
Brealey & Myers – ch 25.
Watson & Head – ch 12.

Other

Buckley, A (2000) *Multinational Finance* (Pearson Education).

CIMA (2002) *Risk Management: a Guide to Good Practice*.

'Corporate risk management', Economist Survey, 10 February 1996.

'Enterprise risk management: implementing new solutions' (2001). The Economist Intelligence Unit and MMC Enterprise Risk, Inc.

ICAEW (2000) 'Risk Management and the Value-Added by Internal Audit', June.

Isaac, T and Connell, B (2002) 'Risk management: risks and strategy: A BOC case study', *Managing Risk to Enhance Shareholder Value* (IFAC/CIMA). See: www.ifac.org *and* www.cimaglobal.com.

Laws, D (February 2002) 'Changing culture, changing minds', www.erisk.com

Smullen, J (2001) *Risk Management for Company Executives* (FT Prentice Hall).

Mini-case studies

Mini-case study – Rover

Rover offered all those who bought its new cars at the start of 2003 free fuel for the year. This introduced considerable risk since the start of the year was a period of great international tension over Iraq, with the potential for a considerable rise in world oil prices that would feed into domestic petrol prices.

Required
Identify the risks that Rover should have evaluated if it were utilising an integrated risk system. To what extent are these offsetting?

Mini-case study – EuroDisney

Disney's decision to build a new theme park in Paris in 1992 was a bold strategic move. By moving into Europe, the company was attempting to 'stretch' its hugely successful US brand into a new economic context. The idea followed from the successful opening of a park in Japan.

Initially, Disney had a choice of siting the new park near Paris or near Barcelona. The benefits of Spain were the weather and higher attendance projections. Influential in the ultimate choice of Paris, however, was its proximity to large population centres, the number of visitors to the city, and the fact that the French government made land available to the company at a low price. Also rather surprisingly, Disney products were more popular in France than in any other European country. However, there was a certain hostility among some sections of French public opinion about this invasion of classic Americana; one French film director called the project a 'cultural Chernobyl'.

The company financed the park with loans from the French government and share issues. EuroDisney, as it was then called, paid a royalty to the parent US company. The early history of the park was a troubled one as the US model fitted sometimes uneasily into the European dimension. This had not been the case in Japan where there was little concession to Japanese culture, with signs in English, and American food sold. Clearly, Disney and Europe had to get used to each other's ways.

Disney anticipated some problems – it used French as the first language of the park, and emphasised the European origins of characters like Peter Pan and Pinocchio. But attendances dampened by poor weather and a strong franc at the time impacted adversely on the EuroDisney share price. In its first year of operation, EuroDisney lost $900 million and the share price fell around 60 per cent. The park was seen as expensive due to high entrance charges, a situation not helped by the strong French franc and economic recession. None of this encouraged Europeans to develop the same habit of attending theme parks as Americans. In addition, other attractions opened in competition, including Parc Asterix based on a French cartoon character, north of Paris. In fact, the French did not attend in great numbers, resistance being fuelled by a trade dispute between France and the USA, and striking farmers upset by their land being taken by the government to build the park in the first place.

Further rights issues and borrowing to fund the deficits were difficult to manage and the company attempted to cut costs, which included renegotiation of the royalty payments to be made to its American parent.

Disney was quick to learn from these early setbacks and set about improving performance. It introduced a more competitive pricing strategy, including lower charges during winter, and provided better facilities to deal with bad weather. It even agreed to serve wine within the park, completely at odds with the no-alcohol rule that applied to its other parks. Over time, there has been a greater acceptance of the park within Europe.

So after a shaky start, the park has become a success. Disney has added to its parks portfolio, increased attendances and boosted the demand for its numerous products. In 2002, it opened an additional attraction, a Universal Studios complex.

Required

(a) Identify the key operational and financial risks that Disney took on by opening the new park in Paris.

(b) How could the problems that emerged have been anticipated?

(c) What were the important decisions made by the company to deal with these risks and problems, and why were they generally successful?

Sources: For further information see Peter Curwen (1995) EuroDisney: the mouse that roared (not!), *European Bussiness Review* Vol. 96 No. 5; and John Daniels & Lee Radeburgh (1995) *International Business*, Addison Wesley

Mini-case study - Electrolux

Echoing the catastrophic losses which brought down Barings bank in 1995, Electrolux, the world's biggest maker of washers and spin dryers and other household appliances, announced in 2000 that its 1999 profits would be dented by a currency trading loss of $30 million. Attempting to soften the blow, a senior executive responsible for corporate communications, said that the loss, due to unauthorised currency trading, was tax-deductible and would reduce profits by only about 5 per cent.

The loss stemmed from trading of **forward contracts** by an employee at Electrolux's internal banking operation based in Siegen in Germany, and responsible for foreign exchange trade finance covering imports and exports into Germany. The unnamed employee, under police investigation, confessed after his cumulative deficit had risen to a level he could not cope with, although he claimed he had not been trying to make personal gains.

Forward contracts are a device used by corporates to lock in a set rate of exchange by laying off the exposure to a bank which takes a 'position', i.e. a gamble, on the future course of exchange rates, hoping to profit from the operation. Some corporates have such a volume of foreign exchange moving through their offices that they set up their own foreign exchange speculation units as profit centres. Electrolux has now moved its foreign exchange trading to its Stockholm headquarters.

Required
In the light of the Electrolux experience, discuss the cases for:

(a) foreign exchange speculation rather than hedging

(b) centralised cash and foreign exchange management rather than devolving it to subsidiary units.

Mini-case study - Tomkins plc

This is an extract from the 2002 Annual Report:

'The Directors have overall responsibility for the Group's system of internal control and for reviewing its effectiveness. To fulfil this responsibility the Directors have established a planning, control and performance management framework within which each of the Group's businesses operate. Within this framework, the management of each of the businesses considers strategic, operational, commercial and financial risks and identifies risk mitigation actions. Whilst acknowledging their overall responsibility for the system of internal control, the Directors are aware that the system is designed to manage rather than eliminate the risk of failure to achieve business objectives and can provide reasonable and not absolute assurance against material misstatement or loss.

During the period under review, the Directors were not aware of any control breakdowns, which resulted in a material loss.

The planning, control and performance management framework includes an ongoing process for identifying, evaluating and managing the significant risks faced by the Group and has been in place throughout the period and up to the approval date of the financial statements. Each business identifies and assesses the key business risks affecting the achievement of its objectives. Business unit management also identifies the risk management processes used to mitigate the key risks to an acceptable level and, where appropriate, additional actions required to manage further and mitigate them. The risk summaries developed out of this process are updated at least annually. In addition, Corporate Centre management considers those risks to the Group's strategic objectives that may not be identified and managed at the business level.

In connection with quarterly business reviews, relevant executives discuss risk management activities with Corporate Centre management. The key risks and mitigation strategies are also discussed at least annually with the Audit Committee as well as the full Board.

The risk management framework described above is applied to major initiatives such as acquisitions as well as operational risks within the business including environmental, health and safety risks.

The other key elements of the framework, which constitutes the control environment, include:

- Business strategy reviews - each business is required to prepare a strategic position assessment taking into account the current and likely future market environment and competitive position of the business, with specific consideration given to strategic risk. The Corporate Centre management reviews the strategy with each business and the Board is presented with a summary of the plans.

- Business reviews – on a quarterly basis, Corporate Centre management performs extensive reviews with each business. These reviews consider current financial results, projections and forecasts, and address the progress of key strategic and operating initiatives, the risks affecting their achievement and the actions being taken by business unit management to manage the risks and achieve their objectives.

- Budget and financial plans – each business prepares budgets and financial plans in accordance with a defined format, which includes consideration of risks. To the extent risks are both reasonably estimable and likely to occur, they are reflected specifically in the respective business' budget. Management at the Corporate Centre reviews the budgets and financial plans with the business units and a summary is presented to the Board for approval.

- Capital expenditure authorisation approval – all significant capital expenditure is subject to a formal capital expenditure authorisation process, which takes into account, inter alia, operational, financial and technical risks.

- Reporting and analysis – all businesses are required to report monthly to the Corporate Centre on financial performance compared to budget and to explain significant variances from plan and changes in the business environment.

- Forecasts – monthly each business is required to reassess its forecast for the current and following financial year. These forecasts are subject to reviews on a quarterly basis.

- Financial strategy – the financial strategy includes assessment of the major financial risks related to interest rate exposure, foreign currency exposure, debt maturity and liquidity. There is a comprehensive global insurance programme in place using the external insurance market and some limited involvement of an internal captive insurance company. Group Treasury manages hedging activities, relating to financial risks, with external cover for net currency transaction exposures. The Board oversees the financial strategy as well as the tax strategy and considers the associated risks and risk management techniques being used by the Group. The Group Tax function manages tax compliance and tax risks associated with the Group's activities.

- Reporting certifications – in connection with the preparation of the annual and quarterly financial statements, senior business general management and financial management sign a certificate which includes a declaration regarding the existence of internal controls, the proper recording of transactions and the identification and evaluation of significant business risks.

The Group established an internal audit function in 2001 via a co-sourcing arrangement. The Vice President – Business Risk Assurance directs the activities of the internal auditors on a day-to-day basis and reports direct to the Audit Committee of the Board at least four times a year. As part of their financial audit responsibilities, the external auditors also provide reports to the Audit Committee on the operation of internal controls affecting key financial processes. The Directors confirm that the effectiveness of the system of internal control for the eight months ended 31 December 2002 has been reviewed in line with the criteria set out in the Combined Code "Internal Control" guidance for Directors, issued in September 1999.'

Source: Tomkins plc Annual Report 2002

Required
Comment on the risk management framework of Tomkins plc from this extract.

Self-assessment answers

All but two of these SAAs involve personal research and observation. The exceptions are:

12.3
If the forward rate is falling (rising), i.e. fewer (more) units of the foreign currency are quoted per pound, this means that the pound is expected to depreciate (appreciate), probably due to people expecting a higher (lower) rate of inflation in the UK relative to that in other countries.

12.6
If the spot rate is $1.60 = £1, the option is said to be 'at the money'. The holder would be indifferent in financial terms whether to exercise it or not, although to save time and trouble he would probably not do so. Either way, he has paid the premium which is a sunk cost.

MEASURING PERFORMANCE

A valuable survey

The Department of Trade and Industry publishes an annual 'Value Added Scorecard' of companies. Value added is defined for this survey as revenues less the cost of bought-in materials, components and services. This added wealth is then distributed to employees (wages and salaries), to providers of finance (interest and dividends), to governments (as taxes) and for reinvestment to sustain and develop the business (R&D).

The relative amounts of these distributions of wealth created were shown to vary between countries, as follows:

(Figures are per cent of value added.)

	Employee costs	Dividends	Operating profit
Germany	63.9	3.8	13.9
France	61.7	4.3	19.9
UK	48.5	11.1	19.9

The 2003 survey confirms that 2002–3 was a difficult year for business, with the value added for Europe's top 600 companies decreasing by 1 per cent, compared with a 17 per cent increase the previous year. During the year, operating profits fell by 35 per cent. These results provide some reasons why stock markets fell so much during 2002 – the London market alone falling around 25 per cent.

The top 10 European companies for adding value in the 2003 survey are:

		£bn
1	Daimler-Chrysler	21.2
2	Siemens	21.1
3	Shell	19.7
4	Deutsche Telekom	19.1
5	BP	19.1
6	Volkswagen	16.5
7	TotalFinaElf	16.3
8	Allianz	13.3
9	UBS	13.2
10	France Telecom	12.7

The highest value-added sectors were calculated to be banks, telecoms, automotive, and oil and gas.

Source: Both tables Copyright © Crown Copyright 2002, Crown Copyright material is reproduced with the permission of the Controller of HMSO

13.1 Introduction

The emphasis of this book has been on how to manage a business and make decisions that will add value by improving the financial prospect is for the future. The concept of value-adding decisions was discussed in the first chapter. Although an easy principle to write, it is difficult to operate in practice because of the complexity surrounding many decisions. Nevertheless throughout the book, we have attempted to articulate the key principles involved in order to make the value-adding decision when faced with any situation.

Having asserted that financial management is about making decisions that add value, it is appropriate that we conclude this book by analysing the various approaches which are used to measure whether value has been added or not. This is the primary variable in determining the financial performance of a business over time. Having established the assumed financial objective of adding value in the first chapter, we will now conclude by looking further at how to measure value added (the introductory cameo represents one definition), and revisit some of the objectives identified at the beginning of this book.

13.2 Problems with profit-based measures of performance

Until recently, many lay people might have regarded accounting profit as an accurate and objective measure of a firm's performance. Indeed, many analysts still focus on a firm's total profit as a useful measure of financial performance. Related measures that also use accounting profit are:

- earnings per share (EPS) – the profit that belongs to shareholders, i.e. after interest and after tax, divided by the number of shares in issue

- rate of return ratios, such as return on capital employed, return on equity, etc. In all of these cases, accounting profit is used as 'the return'.

Unfortunately, although profit may be a useful measure of performance, it is a number that is likely to carry with it a number of qualifications. This was starkly shown when Enron, a highly 'profitable' company, collapsed in 2002 with debts totalling $60 billion. There are three main elements that can lead to an Enron situation:

(a) Accounting profit is not a reliable measure of performance – simply showing profits in the accounts does not prove that value has been created.

(b) There is more than one profit figure shown in a set of company accounts – it may be unclear which one is the most indicative of value added.

(c) However profitable (or valuable) a business may be, survival requires managing cash flow such that, as in ordinary life, debts can be paid when they become due. Profitable businesses can and do fail.

The unreliability of profit as a measure of performance is due to many reasons, some of which we will now examine in more detail.

1 The calculation of accounting profit is the result of many subjective policies and assumptions that leaves it open to manipulation. Readers who have studied financial accounting will know that it is possible to apply different approaches when drawing up accounting statements, for example:

- The valuation of closing stock can assume different flows of stock, such as FIFO (first in first out) or LIFO (last in first out), i.e. the same physical amount of stock can be valued in different ways to produce different amounts. The higher the value placed on closing stock, the higher will be the reported profit.

- It is well known that fixed assets, like cars, lose value, or depreciate, over time. Firms have great latitude over the method and the amount of depreciation that they charge against profit in the accounts.
- Many businesses recognise that there is a risk that some of their customers who owe them money (debtors) will not in fact pay. It is reasonable to make a provision for these expected bad debts in the accounts now (so as not to spend money that will not in fact be received). However, the amount of this provision, which is largely at the discretion of the accountant, will directly affect reported profit.
- Some firms may choose not to write off all expenses incurred in any one year against profit, such as marketing expenses or research and development, because it will help generate revenues in the future. If the expense is not written off against profit in the current year, it will be carried forward as an asset on the balance sheet. It is easy to see the temptation to carry these costs forward so that current profit is kept higher than otherwise, and at the same time, the balance sheet looks stronger.

These are just a small sample of situations where the decision of the accountant dealing with a particular financial issue can affect the profit declared. None of this is illegal – it is simply that there is a lot of room for manoeuvre. UK auditors sign off accounts as showing a 'true and fair view' – this must ultimately be a matter of opinion rather than a matter of fact.

2 Accounting profit does not take full account of the cost of equity in its calculation. In deriving profit, the accounts show the full cost of debt (i.e. interest incurred is charged as an expense against profit). However, the full cost of equity is unlikely to be shown. At an extreme, some companies pay no dividends and hence record no financing charge for equity at all in the profit and loss account. However, shareholders in all companies require a return on their investment. The fact that this is not shown in the accounts is a major reason why accounting profit fails to measure the amount of value added. For example, assume that a company has £100 million of equity finance, on which shareholders require a 10 per cent return. If this company pays no dividend and records an after-tax profit of £8 million, this company is in fact losing value – it is not generating enough after-tax profit to meet shareholders' requirements. It is likely that even though this company has declared a 'profit', its share price will have fallen.

3 Performance measurement needs to recognise that investors need to be rewarded for risk. It is possible that a company has recorded an increase in its accounting profit but that this increase has taken place because it has taken on much more risky investments. Both lenders and shareholders will want a higher return for financing this extra risk. Because of this, if the profit fails to rise by an amount that will cover this extra requirement, it is again possible for an increase in profit to result in a fall in the share price. Before using profit as a measure of performance, any change in the risk profile of the business must be taken into account.

4 For performance measurement, profit needs to be related to the size of the investment. The press and the public can get very excited when companies declare big profit numbers. But if a company with a market value of £50 billion declares a profit of £1 billion, this is no big deal – this represents a paltry 2 per cent return. Currently (2003), investing in government securities will produce nearly double that return – and they have little or no risk.

5 Accounting numbers often need serious qualification:

- Some are affected by inflation. If inflation is running at 20 per cent p.a., revenues have to increase by this amount just to stand still. In high-inflation countries, such as South America, accounting numbers are best viewed in real terms to exclude the effects of inflation, particularly on revenues and expenses.
- Some are expressed in historic cost terms. Accountants do not have to revalue fixed assets, whereas the market always will. Imagine that a company starts up by selling 500 shares at £2 each, and borrowing £1,000. It uses the £2,000 finance to buy a piece of land. The balance sheet will look like this:

	£		£
Share finance	1,000	Land	2,000
Borrowing	1,000		
	2,000		

Assume that the market value of the land doubles to £4,000. The accounts are not required to reflect this increase in value (following the historic cost principle). But the market will. In fact, the share price will reflect the fact that this company now has an asset worth £4,000, against which there is borrowing worth £1,000. The remaining £3,000 belongs to the shareholders, i.e. the 500 shares will now be worth £6 each.

- This example also demonstrates why gearing is more informative using market values and not book values. Using debt/equity, the above balance sheet gives a gearing ratio of 100 per cent. Using market prices after the increase in the value of the land, this ratio falls to (£1,000/£3,000) = 33.3%. This fall demonstrates that this company's 'ability to borrow' has significantly increased, which is perfectly true since the value of the land has increased. This signal will be lost if balance sheet values for debt and equity are used rather than market values.
- In addition, the accounts may exclude liabilities and assets. The market value of equity will take account of liabilities that are real enough, but

that may not be shown on the balance sheet (such as those acquired by operating lease finance), and intangible assets which may have a high value but which again may not be shown on the balance sheet (such as internally generated goodwill, or a well-known brand name).

Thus, accounting profit is an unreliable guide to the actual performance of a business. Indeed, it is not unusual to see an increase in accounting profit producing a fall in share price. This could be due to the company taking short-term cost-cutting measures which, although increasing profit in the short term, could lower value by reducing the financial prospects for the future, e.g. Glaxo could easily increase profit by cutting back on its £3 billion annual expense for research and development. But if the company does this, it will reduce its potential to earn future incomes and thereby reduce the present value of the company. There could be similar effects if companies reduce 'investment' expenses such as staff training or marketing. In all of these cases, if the market is convinced that these expenditures will increase future cash inflows, the share price will rise even if the accountant treats them as an expense and writes them off against profit.

For many 'New Economy' businesses, accounting profit is irrelevant to company valuation, e.g. internet firms or bio-technology companies. The value in such business is predominantly embedded in the potential of future prospects rather than assets currently owned. This emphasis on the future, and the lack of a bedrock of tangible assets, makes valuing these types of business a highly complex exercise.

For all of these reasons, it is no surprise that studies have failed to find a strong correlation between changes in accounting profit and changes in the share price. This would appear to confirm that accounting profit is not a reliable guide to the measurement of performance.

13.3 The value-action pentagon model

The Efficient Markets Hypothesis states that market prices fully reflect all publicly available information. The basic valuation model suggests that the market prices the shares of any company by:

- generating expectations of the *amount* and the *timing* of future cash flows
- discounting these expected cash flows by a risk-adjusted required return.

Share prices are volatile because all three of these variables – the expected amount of future cash, the expected timing of future cash, and the discount rate reflecting risk – are subject to continuous reappraisal. It is entirely possible that the market's optimism about the future financial prospects of a company can change from one minute to the next because something happens to alter the market's view. This could be caused by an event specific to the company (an unsystematic factor) or something which affects the economy as a whole (a systematic factor).

The above model shows us that value is added by:

- improving the prospects for future cash flows, and/or
- reducing the required return.

It is possible to break down these two broad factors into more component parts, such as the value pentagonal model in Figure 13.1 which highlights five ways to increase value.

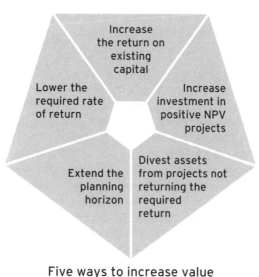

Five ways to increase value

Figure 13.1 The value-action pentagon

Source: Adapted from Arnold (2002, p 674)

It is possible to start anywhere on this pentagon, but let us take it from the very top.

1 Increasing the return on existing capital can be achieved by increasing incomes, reducing costs and reducing the investment in assets earning the returns. Improving the time profile of cash flows is also important – the sooner the cash incomes occur, the more valuable they are. Similarly, businesses will try to delay making payments.

2 Increasing investment in positive NPV projects means exploiting those areas of value where the business is earning returns in excess of required risk-adjusted returns. These areas must be exploited to the full before they disappear (e.g. customers demand changes) or competitors move in.

3 Divesting and selling off poorly-performing divisions or subsidiaries is a critical aspect of increasing value. It used to be thought that as far as business is concerned 'bigger is best'. However, this is not the case if significant parts of the empire are destroying value as fast as the other parts are creating it. It can be difficult to identify the value-destroyers, but once identified, these parts must be turned round or removed (ideally by selling them to a company that has the competences to add value).

4 Extending the time horizon of the cash inflows is important. The longer the total period over which value can be created, the better. Star Wars merchandise is still being sold more than 25 years after the first film was shown. This has been achieved by a combination of a series of popular films, shrewd marketing and legal protection of trademarks. The producers of Harry Potter and Lord of the Rings will have noted this phenomenal achievement in sustained value-creation.

5 Reducing the required return is a little more complex. The lower the discount rate, the higher the present value of future cash flows. This is achieved by reducing the return required by lenders and shareholders, the financiers of the company. At its simplest, this can be achieved by moving into low-risk business areas. However, other things being equal, there is less potential for adding value in safer rather than riskier business areas. Thus, businesses must try to look for projects that will generate good returns without adding to the expectations of return from lenders and shareholders. This is one of the reasons why companies are concerned to maintain their credit ratings as independently assessed by agencies such as Moody's and Standard and Poor's. A high credit rating will lower the company's cost of finance. Sometimes, companies will get a helping hand in this regard from macro-economic policy. It is no surprise that, when central banks lower interest rates, share prices usually rise. This is because a lower bank rate, other things being equal, will reduce the required return for both lenders and shareholders. This will reduce the discount rate and hence increase the present value of future cash flows.

It is therefore important for businesses that manage for value to concentrate on the two main elements of cash flow and the discount rate. It is easy to become distracted by everyday events from these two key variables. Some of the following common performance measures may actually reduce value:

- maximise sales growth – this is most easily achieved by reducing selling price and reducing profit margins

- increase market share – this may cost more to achieve than it is worth, e.g. expensive advertising campaigns

- maximise accounting profit or earnings per share – as we have already seen, both of these factors can be manipulated without any value being added

- widen the product range – will the new products add value or will they cost money to get them to the market?

- expand the size of department – this may be at the expense of another department in the organisation. There is no point in adding value in one department at the expense of another.

It is important to stress at this point that all of the above targets can add value if they improve future cash flows and/or reduce the required return through lowering risk. However, the target should be seen only as a means to an end (i.e. adding value), not as an end in itself. This demonstrates how important it is to set appropriate targets, namely ones that can be relied upon to add value.

As we saw in the first chapter, because many companies accept that their main financial objective is to maximise shareholder wealth, they now specifically focus on value in their published objectives as the way to achieve this goal.

Apple computers famously lost its technological lead over Microsoft by refusing to license out its superior Macintosh operating system. Microsoft, on the other hand, was happy to license out its Windows system, so that soon it became the industry standard. As a result of this critical strategic decision, Microsoft has gone on to become the most valuable company in the world, while Apple lost several billion dollers in value between 1991 and 1996

Source: for further information see Paul Finlay (2000) *Strategic Management*, FT Prentice Hall

Self-assessment activity 13.1

Using a search engine on the internet, find examples of companies that claim to 'manage for value'. Find out what they mean by the term.

13.4 Shareholder value analysis

The work of Rappaport in defining the determinants of a firm's value was examined in Chapter 10. He expanded the valuation model described above into a set of 'value drivers' on which managers could focus their attention. These are shown in Figure 13.2.

This approach provides a structure for the valuation model already described and the key decision areas in the model.

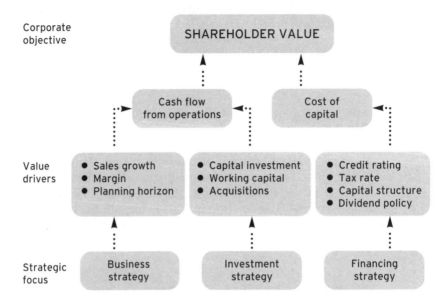

Figure 13.2 Rappaport's value pyramid

Source: Adapted with the permission of The Free Press, a Division of Simon & Schuster Adult Publishing Group, from Figure 2.1, p 56 from *Creating Shareholder value: a Guide for Managers and Investors*, by Alfred Rappaport. Copyright © 1986, 1998 by Alfred Rappaport. All rights reserved; also adapted from Pike and Neale (2003)

Maximising shareholder value

Rappaport's SVA has at its pinnacle the maximisation of value for shareholders. This is being increasingly emphasised in company annual reports. There are many possible reasons for this:

1 Managers now recognise that poorly performing companies risk being taken over. Shareholders of such companies are always likely to be influenced by a predator company promising them better financial returns, whatever other objectives are currently being met.

2 Institutional shareholders take a more aggressive stance against poorly performing management (particularly during the downturn in the share markets 2000–3). This is demonstrated by this press release of October 2002:

'City institutions today gave new impetus to effective shareholder activism through the launch of new principles drawn up by the Institutional Shareholders' Committee (ISC), whose associations represent virtually all UK institutional investors. The principles are the first comprehensive statement of best practice governing the responsibilities of institutional shareholders and investment managers in relation to the companies in which they invest. They aim to secure value for ultimate beneficiaries – pension scheme members and individual savers – through consistent monitoring of the performance of those companies. This is to be backed up by direct engagement where appropriate. The principles make it clear that if companies persistently fail to respond to concerns, institutional shareholders and investment managers, ISC members will vote against the Board at general meetings.'

Source: Press release from the Institutional Shareholders Committee, 21 October 2002

3 Many agree with the view expounded by Milton Friedman that society as a whole benefits from value creation – the bigger the cake, the more there is for everyone.

4 The increasing realisation, including lessons learned from recent corporate failures, that measures that imply higher shareholder wealth do not always deliver value, e.g. higher market share may lower value; or that accounting measures such as profit and EPS may have resulted from a manipulation of the figures rather than representing real increases in value, as the notorious example of WorldCom demonstrated.

Managing for value firmly re-establishes adding value as the primary objective. But given the problems with profit, how can the value that a company adds be measured?

13.5 Measuring value creation

Several measures have been proposed as providing measures of performance. Many of them use market prices since they are seen as being objective and reflective of value given an efficient stock market. Examples of these measures are as follows.

1 Total shareholder return (TSR)

Adding value will benefit shareholders in two ways: cash dividend payments and/or a rising share price (capital gain).

The annual return on an investment in a share can be calculated as follows:

$$\frac{\text{Dividend} + (\text{closing share price} - \text{opening share price})}{\text{Opening share price}}$$

For example, if an investor buys a share for 100p, and during the year receives a dividend of 10p, and at year-end the share is worth 115p, the return on this investment for the year is:

$$\frac{10p + (115p - 100p)}{100p} = 25\%$$

As discussed in Chapter 6, the return on the market portfolio of shares exceeded the returns achieved on government securities by around 5 per cent p.a. during the last century. However, as the small print constantly reminds us, share prices can go down as well as up, i.e. because of this risk, investors require a higher expected (but never guaranteed) return. This risk was clearly demonstrated in the period between 2000 and early 2003 when the FTSE 100 share price index fell by 50 per cent. Even worse, the Nikkei index measuring the level of prices on the Tokyo Stock Market had fallen by nearly 80 per cent over the past 14 years.

To make a meaningful analysis of the return on a particular share, it is important to take into account:

- the returns achieved by the sector the share is in, or the market as a whole. After all, if the share has fallen by 'only' 5 per cent in a year that the sector has fallen by 10 per cent, then its relative performance is superior to the sector as a whole

- the risk class of the company; higher (systematic) risk companies will be expected to earn higher returns to compensate investors for taking on the extra risk

- the fact that share prices, and therefore the annual returns on shares, can vary considerably over different time periods. This is because there are so many systematic and unsystematic factors continuously affecting shares.

2 Market value added (MVA)

MVA measures the *extra* value that a company has created over time compared with the finance invested in it by shareholders and lenders. The total market value of a company comprises the value of its equity plus the value of its debt. Hence:

> MVA = market value of debt and equity
> less
> the total amount debt and equity financing invested in the business

Thus if, over time, shareholders have invested £1 million in the shares of a company, and lenders have lent £2 million, then a total of £3 million has been invested in the company. If this company is now worth £4.5 million, the MVA is (£4.5m – £3m) = £1.5m.

If the market value of debt is assumed to be equal to the amount lent to the company (usually a reasonable assumption), debt can be deducted from both sides of the equation, which can now be rewritten as:

> MVA = the market value of the company's ordinary shares
> less
> the capital supplied by ordinary shareholders

MVA gives a good indication of how successful managers have been in adding value by investing the finance received in positive NPV projects. However, there are caveats when calculating the MVA of a company:

- It is difficult to estimate the amount of cash invested, especially over a long period of time.

- MVA does not explain when value was created, whether it is still being created or whether it will be created in the future.

- Inflation distorts MVA – market value can increase purely because of inflation, not as a result of real value being added.

- MVA is an absolute number and therefore tends to favour bigger companies. Thus £1 billion MVA on a company with billions of finance may represent a poor performance, whereas £1 million MVA for a small company could be highly impressive. Relating MVA to the size of the business can be shown by calculating a market to book ratio (MBR). This divides the market value by the capital invested so that MVA is expressed as a percentage of the capital invested in the business. In modern economies, service businesses are now more prevalent than manufacturing. Service companies tend to have most of their value tied up in intangible rather than tangible assets. Since valuable intangible assets are often excluded from balance sheets, market to book values in general have increased in recent years.

3 Economic value added (EVA™)

Economic value added (EVA™) attempts to measure the value added over the previous year. It is based on the concept of economic profit – the profit left after the cost of finance has been deducted. EVA can be expressed in two main ways:

$$EVA = NOPAT - (IC \times \text{cost of capital})$$

where NOPAT = net operating profit after tax

IC = all invested capital

An example will demonstrate the basic principles. Assume that a company has invested £100 million in the business, consisting of £50 million from lenders and £50 million from shareholders. Lenders require an after-tax return of 5 per cent, and shareholders a return of 10 per cent. Since they have both invested equal amounts, the average cost of capital for this company is 7.5 per cent. Assume that the company has announced a NOPAT of £10 million.

The EVA created by the company this year can be calculated as follows using the above formula:

$$£10m - (£100 \times 7.5\%) = £2.5m$$

This shows that EVA occurs only after the return to all finance (both debt and equity) is explicitly deducted from the after-tax operating profit. This overcomes one of the disadvantages of using profit as a measure of performance.

The same result can be shown by looking at EVA from a slightly different perspective:

EVA = (return achieved on capital – cost of capital) × invested capital

Using the above example, this produces the same answer:

EVA = (10% – 7.5%) × £100m = £2.5m

This shows that for a company to add value, it must generate a return on capital invested over and above the cost of financing this investment.

The calculation of EVA

We have already seen that EVA is the value added to a business over a period of time after *the cost of financing all investment in the business* has been deducted from the adjusted after-tax operating income. EVA can be calculated from a traditional set of accounts. In practice, this requires many adjustments. Some of the most common ones are:

- research and development costs and marketing costs are regarded as an expense by accountants but as an investment for future cash flows by EVA. As such, EVA will tend to place these expenditures on the balance sheet rather than pass them through the profit and loss account

- similarly, EVA states that there should be no commitment to write off goodwill if there is still the prospect of future cash flows arising from 'intangible' assets such as brand names or know-how.

The following extract is taken from SAB Miller plc, which as well as showing traditional accounts shows this EVA calculation in its annual report.

13.6 How EVA is calculated in practice: SAB Miller plc

The following extract from the 2001 report and accounts of SAB Miller plc (formerly South African Breweries plc) illustrates the rationale of EVA.

Shareholder value

Shareholder value is best measured by the total return to shareholders (TSR), being the appreciation in share price, plus dividends over the long term. From its listing in London to 31 March 2000, SAB delivered a respectable return of 5.3 per cent, which compares favourably with its peer group. Independent research shows that we ended the year in fourth position in a survey of 18 of our peers.

The group uses EVA™ as a key indicator of annual performance in delivering value to shareholders. EVA™ is taxed operating profit less a charge for the cost of capital employed in generating that profit.

In SAB, we have calculated EVA™ using operating profit after tax, adjusted for exceptional and non-recurring items. The cost of capital has been calculated on the opening economic capital (which represents the non-interest bearing assets and liabilities of the group) after adding back the continuing businesses' asset impairments and goodwill previously eliminated against reserves. The capital charge applied on the opening economic capital is the group's weighted average cost of capital (WACC) which the group has computed at 12.5 per cent (1999 – 13 per cent). WACC takes account of individual country risks attributable to the geographies in which we operate and the overall debt profile of the group. The group's WACC has improved due to reduced emerging markets' risk premiums and lower cost of borrowings in the year under review.

Summarised below is the group's EVA™ calculation.

2000 unaudited economic profit statement (US$m)

Profit on ordinary activities before interest and taxation	**844**
Taxation on profit on ordinary activities	**(186)**
Tax deduction on financing costs	**(20)**
Adjustment for non-recurring items	**(58)**
Net operating profit after tax	**580**
Capital charge (see note below)	**(360)**
Economic profit (EVA™)	**220**

Economic balance sheet

Fixed assets	3,510
Working capital	(87)
SPV shareholding (Safari)	(560)
Accumulated adjustment for non-recurring items	192
Economic capital	**3,055**
Non-interest bearing funding	(440)
Provisions	(138)

(continued)

Net operating assets	**2,477**
Capital charge	
Opening economic capital	2,880
Weighted average cost of capital	12.5%
Capital charge	**360**

During the current year, the group again demonstrated its ability to add value, returning EVA™ of US$220 million, a slight improvement compared with the EVA™ of US$218 million in 1999. It is worth noting that it is not unusual that while groups are investing, EVA™ can temporarily fall in the short term – through higher capital charges – while acquisition benefits are still coming on stream and SAB is in such a position with our recent expansion.

(*Source*: SAB Miller plc report and accounts 2001)

13.7 The advantages of EVA

EVA has become an extremely popular strategic tool and performance measure for many global companies. Coca-Cola, Kodak, Polaroid and Unilever rank among firms that now employ this approach. Some of the advantages that these companies are seeking are as follows.

(a) *EVA makes the cost of capital visible to managers*. The model demonstrates to a divisional manager that he can improve EVA by:

- increasing earnings on existing capital
- investing in assets that give a return above the cost of capital
- reducing capital invested without reducing profit by the same percentage.

This latter point is extremely important because it causes managers to justify all investment in assets.

North Carolina Centura Bank, a large US bank, pays bonuses to its 500 salespeople based upon their individual EVAs. Each of the salespeople draws up his/her own EVA account, which might look as follows:

Individual sales revenue achieved on the bank's 56 product offerings
less
Costs incurred including:
- salary
- fringe benefits
- travel
- entertainment
- cost of support staff

- share of overhead
- cost of capital
  = individual EVA

Bonuses are paid at the rate of 10–12 per cent EVA achieved. This approach has encouraged:

- more proactive selling
- a focus on selling high-margin products
- each member of the sales team gives attention to assets that are incurring a charge, e.g. the value of their cars now carries a cost of finance. Salespeople will now want to justify to themselves the need for a big, expensive car on which they will be charged with a high cost of finance. Perhaps a cheaper car will still do the job and yield a higher EVA and a higher bonus. On the other hand, a larger car might allow them to drive more miles in a day. The point is that the decision is now made by the individual on value-adding criteria.

(b) *The principle can be applied to all sections and departments in the business.* One of the advantages of EVA is that it can be 'drilled down' throughout all departments in the organisation so that everybody buys into the new approach to adding value. More than that, managers will no longer have the incentive in an EVA company to add value in their department by taking it from another. Instead, all managers can be incentivised at a company level to ensure that, overall, EVA is encouraged.

One way of restructuring for EVA is to convert individual departments from cost centres into profit centres. For example by converting the training department into a profit centre, this raises the profile of the department (especially as it will no longer be part of the overhead) and will make it responsive to what the customers (the other departments) want, especially as they will now be paying.

(c) *EVA provides a measure of performance consistent with the objective of maximising shareholder wealth articulated in this book in the first chapter.* It measures value added in a more objective and rational way than accounting profit. Indeed, proponents of EVA argue that it is a much more reliable predictor of future share prices than accounting profit.

(d) *EVA can act as the basis of incentive schemes.* As a result, all employees as well as managers should be incentivised to increase EVA. There are two initial factors to consider in this case:

- Since EVA adds value, should bonuses based on EVA be capped?
- Should bonuses based on EVA work both ways? Consider the case example of Hays plc, the UK logistics and consulting firm found in the end of chapter questions, that operated an incentive scheme with a sting in its tail.

⊙ 13.8 The challenge of EVA

Whenever businesses introduce 'managing for value' systems like EVA into their organisations, these are the types of questions that are likely to be asked.

1 Is the rate of return being achieved covering the cost of financing the investment in the business?

2 Are remuneration schemes based on value-added performance measures rather than on accounting or other potentially dysfunctional targets?

3 Can value-added remuneration schemes be applied throughout the organisation?

4 Are any divisions destroying value? One of the big problems with large conglomerates is that the company is often not sure which parts of the business are adding value and which parts are destroying value. EVA requires firms to disaggregate their activities as much as they can so that the relative performance of the different divisions can be made more transparent. If a division is destroying value, EVA suggests that if the situation cannot be rectified, that division should be divested. EVA awards no prizes for size – it is value that is important, not size.

   This rationalisation of activities that often results from an EVA analysis is, of course, likely to produce a defensive reaction from those who may be affected. Any introduction of an EVA approach to value management, measurement and remuneration will need to be carefully managed in order to reduce negative reactions to a minimum.

5 Should cash be returned to shareholders rather than being invested elsewhere? As far as EVA is concerned, cash should be invested only if it can earn a return over and above the risk-adjusted discount rate. If there is no immediate prospect of this, the cash should be returned to shareholders either by a share buy-back or by an increase in dividends. 'Excessive' amounts of cash held will reduce value – EVA will require that there has to be a good reason for large cash balances.

6 Can the business lower its cost of finance? If this can be achieved without changing risk, this is likely to add value. This is one of the reasons why EVA encourages debt as well as equity financing. Because debt is a cheaper source of finance and it provides a tax saving, more borrowing will lower the average cost of capital. Of course, increasing debt will lower the average cost of finance only if the lower cost of debt is not cancelled out by the higher required return of equity-holders as a result of their greater financial risk.

   EVA also favours debt because its commitment to pay interest makes managers less likely to waste money and risk company failure. Because there is not the same financial commitment to pay dividends, equity finance can make managers a little complacent in their decision making. 'Debt is like a dagger; equity is like a pillow.'

Value added, not size, matters!

Stern Stewart offers the following example to demonstrate the fact that being big does not of course mean being more valuable. The following data apply to PepsiCo and Coca-Cola, the two main competitors in the carbonated drinks industry, and fierce rivals.

	Pepsi Sales	Coca-Cola Sales
1981	$7bn	$6bn
1997	$32bn	$19bn

From parity in sales in 1981, Pepsi had grown to be the bigger company in terms of global sales by 1997.

	Pepsi Invested capital	Coca-Cola Invested capital
1981	$2.9bn	$2.5bn
1997	$18.5bn	$11bn

The amount of funds invested in the two businesses had also grown significantly, but Pepsi had invested more. Thus Pepsi is the bigger company by size of sales and capital employed, but the value-added figures tell a significant story.

	Pepsi MVA	Coca-Cola MVA
1981	$1.5bn	$1.8bn
1997	$40.7bn	$158.5bn

From a similar MVA in 1981, Coca-Cola, the smaller company of the two in terms of sales and investment, had generated a massive $158.5 billion of MVA, dwarfing Pepsi's not-insignificant MVA.

However, to prove that nothing is set in stone, a survey from Stern Stewart reversed the roles of these two companies in the five years to December 2001. Stern Stewart has produced a ranking based upon a wealth added index (WAI).

This measures the change in the market capitalisation of companies between 1997 and 2001, adjusted for dividends, share issues and the required return on the company's equity (using CAPM). The following results were given (all in $m):

Top 4:	
Wal-Mart Stores	149,662
Microsoft	93,780
IBM	93,092
General Electric	91,857

Others:	
Dell computers	35,352
Nestlé	34,609
Siemans	23,066
Philips	20,858
L'Oreal	18,810
Pepsico	16,089
Xerox	−19,514
Walt Disney	−31,515
Boeing	−32,651
Deutsche Telekom	−39,868
WorldCom	−67,827
Coca-Cola	−68,211
Vodafone	−104,574

Sources: Tables on pp. 415–16 adapted from table from *Change in Market Capitalization of Companies 1997–2001, and Comparison of Coca-Cola and PepsiCo* from www.sternstewart.co.uk; Stern Stewart, *The Wealth Added Index* 2001, www.sternstewart.co.uk

13.9 **Some problems with EVA**

EVA is a simple principle which contains significant messages as a model. Nevertheless, it has limitations which need to be recognised. Significantly high EVA companies do not seem to provide any higher stock returns than other companies. One of the main reasons for this is the fact that EVA is calculated by adjusting accounting figures. Inevitably these adjustments – and there are a possible 164 of them according to Stern Stewart – produce figures which are themselves subjective in assumption and amount, just like the profit figures they are trying to replace. EVA can also be criticised for its focus on invested capital rather than current value. A £600,000 p.a. return on a building bought for £5 million gives an EVA of £100,000 if the cost of finance is 10 per cent, but if this building now has a market value of £10 million, the return is less than the cost of finance.

EVA is also difficult to implement in a meaningful way. Allocating revenues and costs can be arbitrary if calculating the EVA of a particular department. In addition, tying remuneration schemes to EVA achieved relies critically on a meaningful measure of it; otherwise, the business may create a lot of dissatisfied employees and managers.

◯13.10 A broader perspective: the balanced scorecard

In some eyes, overtly financial measures of performance suffer from several serious drawbacks. Their focus is backward-looking, and they omit recognition of the need for continuous improvement and the importance of serving customer needs. Albeit critical measures of outcomes, they overlook the supporting processes which contribute to financial success.

The balanced scorecard (BSC) was developed by Kaplan and Norton (1996) in response to growing dissatisfaction with traditional, financially-oriented performance measures. According to Kaplan and Norton, a more broadly based approach is needed to include non-financial as well as financial indicators of success – 'the BSC enables companies to track financial results while simultaneously monitoring progress in building capabilities and acquiring the intangible assets they need for future growth.'

The original BSC incorporated four groupings of performance measures (or 'metrics') – one set was 'financial' and the others were 'non-financial'. The last three areas distinguish between outcome measures (results) and 'drivers' – measures of factors which determine or drive the outcomes. This is an attempt to identify the key success factors at which the successful firm should excel. These four perspectives are shown in Figure 13.3, which portrays the scorecard used by the US company Brown & Root, the oil industry supplier.

- *The financial perspective* covers measures such as levels and growth in profitability and share price, reflecting the fundamental concerns of owners. The measures are inevitably, and quite properly, backward-looking, i.e. they highlight the financial results of past management actions.

- *The customer perspective* reflects competitive strategies, such as customer orientation, delivery times, quality and before- and after-sales service. The drivers chosen should reflect contact with customers who specify what they particularly value and require in their relationship with the firm, i.e. these factors drive the outcome measures such as indicators of customer satisfaction, market share, customer retention and profitability by customer.

- *The internal business perspective* highlights the things at which the organisation must excel – those internal processes, decisions and actions necessary to meet customer requirements. As such, it reflects the core skills and the key technology involved in adding value to the customer's business. Typical outcome measures relate to both process and product innovation and operations (cycle times, defect rates), and need sub-division into unit and departmental measures.

Balanced scorecard: summary of strategy perspectives

Strategy perspective	Example	Example of scorecard measure
Financial perspective	Shareholders' views of performance	• Return on capital • Economic value added • Sales growth • Cost reduction
Customer perspective	Customer satisfaction	• Customer satisfaction • Customer retention • Acquisition of new customers
Internal perspective	Assess quality of people and processes	• Training and development • Job turnover • Product quality • Stock turnover
Future perspective	Examine how an organisation learns and grows	• Employee satisfaction • Employee retention • Employee profitability

Figure 13.3 A version of Kaplan and Norton's balanced scorecard

Source: adapted from Lynch (2003) and also based on information from Kaplan and Norton (1996)

- *The learning and growth perspective* focuses on the infrastructure which the firm must build to foster long-term growth and improvement, i.e. the capabilities necessary to attain the long-term targets for the customer and internal business process perspectives. Outcome measures may include measures of employee satisfaction, training and retention. (Note that this is called the 'future' perspective in Figure 13.3.

Ideally, the chosen measures would be those that contributed greatest to ultimate financial success. In other words, the intention is not to divert attention from the primacy of the financial goal – without financial success, firms do not survive – but to develop measures of performance to which operating managers can more easily relate, i.e. to remove their remoteness from the financial sphere and enhance their involvement. The trick is to settle on a set of critical metrics which influence the financial results. This requires thorough understanding of the internal mechanics of the business, an understanding which many firms claim is enhanced by the process of discussing what the appropriate measures should be.

Developing and applying a BSC is not problem-free. To operate successfully, it should not only be based upon the over-riding corporate strategy but also reflect clear linkages between success drivers and achievement of financial goals. Ideally, a BSC should be prepared for individual workplaces, and even individuals, to make it meaningful at an operating level. To do this, significant investment in time and other resources is required, and while (as with budgeting) subordinate involvement in the process is helpful, the relationships between identified drivers and financial success are often difficult to establish, and tenuous. Moreover, the chosen metrics need continuous review to ensure that they remain appropriate under changing external and internal conditions.

There is also a danger that employees will over-concentrate on the items specified in the BSC, neglecting other measures which also have important implications for success, operating either singly or in conjunction with the identified metrics. This danger is compounded if employees are compensated according to performance in their particular measured areas.

Finally, there is a danger that development and distribution of a BSC may tend to obscure the primacy of the financial objective. This is why representations of the BSC usually show the financial perspective at the head of the diagram or list of metrics. Maybe 'perspective' is too anodyne a word for financial aims – 'imperative' is perhaps preferable!

13.11 Summary

Any company that sets out to manage for shareholder value must attempt to measure whether it has succeeded. At the company level, the price of the share in the market provides the market's objective verdict. Within the company, managing for value is best based upon economic profit rather than accounting profit. Although well recognised, accounting profit is in fact a highly subjective number that may not reflect either past performance or future prospects. SVA and EVA provide approaches based upon economic profit in that they both explicitly recognise a charge for financing the business (including the full cost of equity) before value can be said to be added. Both models provide management with the key areas to focus on. The conclusion is clear: based upon these principles, value can be added regardless of size.

References and further reading

Butler, A, Letza, S and Neale C W 'Linking the balance scorecard to strategy', *Long Range Planning*, Vol. 10, No. 2, April, pp. 242–53

Kaplan, S and Norton, D P (1996) *The Balanced Scorecard: Translating Strategy into Action* (Harvard Business School Press).

Knight, J (1998) *Value-Based Management* (McGraw-Hill).

'Loving debt is easy; the role of debt as a driver of value', www.anz.com.

Lynch, R (2003) *Corporate Strategy*, 3rd edn (FT Prentice Hall).

Pike, R H and Neale, C W (2003) *Corporate Finance and Investment* (Prentice Hall)

Rappaport, A (1998) *Creating Shareholder Value* (Free Press).

Stern, J and Shieley, J (2001) *The EVA Challenge* (Wiley).

Wright, P and Bachman, J (1998) *In Search of Value* (FT/Pitman Publishing).

www.sternstewart.com

Young, S and O'Byrne, S (2001) *EVA and Value-Based Management* (McGraw-Hill).

Questions and mini-case studies

1 Reflect upon how EVA could be implemented in your own organisation. Some areas that you might like to consider are:

   - how the type and/or the structure of the organisation that you work for might affect its effectiveness
   - methods of incentivising management and all other workers
   - effect on the type of activities that the business carries out
   - behavioural effects on management and the workforce of introducing such a measure of performance
   - the effects on the investment/dividend policy of the organisation.

   Because you will be from different organisations, you will have different thoughts about how useful EVA might be for your own organisation. Some of you may work in an EVA-type climate; you can give an assessment of how effective it is. Others of you may work in the public sector (such as government or local authority departments, or in health). How applicable might EVA be here?

2 The legendary investor Warren Buffett ('The Sage of Omaha') manages a fund called Berkshire Hathaway. Comment on his strategy for 'investing' to add value, as illustrated by some of his axioms:

   - 'Invest in simple businesses – we don't understand lots of technology.'
   - 'Ensure there is good management in place.'
   - 'Invest in businesses providing a good return on equity, with little or no debt.'
   - 'Invest in businesses that demonstrate consistent earning power – the fund is not interested in future projections or "turnaround" companies.'

3 (a) Briefly explain the difference between economic value added (EVA) and market value added (MVA).
   (b) Campbell plc, an ungeared British company, is one of the few biotechnology firms that have successfully commercialised products developed in-house. It has the following capital structure:

Issued share capital (par value 50p)	£200m
Share premium account	£50m
Profit & loss account	£100m
Revaluation reserve	£80m
5% preference shares	£40m

   The market price per ordinary share is currently £5 (ex-dividend).

   Last year, Campbell earned £80 million profits before tax, which is payable at 30 per cent.

The risk-free rate is 4.5 per cent, Campbell's Beta is 1.5, and investors expect the stock market to offer a premium of 7 per cent p.a. on average in future years.

Required

(i)   What EVA did Campbell achieve last year?

(ii) What is its MVA now? What is the price : earnings ratio?

(iii) Discuss the problems in using EVA as a performance criterion for a firm like Campbell.

(c) Campbell's management expects growth in sales of 10 per cent p.a. on average over the foreseeable time horizon, and the operating profit margin to be roughly constant.

   Campbell pays no dividend at present, all retentions being ploughed back into ongoing R&D. Depreciation and amortisation of fixed assets is £30 million p.a., roughly matched by ongoing replacement investment.

Required

(i)   Value the future free cash flows to obtain the shareholder value.
    (*Hint:* use the perpetuity formula.)

(ii) Suggest some possible reasons why the stock market might appear to undervalue Campbell. In your answer, explain some alternative methods of valuation.

Mini-case study - The bonus scheme that can lose you money!

In 1995, Mr Ronnie Frost, the chairman of Hays plc, the business support services company, launched a bold new executive incentivisation scheme. All senior executives (30 in total) were required to invest up to 20 per cent of their income after tax into the scheme, held as a trust fund. After five years, the trust would pay them back in Hays shares according to the following formula based upon growth in profits. The benchmark comparison used was the average annual growth in earnings of the median FTSE 100 company. (Hays itself is not a member of the FTSE 100.)

- If Hays simply matched this growth, the executives would lose their money.
- If Hays beat the benchmark by 2 per cent, executives would get shares equal in value to their accumulated stake, without interest.
- If Hays beat the benchmark by 4 per cent, executives would get shares valued at $3\frac{1}{2}$ times their accumulated stake.
- If Hays beat the benchmark by 10 per cent, executives would get shares valued at 24 times their accumulated stake.

Mr Frost, who was involved in the MBO that created Hays and its subsequent flotation, said:

> 'I want to pass on the culture of our original buy-out to the next generation. I want to motivate my key executives and lock them in at the same time.'

At the time of this proposal when the benchmark growth rate was expected to be in the range of 5–8 per cent, Hays' recent history had been to grow earnings at around 18 per cent per annum.

The scheme was backed by the company's four biggest institutional shareholders.

The proposed bonus scheme has been introduced as an extra incentive and has not been at the expense of salary increases or eligibility in other bonus schemes.

Required

(a) Highlight how this scheme differs from a share option incentive.

(b) Comment on the use of earnings (profit) as the basis of the incentive.

Self-assessment answers

13.1
Over to you.

Case study: KLM Royal Dutch Airlines

This case was contributed by Maurice Brown, Aviation Consultant, Utrecht, The Netherlands.

The case study traces the recent operating and financial history of one of Europe's leading airlines, KLM. It shows how KLM's strategic stance was largely driven by events in a shifting and often hostile environment, thus raising the question of whether firms are able to follow an unambiguous strategy through time. However, KLM, unlike many of its larger US rivals, is a survivor. Its survival may be due to its readiness to innovate and its flexibility in response to events.

Key issues in this case study are the nature of the competitive advantage enjoyed by KLM, and its suitability to the operating environment, the interplay between corporate/business strategy and financial strategy, and the relationship between a firm's operating environment and its strategic stance.

1 Historical background and overview of KLM

KLM Royal Dutch Airlines was founded on 7 October 1919, as the state airline of the Netherlands. It remains the oldest scheduled airline in the world, still flying under its original name. Its first flight and scheduled service began on 17 May 1920 with the Amsterdam to London route, which still forms a key strength of KLM's European network and operations. For the financial year 2001–2, KLM transported 16 million passengers, 490,000 tonnes of cargo and provided maintenance and engineering services to more than 20 airlines. KLM and its partner airlines now serve over 360 cities in 78 countries on six continents. KLM holdings in associate companies are shown in Table 1.

KLM's core revenue-earning activities are passenger and cargo transport, aircraft maintenance and engineering. Its main hub airport is Schiphol, Amsterdam, the fourth largest in Europe in terms of passengers and cargo traffic. KLM holds the majority of take-off and landing slots at Schiphol, and therefore accounts for the majority of the passengers and cargo traffic generated there. As domestic air travel within the Netherlands is minimal, KLM feeds extensively from its European neighbours in order to generate passenger traffic, and earns approximately 60 per cent of its revenue from transfer traffic.

KLM's shares are listed on three stock exchanges – Amsterdam, New York and Frankfurt. It was one of the first airlines in Europe to be publicly traded when it listed simultaneously on the Amsterdam (AEX) and the New York (NYSE) exchanges in May 1957. The state of the Netherlands continues

Table 1 Major KLM holdings as of 31 March 2002

Holding	KLM stake in percentage
KLM Cityhopper BV	100
KLM UK Holdings Ltd	100
KLM Catering Services Schiphol BV	100
KLM Luchtvaartschool BV	100
KLM Arbo Services BV	100
KLM Equipment Services BV	100
KLM Financial Services BV	100
Cygnific BV	100
KLM Ground Services Ltd	100
Transavia Airlines BV	80
Martinair Holland NV	50
Polygon Insurance Company Ltd	31
Kenya Airways Ltd	26
Travel Unie International Nederland NV	9

Table 2 KLM consolidated fleet as of 31 March 2002

Aircraft type	Average age	Owned	Financial lease	Operational lease
Boeing 747-400 Pax	11.3	2	3	
Boeing 747-400 Combi	8.6	2	14	
Boeing 747-300 Pax	21.8	2		
Boeing 747-300 Combi	20.9	5	1	2
Boeing 747-300 Freighter	26.3	2		
Boeing MD-11	7	2	8	
Boeing 767-300 ER				12
Boeing 757-200	8.7		3	1
Boeing 737-900	0.6	3	1	
Boeing 737-800	2.2	3	22	
Boeing 737-700				1
Boeing 737-400	11	12	2	
Boeing 737-300	9.5	4	3	13
Fokker 100	12.9	1	14	
Fokker 70	5.7	14		1
Fokker 50	11.2	4	6	12
BAe 146-300	12.3		2	6
ATR 72	4	5		
Training aircraft		27		
Total	**8.7**	**88**	**79**	**48**

Source: Tables 1 and 2 from Report and Accounts of KLM Royal Dutch Airlines, 2001/2002

to hold a 14.1 per cent minority stake. However, in turbulent aero-political conditions, the state, if required, can increase its ownership stake in the airline to 50.1 per cent.

KLM is a member of the International Air Transport Association (IATA), ranking seventh among the association's 260-plus members when measured by international revenue tonne-kilometres. In 2001, *Airline Business* ranked KLM twenty-third in the world and seventh in Europe by number of passengers transported. In air cargo, KLM is ranked eighth in the world and third in Europe by cargo tonne-kilometres transported. Its fleet configuration is shown in Table 2.

As a major airline and brand, KLM commands respect among its industry peers and with the air-travelling public, its brand and image ranks among the top echelon of the airline industry. KLM was one of the first airlines to pioneer a global airline alliance when it formed a joint working partnership with Northwest Airlines of the USA in 1989. In terms of total number of passengers transported globally, this alliance is ranked the fourth largest in the world today. In 1998, the alliance was expanded to Alitalia of Italy. However, in April 2000, after 18 months, the alliance was disbanded, as certain conditions stipulated in the partnership agreement were not satisfied.

After failed merger talks with British Airways in September 2000, KLM's management temporarily suspended its search for a European partner airline and concentrated on strengthening its European operations, and on focusing on its own development and profitability. The Chief Executive Officer at the time of writing, Leo van Wijk, has reiterated that KLM will continue to meticulously review strategic options, which will strengthen its European and global network, when the right opportunity arises.

2 A brief overview and analysis of the aviation industry

In order to understand the competitive forces affecting an airline, it is important to define the nature of the business and the market in which it operates. Airlines are involved primarily in the transportation of passengers to destinations of choice. A passenger, choosing to travel by air, places a monetary value on the benefit or advantage derived from this mode of transport. The benefits derived for a passenger may constitute time saved in arriving at their destination, price, safety, passenger comfort, reliability, and availability and frequency of service. These benefits constitute the competitive advantage that an airline is able to exploit against its competitors. The competitive advantage it can exploit is therefore determined by the financial resources at the airlines disposal and the specific target markets and/or destination it serves. Therefore, the competitive forces that affect the profitability of the airline industry in Europe may well vary from those that affect the industry in the USA.

In Europe, transport of passengers is not restricted solely to competition among airlines but also encompasses Europe's highly developed rail and road network. Therefore, in order for an airline to compete successfully within the European domestic marketplace, it needs to hold a significant competitive advantage or benefit over existing modes of transportation. European airlines should therefore price their product at fares which reflect the competitive advantage of the service they provide. The introduction of high-speed train links between major European cities has been especially problematic, as this has eroded some of the competitive advantage held by some airlines. The CEO of Air France, at the time of writing, Jean Cyril Spinetta, was quoted as saying: 'We all compete with a low-cost carrier – the TGV.' Where there is little advantage in price to be gained by travelling by air, the passenger determines whether there is a sufficient benefit in time saved to the destination and/or comfort level provided to offset the premium paid for air travel.

Competition in the airline industry and for the transport of passengers in Europe will therefore be driven by airlines that can offer passengers attractive fares, while meeting the service expectations of the passenger. Success of an airline will therefore be determined by its ability to maintain a low operating cost base and to pass on this benefit in cost saving to the passenger. Current air travel trends show that passengers are prepared to sacrifice specific expectations in service for the advantage of a lower air fare. This has led to a product and service differentiation within the airline industry, giving rise to the rapid growth of the vacation charter and low-cost airlines of Europe.

Low-cost airlines in Europe are modelled primarily on the Southwest Airlines concept, pioneered in the USA and adapted to the European market. Three low-cost airlines dominate this market segment – Ryanair, easyJet and Virgin Express. Low-cost airlines reduce costs by facilitating the direct booking of flights for the passenger, bypassing the travel agents who would collect a commission from the airline for flight booking. The elimination of meal service on flights, the standardisation of aircraft fleets and the use of alternative airports such as London Stansted, that impose lower landing and take-off charges, are all strategies used by low-cost airlines to reduce costs.

The aviation industry as a whole is not renowned for generating a high return on investment (see Table 3). It can be regarded as being both labour- and capital-intensive, it is in essence a service industry that requires large amounts of capital investment to fund its operations. Most airlines raise capital via debt financing and, when possible, through share issues. The large amounts of long-term debt needed to finance aircraft acquisition means that airlines tend to have high gearing ratios.

The limitations of debt financing have led airlines to consider alternative ways of achieving growth and dominance within the industry. This has led to the formation of strategic working alliances between airlines, allowing them to make inroads to markets where they previously may not have had a strong presence. The industry may be on the threshold of large-scale consolidation, as size and economies of scale begin to play a more important role in the future of the industry.

In order to examine the influences impacting on any industry, a PEST analysis may be undertaken. This analyses the Political, Economic, Social and Technological forces that help shape the operating environment of that industry and thus occupy the attentions of the managers attempting to define and implement strategy. A modified PEST analysis is applied to the airline industry, incorporating an extra dimension, Environmental.

Political

Most airlines began life under state ownership and management, operating in regulated markets enjoying large subsidies. Deregulation of the industry beginning in the USA in the early 1980s, and in Europe during the late 1980s and 1990s, has forced more airlines to make themselves financially viable, and upon privatisation, accountable to shareholders.

The role of the state, however, is still evident in areas such as route rights between countries. State involvement also extends to the granting of take-off and landing slots at major airports. Discussions are under way in Europe, paving the way for the privatisation of more airports and the trading of airport take-off and landing slots held by airlines. If this happens, route rights will be treated as intangible assets held by airlines, with some routes attracting a higher valuation than others. The continuing discussions between Europe and the USA on the creating of an 'open skies' policy between the two continents will impact on airlines which currently hold a domestic and national advantage, exposing them to the full forces of free market competition from foreign rivals.

Economic

The price of oil plays a significant factor in the operating cost of an airline. The purchase price of aviation fuel is usually benchmarked or denominated in US dollars. Therefore, changes in exchange rates or rising fuel prices will have an adverse effect on the cost base of an airline. In an effort to minimise the effects of changes in fuel prices, airlines tend to engage in currency hedging and forward purchasing of aviation fuel. Airlines that

Table 3 Comparative performance indicators for seven airlines

	British Airways 2001/2002 £	Continental Airlines 2001 $	Delta Airlines 2001 $	KLM 2001/2002 €	Lufthansa 2001 €	Northwest Airlines 2001 $	SAS 2001 SEK
millions							
Operating Revenues	8,340	8,969	13,879	6,532	16,690	9,905	51,433
Operating Income	(110)	144	1,602	(94)	(316)	(868)	743
Net Income	(142)	(95)	(1,216)	(156)	(633)	(423)	(1,064)
Free Cash Flow	960	(87)	(2,460)	292	(695)	(84)	(3,644)
EPS	0.13	(1.72)	(9.90)	(3.37)	(1.66)	(5.03)	(6.58)
Dividend per Share (pence/cents)	0.0	0.0	0.10	0.20	0.0	0.0	0.0
No. of Shareholders (millions)	1,077	55.2	123.2	46.8	381.6	85.3	161.8
Operating Margin (%)	(1)	2	10	(1)	(2)	(9)	1
Current Ratio	0.8	0.7	0.6	1.2	1.6	0.9	0.9
ROE (%)	(6)	(8)	(32)	(8)	(18)	(1)	(7)
millions							
Current Assets	2,559	2,144	3,567	2,519	4,962	3,790	20,355
Fixed Assets	11,103	7,647	20,038	6,524	13,244	9,165	42,407
Total	13,662	9,791	23,605	9,043	18,206	12,955	62,762

Current Liabilities	3,201	3,191	6,403	2,092	3,028	4,146	22,386
Long-term Debt	7,097	4,198	12,349	4,417	4,446	5,221	19,284
Provisions	126	243	255	277	6,863	719	5,285
Deferred Credits	1,031	998	829	265	341	3,300	15,544
Group Equity	2,207	1,161	3,769	1,992	3,528	(431)	
Total	13,662	9,791	23,605	9,043	18,206	12,955	62,499
Passenger Load Factor (%)	65	75	77	79	72	74	65
Revenue Passenger Kilometres/Miles (RPK/M) millions	106,270	61,140	101,717	56,891	90,388	73,126	23,296
Available Seat Kilometres/Miles (ASK/M) millions	151,046	84,485	147,873	72,288	126,400	98,356	35,981
Passengers (millions)	40.0	44.2	104.9	15.9	45.7	54.1	23.2
Number of Aircraft	360	352	814	215	345	428	200
Number of Staff	60,468	42,900	76,273	33,265	87,975	45,708	

Source: Report and Accounts of KLM Royal Dutch Airlines

have not sufficiently reduced their risk to the volatility of currency and fuel prices fluctuations are forced to pass on this increase in their operating costs to the passenger in the form of increased fares.

Macro-economic forces also play an important role in determining the profitability of an airline. The demand for air travel tends to peak when the economy of a country is on an uptrend. Therefore, air travel occurs at its highest in countries where the population has a high amount of disposable income available.

Social

Over time, passenger expectations have had a growing influence on the way in which airlines approach their operations. The liberalisation of the aviation industry has led to the travelling public having a greater range of airlines to choose from. This has resulted in airlines having to shape their business and competitive strategies around the expectations of passengers in order to keep the loyalty of existing passengers and/or to generate new passenger traffic. Today's passenger is more sensitive to price, yet demands a high level of customer service and passenger comfort, and more flexibility in departure times. This means that airlines face a financial dilemma: reducing operating costs, while having to invest regularly in passenger comfort and services. This is particularly so for airlines providing long-haul flights.

Technological

Technological advancement in the aerospace industry has a direct influence on the operations of the commercial aviation industry. Advancements in cockpit technology, aircraft engines and composite materials have produced aircraft that are safer, more fuel-efficient and that generate less noise than their predecessors. Savings brought about through the creating of commonalities between aircraft have also led to a reduction in maintenance and crew training costs.

Airlines that are financially able to incorporate new technology into their aircraft tend to be one step ahead of the competition and the industry's legislative curve. Many technological advances have improved the operational safety of aircraft and have later become mandatory requirements by IATA and the ICAO, the aviation industry's two governing bodies. While the initial investment in new technology may be high, it often generates operational cost savings for the airline in the medium to long term. Technological advancements that bring about no direct operational cost savings, such as safety enhancements, tend to be marketed by airlines to the flying public to garner patronage.

The commercialisation of the internet in 1996 has also had a substantial impact on the airline industry. Airlines that have developed internet reservation sites have been able to reach their customers directly. In an e-travel commerce survey carried out by PhoCusWright 2000, combined sales of internet bookings in 2000 surpassed US$12.9 billion, while reservations by online agencies reached 55 per cent and were expected to grow further. This has led to a reduction in distribution and procurement costs for airlines. Some of these cost savings have been passed on to the customer in the form of lower airfares, primarily by promoting reservations via the airline's internet site.

Environmental

The 1990s saw increasing pressure on airlines to be responsible corporate citizens regarding the community and the environment. Regulations governing the exhaust and noise pollution levels of aircraft are set by IATA and the ICAO. In Europe, some airports have already introduced stricter regulations than those stipulated by these bodies. This has been achieved by limiting the take-off and landing of aircraft to specific periods of the day, and by levying higher airport charges to airlines using aircraft that violate the airport's stated noise restrictions.

The European Union is currently reviewing a proposal for the creation of a new tax to be levied on airline fuel. The initiative is seen as an effort to make the industry more accountable for its impact on the environment. It is also seen as a way to encourage airlines to use more modern aircraft that have a less damaging impact on the environment. Such a tax proposal would impact significantly on the cost base of airlines that operate to and within Europe.

3 Where KLM stands in 2003 and how it got there

Throughout the 1990s and beyond, KLM has had to adopt certain strategies in order to maintain its profitability and increase its shareholder value. It has had to weather increased competition in both its domestic European and international markets in the face of a higher demand in service levels from passengers, at lower fares. This has led to unrelenting pressure on profit yields for all airlines. As the European aviation market continues to move towards full deregulation, KLM will have to continue to re-evaluate its strategies in order to keep abreast of the evolving marketplace.

Table 4 gives a time profile of KLM's financial and operating performance indicators.

The 1990s began with KLM facing some difficulties. After having closed a far-reaching partnership agreement with Northwest Airlines of the USA in 1989, KLM came to Northwest's assistance with a $400 million leveraged buy-out. The agreement also gave KLM a 19 per cent equity stake in the airline and included a number of seats on the management board of Northwest.

The global uncertainty which followed the 1991 Gulf War led to a downturn in air travel that had a profound effect on the airline industry. The resulting disruption to oil production in the Middle East triggered a rise in the price of oil, which led to global recession and a rise in aviation fuel prices. In 1992, KLM again came to the financial assistance of Northwest, with a $200 million loan. The loan included an optional clause which allowed KLM to increase its equity stake in Northwest to 25 per cent, when it deemed fit.

During this period, KLM had to adjust its operations to counter the effects of the increase in fuel prices. It also restructured its schedules and capacity to cope with the slowing of the global economy. The airline came under increasing criticism and scrutiny from the markets for its investment in Northwest. KLM's net income fluctuated between profitability and loss during the financial years 1990 to 1993, with the airline posting positive net income only in the financial year 1991–2. Although revenues grew during this period, rising operating expenses placed pressure on operating income. Rising financial expenses and declining results in associate firms further pressured pre-tax income. Payment of dividends to share holders was suspended through financial years 1990–1 to 1993–4, except for 1991–2.

By late 1993, world economies began to emerge from recession. Rising consumer confidence, along with falling oil prices, provided the right conditions for stimulating growth in air travel. Strong economic growth in the Asia-Pacific countries led to an increase in demand for air travel within and to the region. Northwest's strong market presence in the Asia-Pacific region from the US market helped to bolster KLM's access and impact in the region. The more stable global economic environment of the mid 1990s allowed KLM to grow its operating revenues during this period. The airline's strengthening financial performance was further enhanced by its equity investment in Northwest. Northwest's vastly improved financial performance and high customer satisfaction ratings were now being reflected in its share price. Its contribution towards KLM's financial performance was significant, so much so that it prompted one Dutch financial journalist to jokingly describe KLM as an investment company rather than an airline.

Table 4 Time profile of KLM performance indicators

KLM Consolidated Statement of Earnings	1992/1993	1993/1994	1994/1995	1995/1996	1996/1997	1997/1998	1998/1999	1999/2000	2000/2001	2001/2002
€ millions										
Traffic Revenue										
Passenger	2,600	2,693	2,867	3,006	3,305	4,452	4,431	4,563	5,017	4,810
Cargo	556	653	717	753	790	898	870	945	1,109	1,016
Other Revenue	574	589	586	568	605	714	746	788	834	706
Operating Revenue	3,731	3,935	4,169	4,327	4,700	6,064	6,047	6,296	6,960	6,532
Operating Expenses	3,687	3,723	3,819	4,122	4,791	5,696	5,854	6,201	6,683	6,626
Operating Income (Loss)	44	212	350	206	(95)	368	193	95	277	(94)
Financial Income and Expense	(158)	(173)	(128)	(87)	(98)	(127)	(82)	(112)	(138)	(134)
Result on Sale of Assets	26	7	21	43	7	22	32	(8)	27	10
Result on Sale of Holdings	(176)	4	13	145	235	111	116	54	(17)	(6)
Pretax Income (Loss) Before Extraordinary Items	(264)	50	255	307	53	374	259	29	149	224
Taxes	-	-	(36)	(59)	54	(99)	(52)	(26)	(73)	68
After Tax Income (Loss) Before Extraordinary Items	(264)	50	219	248	107	275	207	3	76	(156)
Extraordinary Items After Tax	10	-	-	-	-	726	-	334	-	-
Share of Third Parties	(0)	(3)	(6)	0	-	(1)	-	-	1	-
Net Income	(255)	47	213	248	107	1,000	207	337	77	(156)
Free Cash Flow	(189)	(80)	29	35	308	258	604	90	4	292
Stockholders Equity										
Issued Common Shares (×1,000)	52,818	85,126	85,126	86,119	68,828	69,136	61,485	46,810	46,810	46,180
Issued Participation Certificates (×1,000)	-	4,749	4,749	4,781	4,828	4,845	-	-	-	-

(continued)

Table 4 Continued

KLM

Consolidated Statement of Earnings	1992/ 1993	1993/ 1994	1994/ 1995	1995/ 1996	1996/ 1997	1997/ 1998	1998/ 1999	1999/ 2000	2000/ 2001	2001/ 2002
Key Financial Figures										
Operating Margin	1	6	9	5	(2)	7	8	2	4	(1)
Return on Equity	(26)	3	12	13	7	18	9	16	4	(8)
Net Income (Loss) as a Percentage of Operating Revenue	(6.8)	1.2	5.1	5.7	2.3	4.5	3.4	5.4	1.1	(2.4)
Interest Coverage Ratio	(0.7)	1.3	3.0	4.5	2.9	3.9	4.2	1.3	2.1	(0.7)
Capital Expenditure (Net)	503	491	427	331	49	841	(336)	89	(520)	(0.7)
Net Income Plus Depreciation	85	396	591	643	498	1,347	577	739	506	(234)
Net Debt-to-Equity Ratio	292	147	124	111	126	84	82	107	138	131
Data per Common Share										
Net Income (Loss)	(4.83)	0.46	2.31	2.66	1.37	3.68	4.02	0.04	1.61	(3.37)
Net Income (Loss) Plus Depreciation	1.60	4.35	6.50	7.00	6.67	18.21	11.33	15.79	10.81	7.08
Dividend	0.00	0.00	0.68	0.91	0.45	1.36	0.68	0.00	0.60	0.20
Stockholders' Equity	16.53	16.56	17.82	19.69	20.62	32.55	41.38	42.73	43.93	42.61
Highest Price	18.42	24.14	26.00	27.82	28.95	40.34	44.33	30.91	32.65	23.00
Lowest Price	10.03	11.34	18.88	20.87	18.29	24.50	19.65	18.25	18.15	8.50
Price at Year End	12.89	21.65	20.60	26.09	25.41	37.85	26.00	22.35	21.00	16.48

Consolidated Balance Sheet

Current Assets	1,263	2,139	2,243	2,172	2,071	2,778	2,289	2,467	2,467	2,519
Fixed Assets	4,929	5,093	5,125	5,309	5,228	5,937	6,010	6,180	6,123	6,524
Total	6,192	7,232	7,368	7,481	7,298	8,715	8,299	8,647	8,590	9,043
Current Liabilities	1,150	1,344	1,416	1,545	1,858	1,912	1,999	2,243	2,057	2,092
Long-Term Debt	3,495	3,755	3,705	3,454	3,290	3,628	3,503	3,712	3,686	4,417
Provisions	163	140	154	239	310	473	413	458	499	277
Deferred Credits	398	373	373	336	285	267	227	215	287	265
Group Equity	985	1,620	1,720	1,907	1,554	2,435	2,157	2,019	2,061	1,992
Total	6,192	7,232	7,368	7,481	7,298	8,715	8,299	8,647	8,590	9,043

Operational Data

Passenger Load Factor (%)	71	71	73	74	76	78	77	77	80	79
Revenue Passenger Kilometres/Miles (RPK/M) millions	33,064	38,605	41,767	45,531	50,350	56,171	57,334	58,903	60,047	56,891
Available Seat Kilometres/Miles (ASK/M) millions	46,773	54,213	57,193	61,196	66,361	71,802	74,155	76,054	75,222	72,288
Passengers (millions)	9.5	11.2	11.9	12.3	13.3	14.7	15	15.7	16.1	15.9
Cargo (tonnes)	422	471	541	598	612	621	578	576	502	490
Number of Aircraft	148	152	151	159	178	195	199	207	213	215
Number of Staff	28,911	29,047	29,206	31,312	31,912	35,521	33,892	35,348	33,763	33,265

Source: Report and Accounts of KLM Royal Dutch Airlines 1992–2002

During 1993–7, KLM maintained a positive net income, peaking at NLG 547 million in financial year 1995–6. Its strengthening performance led to the resumption of regular dividend payments for 1993–4. Operating income and pre-tax income during this period remained positive, except for financial year 1996–7. A rise in oil prices during 1996 placed pressure on operating expenses, resulting in an operating loss. However, a positive net income was attained due to the performance of KLM associate companies.

In 1996, tensions began to surface between the senior management of KLM and Northwest, after KLM expressed its intention to exercise its right to increase its equity stake in Northwest to 25 per cent. Top management at Northwest objected, on the grounds of what they saw as a growing control by KLM over the airline. The relationship between the management of both airlines remained strained for close to a year before finally being resolved in 1997. A new 13-year alliance agreement, strengthening the working partnership between both airlines, was signed in September 1997. Under the new agreement, KLM agreed to reduce to zero its equity stake in Northwest by 2000. The year also saw a change in leadership at KLM, with the retirement of then chief executive officer Pieter Bouw, and the succession of a long-serving KLM veteran, Leo van Wijk, to the position.

Nineteen ninety-seven saw major changes in the aviation industry which would affect Europe's major airlines. In April, Europe's aviation industry was officially opened to the forces of free market competition. In the same month, UK low-cost airline easyJet began scheduled passenger flights from London's Luton airport to Schiphol. Later that year, easyJet would file a legal suit against KLM in the European courts, on the grounds of unfair competitive practices through the use of predatory pricing. The onus was now on KLM to prove to the European Union courts that it was economically viable for the airline to offer lower fares between Amsterdam and London, and that it was operating within its established cost structures.

The growing prominence of low-cost airlines in Europe, coupled with the poor financial performance of the previous year, saw KLM adopt new strategic initiatives to improve its competitive advantage, the most noticeable being Focus 2000. The aim of this initiative was to create a simpler and more flexible organisation, while generating NLG 1 billion in cost savings by 2000. The next initiative was market-specific in nature, with KLM taking steps to strengthen its position in its domestic European market. This was achieved through a combination of organic growth, equity purchases, and alliance partnerships with a number of smaller European domestic airlines. To consolidate the airline's image and service to the customer, the new partner airlines adopted the KLM name and colour scheme. The year also saw the use of internet technology enter the mainstream.

Airlines were quick to realise the technology's potential to expand their customer base while reducing costs. KLM was early in adopting the new technology and committed substantial financial resources to providing a complete range of internet-related services.

The last quarter of 1997 saw the beginning of the Asian economic crises. The collapse of the Asian economies led to a substantial decline in passenger traffic originating from within these markets. Airlines' heavy targeting of the Asia-Pacific market during the early 1990s meant that the region was now facing excess capacity in a shrinking market for air travel. KLM's response was similar to that taken by other airlines. Excess capacity was redirected to other markets, primarily to the North American market. The resulting overcapacity to this region led to price discounting and a subsequent decline in revenue yields as airlines tried to improve their passenger load factors. This was not only limited to passenger traffic but was repeated in the air cargo segment of the industry.

In spite of this, 1997–8 was a good year for KLM as it recorded its best operating income and pre-tax income for the whole decade. This was achieved by strongly growing passenger revenues while tempering growth in operating expenses. The airline's net income was further enhanced by an extraordinary gain of NLG 1,600 million, resulting from the sale of part of its equity holding in Northwest. The financial markets were impressed with KLM's performance, sending the airlines share price to an unprecedented high of NLG 89. KLM-Northwest's efforts were recognised in February 1998 by receiving 'The Airline of the Year Award' by the influential US magazine, *Air Transport World*.

The financial year 1998–9 saw the airline industry still struggling to cope with the fall-out from the Asian economic crisis. As airlines fought to remain profitable, the situation at KLM was further compounded by the introduction of new noise, take-off and landing restrictions at the Schiphol hub. The impact of the new restrictions would be financially disadvantageous for KLM and raised questions by its partner airline, Northwest, as to the future of their alliance.

Despite the difficulties faced by KLM, the airline would announce during 1998 the start of a new and highly promising alliance partnership with Alitalia of Italy which would give KLM the opportunity to increase its passenger base while developing new routes. There was also the opportunity to considerably strengthen its cargo operations. The agreement would see KLM bring not only its management expertise and discipline to Alitalia but also substantial financial and human resources. The success and development of the alliance was underpinned by commitments by the Italian government to the development of the new Malpensa airport in Milan and the privatisation of Alitalia before the end of June 2000. The announcement of the alliance was well received by the markets, being seen as a positive strategic step by KLM to strengthen both its European and international position within the industry.

For the financial year, KLM's operating revenues remained flat compared with the previous year, with operating expenses showing a moderate increase. With no extraordinary gains for the year, net profit compared with the previous year seemed somewhat lacklustre. The KLM share price fluctuated wildly during the year, at one point reaching a new high of NLG 98, yet recording a low of NLG 43.

The remainder of 1999 would prove to be a testing time for KLM. The spring announcement by OPEC of new oil production quotas led to a gradual but constant rise in oil prices throughout the year. As with most airlines in the industry, KLM announced that it would increase cargo and passenger fares to offset increased fuel costs. A strong US dollar and costs incurred for IT projects, related to the turn of the millennium, would also impact negatively on the airline's cost base. Steps were also taken to reduce capacity through changes to the airline's route network.

KLM embarked on a number of strategic initiatives during the year in order to firm up its shareholder value and competitive position in the industry. In spring 1999, it announced it would increase its stake in the Dutch scheduled and charter airline Martinair, to take a controlling interest in the company. This initiative was abandoned only a month later, with the realisation that obtaining regulatory approval from the European Union competition authorities would prove difficult, with no guarantee of success. During this period, the airline announced to the markets that it had plans to reduce the number of shares outstanding by 25 per cent. This would be accomplished through a reverse share split and capital redemption to shareholders to commence in the autumn of that year.

Alliance plans with Alitalia were also announced to be on track, with the continued integration between passenger and cargo operations and commercial plans. The alliance was granted regulatory approval by the European Union competition authorities in the summer, and plans to begin the global joint venture under a unified management structure would begin by 1 November of the same year. In early autumn, KLM announced that its UK division would launch its own low-cost airline brand, to be called 'Buzz'. The airline would begin operations in January 2000 and would be based at London Stansted airport. The new airline would initially begin services to seven European destinations; however, it was made clear to the markets that Buzz would not operate on the London to Amsterdam route. The formation of the airline was seen as KLM's response to the upsurge of the low-cost airlines in Europe, and the threat posed by British Airway's low-cost alternative airline Go, also based at Stansted. In December 1999, KLM became the first airline to receive the ISO 14001 certification for its environmental care system.

By quarter four, the harsh economic environment was evident in the company's financial performance. It responded with a further increase in passenger fares and the launch of a new company-wide cost reduction programme in February 2000 to be called Operation Baseline. The aim was to focus on the key factors which had pressured the airline's results during the financial year, and to negate their impact in the upcoming financial year. Operating and pre-tax results for the year remained positive but were substantially reduced by a 6 per cent rise in operational expenses and a further rise in financial expenses. However, the airline did maintain a sizeable net profit but this was due solely to extraordinary gains made by the sale of its stake in the airline reservation system, Galileo International. In view of the company's financial performance and the continuing harsh economic climate in prospect, the board decided to suspend payment of dividends.

The financial year 2000–1 began with the termination of the airline's alliance with Alitalia in April. The alliance was contingent on the development of Milan's new airport Malpensa into a hub for both airlines. However, uncertainty concerning the future of Malpensa and the privatisation of Alitalia constituted too high a business risk for KLM, so its management decided to terminate the alliance. The airline's strategic focus for the financial year remained on cost management, margin improvement and a stronger focus on markets and customers. This was achieved thorough staff reductions, reducing capacity and route rationalisation. In June, KLM and British Airways entered into discussions about combining operations and services possibly leading to a full partnership agreement. However, the talks ended in September without agreement. In spite of a 60 per cent increase in fuel prices and an overall 8 per cent increase in operating expenses, the airline managed to grow its operating income compared with the previous year. With a 7 per cent seat yield increase, KLM achieved a positive net income of €77 million.

KLM remained committed to its continuing strategy of cost reduction and downsizing capacity in the financial year 2001–2. It announced a fleet renewal strategy which would see older aircraft being replaced with newer and more efficient equipment. Several new strategic partners were signed up, including Malev Hungarian Airlines, Malaysian Airlines and Continental Airlines in the USA. An important cargo agreement partnership was also concluded with TNT Express delivery. The year saw the restructuring of its domestic partnerships, the disposal of equity in Braathens to Scandinavian Airlines, and the ending of its partnership with Eurowings on routes to the

German market. Routes from both airlines were transferred to KLM Cityhopper, while Transavia (a Dutch airline, partly owned by KLM) developed its own low-cost, no-frills service within its existing operation called BASIQAIR. The launch of BASIQAIR with services from Schiphol to leisure destinations in Europe provided direct competition to no-frills carrier easyJet.

By far the greatest blow to the industry that year came on September 11th in the form of the terrorist attacks on the World Trade Centre in New York and the Pentagon in Washington DC, using scheduled passenger aircraft. The resulting loss in confidence in air travel severely damaged the global aviation industry. KLM like all other global airlines was faced with an instant decline in passenger and freight traffic and reduced maintenance outsourcing revenues. The industry was also faced with an immediate and mandatory increase in accident and terrorism insurance. KLM responded by further cutbacks to capacity to those already planned, and a reduction in work hours and number of employees. Passenger and cargo traffic declined by 4 per cent and 8 per cent respectively, while total revenues for the year declined by 6 per cent and expenses increased by 1 per cent. KLM went on to make an operating loss of €94 million and a net loss of €156 million for the financial year, yet maintained a dividend payment for the year.

The reduction in air travel continued throughout 2002. The decline in passenger traffic and the fierce competitive environment exposed weaknesses in strategy and finances of several prominent major airlines. In Europe, the resulting crisis in travel led to the insolvency and liquidation of Swissair, and Sabena of Belgium, while in the USA, which accounts for about 50 per cent of world air traffic and movements, it precipitated the bankruptcy filings of two major carriers, US Airways and United Airlines. The combined total loss of US airlines as a result of 9/11 was US $18 billion. The year 2002 was also clouded by looming hostilities in Iraq which had a negative effect on passenger traffic and reduced the chances of a fast recovery for the industry. However, while the traditional airlines failed to deliver profits, low-cost airlines like Ryanair and easyJet recorded double-digit growth in passenger and net profitability. Ryanair became the largest airline in Europe by stock market value. For the financial year 2002–3, KLM, like most major carriers, was not expected to improve significantly its net profitability. In February 2003, after announcing a review of its strategic position and of the low-cost airline market, KLM sold Buzz to Ryanair for approximately €30 million.

4 Prospects for future shareholder value creation by KLM

As a publicly traded company, KLM is obliged to pursue a policy of creating and delivering shareholder value. Its management is therefore answerable to its shareholders, and its policies and strategies should therefore be geared to exploiting market opportunities that promise value for shareholders. Its commitment to creating shareholder value is expressed in its articles of association and forms the core of its business strategy. Key elements of this strategy are a strong focus and concentration of resources on core business, a growth strategy based on internal capacity growth and alliances, divestment of non-core holdings, outsourcing of non-core competences, rigorous cost control, and sound business and financial risk management.

KLM's aim of growing shareholder value involves commitment to achieving the following financial targets:

- an average return on equity of 14 per cent
- an average return on capital employed of 12 per cent
- a net debt-to-equity ratio of 100 per cent.

Over time, KLM has employed a number of strategies aimed at attaining these financial targets. This has involved focusing on strategies aimed at influencing the airline's value drivers. A number of these strategies have been planned and controlled initiatives, while others have emerged out of responses to unforeseen changes in the operating environment.

While KLM has achieved measurable success in restoring shareholder value through the use of its cost-reduction strategies, such strategies do have their limitations. In an interview with *Air Transport World Magazine*, CEO Leo van Wijk reinforced this point.

> 'We are are nearing the end of what we can do in-house. Maybe we still can find a million euros left and a million right, but the hundreds of millions needed to create a decent shareholder return in this industry can only be found through consolidation.'

The real challenge ahead for KLM is to find new and innovative ways of generating shareholder value. The events of 9/11 and the second Gulf War have served only to hasten the need for rationalisation and consolidation of the airline industry.

Future strategies aimed at unlocking shareholder value at KLM will have to incorporate fundamental structural changes in the way the airline faces the aviation industry and how it secures and positions its resources to attain these goals. As with all business strategies, timing, speed and execution are critical to its implementation and success. However, strategy creation is effective only once the following questions have been answered: 'Where and what do we want to be as a company or organisation, and is the environment in which we operate conducive to realising and achieving these goals?' KLM could be described as operating within three major environments that could be classified as:

- global, socio-economic
- the transport/aviation industry
- KLM's internal organisational.

The creation and analysis of the strategy should be a progressive one, beginning with an analysis of the bigger working environmental picture and identifying what trends are occurring globally and their potential effects on Europe and the Netherlands. The second working environment focus should be on the transport industry as a whole and the airline industry specifically, as a subset of the transport industry. Changes occurring in the transport environment should be charted and compared with the global economic environment. The third working environment focuses on KLM and the internal changes occurring within the organisation. Each working environment should be analysed with the use of appropriate analytical tools, taking into consideration varying elements such as economic, technological, political, social and competitive forces.

Airlines should therefore design and apply their strategic focus in the context of the changes occurring in these three working environments. Throughout the analysis and the creation of its strategy, links between the three working environments should be identified and their impact on the airline determined. By charting the changes occurring in the various environments, an airline will be in a better position to foresee and manage the changes that will impact on the aviation industry and on its value drivers. This allows it to take a more proactive stance to strategy design and implementation.

Companies that succeed in creating shareholder value are those that have taken a more proactive stance to changes occurring in their environment. This has been achieved by harnessing strengths to exploit changes, while taking steps to minimise their impact on the firm's weaknesses. Instances where KLM has been proactive in strategy design and implementation, such as its visionary alliance formation with Northwest Airlines and with its introduction and use of the internet, have been successful in creating shareholder value and passenger loyalty in the long run. The future financial success of KLM and its ability to create further shareholder value will lie in its ability to create savings though intelligent operational efficiencies, either organically or through acquisitions and alliances, while focusing on its core activities.

Questions

Using the figures provided and the tables in the Appendix to this case, analyse the following questions:

1 Determine the return on investment achieved by KLM as compared to other airlines.

2 Analyse the movements in KLM gearing ratios. Why do airlines tend to have such high gearing? Can you infer anything about KLM's operating gearing?

3 Determine the TSR achieved by KLM over this period.

4 Identify the key value drivers for airline companies in general, and for KLM in particular.

5 Explain the type of competitive advantage achieved and exploited by KLM.

6 Why do you think KLM could not make a go of Buzz?

7 In order to achieve its objectives, what performance indicators do you think KLM should closely monitor?

8 Do you think KLM has followed a clear, consistent strategy? Or has strategic decision-making merely been driven by events?

Appendix to the KLM case

Five-year overview of six competing airlines, 1997–2001/2

Northwest Airlines

	1997	1998	1999	2000	2001
$ millions					
Operating Revenues	10,133	8,928	10,133	11,240	9,905
Operating Income	1,157	(191)	714	569	(868)
Net Income	597	(285)	300	256	(423)
Free Cash Flow	721	(1,025)	286	314	(84)
EPS ($)	5.29	(3.48)	3.26	2.77	(5.03)
Dividend per Share (cents)	0	0	0	0	0
No. of Shareholders (millions)	97	84.0	84.6	85.1	85.3
Operating Margin (%)	11	(2)	7	5	(9)

Current Ratio	0.8	0.5	0.6	0.6	0.9
ROE (%)	(2)	(1)	(6)	1	(1)

$ millions

Current Assets	2,598	1,870	2,063	2,014	3,790
Fixed Assets	6,738	8,411	8,521	8,863	9,165
Total	9,336	10,281	10,584	10,877	12,955
Current Liabilities	3,272	3,462	3,577	3,518	4,146
Long-term Debt	2,491	4,279	3,891	3,545	5,221
Provisions	1,641	825	869	790	719
Deferred Credits	2,243	2,192	2,299	2,793	3,300
Group Equity	(311)	(477)	(52)	231	(431)
Total	9,336	10,281	10,584	10,877	12,955
Passenger Load Factor (%)	74	73	75	77	74
Revenue Passenger Miles (RPM) millions	72,031	66,738	74,168	79,128	73,126
Available Seat Miles (ASM) millions	96,964	91,311	95,446	103,356	98,356
Passengers (millions)	54.7	50.5	56.1	58.7	54.1
Number of Aircraft	405	409	410	424	428
Number of Staff	48,984	50,565	51,823	53,491	45,708

Delta Airlines

	1997	1998	1999	2000	2001
$ millions					
Operating Revenues	13,868	14,312	14,883	16,741	13,879
Operating Income	1,628	1,803	1,318	1,637	1,602
Net Income	934	1,078	1,208	828	(1,216)
Free Cash Flow	98	592	(1,315)	(498)	(2,460)
EPS Diluted ($)	6.02	6.87	8.52	7.05	(9.90)
Dividend per Share (cents)	0.10	0.10	0.10	0.10	0.10
No. of Shareholders (millions)	149.0	141.5	132.9	123.0	123.2
Operating Margin (%)	13	14	10	11	10
Current Ratio	0.7	0.7	0.5	0.6	0.6
ROE (%)	0.31	0.27	0.27	15	(32)
$ millions					
Current Assets	2,867	3,362	2,672	3,205	3,567
Fixed Assets	9,874	11,241	14,078	18,726	20,038
Total	12,741	14,603	16,750	21,931	23,605

Current Liabilities	4,083	4,577	5,392	5,245	6,403
Long-term Debt	4,644	5,079	5,791	10,251	12,349
Provisions	156	175	195	234	255
Deferred Credits	851	749	924	858	829
Group Equity	3,007	4,023	4,448	5,343	3,769
Total	12,741	14,603	16,750	21,931	23,605
Passenger Load Factor (%)	72	73	72	73	69
Revenue Passenger Miles (RPM) millions	99,689	103,342	106,165	112,998	101,717
Available Seat Miles (ASM) millions	138,831	142,154	147,073	154,974	147,837
Passengers (millions)	103.2	105.3	110.1	119.9	104.9
Number of Aircraft	553	569	676	831	814
Number of Staff	65,383	70,846	74,000	83,952	76,272

Lufthansa German Airline

	1997	1998	1999	2000	2001
€ millions					
Operating Revenues	11,049	11,737	12,794	15,200	16,690
Operating Income	1,090	1,455	1,012	1,482	(316)
Net Income	551	732	630	689	(633)
Free Cash Flow	1356	773	(432)	444	(695)
EPS (Euros)	1.44	1.92	1.65	1.81	(1.66)
Dividend per Share (cents)	0.46	0.56	0.56	0.60	0.00
No. of Shareholders (millions)	381.6	381.6	381.6	381.6	381.6
Operating Margin (%)	11	14	9	11	(2)
Current Ratio	2.7	2.8	2.1	1.8	1.6
ROE (%)	20	22	17	17	(18)
€ millions					
Current Assets	3,712	3,579	3,216	3,728	4,962
Fixed Assets	7,948	8,713	9,672	11,082	13,244
Total	11,660	12,292	12,888	14,810	18,206
Current Liabilities	1,400	1,267	1,512	2,053	3,028
Long-term Debt	2,988	2,375	2,300	2,408	4,446
Provisions	4,307	5,076	5,083	5,943	6,863
Deferred Credits	272	260	259	241	341
Group Equity	2,693	3,314	3,734	4,165	3,528
Total	11,660	12,292	12,888	14,810	18,206
Passenger Load Factor(%)	72	73	73	74	72

Revenue Passenger Kilometres (RPK) millions	70,581	74,668	84,443	92,160	90,388
Available Seat Kilometres (ASK) millions	98,750	102,354	116,383	123,800	126,400
Passengers (millions)	37.2	40.5	43.8	47.0	45.7
Number of Aircraft	286	302	306	331	345
Number of Staff	55,520	54,867	66,207	69,523	87,975

Continental Airlines

	1997	1998	1999	2000	2001
$ millions					
Operating Revenues	7,194	7,927	8,639	9,899	8,969
Operating Income	716	701	615	729	144
Net Income	385	383	455	342	(95)
Free Cash Flow	303	178	117	836	(87)
EPS Diluted $	4.99	5.02	6.20	5.45	(1.72)
Dividend per share (cents)	0	0	0	0	0
No. of Shareholders	77.2	76.3	73.4	62.8	55.2
Operating Margin (%)	8	8	7	8	2
Current Ratio	0.8	1.0	0.9	0.8	0.7
ROE (%)	42	32	29	29	(8)
$ millions					
Current Assets	1,728	2,354	2,606	2,459	2,144
Fixed Assets	4,102	4,732	5,617	6,742	7,647
Total	5,830	7,086	8,223	9,201	9,791
Current Liabilities	2,285	2,442	2,775	2,980	3,191
Long-term Debt	1,568	2,480	3,055	3,374	4,198
Provisions	242	111	–	692	243
Deferred Credits	819	860	800	995	998
Group Equity	916	1,193	1,593	1,160	1,161
Total	5,830	7,086	8,223	9,201	9,791
Passenger Load Factor (%)	71	72	73	75	72
Revenue Passenger Miles (RPM) millions	47,906	53,910	60,022	64,161	61,140
Available Seat Miles (ASM) millions	67,576	74,727	81,946	86,100	84,485
Passengers (millions)	41.2	43.6	45.5	46.8	44.2
Number of Aircraft	337	363	363	371	352
Number of Staff	39,300	43,900	51,275	54,300	42,900

British Airways

	1997/ 1998	1998/ 1999	1999/ 2000	2000/ 2001	2001/ 2002
£ millions					
Operating Revenues	8,642	8,892	8,940	9,278	8,340
Operating Income	504	442	84	380	(110)
Net Income	365	171	(62)	67	(142)
Free Cash Flow	897	1,123	1,040	794	960
EPS Diluted (pence)	0.35	0.16	0.06	0.06	0.13
Dividend per Share (pence)	0.17	0.18	0.18	0.18	0.0
No. of Shareholders (millions)	1,132	1,054	1,074	1,085	1,077
Operating Margin (%)	6	5	1	4	(1)
Current Ratio	0.8	0.9	0.8	0.8	0.8
ROE (%)	16	7	(3)	3	(6)
£ millions					
Current Assets	2,303	2,645	2,659	2,550	2,559
Fixed Assets	8,997	10,179	10,856	11,148	11,103
Total	11,300	12,824	13,515	13,698	13,662
Current Liabilities	2,821	3,048	3,366	3,308	3,201
Long-term Debt	5,128	6,356	6,728	6,901	7,097
Provisions	30	65	81	70	126
Deferred Credits	971	1,006	1,047	1,094	1,031
Group Equity	2,350	2,349	2,293	2,325	2,207
Total	11,300	12,824	13,515	13,698	13,662
Passenger Load Factor (%)	71	70	70	71	70
Revenue Passenger Kilometres (RPK) millions	113,045	125,951	127,425	123,197	106,270
Available Seat Kilometres (ASK) millions	159,921	178,820	183,158	172,524	151,046
Passengers(millions)	40.9	45.0	46.5	44.4	40.0
Number of Aircraft	330	335	366	338	360
Number of Staff	60,770	64,051	65,640	62,844	60,468

Scandinavian Airline Systems

	1997	1998	1999	2000	2001
MSEK					
Operating Revenues	38,928	40,946	43,746	47,540	51,433
Operating Income	4,118	4,115	2,747	3,723	743
Net Income	1,666	2,134	1,379	2,135	(1,064)
Free Cash Flow	1,252	385	2,481	(378)	(3,644)
EPS (SEK)	10.13	12.97	8.38	12.98	(6.58)
Dividend per Share (SEK)	4.00	4.00	4.00	4.50	0.00
No. of Shareholders (millions)	164.5	164.5	164.5	164.5	161.8
Operating Margin (%)	11	10	6	8	1
Current Ratio	1.4	1.0	1.0	0.9	0.9
ROE (%)	12	14	9	12	(7)
MSEK					
Current Assets	14,661	13,982	15,628	16,003	20,355
Fixed Assets	23,003	26,491	28,587	33,422	42,407
Total	37,664	40,473	44,215	49,425	62,762
Current Liabilities	10,474	13,926	15,652	16,879	22,386
Long-term Debt			10,194	10,132	19,284
Provisions	377	354		4,763	5,285
Deferred Credits					
Group Equity	13,719	15,340	16,011	17,520	15,544
Total	24,570	29,620	41,857	49,294	62,499
Passenger Load Factor (%)	65	66	64	67	65
Revenue Passenger Kilometers					
(RPK) million	20,339	20,883	21,707	22,923	23,296
Available Seat Kilometers					
(ASK) millions	31,333	31,766	33,910	34,189	35,981
Passengers (millions)	20.7	21.7	22.2	23.4	23.2
Number of Aircraft	178	185	190	203	200
Number of Staff	25,057	27,071	30,310	30,943	31,035

Source: Prepared by the author from airlines' Annual Report and Accounts and respective internet sites, including *Report and Accounts of: British Airways 2001 and 1997 to 2001; Delta Air Lines 2001 and 1997 to 2001; Continental Airlines 2001 and 1997 to 2001; Deutsche Lufthansa AG 2001 and 1997 to 2001; SAS Group 2001 and 1997 to 2001; Northwest Airlines 2001 and 1997 to 2001*

APPENDICES

Appendix 1

Present value interest factor (PVIF) per £1.00 due at the end of n years for an interest rate of:

n	1%	2%	3%	4%	5%	6%	7%	8%	9%	10%
1	0.99010	0.98039	0.97007	0.96154	0.95238	0.94340	0.93458	0.92593	0.91743	0.90909
2	0.98030	0.96117	0.94260	0.92456	0.90703	0.89000	0.87344	0.85734	0.84168	0.82645
3	0.97059	0.94232	0.91514	0.88900	0.86384	0.83962	0.81630	0.79383	0.77218	0.75131
4	0.96098	0.92385	0.88849	0.85480	0.82270	0.79209	0.76290	0.73503	0.70843	0.68301
5	0.95147	0.90573	0.86261	0.82193	0.78353	0.74726	0.71299	0.68058	0.64993	0.62092
6	0.94204	0.88797	0.83748	0.79031	0.74622	0.70496	0.66634	0.63017	0.59627	0.56447
7	0.93272	0.87056	0.81309	0.75992	0.71068	0.66506	0.62275	0.58349	0.54703	0.51316
8	0.92348	0.85349	0.78941	0.73069	0.67684	0.62741	0.58201	0.54027	0.50187	0.46651
9	0.91434	0.83675	0.76642	0.70259	0.64461	0.59190	0.54393	0.50025	0.46043	0.42410
10	0.90529	0.82035	0.74409	0.67556	0.6139	0.55839	0.50835	0.46319	0.42241	0.38554
11	0.89632	0.80426	0.72242	0.64958	0.58468	0.52679	0.47509	0.42888	0.38753	0.35049
12	0.88745	0.78849	0.70138	0.62460	0.55684	0.49697	0.44401	0.39711	0.35553	0.31863
13	0.87866	0.77303	0.68095	0.60057	0.53032	0.46884	0.41496	0.36770	0.32618	0.28966
14	0.86996	0.75787	0.6612	0.57747	0.50507	0.44230	0.38782	0.34046	0.29925	0.26333
15	0.86135	0.74301	0.64186	0.55526	0.48102	0.41726	0.36245	0.31524	0.27454	0.23939
16	0.85282	0.72845	0.62317	0.53391	0.45811	0.39365	0.33873	0.29189	0.25187	0.21763
17	0.84438	0.71416	0.60502	0.51337	0.43630	0.37136	0.31657	0.27027	0.23107	0.19784
18	0.83602	0.70016	0.58739	0.49363	0.41552	0.35034	0.29586	0.25025	0.21199	0.17986
19	0.82774	0.68643	0.57029	0.47464	0.39573	0.33051	0.27651	0.23171	0.19449	0.16351
20	0.81954	0.67297	0.55367	0.45639	0.37689	0.31180	0.25842	0.21455	0.17843	0.14864
21	0.81143	0.65978	0.53755	0.43883	0.35894	0.29415	0.24151	0.19866	0.16370	0.13513
22	0.80340	0.64684	0.52189	0.42195	0.34185	0.27750	0.22571	0.18394	0.15018	0.12285
23	0.79544	0.63414	0.50669	0.40573	0.32557	0.26180	0.21095	0.17031	0.13778	0.11168
24	0.78757	0.62172	0.49193	0.39012	0.31007	0.24698	0.19715	0.15770	0.12640	0.10153
25	0.77977	0.60953	0.47760	0.37512	0.29530	0.23300	0.18425	0.14602	0.11597	0.09230

n	11%	12%	13%	14%	15%	16%	17%	18%	19%	20%	n
1	0.90090	0.89286	0.88496	0.87719	0.86957	0.86207	0.85470	0.84746	0.84034	0.83333	1
2	0.81162	0.79719	0.78315	0.76947	0.75614	0.74316	0.73051	0.71818	0.70616	0.69444	2
3	0.73119	0.71178	0.69305	0.67497	0.65752	0.64066	0.62437	0.60863	0.59342	0.57870	3
4	0.65873	0.63552	0.61332	0.59208	0.57175	0.55229	0.53365	0.51579	0.49867	0.48225	4
5	0.59345	0.56743	0.54276	0.51937	0.49718	0.47611	0.45611	0.43711	0.41905	0.40188	5
6	0.53464	0.50663	0.48032	0.45559	0.43233	0.41044	0.38984	0.37043	0.35214	0.33490	6
7	0.48166	0.45235	0.42506	0.39964	0.37594	0.35383	0.33320	0.31392	0.29592	0.27908	7
8	0.43393	0.40388	0.37616	0.35056	0.32690	0.30503	0.28487	0.26604	0.24867	0.23257	8
9	0.39092	0.36061	0.33288	0.30751	0.28426	0.26295	0.24340	0.22546	0.20897	0.19381	9
10	0.35218	0.32197	0.29459	0.26974	0.24718	0.22668	0.20804	0.19106	0.17560	0.16151	10
11	0.31728	0.28748	0.26070	0.23662	0.21494	0.19542	0.17781	0.16192	0.14756	0.13459	11
12	0.28584	0.25667	0.23071	0.20756	0.18691	0.16846	0.15197	0.13722	0.12400	0.11216	12
13	0.25751	0.22917	0.20416	0.18207	0.16253	0.14523	0.12989	0.11629	0.10420	0.09346	13
14	0.23199	0.20462	0.18068	0.15971	0.14133	0.12520	0.11102	0.09855	0.08757	0.07789	14
15	0.20900	0.18270	0.15989	0.14010	0.12289	0.10793	0.09489	0.08352	0.07359	0.06491	15
16	0.18829	0.16312	0.14150	0.12289	0.10686	0.09304	0.08110	0.07078	0.06184	0.05409	16
17	0.16963	0.14564	0.12522	0.10780	0.09393	0.08021	0.06932	0.05998	0.05196	0.04507	17
18	0.15282	0.13004	0.11081	0.09456	0.08080	0.06914	0.05925	0.05083	0.04367	0.03756	18
19	0.13768	0.11611	0.09806	0.08295	0.07026	0.05961	0.05064	0.04308	0.03669	0.03130	19
20	0.12403	0.10367	0.08678	0.07276	0.06110	0.05139	0.04328	0.03651	0.03084	0.02608	20
21	0.11174	0.09256	0.07680	0.06383	0.05313	0.04430	0.03699	0.03094	0.02591	0.02174	21
22	0.10067	0.08264	0.06796	0.05599	0.04620	0.03819	0.03162	0.02622	0.02178	0.01811	22
23	0.09069	0.07379	0.06014	0.04911	0.04017	0.03292	0.02702	0.02222	0.01830	0.01509	23
24	0.08170	0.06588	0.05322	0.04308	0.03493	0.02838	0.02310	0.01883	0.01538	0.01258	24
25	0.07361	0.05882	0.04710	0.03779	0.03038	0.02447	0.01974	0.01596	0.01292	0.01048	25

n	21%	22%	23%	24%	25%	26%	27%	28%	29%	30%	n
1	0.82645	0.81967	0.81301	0.80645	0.80000	0.79365	0.78740	0.78125	0.77519	0.76923	1
2	0.68301	0.67186	0.66098	0.65036	0.64000	0.62988	0.62000	0.61035	0.60093	0.59172	2
3	0.56447	0.55071	0.53738	0.52449	0.51200	0.49991	0.48819	0.47684	0.46583	0.45517	3
4	0.46651	0.45140	0.43690	0.42297	0.40960	0.39675	0.38440	0.37253	0.36111	0.35013	4
5	0.38554	0.37000	0.35520	0.34111	0.32768	0.31488	0.30268	0.29104	0.27993	0.26933	5
6	0.31863	0.30328	0.28878	0.27509	0.26214	0.24991	0.23833	0.22737	0.21700	0.20718	6
7	0.26333	0.24859	0.23478	0.22184	0.20972	0.19834	0.18766	0.17764	0.16822	0.15937	7
8	0.21763	0.20376	0.19088	0.17891	0.16777	0.15741	0.14776	0.13878	0.13040	0.12259	8
9	0.17986	0.16702	0.15519	0.14428	0.13422	0.12493	0.11635	0.10842	0.10109	0.09430	9
10	0.14864	0.13690	0.12617	0.11635	0.10737	0.09915	0.09161	0.08470	0.07836	0.07254	10
11	0.12285	0.11221	0.10258	0.09383	0.08590	0.07869	0.07214	0.06617	0.06075	0.05580	11
12	0.10153	0.09198	0.08339	0.07567	0.06872	0.06245	0.05680	0.05170	0.04709	0.04292	12
13	0.08391	0.07539	0.06780	0.06103	0.05498	0.04957	0.04472	0.04039	0.03650	0.03302	13
14	0.06934	0.06180	0.05512	0.04921	0.04398	0.03934	0.03522	0.03155	0.02830	0.02540	14
15	0.05731	0.05065	0.04481	0.03969	0.03518	0.03122	0.02773	0.02465	0.02194	0.01954	15
16	0.04736	0.04152	0.03643	0.03201	0.02815	0.02478	0.02183	0.01926	0.01700	0.01503	16
17	0.03914	0.03403	0.02962	0.02581	0.02252	0.01967	0.01719	0.01505	0.01318	0.01156	17
18	0.03235	0.02789	0.02408	0.02082	0.01801	0.01561	0.01354	0.01175	0.01022	0.00889	18
19	0.02673	0.02286	0.01958	0.01679	0.01441	0.01239	0.01066	0.00918	0.00792	0.00684	19
20	0.02209	0.01874	0.01592	0.01354	0.01153	0.00983	0.00839	0.00717	0.00614	0.00526	20
21	0.01826	0.01536	0.01294	0.01092	0.00922	0.00780	0.00661	0.00561	0.00476	0.00405	21
22	0.01509	0.01259	0.01052	0.00880	0.00738	0.00619	0.00520	0.00438	0.00369	0.00311	22
23	0.01247	0.01032	0.00855	0.00710	0.00590	0.00491	0.00410	0.00342	0.00286	0.00239	23
24	0.01031	0.00846	0.00695	0.00573	0.00472	0.00390	0.00323	0.00267	0.00222	0.00184	24
25	0.00852	0.00693	0.00565	0.00462	0.00378	0.00310	0.00254	0.00209	0.00172	0.00152	25

Appendix 2

Present value interest factor for an annuity (PVIFA) of £1.00 for n years for an interest rate of:

n	1%	2%	3%	4%	5%	6%	7%	8%	9%	10%	n
1	0.9901	0.9804	0.9709	0.9615	0.9524	0.9434	0.9346	0.9259	0.9174	0.9091	1
2	1.9704	1.9416	1.9135	1.8861	1.8594	1.8334	1.8080	1.7833	1.7591	1.7355	2
3	2.9410	2.8839	2.8286	2.7751	2.7232	2.6730	2.6243	2.5771	2.5313	2.4868	3
4	3.9020	3.8077	3.7171	3.6299	3.5459	3.4651	3.3872	3.3121	3.2397	3.1699	4
5	4.8535	4.7134	4.5797	4.4518	4.3295	4.2123	4.1002	3.9927	3.8896	3.7908	5
6	5.7955	5.6014	5.4172	5.2421	5.0757	4.9173	4.7665	4.6229	4.4859	4.3553	6
7	6.7282	6.4720	6.2302	6.0020	5.7863	5.5824	5.3893	5.2064	5.0329	4.8684	7
8	7.6517	7.3254	7.0196	6.7327	6.4632	6.2098	5.9713	5.7466	5.5348	5.3349	8
9	8.5661	8.1622	7.7861	7.4353	7.1078	6.8017	6.5152	6.2469	5.9852	5.7590	9
10	9.4714	8.9825	8.5302	8.1109	7.7217	7.3601	7.0236	6.7101	6.4176	6.1446	10
11	10.3677	9.7868	9.2526	8.7604	8.3064	7.8868	7.4987	7.1389	6.8052	6.4951	11
12	11.2552	10.5753	9.9539	9.3850	8.8632	8.3838	7.9427	7.5361	7.1607	6.8137	12
13	12.1338	11.3483	10.6349	9.9856	9.3925	8.8527	8.3576	7.9038	7.4869	7.1034	13
14	13.0038	12.1062	11.2960	10.5631	9.8986	9.2950	8.7454	8.2442	7.7861	7.3667	14
15	13.8651	12.8492	11.9379	11.1183	10.3796	9.7122	9.1079	8.5595	8.0607	7.6061	15
16	14.7180	13.5777	12.5610	11.6522	10.8377	10.1059	9.4466	8.8514	8.3125	7.8237	16
17	15.5624	14.2918	13.1660	12.1656	11.2740	10.4772	9.7632	9.1216	8.5436	8.0215	17
18	16.3984	14.9920	13.7534	12.6592	11.6895	10.8276	10.0591	9.3819	8.7556	8.2014	18
19	17.2261	15.6784	14.3237	13.1339	12.0853	11.1581	10.3356	9.6036	8.9501	8.3649	19
20	17.8571	16.3514	14.8774	13.5903	12.4622	11.4699	10.5940	9.8181	9.1285	8.5136	20
21	18.0457	17.0111	15.4149	14.0291	12.8211	11.7640	10.8355	10.0168	9.2922	8.6487	21
22	19.6605	17.6580	15.9368	14.4511	13.1630	12.0416	11.0612	10.2007	9.4424	8.7715	22
23	20.4559	18.2921	16.4435	14.8568	13.4885	12.3033	11.2722	10.3710	9.5802	8.8832	23
24	21.2435	18.9139	16.9355	15.2469	13.7986	12.5503	11.4693	10.5287	9.7066	8.9847	24
25	22.0233	19.5234	17.4131	15.6220	14.0939	12.7833	11.6536	10.6748	9.8226	9.0770	25

n	20%	19%	18%	17%	16%	15%	14%	13%	12%	11%	n
1	0.8333	0.8403	0.8475	0.8547	0.8621	0.8696	0.8772	0.8850	0.8929	0.9009	1
2	1.5278	1.5465	1.5656	1.5852	1.6052	1.6257	1.6467	1.6681	1.6901	1.7125	2
3	2.1065	2.1399	2.1743	2.2096	2.2459	2.2832	2.3216	2.3612	2.4018	2.4437	3
4	2.5887	2.6486	2.6901	2.7432	2.7982	2.8550	2.9137	2.9745	3.0373	3.1024	4
5	2.9906	3.0576	3.1272	3.1993	3.2743	3.3522	3.4331	3.5172	3.6048	3.6959	5
6	3.3255	3.4098	3.4976	3.5892	3.6847	3.7845	3.8887	3.9976	4.1114	4.2305	6
7	3.6046	3.7057	3.8115	3.9224	4.0386	4.1604	4.2883	4.4226	4.5638	4.7122	7
8	3.8372	3.9544	4.0776	4.2072	4.3436	4.4873	4.6389	4.7988	4.9676	5.1461	8
9	4.0310	4.1633	4.3030	4.4506	4.6065	4.7716	4.9464	5.1317	5.3282	5.5370	9
10	4.1925	4.3389	4.4941	4.6586	4.8332	5.0188	5.2161	5.4262	5.6502	5.8892	10
11	4.3271	4.4865	4.6560	4.8364	5.0286	5.2337	5.4527	5.6869	5.9377	6.2065	11
12	4.4392	4.6105	4.7932	4.9884	5.1971	5.4206	5.6603	5.9176	6.1944	6.4924	12
13	4.5327	4.7147	4.9095	5.1183	5.3423	5.5931	5.8424	6.1218	6.4235	6.7499	13
14	4.6106	4.8023	5.0081	5.2293	5.4675	5.7245	6.0021	6.3025	6.6282	6.9819	14
15	4.6755	4.8759	5.0916	5.3242	5.5755	5.8474	6.1422	6.4624	6.8109	7.1909	15
16	4.7296	4.9377	5.1624	5.4053	5.6685	5.9542	6.2651	6.6039	6.9740	7.3792	16
17	4.7746	4.9897	5.2223	5.4746	5.7487	6.0472	6.3729	6.7291	7.1196	7.5488	17
18	4.8122	5.0333	5.2732	5.5339	5.8178	6.1280	6.4674	6.8399	7.2497	7.7016	18
19	4.8435	5.0700	5.3162	5.5845	5.8575	6.1982	6.5504	6.9380	7.3658	7.8393	19
20	4.8696	5.1009	5.3527	5.6278	5.9288	6.2593	6.6231	7.0248	7.4694	7.9633	20
21	4.8913	5.1268	5.3837	5.6648	5.9731	6.3125	6.6870	7.1016	7.5620	8.0751	21
22	4.9094	5.1486	5.4099	5.6964	6.0113	6.3587	6.7429	7.1695	7.6446	8.1757	22
23	4.9245	5.1668	5.4321	5.7234	6.0442	6.3988	6.7921	7.2297	7.7184	8.2664	23
24	4.9371	5.1822	5.4509	5.7465	6.0726	6.4338	6.8351	7.2829	7.7843	8.3481	24
25	4.9476	5.1951	5.4669	5.7662	6.0971	6.4641	6.8729	7.3300	7.8431	8.4217	25

n	21%	22%	23%	24%	25%	26%	27%	28%	29%	30%	n
1	0.8264	0.8197	0.8130	0.8065	0.8000	0.7937	0.7874	0.7813	0.7752	0.7692	1
2	1.5095	1.4915	1.4740	1.4568	1.4400	1.4235	1.4074	1.3916	1.3761	1.3609	2
3	2.0739	2.0422	2.0114	1.9813	1.9520	1.9234	1.8956	1.8684	1.8420	1.8161	3
4	2.5404	2.4936	2.4483	2.4043	2.3616	2.3202	2.2800	2.2410	2.2031	2.1662	4
5	2.9260	2.8636	2.8035	2.7454	2.6893	2.6351	2.5827	2.5320	2.4830	2.4356	5
6	3.2446	3.1669	3.0923	3.0205	2.9514	2.8850	2.8210	2.7594	2.7000	2.6427	6
7	3.5079	3.4155	3.3270	3.2423	3.1611	3.0833	3.0087	2.9370	2.8682	2.8021	7
8	3.7256	3.6193	3.5179	3.4212	3.3289	3.2407	3.1564	3.0758	2.9986	2.9247	8
9	3.9054	3.7863	3.6731	3.5655	3.4631	3.3657	3.2728	3.1842	3.0997	3.0915	9
10	4.0541	3.9232	3.7993	3.6819	3.5705	3.4648	3.3644	3.2689	3.1781	3.1090	10
11	4.1769	4.0354	3.9018	3.7757	3.6564	3.5435	3.4365	3.3351	3.2388	3.1473	11
12	4.2785	4.1274	3.9852	3.8514	3.7251	3.6060	3.4933	3.3868	3.2859	3.1903	12
13	4.3624	4.2028	4.0530	3.9124	3.7801	3.6555	3.6381	3.4272	3.3224	3.2233	13
14	4.4317	4.2646	4.1082	3.9616	3.8241	3.6949	3.5733	3.4587	3.3507	3.2487	14
15	4.4890	4.3152	4.1530	4.0013	3.8593	3.7261	3.6010	3.4834	3.3726	3.2682	15
16	4.5364	4.3567	4.1894	4.0333	3.8874	3.7509	3.6228	3.5026	3.3896	3.2832	16
17	4.5755	4.3908	4.2190	4.0591	3.9099	3.7705	3.6400	3.5177	3.4028	3.2948	17
18	4.6079	4.4187	4.2431	4.0799	3.9279	3.7861	3.6536	3.5294	3.4130	3.3037	18
19	4.6346	4.4415	4.2627	4.0967	3.9424	3.7985	3.6642	3.5386	3.4210	3.3105	19
20	4.6567	4.4603	4.2786	4.1103	3.9539	3.8083	3.6726	3.5458	3.4271	3.3158	20
21	4.6750	4.4756	4.2916	4.1212	3.9631	3.8161	3.6792	3.5514	3.4319	3.3198	21
22	4.6900	4.4882	4.3021	4.1300	3.9705	3.8223	3.6844	3.5558	3.4356	3.3230	22
23	4.7025	4.4985	4.3106	4.1371	3.9764	3.8273	3.6885	3.5592	3.4384	3.3254	23
24	4.7128	4.5070	4.3176	4.1428	3.9811	3.8312	3.6918	3.5619	3.4406	3.3272	24
25	4.7213	4.5139	4.3232	4.1474	3.9849	3.8342	3.6943	3.5640	3.4423	3.3286	25

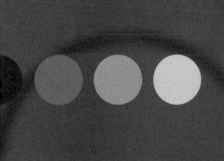

GLOSSARY AND USEFUL TERMS

Accounting rate of return (ARR) a profitability ratio, commonly defined as (average annual profit/average investment) – but other definitions abound. Also known as return on capital employed (ROCE).

Acquirers firms that make takeovers. Also, **Predators**.

Agency costs costs that owners (principals) have to incur in order to ensure that their agents (managers) make financial decisions consistent with their best interests.

Agency relationships the separation of ownership and control whereby an agent runs an operation on behalf of a principal, e.g. managers run companies on behalf of shareholders. Conflicts of interest can emerge that may involve agency costs as the owners attempt to 'manage' the managers.

Aggressive stocks shares whose returns vary by a larger proportion than overall market returns. Their Betas exceed 1.0.

Annuity an investment activity having identical payments or receipts in future time periods.

Arbitrage the profitable exploitation of divergence between the prices in different markets, e.g. different exchange rates for the same currency. Hence, **Arbitrageur**.

Articles of association a document drawn up at the formation of an enterprise, detailing the rights and obligations of shareholders and directors.

Asset (or **Activity**) **Beta** the inherent systematic riskiness of a firm's operations, before allowing for gearing. Also known as firm Beta, company Beta, or ungeared Beta.

Asset-backed securities bonds issued on the security of a stream of highly certain income flows, e.g. mortgage payments to a bank, out of which interest payments are made.

Asset-stripping the selling off the assets of a taken-over firm, often in order to recoup the initial outlay.

Bank loan usually fixed-term borrowing with a pre-agreed schedule of interest and capital prepayments. Interest is usually payable on the initial amount borrowed, regardless of the falling balance as repayments are made.

Beta (or **Beta coefficient**) measurement of the responsiveness of the returns on individual securities to variations in the return on the overall market portfolio.

Bird-in-the-hand fallacy the mistaken belief that dividends paid early in the future are worth more than dividends expected in later time periods, simply because they are nearer in time.

Bonds any form of borrowing that firms can undertake by selling a medium- or long-term security, committing them to specific repayment dates, at fixed or variable interest.

Bonus (or **Scrip**) **issues** issues of free shares to existing shareholders in lieu of, or in addition to, cash dividends. Reflected in lower reserves, hence the alternative label, capitalisation issues.

Break-Up Value (BUV) the value that can be obtained by selling off the firm's assets piecemeal to the highest bidders.

Call option an option that gives the right to buy the underlying security or asset.

Capital strictly, the funds invested in a firm by shareholders when they purchase ordinary shares, but often used to indicate all forms of equity, and often to refer to any form of finance, whether equity or debt (as in 'the capital market').

Capital allowances tax allowances given on the depreciation of particular assets, such as plant and machinery. Such allowances can be set against taxable profit thereby reducing tax liability. Presently, available most commonly at 25 per cent p.a. on a reducing balance basis.

Capital asset any investment that offers a prospective return, with or without risk. However, in finance, the term is applied to securities in general, but to ordinary shares in particular.

Capital Asset Pricing Model (CAPM) a theory used to explain how efficient capital markets value securities. The expected returns on any security will correspond to its level of systematic risk.

Capital expenditure expenditure on fixed assets, i.e. those that remain on the balance sheet for more than one accounting period.

Capital gains tax is paid on realising an increase in share value. Capital gains are currently treated as income in the UK.

Capital gearing the mixture of debt and equity in firm's capital structure, which influences variations in shareholders' profits in response to sales and EBIT variations. Also called **balance sheet gearing**.

Capital rationing a situation of limited access to funds so that a company is unable to invest in all of the good projects available to it. Can be 'hard' (imposed by the external market) or 'soft' (imposed internally by the company itself).

Capital structure the mixture of debt and equity resulting from decisions on financing operations.

Capitalisation the procedure of converting (by discounting) a series of future cash flows into a single capital sum. Also, applied to the (market) capitalisation of a firm, i.e. its equity.

Capitalisation rate a discount rate used to convert a series of future cash flows into a single capital sum.

Cash cycle (or **cash conversion cycle**) the period of time after cash has been paid to creditors before cash is received from debtors after the goods have been held and sold.

Cash discounts discounts given to customers who pay their invoices within a certain period of time.

Characteristics line (CL) relates the periodic returns on a security to the returns on the market portfolio. Its slope is the Beta of the security. The regression model used to estimate Betas is called the market model.

Chartists see technical analysts.

Classical tax system a system which initially taxes company profits, and then also taxes any dividend income. This double taxation of dividends thus provides an incentive to retain profits.

Clientele effect the notion that a firm attracts investors by establishing a set dividend policy that suits a particular group of investors.

Competitive advantages the business advantages companies enjoy over their competitors in the product market through the exploitation of core competences, enabling them to achieve abnormal returns.

Contra-cyclical a term applied to an investment whose returns fluctuate in opposite ways to general trends in business activity, i.e. contrary to the cycle.

Convertible loan stock a debenture that can be converted into ordinary shares, often on attractive terms, usually at the option of the holder.

Core competence distinctive skills and technologies that a business owns that can be exploited in the product market.

Cost of capital the cost of company long-term finance – incorporating the two main costs: debt and equity. Often used as a discount rate in investment appraisal.

Cost of debt the yield a firm would have to offer if undertaking further borrowing at current market rates.

Cost of equity the minimum rate of return a firm must offer owners to compensate for waiting for their returns, and for bearing risk.

Counter-party risk the risk that the opposite party to a contract defaults on its obligations.

Coupon rate the rate of interest shown on a debenture or a gilt indicating the amount paid each year as annual interest. It is based on the nominal value of the security – usually £100 in the UK. Hence, a debenture with a 6% coupon rate will pay £6 a year until redemption.

Creative accounting the manipulation of accounting figures usually to exaggerate profit.

Credit control the process of managing debtor collection.

Credit insurance the insurance of some, or all, debtor accounts against non-payment.

Critical mass the minimum size of firm thought necessary to compete effectively, e.g. to finance R&D.

Currency futures contract a commitment to deliver a specific amount of foreign exchange at a specified future date at an agreed price incorporated in the contract. Contracts can be traded on an exchange in standard sizes.

Debentures in law, any form of borrowing that commits a firm to pay interest and repay capital. In practice, usually applied to long-term loans that are secured on a firm's assets.

Debt borrowing, short or long term, usually with an interest commitment.

Debt capacity the maximum amount of debt finance, and hence interest payments that a business can support without incurring financial distress.

Deep discount the gap between market value (equities) and face value (bonds) and the selling price of the security in question.

Default the failure by a borrower to adhere to a pre-agreed schedule of interest and/or capital payments on a loan.

Defensive stock a share that generates returns that vary by a smaller proportion than overall market returns on average. Its Beta is less than one.

Discount rate the rate of interest representing the required return used to convert future cash amounts to a present equivalent value.

Discounted payback using the present value of future cash inflows, the number of years required to pay back the cost of the original investment.

Diversifiable risk the unsystematic risk that can be removed by efficient portfolio diversification.

Diversification extension of a firm's activities into new and unrelated fields; or including a variety of different securities in an investment portfolio. The fundamental motive for diversification is to reduce exposure to fluctuations in economic activity.

Divestment the selling off of parts of a conglomerate business (often to leave just the core business).

Dividend irrelevance the theory that, when a firm has access to external finance, it is irrelevant to its value whether it pays a dividend or not.

Dividend valuation model a way of assessing the value of shares by capitalising the future dividends. With an assumption of growing dividend payments, it becomes the **Dividend growth model**.

Dividend yield dividend paid per ordinary share (including both interim and final payments) divided by current share price.

Earnings before interest, tax, depreciation and amortisation (EBITDA) a rough measure of operating cash flow; effectively, operating profit with depreciation added back.

Earnings dilution the dampening effect on EPS of issuing further shares at a discount as in a rights issue.

Earnings per share (EPS) profit attributable to ordinary shares (i.e. after interest, tax, preference share dividends and minority interest) divided by the total number of shares in issue.

Earnings yield EPS divided by current share price. Sometimes, it refers to expected or 'prospective' EPS, becoming the 'prospective earnings yield'. It is a simple way of expressing the investor's return on investment on the share.

EBIT earnings (i.e. profits) before interest and taxation. Also, PBIT.

Economic order quantity (EOQ) model a model that calculates the most economic amount of stock to order each time an order is placed.

Economic value added (EVA) post-tax accounting profit generated by a firm reduced by a charge for using the equity (usually, cost of equity times market value of equity).

Economies of scale cost efficiencies, e.g. bulk-buying, stemming from an increase in a firm's size of operation.

Efficient market a market in which prices fully and instantaneously reflect all available relevant information. Three forms have been defined – weak, semi-strong and strong.

Enhanced scrip dividends scrip alternatives offered to investors that are worth more than the alternative cash payment.

Enterprise value the value of the whole firm, i.e. the value of its assets.

Equities ordinary shares.

Equity (or **Owners' equity**) long-term finance for companies provided by the owners, either directly by the sale of shares (especially ordinary shares), or indirectly by the reinvestment of retained profits.

Equity Beta indicates the systematic riskiness attaching to the returns on ordinary shares. It equates to the asset Beta for an ungeared firm, or is adjusted upwards to reflect the extra riskiness of shares in a geared firm, i.e. the 'geared Beta'.

Equity premium the return on equities in excess of that on risk-free assets such as government stock hence, the reward for bearing risk, or risk premium.

Ex-dividend (**ex-div.** or **xd**) when subsequent purchasers no longer qualify for the forthcoming dividend payment on a share. Until this point, the shares are quoted cum-dividend (with dividend).

Exercise price the fixed price at which derivatives, such as options, can be bought and sold in the future.

Expected net present value (ENPV) the theoretical average NPV if an investment were carried out many times; found by multiplying all possible NPVs by their probabilities and summing the resulting products.

Factoring the process of obtaining finance using debtors as security. The factor may also collect outstanding accounts payable and administer debtors' accounts.

Financial distress in narrow terms, the difficulty that a firm encounters in meeting obligations to creditors. More broadly, it refers to the adverse consequences, e.g. restrictions on behaviour, that result from excessive borrowing by a firm.

Financial gearing the ratio of the value of a firm's debt to the value of its equity finance.

Financial leverage the percentage change in profits attributable to ordinary shareholders relative to the percentage change in operating profit (before interest); the higher the amount of interest payable, the higher the leverage.

Financial risk the risk incurred by equity-holders resulting from firms having to pay interest on their debt finance regardless of what levels of profit are achieved.

First mover's advantage the advantages enjoyed by being the first into the market e.g. reputation, ability to set a premium price, control over resources, etc.

Five Forces Model see **Porter's Five Forces Model**.

Fixed charge this applies when a lender can force the sale of pre-specified company's assets in order to recover debts in the event of default on interest and/or capital payments.

Floating charge applies when a lender can force the sale of any, i.e. unspecified, of a company's assets in order to recover debts in the event of default on interest and/or capital payments.

Floating Rate Note (FRN) a bond issue where interest is paid at a variable rate.

Foreign direct investment (FDI) investment in fixed assets located abroad for the purpose of operating distribution and/or production facilities.

Foreign exchange exposure the risk of loss stemming from exposure to adverse foreign exchange rate movements.

Forward contract (Forward rate agreement) a legal obligation to deliver (pay) a specified amount of currency (rate of interest) at some specified future date. The rate of exchange (interest) is fixed at the date of the contract.

Forward rate of exchange the rate fixed for transactions that involve delivery and settlement at some specified future date.

Free cash flow (FCF) a firm's cash flow free of obligatory payments. Strictly, it is cash flow after interest, tax and replacement investment, although it is measured in many other ways in practice.

Fundamental analysis thorough analysis of all relevant information relating to a firm's business operations, and hence its financial prospects.

Geared Beta the Beta attaching to the ordinary shares of a geared firm that bear a risk higher than the firm's basic activity.

Gearing see financial gearing and operating gearing.

Gilts short for gilt-edged securities, or government stock which used to be printed on paper with a gold-coloured surround.

Global companies firms that serve a range of overseas markets both by exporting and by direct investment.

Going concern value (GCV) the value of a firm's assets as stated in the accounts assuming that the firm will continue to operate as a viable entity as it stands, i.e, as an ongoing activity.

Government stock securities issued by the government to finance its expenditures. If held to redemption, they are regarded as 'risk-free' and the rate of return earned on them is regarded as a 'risk-free rate of interest'.

Hedging attempting to minimise the risk of loss stemming from exposure to adverse contingencies, e.g. foreign exchange rate movements.

Home-made dividends cash released when an investor realises part of his investment in a firm in order to supplement his/her income.

Horizontal integration the acquisition of a competitor in pursuit of market power and/or scale economies.

Hybrid a security that embodies features of both equity and debt, and is thus difficult to classify under either category.

Imputation system an integrated system of corporate and personal taxation that offers shareholders a tax credit (maybe in full or partially) in respect of company tax already paid when assessing income taxation due on dividends paid out.

Income gearing the proportion of EBIT pre-empted by prior interest commitments, i.e. the inverse of interest cover.

Information asymmetry the imbalance in access to information about a firm's affairs as between directors and owners.

Information content the extra, unstated intelligence that investors deduce from the formal announcement by a firm of any financial news, i.e. what people read 'between the lines', or 'financial body language'.

Initial public offering (IPO) the first issue of shares by an existing, or a newly formed firm to the general public.

Institutional investors the pension funds, insurance companies, investment trusts, finance companies and unit trusts that between them now own over 60 per cent of all company shares on the London Stock Exchange.

Internal rate of return (IRR) the rate of interest which discounts an investment's future cash flows to an NPV of zero. If the IRR of an investment exceeds the investor's required return, accepting it will increase wealth.

Introduction method whereby shares of a private company can obtain a quotation on the stock market without releasing any shares.

Investment appraisal application of the various methods to assist the investment decision.

Invoice discounting a service less comprehensive than factoring, involving the sale for cash of approved invoices to a financial institution.

Issuing house a financial institution, often a merchant bank, that arranges a company share issue.

Joint venture a strategic alliance involving the formal establishment of a new marketing and/or production operation involving two or more partners.

Junk bonds high risk, unsecured, high-yielding bonds often issued by companies to finance takeovers. Also, called 'sub-investment grade' bonds.

Just-in-time (JIT) an operating system built around the delivery of supplies only as and when required in order to reduce levels of stockholding.

Leverage the amplification of changes in operating profit and profit after tax relative to changes in sales stemming from the existence of 'fixed' expenses and interest charges.

Linear interpolation calculation of the IRR of a project based on two NPVs using two different discount rates.

Management buy-in (MBI) acquisition of an equity stake in an existing firm by new management that injects expertise as well as capital into the enterprise.

Management buy-out (MBO) acquisition of an existing firm by its existing management usually involving substantial amounts of straight debt and mezzanine finance.

Marginal efficiency of investment (MEI) a schedule listing available investment in declining order of attractiveness.

Market capitalisation the market value of a firm's equity, i.e. number of ordinary shares issued times market price.

Market efficiency the extent to which any market incorporates information into prices.

Market portfolio includes all securities traded on the stock market weighted by their respective capitalisations. Usually, a more limited portfolio such as the FT All Share Index is used as a proxy.

Matching offsetting a currency inflow in one currency, e.g. a stream of revenues, by a corresponding stream of costs, thus leaving only the profit element unmatched. Firms may also match operating cash flows against financial flows, e.g. a stream of interest and capital payments resulting from overseas borrowing in the same currency.

Mergers pooling by firms of their separate interests into a newly constituted business, each party participating on roughly equal terms.

Mezzanine finance subordinate or secondary debt (i.e. gets paid after main debt finance such as bank loans and debentures), unsecured, higher-risk, higher-yield debt often used to finance management buy-outs (MBOs). Includes hybrids such as convertibles that embody both debt and equity features.

Money market the market for funds with maturity (i.e. having to be repaid) of less than one year.

Multi-National Company (MNC), or **Multi-National Enterprise (MNE)** one that conducts a significant proportion of its operations abroad.

Mutually exclusivity where only one selection can be made from a set of (mutually exclusive) alternatives.

Net Asset Value (NAV) the value of the owners' stake in a firm, found by deducting total liabilities (i.e. debts) from total assets.

Net debt a firm's net borrowing including both long-term and also short-term debt, offset by cash holdings. Expressed either in absolute terms, or in relation to owner's equity.

Neutral stocks generate returns that vary by the same proportion as overall market returns. Their Betas equal 1.0. Also called market-tracking investments.

New issue market the market for selling and buying newly issued securities. It has no physical existence.

Nil-paid rights price the market price at which the right to buy ordinary shares in a rights issue can be traded separately from the security in question.

Off-balance sheet financing any liability that does not have to be shown on a company balance sheet, and which will not therefore be included in a balance sheet gearing ratio, e.g. operating leasing.

Offer for sale the sale of company shares to the general public by an issuing house.

Operating cycle the time elapsing between the cash outflow to creditors for materials and the cash inflow from debtors from the sale of the final product. Also known as the cash cycle.

Operating gearing relates to the importance of fixed expenses within a firm's overall cost structure. It increases the responsiveness of operating profit to sales variations (also known as operating leverage).

Operating gearing factor a ratio that compares the operating gearing of a particular activity, e.g. a product division within a larger firm, to that of a larger entity such as the whole firm.

Operating lease a method of hiring assets over periods less than the expected lifetime of those assets.

Opportunity cost the value of the alternative forgone by undertaking a particular course of action.

Optimal capital structure the financing mix that minimises the overall cost of finance and maximises market value.

Ordinary shares (USA: **Common stock**) shares sold to finance a company's activities - also known as equity or risk capital.

Overcapitalisation a business characterised by too much long-term finance and too heavy an investment in fixed assets relative to the level of activity.

Overdraft short-term finance extended by banks subject to instant recall. A maximum deficit balance is pre-agreed and interest is paid on the actual daily balance outstanding.

Overtrading a feature of fast-growing businesses whereby there is insufficient long-term finance and liquidity for the level of activity.

Owners' equity in accounting terms, simply the NAV, but can also be expressed in market value terms, i.e. share price times number of ordinary shares issued, or capitalisation.

Payback period the number of years it takes for the net cash inflows of an investment to cover the original cost.

Perpetuity an investment with the same annual cash inflow or outflow each year for ever.

Placing the sale of shares to a select number of institutions and investors.

Porter's Five Forces Model a set of five factors that collectively determine the strength of competition, and hence the prospects for earning abnormal profits, within any market.

Portfolio a combination of investments – securities or physical assets – into a single bundled investment. A well-diversified portfolio has the potential capacity to lower the investor's exposure to the risk of fluctuations in the overall economy.

Portfolio effect the tendency for the risk on a well-diversified holding of investments to fall below the risk of most, and sometimes all, of its individual components.

Preference shares hybrid securities that rank ahead of ordinary shares for dividend payment, usually at a fixed rate, and also in distributing the proceeds of a liquidation. Normally, they carry no voting rights. Found in many forms, e.g. convertible, cumulative, participating.

Present values the equivalent value now of a future cash flow(s). Found by discounting the future cash flow(s) by a discount rate.

Price : earnings (P : E) ratio price per share divided by earnings per share; an important market ratio indicating the expected future prospects of a company – the higher the P : E ratio, the higher the market's rating of the firm.

Primary debt (or **Senior debt**) debt (usually secured) having priority of repayment.

Probability tree a pattern of outcomes with associated probabilities that may occur from a decision (hence decision tree) through future time periods.

Profitability index the NPV of a project relative to its original cost. Used to rank projects under capital rationing.

Prospectus document giving financial and other details of a company; required when a share issue is being made to the public.

Provision a notional deduction from profits to allow for some highly likely future financial contingency. In accounting terms, an appropriation of profit after taxation.

Proxy (or **surrogate**) **Beta** is used when the firm has no market listing and thus no Beta of its own. It is taken from a comparable listed firm, and adjusted as necessary for relative financial gearing levels. Hence, proxy discount rate.

Public company a limited company that can sell shares to the public.

Public issue direct sale of shares by a company to the market without the use of an issuing house.

Put option an option that gives the right to sell the underlying security or asset.

Record day the cut-off date beyond which further entrants to the shareholder register do not qualify for the next dividend.

Redeemables securities (debentures always, preference shares sometimes, and ordinary shares very rarely) that will be eventually be repaid by the company.

Relevant risk is systematic risk, that component of total risk taken into account by the stock market when assessing the appropriate risk premium for determining capital asset values.

Reserve the funds that shareholders invest in a firm in addition to their initial subscription of capital.

Residual theory of dividends asserts that firms should pay cash dividends only when they have financed new investments. It assumes no access to external finance.

Retained earnings reserves represented by retention of profits. Often (confusingly) labelled 'profit and loss account' on the balance sheet. Also called revenue reserves.

Revolving credit facility this enables a firm to borrow up to a pre-specified amount usually over 1–5 years. As repayments of outstanding balances are made, the loan facility is replenished.

Rights issues sales of further ordinary shares (usually) below market price to existing shareholders who are usually able to sell the rights on the market should they not wish to purchase additional shares.

Risk-free assets securities with zero variation in overall returns, i.e. their future nominal returns are certain.

Risk premium the additional return demanded by investors above the risk-free rate to compensate for exposure to systematic risk.

Safety stock stock held to reduce the risk of a stock-out if order lead times and/or usage of stock differ from that expected.

Scrip dividends dividends that are offered to investors in lieu of the equivalent cash payment. Also called a scrip alternative.

Securitisation the technique of packaging otherwise non-tradable claims, such as future cash flows from mortgage contracts, into a traded security.

Security an instrument issued by a firm or other organisation in order to raise finance, and (usually) market-traded, and (usually) carrying the right to enjoy a stream of income.

Security Market Line (SML) an upward-sloping relationship tracing out all combinations of expected return and systematic risk, available in an efficient market. All traded securities locate on this schedule. In effect, the Capital Market Line adjusted for systematic risk.

Sensitivity analysis the technique of assessing the impact on a project's NPV of potential changes in the values of variables fed into the calculation.

Share buyback the repurchase by a firm of its existing shares, either via the market or by a tender to all shareholders.

Shareholder Value Analysis (SVA) a way of assessing the inherent value of the equity in a company, taking into account the sources of value creation and the time horizon over which the firm enjoys competitive advantages over its rivals.

Shareholder wealth maximisation the assumption that the primary financial objective of any company is to maximise firm value for the ultimate benefit of shareholders.

Share premium account a reserve set up to account for the issue of new shares at a price above their par value.

Share splits (USA: **Stock splits**) a way of reducing the share price of 'heavyweight' shares (prices above £10). Achieved by reducing the par value of issued shares, e.g.

two shares of par value 50p to replace one share at £1 is a one-for-one split, halving the share price.

Signalling the use of financial announcements to deliver more information than is actually spelt out in detail.

Simulation the use of different cash flow estimates and their respective probabilities to calculate a range of possible NPVs. Monte Carlo simulation uses computer-generated random numbers to derive the frequency distribution of possible NPVs.

Specific risk the variability in the return on a security due to exposure to risks relating only to that security, e.g. risk of losing market share due to poor marketing decisions.

Spot rate the rate of exchange quoted for transactions involving immediate settlement. Hence, spot market.

Spread the difference between the exchange rates (interest rates) at which banks buy and sell foreign exchange (lend and borrow).

Stakeholders interested groups in any organisation that may wish to influence objectives and decisions.

Stakeholder approach to management the approach whereby decisions are made only after a careful analysis of the effect of the decision on all stakeholders.

Stock turnover the number of times a year average stock is sold.

Straight, (or **plain vanilla**) **debt** fixed rate borrowing with no additional features such as convertibility rights or warrants.

Striking, (or **strike**) **price** the price at which all shares are cleared in a tender; all applicants usually pay this price.

Synergies gains in revenues or cost savings resulting from takeovers and mergers, not resulting from firm size, i.e. stemming from a 'natural match' between two sets of assets.

Systematic risk variability in a security's return due to exposure to risks affecting all firms traded in the market (hence, market risk), e.g. the impact on a business due to changes in macro-economic variables such as exchange rates, the economic cycle and inflation.

Takeover acquisition of the share capital of another firm, resulting in its identity being absorbed into that of the acquiror.

Tax breaks tax concessions, e.g. relief of interest payments against profits tax.

Tax credit see imputation system.

Tax shelter a method of sheltering profits from corporate tax. It is measured by the discounted value of future tax savings generated by the available tax reliefs. Also called a **tax shield**.

Taxable written-down value the value of an asset for tax purposes after capital allowances have been deducted from the original cost.

Technical analysts analysts who attempt to predict the future pattern of share prices by studying past share price movements.

Term structure of interest rates (TSIR) the configuration of market's expectation of the level of interest rates according to time to maturity of securities (usually based on government securities; in which case it profiles expected risk-free rates).

Theoretical Ex-Rights Price (TERP) the market price at which the ordinary shares 'ought' to settle following the completion of a rights issue.

Total Quality Management (TQM) an emphasis on the eradication of faults and errors in any process.

Total Shareholder Return (TSR) the overall return enjoyed by investors, including dividend and capital appreciation, expressed as a percentage of their initial investment. Related to individual years, or to lengthier time periods, and then converted into an annualised, or equivalent annual return.

Trade credit temporary financing extended by suppliers of goods and services pending settlement by customers.

Traditional theory of capital structure the theory that an optimal capital structure exists, where the WACC is minimised and market value is maximised.

Treasury Bills short-dated (up to three months) securities issued by the Bank of England on behalf of the UK government to cover short-term financing needs.

Treasury management definitions differ, but essentially, the control and management of cash and other liquid assets in a business.

Underwriting the facility provided by financial institutions that agree for a fee to buy up any shares left unsold after a share issue.

Ungeared Beta the geared Beta stripped of the effect of gearing. Corresponds to the activity Beta in an equivalent ungeared firm.

Unsystematic risk risk that arises from factors specifically affecting the company or the sector it is in. This risk can be diversified away by holding securities in a portfolio.

Vertical integration the extension of a firm's activities further back, or forward, along the supply chain from existing activities.

Venture capital finance, usually equity, offered by specialist merchant banks wanting to take a stake in firms with high growth potential, but involving a high risk of loss.

Warrants options to buy ordinary shares at a predetermined 'exercise price'. Usually attached to issues of loan stock.

Weighted Average Cost of Capital (WACC) the overall return a firm must achieve in order to meet the requirements of all its investors.

Working capital a firm's investment in items like stock that continually turn over, i.e. enter and exit the firm. Defined as current assets less current liabilities (= net working capital).

Yield curve another name for the term structure of interest rates.

Zero coupon bonds bonds issued below face value that pay no interest, delivering all their returns in the form of capital gain upon redemption.

INDEX

Note: Page references in **bold** refer to definitions in the Glossary